# REQUIEM FOR REVOLUTION

# Requiem for Revolution

## The United States and Brazil, 1961–1969

*Ruth Leacock*

THE KENT STATE UNIVERSITY PRESS
Kent, Ohio, and London, England

©1990 by The Kent State University Press, Kent, Ohio 44242
All rights reserved
Library of Congress Catalog Card Number 89-20054
ISBN 0-87338-401-6
ISBN 0-87338-402-4 pbk.
Manufactured in the United States of America

**Library of Congress Cataloging-in-Publication Data**

Leacock, Ruth.
   Requiem for Revolution : the United States and Brazil, 1961–1969 /
Ruth Leacock.
     p.    cm. —(American diplomatic history)
   Includes bibliographical references.
   ISBN 0-87338-401-6 (alk. paper).∞ —ISBN 0-87338-402-4 (pbk. : alk.
paper)∞
   1. United States—Foreign relations—Brazil. 2. Brazil—Foreign relations—
United States. 3. United States—Foreign relations—1961-1963.
4. United States—Foreign relations—1963-1969. 5. Brazil—History—
Revolution, 1964.
   I. Title.
   E183.5.B6L4   1990
   327.73081—dc20                                     89-20054
                                                   CIP

British Library Cataloging-in-Publication data are available.

# Contents

# BRAZIL
# 1964

RORAIMA

AMAPÁ

MARANHÃO

CEARÁ

Manaus

Belém São
Luis

Fortaleza

RIO GRANDE
DO NORTE

AMAZONAS

PARÁ

PARAÍBA

ACRE

PIAUÍ

Recife PERNAMBUCO

ALAGOAS

GOIÁS

SERGIPE

RONDÔNIA

BAHIA

Salvador

MATO
GROSSO

Brasília

MINAS
GERAIS

Belo Horizonte

ESPÍRITO SANTO

SÃO
PAULO

RIO DE JANEIRO (state)

GUANABARA

PARANÁ

São
Paulo

Rio de Janeiro (city)

SANTA
CATARINA

Curitiba

Porto
Alegre

RIO GRANDE
DO SUL

SOUTH AMERICA

SCALE

0    250    500

MILES

N

# Preface

This book examines an effort to introduce a new American policy in Brazil at a time when the limits to American influence had not yet been clearly demonstrated. Today, although we have been assured that America is standing tall once again, the posture seems somewhat in doubt. There is a rather defensive, even truculent, ring to the rhetoric. The evidence seems thin.

No such doubt clouded the perception of America's international standing in the late 1950s, when some members of the eastern establishment met to discuss foreign policy. Very much aware of American power but also convinced that power should be employed for constructive ends, the liberal academics proposed a new approach to the persistent problems of the world's underdeveloped countries. The new approach, called nation building, was heralded as the democratic counterpoint to international communism. If the Soviet Union could capture hearts and minds with its grim Marxist ideology, surely the United States could export the American Dream.

A concerted effort to do that was made in Brazil during the Kennedy-Johnson administrations. Latin America impinges on the consciousness of the North American public only infrequently, in fits and starts. Complacent indifference is shattered only when the internal problems of a Latin country seem to spill over its borders and pose some kind of threat to American interests. The period from 1960 to 1967 represented one of those awareness intervals. The Cuban Revolution in 1959 had shattered the illusion that all of the Western Hemisphere could be automatically counted as part of the American sphere of influence. It seemed vital to U.S. national interests to counter the appeal of Fidel Castro's revolution by urgently offering an alternative, devising a crash program that would slice through the accumulated debris and barriers of underdevelopment in order to breast the flood of rising expectations on the part of the Latin American masses.

Within a few years the Brazilian revolution of 1964 did provide an alternative model that other Latin countries might emulate. A number of them did. In particular, there was a replay in Chile in the next decade— with extremist variations. And in Central America today, in the reports of death squads and the disappearances of civilians, there are still echoes of the Brazilian experience.

In analyzing the 1964 revolution and pondering the extent to which American policies contributed to it, I have attempted to present the Brazilian perspective as well as the American. I first became sensitized to a Brazilian point of view while in that country in 1956–57, when I was startled to discover that many Brazilians thought that it was the United States, not the Soviet Union, that was an evil empire. On a subsequent visit in 1962–63 I also became aware of some of the social dimensions of the country's enormous economic problems, as well as of the cumbersome complexity of a federal political system that was weighted in favor of local vested interests. Struggling to run the system was a recently installed, unstable government. I did not witness the final chaotic year of that government or the revolution itself, but travels in Brazil in 1965, 1971, and 1983 provided a firsthand, if limited, view of some of the consequences.

As they attempted to introduce the new American policy, American officials also labored under constraints, constraints that have not perhaps been adequately emphasized in earlier analyses. The Alliance for Progress blueprint was soon modified in response to pressures from Congress, from entrenched Washington bureaucracies, and from businessmen's groups. Especially in the Brazilian case, American corporations played an important role in altering policy guidelines and establishing new performance tests for the beleaguered Brazilian government. If the part played by the multinationals has been overemphasized by some Brazilian analysts, it has been definitely underreported in American accounts. American anticommunist ideology in the 1960s has also, in my opinion, been underemphasized. Since it narrowed or distorted the perception of ongoing events and warped understanding of the underlying problems, it was perhaps the greatest constraint of all on policy implementation.

In this account I attempt to correct these distortions and omissions. The paper trail on the American side of this case history is fairly wide and well blazed, thanks in large part to Phyllis R. Parker, who in 1975 initiated the declassification of pertinent documents in order to complete her book, *Brazil and the Quiet Intervention, 1964*. On the Brazilian side, few official documents are available, but the deficiency is partly overcome by the large number of personal memoirs and special studies by Brazilian participants or witnesses to the revolution.

Research for this book was facilitated by travel grants from the Lyndon Baines Johnson Library and from the National Council for the Humanities. I would also like to thank the archivists of the Kennedy, Johnson, and Eisenhower libraries, as well as the staffs of the Library of Congress and the Agency for International Development (AID) Reference Center for their assistance in locating materials.

# Abbreviations

| | |
|---|---|
| ADEP | Ação Democrática Popular (Popular Democratic Action) |
| AFP | Alliance for Progress |
| AFL-CIO | American Federation of Labor-Congress of Industrial Organizations |
| AID | Agency for International Development |
| AIFLD | American Institute for Free Labor Development |
| AMFORP | American & Foreign Power Company |
| BAC | Business Advisory Council |
| BNDE | Banco Nacional de Desenvolvimento Econômico (National Economic Development Bank) |
| CAMDE | Campanha da Mulher pela Democracia (Women's Campaign for Democracy) |
| CGG | Comando Geral da Greve (General Strike Command) |
| CGT | Comando Geral dos Trabalhadores (General Workers Command) |
| CIA | Central Intelligence Agency |
| CNTI | Confederação Nacional dos Trabalhadores na Indústria (National Confederation of Industrial Workers) |
| COMAP | Commerce Committee for the Alliance for Progress |
| CONCLAP | Conselho Nacional de Classes Produtores (National Council of Productive Classes) |
| CVRD | Companhia Vale do Rio Doce (Rio Doce Valley Company) |
| DOPS | Departamento de Ordem Política e Social (Department of Political and Social Order) |
| ESG | Escola Superior de Guerra (Superior War College) |

| | |
|---|---|
| Eximbank | Export-Import Bank |
| IBAD | Instituto Brasileiro de Ação Democrática (Brazilian Institute for Democratic Action) |
| IMF | International Monetary Fund |
| IPES | Instituto de Pesquisas e Estudos Sociais (Institute of Research and Social Studies) |
| IPM | Inquérito Policial Militar (Military Police Investigation) |
| ITT | International Telephone & Telegraph Company |
| LIMDE | Liga da Mulher pela Democracia (Women's League for Democracy) |
| MAC | Movimento Anti-Communista (Anti-Communist Movement) |
| OAS | Organization of American States |
| ORIT | Organización Regional Interamericana de Trabajadores (Interamerican Regional Labor Organization) |
| PCB | Partido Comunista Brasileiro (Brazilian Communist Party) |
| Petrobrás | Petróleo Brasileiro S.A. (Brazilian Petroleum, Inc.) |
| PSD | Partido Social Democrático (Social Democratic Party) |
| PTB | Partido Trabalhista Brasileiro (Brazilian Labor Party) |
| SUDENE | Superintendência de Desenvolvimento do Nordeste (Superintendency of Northeast Development) |
| SUPRA | Superintendência de Política Agraria (Superintendency of Agrarian Policy) |
| UCF | União Cívica Feminina (Women's Civic Union) |
| UDN | União Democrática Nacional (National Democratic Union) |
| UNE | União Nacional dos Estudantes (National Students Union) |
| USIS | United States Information Service |
| UST | União Syndical dos Trabalhadores (Union of Organized Workers) |

# REQUIEM FOR REVOLUTION

# 1

# Inaugurations

---

On January 20, 1961, the youngest president ever elected in the United States was inaugurated. The day before, an eight-inch snowfall had immobilized Washington, but most of the streets and the parade route from the Capitol to the White House had been cleared by noon. Bright sunshine had replaced the heavy snow clouds. Still, there was a biting northwest wind, and the temperature remained in the twenties. Despite the numbing cold, John F. Kennedy removed his overcoat to stand before Chief Justice Earl Warren and take the oath of office. A young and activist administration, undaunted by the elements, was taking over.

There was one ill omen of sorts. While Boston's Cardinal Richard Cushing was delivering the invocation ("of extraordinary length," sniffed a reporter from the *Washington Post*), a short circuit in the lectern sent up a billow of smoke.

Eleven days later, on January 31, Jânio Quadros, the youngest president ever elected in Brazil, was inaugurated. Jânio,[1] who had just turned forty-four on January 25, was four months and four days older than Kennedy. His inauguration took place in Brasília, the partially completed new capital of Brazil. At first it appeared that the weather would not be auspicious for this inauguration either. A steady rain had begun the evening before. It turned the still raw earth of Brasília into red mud and gouged deep gullies in the carefully laid out, but still grassless knolls and slopes of the futuristic new city. But shortly before the outgoing president, Juscelino Kubitschek, was to turn over the sash of office to Quadros, the clouds parted and a brilliant summer sun beamed on the crowd jammed into the Praça de Tres Poderes to witness the ceremony.

In his inaugural address Kennedy concentrated on American foreign policy. Speaking for his entire generation, he welcomed the role of defending freedom around the globe, promising to pay any price, bear any burden, meet any hardship in playing that role. In addition, he offered a special pledge "to our sister republics south of our border," a pledge to create a new alliance for progress, one aimed at eradicating poverty and pursuing development. At the same time he warned that the United States would "oppose aggression or subversion anywhere in the Americas." This lofty summons to a new crusade struck a responsive chord with the American public. The speech was praised and quoted as are few inaugural addresses.

For quite different reasons, Jânio's inaugural address also attracted considerable attention. He delivered his principal inaugural speech on the radio in the evening of January 31. Earlier, at the ceremony when the sash of office was turned over to him, he had made only a four-minute speech. In his radio address he concentrated on domestic affairs, especially on Brazil's immediate fiscal problems. He enumerated figures: Brazil's foreign debt stood at $3,802,000,000; by 1965, $1,853,650,000 would have to be paid on this debt in interest and principal. However, the budget deficit of the federal government was steadily widening. The gap between revenues and expenditures had increased to such an extent that Brazil was unable to meet the payments currently due to the International Monetary Fund (IMF) and to the U.S. Export-Import Bank (Eximbank). Who was responsible for such a mess? His predecessor, Juscelino Kubitschek. The previous administration was also responsible for widespread corruption, "an alarming list of official scandals, encouraged by the most shocking failure to punish."[2]

During the election campaign Quadros had carefully refrained from attacking the popular Kubitschek.[3] Most Brazilians felt it was unseemly to use an inaugural address to initiate such an attack. Even newspapers that had enthusiastically supported Quadros's candidacy saw the speech as petty and vindictive. Jânio spoke like a candidate for office, not like a president who had just taken the helm, according to the influential Rio daily, *Correio da Manha*.[4] Congressional leaders of Kubitschek's party, the PSD (Social Democratic Party) immediately maneuvered the Congress into a special session in order to counterattack and criticize the new president. The PSD was still the largest party in the Congress. So much for the honeymoon. Prospects for smooth cooperation between the legislative and executive seemed dim. It was an odd beginning.

As was the custom among heads of state, Kennedy sent a message of congratulations to Quadros on his inauguration. "Once in twenty years," the Kennedy message noted, "presidential inaugurations in your country and mine occur within days of each other. This year of 1961 is signalized by that happy coincidence."[5]

The statistic, so confidently tossed out, is a little puzzling. It suggests that Brazil had a long-standing tradition of inaugurating presidents in January, under a constitution as stable as that of the United States. But the constitution that Brazil had at that moment was not yet fifteen years old and would not, in fact, last twenty. For fifteen years prior to 1946 Brazil had no elected president at all, and under the pre-1930 constitution the chief executive had been inaugurated in November. In addition, until 1937 the United States had installed its presidents in March. In short, the happy twenty-year coincidence the telegram referred to had never occurred before.

Although the Kennedy message thus managed to suggest American ignorance of Brazilian history, no doubt the State Department official who wrote it merely wanted to underline the fact that the United States, like Brazil, had a brand new administration, one that was conscious of parallels between Brazil and the United States. Parallels there were. Both countries were continental in size and rich in resources. Both were New World countries with a history of European colonization, forced African immigration, and later waves of voluntary European and Asian immigration. Both had struggled for independence from the European mother country. Both had been torn for a time by an internal struggle over the abolition of slavery.

Although there were similarities, they were superficial. In 1961 the United States and Brazil were distant from each other geographically and culturally. At the popular level in the United States a profound ignorance about, and indifference to, all Latin Americans blurred distinctions. Weren't they all Latinos who believed in mañana, siestas, and rhumba? To most Americans, Brazil was just another small banana republic where the natives spoke Spanish and had a lot of coffee.

The perception that most Brazilians had of Americans was equally unflattering. Americans were thought of as wealthy in material possessions but lacking in civility—essentially uncultivated, very much inclined to be loud and boastful.

Brazilians who considered themselves nationalists held an even more negative view of the United States. By the time of the 1960 presidential campaigns, a new type of nationalism—developmental nationalism—was stirring the urban, literate public. The basic ideas dated back to the eighteenth century: Brazil should abandon the role of supplier of raw materials and develop its own potential as an industrialized power. As a popular mass movement, developmental nationalism dated back only to the 1951–53 campaign to create Petrobrás, the state oil company. That campaign had been led by President Getúlio Vargas. His successor, Juscelino Kubitschek, did even more to fan development fervor by actually delivering on his campaign slogan, "Fifty years progress in five." Despite the fiscal and social costs of such rapid development, the public was captivated by the notion that the sleeping giant, Brazil, was finally on the move, marching toward its destiny as a major world power.[6]

Nationalism cut across the political spectrum, but the most vocal of the developmental nationalists were located left of center. They employed a Marxist terminology to argue that the explanation for Brazil's backwardness lay in centuries of exploitation by foreign imperialists. Earlier it had been Portugal, the Dutch Republic, Spain, Great Britain. Now it was American monopolies that were trying to tighten a grip on the Brazilian economy with the aim of preserving Brazil as a supplier of cheap raw materials.

A degree of antipathy to other nations is implicit in any nationalism. National self-definition depends upon comparison, usually invidious, with other nations. It helps to have one sharply defined opponent against whom we can see ourselves. For the Brazilian nationalists the United States was the obvious foil. Ever since World War I, the United States had replaced Britain as the largest investor in Brazil, as well as its best customer and supplier. Americans—missionaries, businessmen, tourists, officials, students—kept turning up in every corner of Brazil. What were they all looking for? Gold, oil, diamonds, unknown mineral resources? In addition, as it assumed "the leadership of the Free World," the United States seemed to parade its power and flaunt its wealth. Apprehension, envy, and resentment were natural reactions on the part of the less affluent and the weak. "Why is the standard of living so high in the United States and so low in Brazil?" Journalist Gondin da Fonseca posed that question in 1961 and of course supplied the answer: it wasn't because the Yankee worked harder than the Brazilian but because the United States robbed and pillaged the entire world.[7]

Similar charges of rampant American imperialism were being aired frequently by 1960, and more moderate Brazilians said little to contradict them. There was no discernible rush to defend the Good Neighbor of the North. Instead, any Brazilian courting votes or public support was likely to join the nationalist chorus. Therefore, during the campaign, when Quadros praised Castro, proposed the recognition of Communist China, promised to renew diplomatic relations with the Soviet Union, and criticized unnamed foreign corporations for bleeding Brazil, it was all put down to political expediency. The conservative parties supporting him did not think that he really meant any of it.

The United States had its own "ism" to interpret the world by. Anti-communism was still the cement that tightened bonds within American society and glued together the diverse strands of foreign policy. Young and old, management and labor, WASP and ethnic, virtually all Americans could agree that communism was a bad thing, and the price of liberty was eternal vigilance with respect to the Soviet Union.[8] In 1961, communism was still seen as a monolithic force, with leaders in the Kremlin moving the chess pieces of their empire, inexorably plotting world conquest, sacrificing a pawn here and there, but ever pressing on toward the ultimate objective. Nearly superhuman powers of infiltration and subversion were attributed to the communist bloc.

In the early Cold War worldview, Latin America had been seen as a safe area, under American protection, outside the theater of superpower competition. The containment lines had to be drawn and held in Eastern Europe and Asia. Minor aid such as technical assistance might be funneled south of the border, but the bulk of development capital there would have to come from private corporate investment. American diplomats were asked to explain to the Latins that more governmental assistance could not be offered because American resources were limited; the nuclear umbrella had to be financed, in addition to the major expenditures along the containment lines in Europe and Asia. But Latin America benefited from the American facedown of Russian imperialism just as much as the United States benefited. Latins, it was believed, understood this and approved.[9]

It was the Cuban Revolution that had led the Eisenhower administration to initiate a change in policy. Not until Castro's band of guerrillas defeated an army equipped and trained by the United States did the administration become concerned about the hearts, minds, and aspirations of the Latin masses. Earlier signs of dissatisfaction with America, such as the mob attacks on Vice President Richard Nixon during his

5

1958 tour of the region had caused alarm but were not followed up. After that Nixon tour, Brazilian President Kubitschek suggested that it was time for a Marshall Plan for the Western Hemisphere, an Operation Pan-America. His proposal was politely buried in Organization of American States (OAS) committees. It was thought that he made such a proposal just to distract attention from Brazil's looming debt crisis.

As the Castro-led forces were winning ever-increasing support during that same year of 1958, the Eisenhower administration switched to a policy of neutrality in the Cuban conflict. Arms shipments to Fulgencio Batista were suspended in March. At the time, Castro was regarded as a romantic liberator figure. It was not until the final days of 1958, Dwight D. Eisenhower noted regretfully in his memoirs, that the CIA suggested that the communists had joined the Castro movement, and a Castro victory might not be in the best interests of the United States.[10] By then it was too late to prevent it. Batista fled to the Dominican Republic on New Year's Day of 1959. During the next twelve months, Eisenhower's glum fear that communism had penetrated this hemisphere seemed to be confirmed by Castro's actions, although the new dictator of Cuba did not actually proclaim his conversion to Marxism until late 1961.

The CIA would not soon repeat the sin of underestimating communist strength in Latin America.

Like the Eisenhower team, Kennedy and his future advisors had paid little attention to Latin America before the Cuban Revolution. True, Eisenhower critics such as Walt W. Rostow were belaboring the administration for a sluggish foreign policy, especially with respect to underdeveloped nations. Rostow believed that the United States must become involved in the modernization of these areas before the communists moved into them in force. But the parts of the Third World that Rostow believed critical to the American position in the Cold War were Asia, the Middle East, and Africa. The Latin American states, he opined in 1958, were protected "by geography and the Monroe Doctrine from all but occasional involvement in the world's power struggles" and therefore could proceed with modernization "at a leisurely pace." As he saw it, "the inevitable periods of vicissitude and crisis" in Latin America "rarely raised issues which seriously touched the American national interest."[11] Presumably, then, Eisenhower was not to be faulted for ignoring Latin America.

President Kennedy had also shown little interest in that region while in the Senate. He was a member of the Senate Foreign Relations Subcommittee on Latin America but devoted most of his attention to the

Subcommittee on Africa, which he chaired. In his 1960 campaign book, *The Strategy of Peace,* he still saw Fidel Castro as a reformer and "part of the legacy of Bolivar" and suggested that Castro might have taken a "more rational course after his victory had the United States Government not backed the dictator Batista so long and so uncritically, and had it given the fiery young rebel a warmer welcome in his hour of triumph."[12]

Although he still did not focus on Latin America, by 1960 Kennedy, like Rostow, was convinced that the next "real struggle" in the Cold War was going to take place in the underdeveloped world. Russia was now attempting to conquer Europe "by the indirect route of winning the vast outlying raw materials region."[13] The periphery of the Free World would be slowly nibbled away, and the Cold War balance would gradually shift against the United States.

This theory of a new ("post-Sputnik") Soviet offensive against the underdeveloped world was to dominate Kennedy's conduct of foreign affairs.[14] Kennedy believed that a speech that Nikita Khrushchev delivered on January 6, 1961, provided proof positive of that scheme. Kennedy insisted that all of his White House aides read the speech. One can sympathize with them. The address, a report of a November 1960 meeting of the world's communist parties, is rambling, repetitive, and of inordinate length. The style is Khrushchev at his most turgid, with the text enlivened only by bursts of improbable exaggeration: "Hundreds of millions of people all over the world were deeply satisfied when they learned the results of the Meeting."[15]

Actually, this Khrushchev performance represented a presentation of the Russian point of view in the ongoing debate with Mao Tse-tung. Kennedy did not realize that, although he had been briefed the month before on the latest evidence of a Sino-Soviet split.[16] He took the speech at face value as a celebration of communist unity. Even so, it is hard to find what Kennedy saw in it. True, Khrushchev did mention the "national-liberation movement" in Asia, Africa, and Latin America in two different sections of his speech. He also happily reported that "the thunder of the glorious Cuban revolution has reverberated throughout the world" and suggested that Latin America was "reminiscent of an active volcano." But there was no hint of any new Soviet initiative to further revolution there or in any other underdeveloped region. There were vague assurances to Asian, African, and Latin American peoples of Soviet solidarity and support. But, in fact, there was the suggestion that the most important part of such aid consisted of setting a glorious example, providing "a vast store of experience in applying Marxist-Leninist theory to the conditions existing in countries and areas which capitalism had doomed to age-long backwardness."[17]

Most of the speech, however, deals with other matters, not with conditions in the Third World. The basic theme is that since nuclear world war is unthinkable, the major task for the socialist states is to prevent any capitalist country from unleashing one. The best way to do this is to present the West with a view of socialist unity and strength, while pursuing a policy of peaceful coexistence. Economic competition with the capitalist world would expose its contradictions and advance the cause of world revolution. To demonstrate the strength of the Soviet economy, Khrushchev devoted a lengthy section of his speech to a narration of its past accomplishments and future prospects. The two concluding sections of his address dealt with the problems of maintaining unity within communist ranks and seem rather clearly directed to Communist China.

Kennedy "accepted Khrushchev's rejection of nuclear war as honest enough," his White House aide Arthur Schlesinger, Jr., informs us. But he apparently dismissed every other indication in the speech that Khrushchev might be sincerely seeking détente. He thought the whole tone of the address was one of "bellicose confidence" and concluded that Moscow was declaring its "faith in victory through rebellion, subversion, and guerrilla warfare," even though Khrushchev had not exactly mentioned any such faith.[18]

Even before he read this speech, Kennedy had decided that the most critical outlying raw materials region lay south of the Rio Grande. He announced that Latin America would have a priority second only to defense in his administration.[19] New developments in Cuba had led him to this conclusion. Stories of summary executions of Castro's opponents continued to be featured in the media. Private property, including the property of American firms in Cuba, was expropriated without the prior negotiation of compensation. Castro periodically indulged in lengthy anti-American harangues, shrilly protesting that the United States planned to invade his country. He also charged that the Americans were equipping and training an army of Cuban exiles to spearhead a U.S. invasion. On January 3, 1961, a few weeks before the inauguration of Kennedy, Castro ordered the staff of the American embassy in Havana reduced to eleven. The embassy, he claimed, was full of spies. Eisenhower responded the next day by breaking diplomatic relations. Most trade relations had already been severed.

Many Americans who had initially sympathized with the Cuban Revolution by now had second thoughts. But in Latin America, Castro's popularity seemed undiminished, at least insofar as Latin students and intellectuals were concerned. They believed that Cuba stood on the threshold of a period of rapid economic growth. Were some bloodshed, violence, disorder, food shortages, too high a price to pay for an end to dependence and exploitation?

Such an attitude thoroughly frightened American officials in charge of foreign policy and national security. Cuba was not the only Latin nation with an impoverished peasantry and an economy dominated by a tiny elite. The entire hemisphere might explode at any moment. "There is absolutely no doubt in my mind that revolution is inevitable in Latin America," wrote Milton Eisenhower, who had served as his brother's special representative to that region. He hoped that an alternative to the Communist-Castro type of revolution could be found urgently, in time.[20]

It was one minute to midnight for Latin America, observed José Figueres, a former president of Costa Rica. The phrase caught on.

In short, as he took office, Kennedy believed that he faced a crisis situation in Latin America. That did not dismay him. He was eager to prove his mettle. At the time, presidential candidates were seriously evaluated on their imagined ability to deal with a crisis in a macho, cool way. There was the feeling that the "fate of mankind for centuries to come" depended on the crisis-management ability of one man, the president of the United States.[21]

The view of a hemisphere under the gun of communism perfectly suited the mood of the American public, still enthralled by fervent anticommunism. By 1961, McCarthyism might be spoken of as a phenomenon of the past, its star performer not only censured but already dead, the hunt for security risks in government agencies no longer making headlines, the use of special loyalty oaths for teachers declining. But the nation was far from free of its fear of Marxism, nonconformity, and freedom of thought and expression. In fact, a new flowering of strident anticommunism coincided with the New Frontier. The John Birch Society was founded by candy manufacturer Robert Welch in December 1958. By 1961 the society claimed 60,000 members across the country, despite its transparently crank nature.[22] In addition to its card-carrying, dues-paying members, the Birch Society had hundreds of thousands of sympathizers who joined Birch campaigns against Polish hams, fluoridated water, urban renewal, the United Nations, and Chief Justice Earl Warren. A number of other new right-wing organizations, such as the Christian

January 1956. President Dwight D. Eisenhower welcomes Brazilian President-elect Juscelino Kubitschek on a visit to the United States in Key West, Florida. Latin America was not yet a major U.S. concern. Dr. Milton Eisenhower, the president's brother and advisor on Latin America, stands in upper left. (Courtesy Dwight D. Eisenhower Library.)

Anti-Communist Crusade and the Young Americans for Freedom made use of Birch publications and films. General Motors, R. J. Reynolds, Alcoa, and Goodyear were among the blue-chip corporations setting up programs to educate their employees in anticommunism and Americanism; the programs might also have utilized Birch material. And, on the fringe of legality, a Birchite organized the Minute Men, a heavily armed group of would-be guerrilla fighters against communist invasion.[23]

"Everybody's against Communism," Kennedy told deLesseps Morrison. "You don't have to sell that."[24] He was chiding the ambassador to the Organization of American States for making unnecessarily "hard" statements in opposition to White House aides Richard Goodwin and Arthur Schlesinger during a White House conference on U.S. strategy at an upcoming inter-American meeting to be held at Punta del Este, Uruguay. Kennedy obviously felt that communist infiltration or subversion was no longer a domestic problem. In Brazil, in Latin America generally, in Southeast Asia, in Africa, yes; not in the United States. In the past he had done his bit to battle communist subversion within the country. He had used his position on the Senate Labor Committee to try to unmask communists in unions. He had refused to condemn fellow senator Joseph McCarthy. In the end, he was the only Democratic senator who did not vote for censure.[25] But now, in 1961, Kennedy felt *that* issue—like race relations, the role of big business in America, women's rights—had been settled.

Given the climate of the times, Kennedy could not, of course, see that it was in fact anticommunism that was a serious domestic problem. Anticommunism was an all-encompassing ideology that distorted reality, smothered creative dissent, skewed the allocation of national resources, and set the country up for a disastrous intervention in a distant civil war.

Both before and after his death, admirers of Kennedy advanced the notion that their man represented something new and fresh, a break away from the tired leadership of the aged generals and bureaucrats who had established the basic structure for the American response to the Cold War. "New men, new ideas," exulted Schlesinger.[26] Schlesinger perhaps exemplified the liberals who supported Kennedy in part because they loathed Nixon the Red-Baiter, the communist hunter who sometimes failed to distinguish between liberals and communists. The liberals hoped that Nixon's opponent was "free of the tired and sterile ideologies of the Cold War."[27]

11

That hope would be unfulfilled. For all of his wit and charm, John Kennedy did not have an original mind. He was a thoroughly conventional, wealthy young man who reflected the basic ideas of the white male establishment. When it came to foreign policy, the mind-set for his generation had been forged during World War II: the greatest sin of a statesman is appeasement; the imperialism of a totalitarian regime is insatiable; there are only two sides, ours and the other; properly organized and channeled, the power of the United States is practically unlimited. If anything, the new young president was much more the perfect Cold Warrior than the old outgoing president. General Eisenhower appeared willing to accept a stalemate in "the long twilight struggle." Kennedy intended to win it.

# 2

# An Independent Foreign Policy

One of the first problems considered by the Kennedy staff after Inauguration Day was the shaky financial position of Brazil.[1] Brazil had been singled out for special consideration for two reasons. One was geopolitical: by virtue of its continental size, strategic location bordering all but two other South American countries, and its population of over 70 million (in 1960), what happened in Brazil might determine what happened in the rest of South America. "Losing" Cuba with its population of 6 million was bad enough. Losing Brazil would be a disaster comparable to losing China. The second reason for the special attention was simply that, of all Latin countries, at that moment it seemed that it was a large section of Brazil that was poised to plunge into a revolution similar to Castro's.

The Americans had discovered the Brazilian Northeast.

The problems of the Northeast had been there for a long time. Disease, malnutrition, illiteracy were endemic. The area had an impoverished peasantry, underemployed urban squatters, an arrogant and corrupt ruling elite. Periodically, these bad conditions got worse when droughts, which sometimes went on for five years, seared the interior, driving the famished survivors into the coastal towns and cities. All of this was an old story. What seemed to be new in the early 1960s was the fact that the formerly docile, defeatist peasants were organizing to push for their rights.

One might have expected American observers to applaud such an exercise. On the face of it, it was just the sort of self-help initiative that Americans cherished. But when *New York Times* reporter Tad Szulc visited the region in October 1960, he discovered, to his horror, that it was pro-Castro Marxists who were doing the organizing. He reported in a dispatch published on October 31, 1960, that extreme leftists were taking advantage of the misery of the Northeast to stir up trouble—trouble for America as well as trouble for the owners of large estates. Fidelista organizers of the new Peasant Leagues were attempting to indoctrinate the peasants with anti-Americanism as well as with revolutionary attitudes. The peasants were told that the United States supported the landowners who exploited them. Szulc quoted one Peasant League organizer delivering a "typical" speech in which he promised that if a peaceful solution to the peasants' problems could not be reached, "we'll come here to ask you to grab weapons and make a revolution. The big landowners, backed by United States imperialism, are sucking your blood." The organizer told his audience that the "great Fidel Castro" and Mao Tse-tung were heroes who fought for the rights of the people. In a dispatch published the next day, November 1, Szulc pointed out that the top leader of the Peasant Leagues, Francisco Julião, was at that very moment on a visit to Communist China. Six months previously he had visited Havana. Szulc concluded that Julião's organization "appeared to be the closest thing to an organized Fidelista movement in Latin America outside Cuba."

In 1960 Americans were not as yet accustomed to hearing their country described as imperialistic or as a bloodsucking satanic force that sided with the wealthy. "Since World War II we have spent a hundred billion dollars trying to help other people...so, regardless of what you hear and regardless of what some of the bellyachers say, we are a much beloved people throughout the world," said Lyndon Johnson, echoing the popular sentiment.[2] Szulc's stories shocked those who read them; only convinced communist agents could make such statements. Kennedy, winding up his presidential campaign, noted the articles and accepted them as concrete new evidence of Cuban subversive activity in the hemisphere.

Szulc's sins were those of omission. His articles left the impression that the Peasant Leagues were springing up in response to a Castroite initiative after the Cuban Revolution. In fact, they dated back to 1955, a year before Castro had even landed in Cuba's Sierra Maestra. The first league had begun as a burial and mutual aid society, with the peasants themselves taking the initiative and approaching the lawyer, Francisco

14

Julião, for legal assistance. Szulc might also have pointed out that the conservative elite in the Brazilian Northeast always identified their critics as communists, whatever their actual political orientation or lack thereof. No doubt Szulc was unaware of this. His research time was limited. In his report of October 31, 1960, he adopted the viewpoint of local notables who argued that the city of Recife was "the stronghold of Communism in Brazil," home of 3,000 card-carrying Communist Party members who exerted influence far beyond their numbers. Szulc solemnly quoted "a high municipal official" warning that unless something was done quickly, the Northeast would go communist.

Kennedy resolved to do something quickly. Ten days after his inauguration, in his State of the Union address, he pledged a new effort to promote "sound development" in Latin America and announced the immediate dispatch of a Food for Peace mission to explore ways in which American food surpluses might be used to relieve hunger and malnutrition in "areas of suffering."

In these early, heady days of taking over the executive branch, every New Frontiersman fervently believed that, with altruistic commitment, Yankee ingenuity, and technological know-how, the administration could take on and pragmatically solve the problems of any underdeveloped area. All that was needed was a minimum of cooperation on the part of the benighted natives. In the case of the Brazilian Northeast, this seemed to be assured. The outgoing Kubitschek administration had already set up SUDENE (Superintendency of Northeast Development) as a planning agency for the region.

Actually, the fact that the Brazilian government had established a federal agency to try to find some solution to the problems of the area did not mean that Brazilians shared the American sense of urgency. Far from it. The Northeast, the periodic drought cycles, famine, the mass migrations out of the area, all were recurrent and familiar problems. The *Nordestinos* were part of the poor we have always with us. During the worst part of every drought cycle the federal government always made gestures toward finding a solution for those problems. SUDENE was the latest gesture. Headed by Celso Furtado, a young, dynamic economist, SUDENE did hold some promise. But Furtado did not share the American perspective. He did not see communism or Castro as any threat to the region. What he saw was poverty, misery, ignorance, and despair. Anyone concerned about combating those conditions was welcome on the SUDENE staff, even if his or her politics happened to be left-wing.

15

Food for Peace director George McGovern and White House aide Arthur M. Schlesinger, Jr., led that first Kennedy mission to Latin America. Schlesinger was delighted to be chosen, believing that his presence would impress the "Latinos" with the fact that the American government was now run by intellectuals, not by "money-grubbing materialists."[3] Schlesinger and McGovern spent one day of their nine-day tour "looking around in person at the squalor of Northeast Brazil," since they thought that would be "the most effective way of dramatizing American humanitarian concern."[4] They also met with SUDENE director Celso Furtado and found him uninterested in humanitarian food relief. Furtado told them of his hopes for a genuine development program instead of relief.[5]

A procession of other New Frontiersmen followed Schlesinger and McGovern to look at the squalor of the Northeast. There was more media attention including several television specials. Congressional delegations on fact-finding tours of South America began to include Northeast Brazil on their itineraries. The American consulate in Recife became a much busier place with a much larger staff. Its political section provided the cover for the CIA's Recife Station. The CIA, of course, was expected to play a key role in fighting communism here among the peasants and urban slum dwellers.[6]

While the Kennedy administration thus very early established a special relationship with Northeast Brazil, its relations with the central government in Brasília remained correct and cordial—but far from special. The major stumbling block seemed to be the new Brazilian president, Jânio Quadros. Jânio was simply not as interested in receiving American advice and assistance as Kennedy was in giving it.

Quadros had built his political career on being independent, enigmatic, and unconventional, on working hard and on getting things done. His eccentricities (such as lunching on a sandwich pulled from his pocket while he worked at his desk, or munching on a dry roll while waiting on a platform to address a rally) endeared him to many voters.[7] He had moved quickly up the political ladder from his position as lawyer and part-time high school teacher to city councilman, to deputy in the state legislature, to mayor of São Paulo, to governor of the state, to congressman, to president—a president elected by a solid plurality over his two major opponents. In all of his campaigns he had used a broom as his symbol, indicating the promise to sweep out corruption, waste, and inefficiency. As mayor and governor, Jânio acquired the reputation of a super-administrator, one able to balance budgets and end deficits while simultaneously proceeding with public improvements such as roads and schools.

Quadros was soon to discover that the problems of Brazil as a whole in 1961 were infinitely greater than the problems of administering the nation's wealthiest city and state during a period of boom, when São Paulo in particular was benefiting from the development policies of Kubitschek.[8] In fact, Quadros was rather poorly prepared to occupy the presidency. He had never held a national office or developed any familiarity with the central machinery of government, having spent his term as congressman either traveling around the world or campaigning for the presidential office while traveling around Brazil.

In some ways the apparent contradictions in the Quadros presidential campaign anticipated the ambiguity of his short term in office. Posing as the opponent of the corruption, wasteful spending, and unbalanced budgets of the "in" parties, he won the endorsement of the major "out" party, the UDN (National Democratic Union), as well as the backing of three small centrist parties. Despite these endorsements, Quadros continued to ignore the endorsers' stand on many issues. To fiscal conservatives in the "out" parties the new capital, Brasília, represented the acme of Kubitschek's spendthrift folly. However, during the campaign Quadros not only vowed to complete the city but promised to live there if elected. Fiscal conservatives generally welcomed foreign investment in the country, and during the campaign Quadros at times spoke out to endorse foreign investment in Brazilian development. But in other speeches he criticized unspecified foreign businesses that were bleeding Brazil and endorsed the idea of stricter legislation to curb the export of profits made in Brazil.

As a candidate, Jânio made repeated gestures to the Left. He frequently referred to the visits he had made to Cuba and to the Soviet Union, praised Castro, vowed to reopen diplomatic relations with Soviet-bloc countries, and promised to establish an independent foreign policy for Brazil, one which would not automatically follow the Cold War lead of the United States but would pursue Brazilian national interests. This last turned out to be one promise that Quadros kept.

Altogether it was a strange campaign.[9] The Brazilian Communist Party never wavered in its support of Quadros's principal opponent, the firmly anticommunist military man, Marshal Henrique Lott. Party leaders insisted that despite his gestures to the Left, Quadros was really the candidate favored by U.S. imperialist interests.[10] On the other hand, the most ardent anticommunists in Brazil warmly endorsed Quadros, the candidate who seemed so determined to have no enemies on the Left.

One incident during the campaign proved to be a portent of things to come. Two weeks after winning the nomination of the UDN, Quadros suddenly resigned as candidate after a minor dispute with his running mate, the UDN nominee for vice president. UDN party leaders, as well as the leaders of the three small center parties, begged him to reconsider the resignation. The Movimento Popular Jânio Quadros, a nonpartisan campaign organization dedicated exclusively to getting Quadros elected, collected 360,000 signatures in less than a week on a petition asking him to resume his candidacy.[11] Several army officers stationed in the state of Goias attempted to get a military coup started, claiming that the resignation of Quadros proved that there could be no political solution to the nation's problems. After a week of negotiation, Quadros consented to be a candidate again, pretty much on his own terms, running as an independent who had the support of various political parties and had only nominal ties to the UDN nominee for vice president.[12] Quadros apparently concluded from this episode that (1) he was an indispensable man, and (2) the resignation ploy enabled him to get his way.

American difficulties in dealing with Quadros began before he took office, during the period between his election on October 3, 1960, and his inauguration on January 31, 1961. A few days after the election, Quadros let it be known that he intended to visit the United States sometime between November 25 and December 25, whether or not he was formally invited and received by President Eisenhower. He also promised to visit Moscow and Peking during the same month.[13] Eisenhower appeared reluctant to take on the chore of entertaining Jânio, but Secretary of State Christian Herter urged him to do so. "... I am concerned," wrote Herter on October 29, "that any substantial delay in the extension of an invitation to Quadros may be taken as an affront by him."[14] During the next week New York governor Nelson Rockefeller and former-Ambassador to Brazil James S. Kemper also pressed Eisenhower to promptly extend a formal invitation to the easily offended president-elect.[15]

It was not until November 10, however, that the White House authorized the State Department to extend an invitation to Quadros to visit Washington on or about December 6. By this time it was difficult to contact him. Preserving his reputation for unpredictability and unconventional behavior, Jânio had suddenly embarked on a sea voyage to Britain without revealing the purpose of his trip or any details of future

18

travel plans. Once in London, he held himself incommunicado. The American ambassador to Britain, John Hay Whitney, finally managed to see Quadros on November 18. Quadros, who now admitted to having come to London for an eye operation, professed to be a great admirer of President Eisenhower and said he was flattered by the invitation. But he refused either to definitely accept or decline it at that time.[16]

In fact, having finally wangled an invitation, Jânio now proceeded to spurn it. Since he never deigned to respond directly, the State Department had to rely on stories in the Brazilian press to learn that Quadros had decided not to visit the United States and was not much interested in meeting his American counterpart, President-elect Kennedy.[17] Perhaps State Department officials found some comfort in the fact that Jânio did not visit Moscow or Peking either but descended unannounced on Lisbon prior to his return to Brazil.

Once back in São Paulo, Quadros secluded himself in his own modest house, receiving only his closest advisors. American ambassador John Moors Cabot (of the Boston Cabots, accustomed to conversing with the highest authorities) had no greater success in gaining an audience with Quadros than did any other diplomat, politician, or journalist.[18] Even after his Inauguration Day, Quadros showed no eagerness to receive the representative of the country that was ready to take up the burden of Brazil. Cabot was forced to deliver Kennedy's letter of congratulations to the Brazilian foreign minister. He tersely explained to Washington that Quadros was "inaccessible."[19]

Undaunted by the odd incivility and aloofness of Quadros, Kennedy was determined to establish closer relations with him and with his country. Handled properly, Brazil could become the key supporting player in the hemisphere. "Brazil might be built up as a counter to Cuba in Latin America," suggested one aide. "Quadros may be difficult to deal with, but deal with him we must, or lose a great opportunity to thwart Castroism in the area."[20] Of course the notion that Brazil needed "building" to measure up to the small island nation of Cuba would have profoundly annoyed even the most pro-American Brazilian; fortunately, they were not aware of it.

On January 23, before the Quadros inauguration, Kennedy had received a careful embassy analysis of the financial situation that would confront the new Brazilian administration.[21] He decided to offer Quadros immediate financial assistance in the form of an Export-Import Bank credit of $100 million. The offer was to serve as a "tangible, immediate expression [of] our willingness [to] assist Quadros during initial months

[of] his government so that he will have time [to] study problems and adopt constructive solutions," Secretary of State Rusk cabled to Ambassador Cabot.[22] Of course American officials already had pretty definite ideas of what constructive solutions Quadros ought to adopt and stood ready to offer suggestions.

In his cable, the secretary of state also cautioned Cabot that the United States wanted to avoid the Brazilian government's tendency "to bargain political cooperation against financial assistance." Nevertheless, he made it clear that the Kennedy administration had Brazilian political cooperation in mind. "Our objectives require constructive GOB (government of Brazil) postures" with respect to Castro and "associated hemisphere problems."

Rusk's instructions were sent on February 3. Ambassador Cabot did not succeed in getting an appointment with Quadros for another two weeks. On February 17 he accompanied that first special Food for Peace mission of the Kennedy administration to the presidential palace in Brasília. During the meeting with Quadros, Cabot offered the $100 million, and Food for Peace director McGovern offered to meet immediate Brazilian needs for wheat and to provide emergency food relief for the Northeast. Schlesinger had been sent along on the mission to sound out Latin leaders on possible sanctions against Cuba, but he decided not to raise the Cuba issue with Quadros because another special White House emissary, Adolf A. Berle, Jr., was due in Brasília in two weeks to explore the same question. By avoidance of the Castro question, the mission avoided any suggestion of quid pro quo (i.e., $100 million for cooperation on Cuba), and the meeting went off smoothly. The mission failed, however, to generate much in the way of favorable publicity within Brazil. The offer of $100 million was not made public, and the promise of emergency food relief did not exactly overwhelm the Brazilians. They had hoped the Kennedy administration was going to push a crash economic development program, not dump more surplus foods.[23]

At this time Adolf A. Berle, Jr., headed a special interdepartmental Task Force on Latin America. He had more diplomatic and Latin American experience than most of Kennedy's advisors; he had served as assistant secretary of state for seven years during the Roosevelt administration and then as ambassador to Brazil for another year. Berle's view of Latin America in 1961 was apocalyptic: "The Caribbean will explode," he confidently predicted. He believed that the Soviet Union had developed plans to take over all of Latin America during that year. Therefore, 1961 was a rerun of 1947, when, as he saw it, the Soviets had attempted to absorb all of Europe.[24] At times he went back even further for a historical parallel: in 1961 Cuba had placed the United States vis-à-vis the Soviet Union in the same position that Munich in 1936 placed England and France vis-à-vis Nazi Germany.[25] In any case, the United States had to work feverishly to alert the Latin Americans to the grave peril they and the entire hemisphere faced.

Berle of course approved of the proposed Bay of Pigs invasion of Cuba, though he felt that the United States, as a great power, should back the Cuban exiles with American forces, a step that President Kennedy was unwilling to take.[26] In diplomatic preparation for the invasion, Berle visited the three larger South American countries that he felt were especially threatened by Cuba: Brazil, Colombia, and Venezuela. Ideally, American assistance to an anti-Castro invasion force would be based on prior approval by "a multilateral group in accord with the rather settled law of the hemisphere."[27] As of February 1961 no such approval had been granted by any Latin country. Not one had asked for American aid against Cuban aggression. Not one seemed to feel threatened by the small island republic. Berle decided that the trouble was that the other American republics did not want to face up to the severity of the situation. He must try to make them see it.

He traveled first to Venezuela. President Rómulo Betancourt seemed receptive to Berle's message, ready to commit his country to battle in Cuba if it came to a showdown. Berle went on to Columbia. President Alberto Lleras Camargo was somewhat less receptive: he promised no more than his sympathy unless the Organization of American States endorsed intervention. Berle journeyed on to Brazil, where President Jânio Quadros was not even ready to promise sympathy.

On the surface level, the Quadros-Berle meeting proceeded quite amicably. Jânio began the meeting on March 2 by delivering what was apparently his opening statement for visiting foreign dignitaries. He deplored the financial and economic condition of his country, put the blame for it on the previous administration, and vowed to be tough in cleaning up the mess. Berle reminded Quadros that the United States was offering a credit of $100 million to help him get started. That was generous and kind, replied Quadros, but he did not think he could accept it. Berle, startled, said there were no strings attached to the offer. Ambassador Cabot, present at the interview, later thought that Berle had been rather tactless, repeatedly coming back to the one hundred million.[28] Quadros made the turn-down more explicit. One hundred million dollars was really nothing in comparison to the financial needs of Brazil, he

21

said. Therefore he must refuse it. "We can consider more if you need it," said Berle, oblivious to the signs of increasing irritation on Jânio's part.

Actually, Quadros knew that there were strings attached to the offer. His foreign minister had briefed him on the real purpose of Berle's visit,[29] and he had taken the trouble to prepare a symbolic answer. Prominently displayed in his office, alongside an engraving of Abraham Lincoln, was a photograph of neutralist leader Marshal Tito and an ebony statue that had been a gift from Che Guevara. But Quadros listened politely as Berle went through his presentation about the imminent Caribbean explosion and the urgent need for the American republics to act together to counter the Cuban threat. Berle urged that Brazil join the United States in boldly meeting the danger that threatened them all. "Jânio's reply, to which he stubbornly clung, was that he could not undertake any bold maneuver in foreign field until he had financial and social crisis now confronting nation under better control," Ambassador Cabot cabled Washington.[30]

"I said this of course left us to meet it, and I did not see how we could walk away from our responsibilities," Berle wrote in his diary. "Since we were getting nowhere I said that I hoped we could count on his sympathy if the moment came."[31]

Quadros responded with soothing words about cooperation with the United States, defense of Christian civilization, and the significance of hemispheric integrity. Berle left the presidential office satisfied that he and Jânio were parting "on the most friendly terms after a very frank and very cordial discussion" during which Quadros had essentially agreed with Berle's basic interpretation of the Cuban threat.

It came as a shock to Berle, therefore, on his return to Washington, to read the *New York Times* account of his meeting with Quadros.[32] According to the newspaper, the meeting had been a cold, formal affair. Quadros had bluntly opposed hemisphere-wide action against Cuba and adopted the Cuban view that the controversy was just between Cuba and the United States and did not concern other nations in the hemisphere. The day before the meeting, according to the *Times* reporter, Jânio had deliberately cold-shouldered Berle by refusing to see him that day in Rio, although he had found time to see the head of the Cuban press agency. Subsequently he had neglected to invite the special emissary from President Kennedy to fly to Brasília on the nearly empty presidential jet. Finally, Quadros chose the day of the Berle interview to authorize release of the announcement that neutralist leader Marshal Tito had

22

accepted an invitation to visit Brazil, and negotiations for economic and cultural exchanges with Yugoslavia were underway. The announcement that Itamarati (the Brazilian foreign office) now favored placing the admission of Communist China on the United Nations agenda had been released a short time before the Berle visit, but it was now reemphasized.

The Brazilian press went even further than the *Times* in portraying the Berle-Quadros encounter as a thoroughly hostile one. It was reported that Quadros had refused to shake hands with Berle and that Itamarati had deliberately neglected to extend the formal farewell courtesies usually paid to a foreign dignitary.[33]

Foreign Minister Afonso Arinos de Melo Franco hastened to assure Washington that the only reason the farewell courtesies had been omitted was because Itamarati did not know when Berle was leaving.[34] Berle was satisfied with the foreign minister's apology and felt the press had irresponsibly manufactured the incident out of whole cloth.

No matter how courteously Quadros had in fact treated the special emissary of President Kennedy, the timing of the announcement of Tito's visit could only be seen as a deliberate swipe at the United States. The most favorable interpretation that could be put on the matter was that Quadros was playing a political game to bemuse his domestic opposition: he was courting the rabidly anti-American Left in Brazil by these gestures in order to win their support for the drastic austerity program that the United States insisted on as a solution to the financial crisis.[35] A less favorable interpretation held that Jânio's actions were definitely calculated to move Brazil out of the United States orbit into the neutralist bloc. Thus, Secretary of State Dean Rusk worried that the United States might in fact be financing such a shift to neutralism via its generous financial aid. "The recent moves of President Quadros in carrying out his 'independent' foreign policy have raised the issue of just how far Quadros intends to go in moving Brazil away from its traditional policy of cooperation with the United States and support for the Inter-American system," he cautioned President Kennedy. "This makes it desirable to couple our expressions of helpfulness with allusions to cooperative action in the mutual interest of both countries."[36]

When he met with American officials, Quadros himself did his best to suggest that his flirtation with neutralism was merely a temporary political tactic. Thus, when he met Secretary of Treasury C. Douglas Dillon on April 12, five days before the Bay of Pigs invasion, he emphasized his determination to concentrate on solving the economic problems of Brazil and asked that the United States trust him on the political front. "While Quadros did not directly say so," Dillon reported to Kennedy, "he very obviously intended to give the impression that his neutralist political activities in the international arena were designed to strengthen his position against the Brazilian left in the battle over his domestic program. He repeated this thought on two separate occasions to be sure we got his point. This same thought had been put to me very directly earlier by the Brazilian finance minister. It was interesting that Quadros himself desired to make the same sort of statement."[37]

Far from being a temporary tactic, however, Quadros's "independent" foreign policy proved to be his one enduring legacy, a legacy only partly and temporarily repudiated during the first few years of the authoritarian military regime in power after the 1964 revolution.[38] The policy obviously appealed to a broad cross section of the Brazilian public, not just to the left-wing nationalists. Quadros's predecessor, Kubitschek, had taken the first steps toward establishing such a policy, and Quadros's foreign minister, Afonso Arinos, a member of the conservative UDN party did much to develop it.[39]

There were three core ideas to the policy. One was that Brazil as a developing country ought to have closer relations with other developing countries in Africa and Asia and with its sister republics in Latin America. Second, since Brazil's primary international concerns were economic, not political, it had no interest in the Cold War. Therefore, diplomatic and commercial relations with the Soviet bloc should be established or expanded. Third, as a part of the inter-American system, Brazil should strive "to give shape and content to the imperative principles of self-determination and non-intervention." What that meant at the moment was "defending with intransigence the sovereignty of Cuba." Brazil would steadfastly oppose military intervention in that country or any sanctions against it.

The policy was called "independent" rather than neutralist because Quadros had no intention of formally joining the neutralist bloc. Joining the bloc would mean that Brazil would have to coordinate its stands on issues with the members of this group. Quadros felt that his country should preserve its "absolute freedom to make our own decisions in specific cases and in the light of peaceful suggestions at one with our nature and history."[40]

Convinced that events were tracking toward some sort of showdown in the Third World between the Communist monolith, led by Moscow, and the Free World, led by Washington, Kennedy and his advisors found the new Brazilian policy quite unsatisfactory. No matter what Quadros called it, the policy seemed indistinguishable from neutralism, and though Kennedy might repeat that he had nothing against a truly neutralist policy, he found it hard to accept. So-called neutralist leaders seemed to be hypercritical of the United States, constantly calling into question the purity of its intentions while ignoring the communist menace. They seemed oblivious to the Sino-Soviet drive for world domination that was so apparent to Americans.

Especially exasperating was the Brazilian attitude toward Cuba. The Quadros administration clearly did not take the Cuban threat seriously; in fact, they behaved as though there were no threat of Castro-Communist subversion in their own impoverished Northeast. Instead they persisted in viewing the matter as a quarrel between Cuba and the United States, a quarrel that Brazil stood ready to mediate. Foreign Minister Afonso Arinos seems to have been genuinely astonished to hear from Berle that the Caribbean was about to explode. Aware of no evidence pointing to such a calamity, he could only conclude that the United States meant to explode it—"Probably within ninety days," he had cautioned Quadros on February 28, 1961. Arinos redoubled his efforts to find a formula which would lead the United States and Cuba to settle their differences at the negotiating table.[41]

"Communism is not negotiable," was the lofty response of the Kennedy administration. To the State Department, any hint of mediation seemed insulting. It suggested some sort of equality between the United States and insignificant little Cuba. Obviously, if the American government was so preoccupied with Cuba, it was only because a much greater power, a suitable opponent, was involved there. The Soviet Union, not Cuba, was the real antagonist. The Kennedy administration was convinced that its hostility toward Castro was totally altruistic, aimed at saving the weak Latin American sister republics from the onrushing Red Tide. American policy was not designed to do anything as grubby as repossess property in Cuba that had once belonged to American firms. But instead of showing a glimmer of gratitude, here was one of the weak sisters refusing to admit that any salvation was needed.

Nevertheless, no matter how noncooperative its leadership at the moment, Brazil, the largest country in Latin America, could not be allowed to slip into bankruptcy in 1961. The Alliance for Progress, Kennedy's plan for a hemisphere-wide *managed* revolution, had not yet been inaugurated; it would never work without Brazil in line. Bankrupt, Brazil would clearly head straight for internal chaos and unmanaged revolution. Therefore, ignoring Quadros's pronouncements on foreign

25

policy, American officials proceeded with the negotiation of a financial rescue package for Brazil. Not until these negotiations were completed, on May 16, did Kennedy signal his personal displeasure with the new independent foreign policy. He delivered a lecture to the Brazilian finance minister on the true significance of Cuba. The minister was in Washington to finalize the financial rescue arrangements.

The President said the United States was interested in the Castro regime because it is a weapon used by international communism in its efforts to take over additional Latin American countries by internal subversion. The President pointed out that the primary threat is not to the United States but to Latin American nations. He declared that the U.S. view is that Castro is not a free agent or a traditional Latin American revolutionary but is for all practical purposes an agent of international communism. The President said that we recognized Quadros' objections to the idea of military intervention in Cuba and that we understand those objections. We strongly believe, however, that this hemisphere must isolate Cuba and frustrate its use by international communism against other Latin American nations. He said that nations of the inter-American system obviously cannot achieve this objective unless they agree on the basic analysis of the situation in Cuba, and that such agreement is seriously prejudiced when the leader of the largest nation in Latin America asserts a strongly divergent view.

In response, Finance Minister Clemente Mariani assured Kennedy that Quadros was "moving with increased rapidity away from his pre-electoral position in favor of Castro." He expressed his belief that in fact the timely American aid would speed up Quadros's move; with the Brazilian economy in better shape, Quadros would no longer have to bend over backward to placate the leftists within Brazil.[42]

Kennedy and his Washington advisors may have believed Mariani. American officials in Rio de Janeiro did not. They were unable to discern the slightest sign of movement away from a "divergent view" on Cuba and glumly pointed out that "announcement [of] massive U.S. aid to Brazil without political conditions has at least temporarily undercut opposition efforts [to] discredit Quadros 'independent' foreign policy."[43] In fact, the size of the loan package did surprise Brazilian officials, since it was twice the sum that the Brazilian finance minister had judged essential.[44]

For his part Quadros continued to underline his dedication to an independent foreign policy. In the next two months he welcomed a Soviet goodwill mission, reestablished diplomatic relations with the Soviet

Union (broken in 1947), sent a special mission to tour East European countries in search of commercial and diplomatic ties, and dispatched Vice President João Goulart to the Far East as his personal representative on a tour that included Communist China. And when Ambassador Cabot remarked (at an embassy press conference) that Brazil was not at the moment in a neutralist position since it had commitments to the United States, Quadros seized the opportunity to publicly chide him. While attending the opening of an exhibit of Argentine art, he departed from the subject of art to say that Brazil "does not tolerate the meddling of anyone, no matter who he might be" in foreign policy. "We consider ourselves born members of the free world; we consider ourselves tied to Christian civilization. But this position does not exhaust the contents of our foreign policy. We demand and require the right and the freedom to take care of our interests wherever their defense may be needed."[45]

Cabot, insisting that he had never made any "effort to tell Brazilian Government what it should do," felt the entire incident had been deliberately manufactured in the same "pattern of affronts which Jânio has given United States for domestic political purposes ever since he assumed office." Cabot then made an effort to tell Kennedy what he should do: "I must point out that if we continue to give undiscriminating aid to Brazil despite series of public affronts we have received, we can only expect these affronts to continue. They may continue in any case, but I believe Jânio's tactics should lead us to more hard-boiled negotiating with Brazilians in connection with aid programs."[46]

Kennedy had already decided to replace Cabot. Although he was a career diplomat with a great deal of prior experience in Latin America, there had been criticism of him for his "obvious refusal" to make "serious personal contact" with the new Brazilian president. According to one report, "the Embassy staff in Rio have been privately laughing about a statement of Cabot to the effect that when Cuadros [sic] changes his attitude toward the United States, I will go call on him again."[47] The public Quadros-Cabot tiff delayed the public announcement of the ambassador's departure until late August, when it was announced that Professor Lincoln Gordon of Harvard's Business School would be his replacement.[48]

At this point, after seven months in office, Kennedy and Quadros scored very differently in terms of popularity with their respective publics. In light of his performance up to that point, Kennedy's rating was surprising. He had been elected over Nixon by the narrowest of margins, with less than 1 percent of the popular vote, and had accomplished little during the political honeymoon months. Facing a Congress still dominated by a conservative Southern Democratic-Republican coalition, he had not pushed domestic reform measures. Foreign affairs absorbed most of his attention, and here, judged by his own Cold War standards, his performance had been abysmal. Not only had he suffered the humiliating defeat of the Bay of Pigs the week after the Russians had put the first man into space, but his face-to-face meeting with Khrushchev in June had not gone as he had expected. Kennedy went to Vienna prepared to debate Communism and perhaps to negotiate some Soviet retreat somewhere. Instead the forty-four-year-old president was harangued, scolded, and threatened by the brusque, sixty-seven-year-old Soviet leader. Nevertheless, the president's standing in the polls steadily improved, topping even the very popular Eisenhower's highest rating. Clearly, with his attractive family, Kennedy had rapidly achieved a media-star status, one that was unaffected by the gritty vicissitudes of politics.

In contrast, Quadros had been elected by a lopsided plurality, gaining 20 percent more votes than his nearest rival. He was extravagantly popular as he took office; expectations about the kind of government he would offer the country ran high. But, as he began his seventh month in office, his popularity had declined drastically. Like Kennedy, he faced a Congress dominated by conservatives. The parties that had opposed his candidacy enjoyed a two-to-one majority over the parties that had supported his election. Of course this did not mean that the Congress would automatically reject the president's initiatives, since each party constantly divided into squabbling factions, and party discipline was virtually nonexistent. But Jânio made little effort to win over Congress. He did not wine and dine the members, invite them to breakfast, or even grant them brief appointments in his office. He made no attempt to strike deals, using the patronage that a president controlled. He made no effort to organize a new political party out of the Movimento Popular Jânio Quadros that had contributed so much to his election. His free use of the veto to quash legislation initiated by Congress was an irritant. So were the investigations of corruption by special presidential committees, investigations that seemed primarily designed to embarrass leaders of the opposition parties. And, though Quadros frequently mentioned the need for major reforms, in his first seven months he submitted only two legislative proposals to Congress.[49]

Jânio seemed to hold Congress in contempt, as a useless organ of government. Oscar Pedroso d'Horta, the minister of justice and chief advisor for domestic politics, announced that Quadros would not attempt to build a working majority in Congress because he believed in the separation of powers and had no wish to impose his will on the legislative branch. With the separation of powers, observed d'Horta, revealing surprising ignorance of the political process, if Congress rejected presidential projects, that would not affect the executive branch, which had its own system of government.[50] The Quadros system was to bypass Congress by relying on presidential decrees and executive action. Thus, he set up an executive agency to promote direct links between local governments and the presidency. The new agency was to coordinate federal assistance to local governments. In addition, Quadros arranged regional meetings with state governors to discuss regional needs. These moves were seen as methods of outflanking the elected congressional representatives of those municipalities and states.[51]

While Congress discussed and debated the reasons for the apparent impotence of the legislative branch, presidential decrees flowed in a steady stream from the Planalto, the presidential palace. One newspaper, the influential *Correio da Manha,* was soon running a special daily column, *"Bilhetes de Jânio,"* just to publish a synopsis of those decrees. The president was undeniably busy, but the impact on public opinion was not exactly what Quadros supporters might have desired. On the one hand, it appeared that Quadros was making major decisions too hastily, without adequate advice and due consideration. On the other hand, the president seemed to be wasting a great deal of time and energy on trivia. In the category of trivia were the decrees banning the wearing of bikinis on public beaches, horse racing on weekdays, playing more foreign tunes than Brazilian in nightclubs, and the manufacture of perfume bombs for Carnaval celebrations. Such edicts, with no provisions for enforcement, served only to bemuse those who had considered Quadros a serious reformer. On the other hand, some presidential decrees had an immediate negative effect on large sectors of the public. This was especially true of the decree of March 13 abolishing the system of multiple official currency exchange rates, a system that had been used to subsidize imports of oil, wheat, fertilizer, and newsprint. Multiple rates had been in use since 1953. Dollars at an artificially low rate had been provided to import these goods, with the federal government making up the difference between the real and the official exchange rate of the cruzeiro. By abolishing the system, Quadros in effect devalued the cruzeiro used for essential imports by 100 percent, and the prices of basic foods and transportation immediately doubled. Foreign economic experts and some businessmen's groups hailed the rate reform as both necessary and courageous, but most Brazilians were bitterly disappointed. They had become alarmed over the accelerating rate of inflation during the later Kubitschek years and had expected Quadros to somehow halt that process quickly and painlessly.[52]

Little was done to offset the erosion of popular support. No doubt the public approved of the new efforts to crack down on smuggling and to expose corruption in high places, but those campaigns had little impact on daily life. The inflation and corruption of the Kubitschek years had been somewhat offset by general euphoria over rapid economic growth and plans for further development. Not only did growth stall under Quadros, so did rhetoric about the future. Quadros seemed unaware of the importance of economic planning and uninterested in any public relations effort to reassure the nation that hopes for rapid industrial development had not been abandoned.

The great majority of Brazilians were preoccupied with the country's domestic problems and paid little attention to international affairs. The cost of living, the quality and quantity of consumer goods in the markets, opportunities for employment, openings for students in the schools, the availability of affordable housing—those were the concerns of most citizens, not Soviet threats to Berlin, chaos in the Congo, civil war in Laos, or Cuban efforts to export revolution. Most Brazilians had never even heard of the Cold War. Aware of no real external threat, the majority of those who followed the national political scene were pleased with Quadros's new foreign policy; it seemed a fitting declaration of Brazil's intention to pursue its own interests rather than those of the United States. In 1961 it was only a minority who perceived the policy as a dangerous tilt toward the Soviet bloc. Unfortunately for Quadros, this minority included one of his staunchest early supporters, the charismatic, highly vocal UDN leader, Governor Carlos Lacerda.

Lacerda had achieved national fame as an outspoken opponent of Getúlio Vargas. Vargas was the president-dictator who dominated Brazilian politics from 1930 to 1945 and again from his election as president in 1950 until his suicide on August 24, 1954. Lacerda's opposition to Vargas dated back to the 1930s. As a law student and young journalist, Lacerda had been jailed on several occasions for participating in left-wing demonstrations. Politically, Vargas was leaning toward fascism at the time, and Lacerda was a member of the Brazilian Communist Party. As he grew older, and as Vargas shifted slightly to the left, Lacerda shifted to the right. By the time he founded his own newspaper, *Tribuna da Imprensa*, in 1949, he had become a fervent anticommunist.

Lacerda dedicated his newspaper to attacking Vargas, the political heirs of Vargas (Juscelino Kubitschek and João Goulart), and other politicians whom he identified as soft on communism or corrupt. He was elected to Congress on the UDN ticket in 1954. In the 1960 election it was Lacerda who persuaded his party to endorse the candidacy of Quadros, even though Jânio was not a member of the UDN. Jânio reciprocated by urging Lacerda to run for governor of the newly created state of Guanabara in the same election. As a governor, Lacerda rose in party standing, and he longed to be the UDN presidential candidate in the 1965 election.

Very much aware of his debt to Lacerda, Quadros treated him with deference after his inauguration as president, frequently inviting him to Brasília. But Lacerda was uncomfortable in the role of one of the "in's." His vocation was to be an "out," attacking those in power. He "rages at friends when there are no more enemies," Afonso Arinos wryly observed.[53] Afonso Arinos, a UDN stalwart, was Lacerda's first target as Lacerda lauched his attack on the new independent foreign policy. From attacking the foreign minister, he soon moved to direct criticism of Quadros.

As Lacerda saw it, with their new policy, Quadros and Afonso Arinos were opening the door for the implantation of communism in Brazil. Their policy toward Cuba was especially heinous. By opposing sanctions against Cuba and by insisting on observation of the principles of self-determination and nonintervention, Brazil was supporting "one of the bloodiest, one of the most vile, one of the dirtiest dictatorships in the world."[54] Lacerda hailed the first news of the Bay of Pigs invasion with "delirious" approval and, after it had collapsed, announced that he favored direct military intervention to overthrow Castro.[55]

As far as American officials were concerned, Lacerda was a dream Third World political leader—articulate, ardently anticommunist, emphatically pro-American. Such men were hard to find in Latin America. The Kennedy White House was delighted to discover him.[56] Lacerda was one of the few Latin politicians whose telegram of congratulations to Kennedy on his inauguration would be acknowledged by the White House. Later in the year he was treated to an interview with Kennedy in the Oval Office.

Following Lacerda's lead, a number of other UDN politicians began criticizing Afonso Arinos and Quadros. Other newspapers joined the *Tribuna da Imprensa* in viewing the new policy with alarm. A number of business leaders and military officers who had formerly supported

Quadros became more and more apprehensive about his tilt toward the East. On the other hand, left-wing politicians, such as Communist Party president Luis Carlos Prestes, who had formerly opposed Quadros, now applauded his initiatives in foreign affairs.

June 12, 1961. In a post–Bay of Pigs damage control effort, UN Ambassador Adlai Stevenson was sent on a tour of Latin America. He was cordially received by Brazilian President Jânio Quadros. (Photograph, UPI/Bettmann Newsphotos.)

"I must note that there was not the slightest difficulty in Brazil–United States relations during the Kennedy administration," wrote Foreign Minister Afonso Arinos. He believed that the New Frontiersmen understood that Brazil's independent foreign policy was not anti-American or pro-communist, but simply pro-Brazilian.[57] He was wrong,[58] but circumstances dictated a subdued American reaction. Other Cold War problems were much more pressing: civil war in Laos, chaos in the Congo, a crisis over the status of West Berlin. In addition, the time was not propitious for the United States to play its usual heavy hectoring role in Latin America. Since limited unilateral American intervention in Cuba had failed, Kennedy now hoped for some sort of multilateral action by the Organization of American States. In late April 1961, all American ambassadors to Latin American countries were instructed to sound out their host governments on possible collective action against Cuba and communist subversion in the hemisphere. The results were not encouraging. "If we publicly declare that Cuba is a threat to our security," said one Mexican diplomat, "forty million Mexicans will die laughing."[59] Not a one of the larger Latin republics, especially not Brazil, saw any need for any type of sanctions whatever.[60]

The Kennedy administration knew better. But apparently the American message of anticommunism could not be imparted easily to the hypersensitive Latin nationalists. Marking time, the administration kept American relations with the Quadros government on a friendly basis. There were polite exchanges of thank-you notes for designating and receiving emissaries. There were exchanges of visits. Celso Furtado, director of SUDENE, was invited to Washington and received at the White House by President Kennedy, despite some misgivings about his possible Marxist beliefs.[61] The American ambassador to the United Nations, Adlai Stevenson, visited Brazil and was warmly received by Quadros and Afonso Arinos. The president's younger brother, Edward Kennedy (with entourage), made an unofficial tour of Latin America. He was received in Brasília by President Quadros and escorted through part of the Northeast by Celso Furtado. The possibility that President Kennedy might visit Brazil in 1961 was discussed, but in the end it was agreed that Quadros would first visit the United States. The public announcement of Quadros's visit was made on August 8.

That visit never took place. It was not Jânio who would make the next official trip to Washington as president of Brazil.

# 3

## The Coup That Collapsed

---

**M**ost of the eastern United States sweltered in a late August heat wave. Cape Cod, with highs in the eighties, was more bearable than Washington, in the humid nineties day after day. President Kennedy spent his August weekends at Hyannis Port.

He was already there on the afternoon of Friday the twenty-fifth when the first report was telephoned: President Quadros of Brazil had just resigned his office, six days short of completing seven months on the job.

The news came as a complete surprise to the White House and the State Department. That week the part of South America that had preoccupied the presidential advisors who "watched" the continent was British Guiana, where an election was taking place. Kennedy and his advisors had decided that the prime minister of the British colony, Cheddi Jagan, was procommunist and therefore a threat to the United States. Despite undercover American efforts to have him defeated, Jagan had easily been reelected.[1] In Brazil, however, everything seemed relatively quiet. It was believed that Quadros had everything under control and as usual was alternating gestures of friendship toward the Soviet bloc with the warmest expressions of appreciation for American aid. Thus, though he had recently committed the serious offense of receiving Che Guevara as Che was on his way home from an Organization of American States conference at Punta del Este, Uruguay, Jânio had received Secretary of Treasury Dillon and OAS Ambassador Morrison with great cordiality on their way to that meeting.[2] There had been no hint that Quadros was contemplating quitting the office he had campaigned for two years to win.

One corollary of the conceit of American world leadership is that a crisis anywhere in the world is a crisis for the United States and particularly for the president, the official in charge of foreign relations. On Sunday, August 27, the *Washington Post* was moved to commiserate wth Kennedy for having his weekend leisure interrupted by these troublesome crises for the third week in a row. Two weeks previously the Russians had suddenly sealed the borders of West Berlin and begun the construction of The Wall. The week after that, Kennedy had returned to Washington early in order to hear Vice President Johnson report on a special trip he had made to Berlin. Now Brazil.

Why had Quadros resigned? Had he been forced out by some group? Had a coup taken place? Was the resignation for real, or was it a ploy of some sort? There were thousands of American citizens in Brazil. Were they in any danger? Kennedy spent a great deal of time on the telephone that Friday evening talking to his White House aides, discussing the implications of the resignation. In Hyannis Port his Air Force aide, Colonel Godfrey McHugh, served as his intelligence officer and relayed the dispatches from the CIA and the State Department as they came in.

The CIA hastened to provide a Cold War explanation and to claim credit for foreseeing some sort of trouble in Brazil:

FM Director CIA
TO White House

Pass Presidential Party at Hyannisport, Attention Col. McHugh, for delivery to President Kennedy.

CONFIDENTIAL

Following memorandum on Quadros resignation prepared by CIA:

1. Quadros attentions to the [sic] Che Guevara and [Cosmonaut Yuri] Gagarin, and more generally his manifest tendencies to draw closer to the bloc, have aroused strong expressions of disapproval from the army and from conservative elements in Brazil. We think it likely that he resigned in the expectation of provoking a strong manifestation of popular support, in response to which he would return to office in a better position against his opponents. (Fidel Castro resigned once for this purpose, and Peron more than once.) Although the higher ranks of the army dislike Quadros, they would probably not block his return in such circumstances.

35

2. If Quadros does not come back, we believe that the next government will follow conservative though nationalist policies, because the army will not tolerate anything else.

3. Vice President Goulart, the constitutional successor, had just left by sea from Communist China, and will not be on hand for at least a few days. He is strongly leftist, and the army would be unlikely to allow him to exert real control of Brazilian policy.

4. The possibility of trouble in Brazil, due to Quadros' flirtation with the bloc and his tendency to hasty and dramatic action, has been recognized for some time; USIB drew attention to it on 24 August, in a "Survey of Cold War Crisis Situations," and in a National Intelligence Estimate on 8 August.[3]

The CIA analysis reflects the researcher's tendency to see only what he is seeking. In reality, Quadros's resignation had little to do with foreign policy, with attentions to Che Guevara or Yuri Gagarin, or with military unhappiness over manifest tendencies to draw closer to the bloc. True, awarding Guevara Brazil's honorary decoration for visiting foreign dignitaries had touched off an uproar in the media. "A small and silly incident," sniffed Foreign Minister Afonso Arinos, "given importance by small and silly people."[4]

Errors of interpretation abound in the CIA memorandum. Few, if any, Brazilians objected to the decoration of Cosmonaut Gagarin, the first man to complete an orbit in space. The suggestion that Quadros might be using Castro or Juan Peron as his political model was ludicrous. Resignation, or the threat of it, was an established Brazilian political tactic. As indicated above, Jânio himself had used it successfully during the campaign to get rid of obligations to political parties. The CIA analysis implies that the Brazilian military at this time spoke with one voice. That was far from true. Although some of the "higher ranks" disliked Quadros and/or his "flirtation with the bloc," other officers supported him and believed his new foreign policy was setting Brazil up as an independent world power. In fact, what was unusual during the first eight months of 1961 was the complete absence of any military plotting against the civilian president. The Brazilian military had nothing whatever to do with Quadros's decision to resign.

There was actually much less to the resignation than meets the eye. It was not the result of subterranean manipulation by hidden socioeconomic forces, nor was it due to Machiavellian maneuvering by any domestic or foreign political power. Its roots do not go deeper than the shallow level of personality. If the vanity of Carlos Lacerda had not been wounded, and if Jânio Quadros had not been an impulsive neurotic, there would have been no resignation.

As indicated in the previous chapter, Governor Lacerda had been leading a public campaign against Quadros's new foreign policy for months prior to August 25. But his personal relations with the president remained quite cordial. Since the new foreign policy had the support of other important state governors (the governors of São Paulo, Minas Gerais, and Rio Grande do Sul), Quadros clearly had no need to take criticism by the governor of Guanabara very seriously. Jânio continued to be solicitous of Lacerda's political and personal needs. He was always ready to receive the governor; other politicians complained of the limited access to the president. When Quadros met on June 29 with the governors of Guanabara, São Paulo, and Rio de Janeiro to discuss regional problems, he readily agreed to help finance capital improvement and educational projects in Guanabara. Lacerda was promised over a billion cruzeiros in federal funds.[5]

According to Lacerda's own version of events,[6] it was at this June 29 meeting that he was given the first hint that Quadros favored some sort of coup d'état to bring about basic changes in the institutions of government. The president seemed to be very upset by the difficulty of working with Congress. His closest political advisor, Justice Minister Oscar Pedroso d'Horta, present at the meeting, told Lacerda that the president might resign if he could not get the legislation he needed through Congress.

Some weeks later (Lacerda did not specify a date) when he was in Brasília, Horta expanded on the idea of "institutional reform." Congress ought to be sent off on permanent paid recess. The public at large could vote on basic policy questions via referendums. According to Lacerda, the justice minister claimed that two of the three ministers for the three branches of the armed forces had been sounded out and were agreeable to such a Napoleonic governmental system, but the president wanted the support of some of the governors before attempting any coup.

After hearing this horrifying tale of a democratically elected president plotting to subvert and overthrow the regime, Lacerda said that he returned to Rio, told absolutely no one about the conspiracy, but wrestled alone with the problem of whether he should resign, leaving the office of governor in order to disassociate himself completely from the Quadros government.

This part of Lacerda's tale is so improbable—that he told no one, not even his closest intimates—that it casts doubt over the entire story.

37

However, Lacerda did reveal more plausible reasons for experiencing a period of depression and thoughts of resignation. He did have problems. One set concerned his newspaper, *Tribuna da Imprensa*. His son had been running the paper since Lacerda became governor and was having a difficult time financially. The *Tribuna*'s burden of debt was increasing monthly. In part, this was probably due to the ending of government subsidies for importing newsprint, decreed by Quadros in early July as a part of the austerity program to reduce federal deficits. Lacerda now chose to consider the move an attack on freedom of the press.[7] He wondered whether he should give up the job of governor in order to devote full time to saving his newspaper and combating such attacks on the press.

A second set of problems revolved around the daily frustrations of administering Guanabara. The state legislature was being difficult. The public clamor for improved services was insistent.[8] The state treasury was bare. A month had passed, but none of the promised federal aid had arrived. Two billion cruzeiros of the five billion that Quadros had promised was to come from American Food for Peace funds and was available for immediate release. But it had not been released. Lacerda began to wonder whether his state was being penalized because he had spoken out against the president's foreign policy. Perhaps he should resign the governorship to spare his state further reprisals. He could then speak out still more forcefully against the drift to the Left.

After brooding about these matters for days, on Friday, August 18, Lacerda decided to have it out with Quadros. He would go to Brasília, threaten to resign, give his reasons in detail, and see what impact this ploy might have. He telephoned Quadros's wife, who was at the presidential residence in Rio, and told her that he must see Jânio in order to discuss a "tremendously serious" personal problem with him.[9] Eloa Quadros telephoned her husband in Brasília. Jânio in turn telephoned Lacerda, invited him to dinner that evening, and had a presidential jet stand by to transport him from Rio to Brasília.

Lacerda may have been somewhat mollified by these attentions, but things that evening did not go as he wished. Although he had been invited to dinner, he found when he arrived that the president had already dined. Then, the tête-a-tête with Quadros did not last as long as he had hoped. Quadros gathered from Lacerda's remarks that the governor was threatening to resign unless he got some bailout assistance for his newspaper and unless the Food for Peace funds promised Guanabara were released promptly. Neither problem struck Quadros as "tremendously serious." Both seemed rather ordinary, the type that Justice Minister Horta handled routinely. Lacerda later claimed that he had also brought up Horta's "institutional reform" plans for discussion, but Quadros begged off, saying that he would not be prepared to discuss that for another month and a half. He then sent Lacerda to see Horta in Horta's apartment. Quadros himself wanted to relax, have a few drinks, and watch an American film. He had a busy day coming up. He was scheduled to meet Che Guevara in the early morning, travel to the state of Espirito Santo to inaugurate some public works in the late morning, and then fly to Rio for the afternoon and evening.

Highly irritated that Quadros preferred to see a silly film rather than discuss the problems of Carlos Lacerda, Lacerda added the inability to get Quadros to talk to him to his list of reasons for resigning the governorship.[10] Horta did his best to soothe the irate governor. He promised to arrange private financing for the *Tribuna da Imprensa* and to expedite the release of aid to Guanabara. He assured Lacerda that the administration did not hold his opposition to the new foreign policy against him. He pointed out that the governor would have a good opportunity for another private talk with Quadros the next evening in Rio. Somewhat appeased, Lacerda left Horta's apartment around midnight.

Then came the matter of the suitcase, a triviality that Lacerda thought important enough to dwell on in his television report the next week. Just as he was leaving Horta's apartment, Lacerda mentioned that his suitcase was still at the presidential palace. To save him the walk from the gate to the palace, Horta telephoned the palace and arranged to have the suitcase brought out to the gate, ready for Lacerda to pick up. Lacerda took this courtesy for another insult. He had somehow gotten the idea that he was to spend the night at the palace. Now the justice minister had canceled the invitation and ordered his belongings put out on the street. Fuming, Lacerda went to a hotel.

> From the hotel, I telephoned the minister just to pass along the receipt and confirm that his eviction order had been carried out. The minister appeared at the hotel. I refused to receive him until he banged on the door, and it was impossible to ignore him. And there, in a more or less bohemian atmosphere, which is the atmosphere in which serious matters are dealt with in Brazil, until 4:40 in the morning the minister attempted to dissuade me from either resigning or refusing to participate in his plot.[11]

Lacerda obviously considered the suitcase affair a serious matter, worthy of a less bohemian atmosphere. To him, in fact, the eviction of the suitcase capped the humiliation of having his tremendously serious personal problem treated in such an offhand way by the president.

By 7:00 A.M. Lacerda was at the airport to catch a flight back to Rio. He thus missed the decoration of Che Guevara. According to Foreign Minister Afonso Arinos, not present in Brasília at the time of Guevara's brief stopover, Quadros used the twenty-minute meeting to urge that the persecution of Cuban Catholics and the nationalization of church schools in Cuba be halted. The papal nuncio had requested Brazilian aid in these matters. In addition, Quadros spoke to Guevara of the "need for Cuba to remain within the continental family."[12] He was probably acting on impulse when he pinned the Southern Cross decoration on Guevara. According to the decree that had created this honor for foreign dignitaries, the award had to be approved by a council that included the foreign minister, the war minister, and the navy minister. None of these officials was aware that it was being awarded to anyone. In fact, the award ceremony was played out before a few reporters and photographers; other than Quadros, no Brazilian official was present.

That afternoon when Lacerda learned of the incident, he rounded up a small group of anti-Castro Cubans in Rio and presented their leader with the key to the city. Lacerda watchers speculated that he had finally broken with the president. But in the evening Lacerda did meet with Quadros and had a long and apparently friendly chat. The Guevara episode was probably not mentioned by either man. Quadros told Lacerda that he would name a committee to distribute the Food for Peace funds immediately. Lacerda agreed to stay on as governor. There was talk of the Lacerdas and Jânio and his wife traveling together the next day to São Paulo. However, by the next morning Lacerda had changed his mind again. The Quadros party flew to São Paulo without the governor. In the evening Lacerda told a radio audience that he was representing Guanabara officially for the last time.

Encouraged by leaks from Lacerda himself, the Rio press, during the next week, indulged in lengthy speculation about the nature of the "serious rift" in Lacerda-Quadros relations and the possibility that Lacerda might really resign.[13] Either Lacerda was, as he later claimed, genuinely undecided as to his next move, or he was biding his time to strike back, waiting for the most dramatic moment. This moment came on Thursday evening, August 24. Seven years earlier on this date, his old opponent, Vargas, had removed himself from the political scene by suicide. Very much a showman, Lacerda chose the date to announce that he was staying in office. He thus underscored the difference between himself and Vargas.

40

He told a large TV-radio audience that although he had been tempted to resign, he had decided to stay on in order to better combat a brewing conspiracy to introduce dictatorship. He gave a detailed account of the conversations he supposedly had with Horta on the subject. He was careful to attribute the plotting for a coup to the justice minister, not to the president, but he made it clear that Quadros had to be aware of the scheme. He suggested that Jânio, shut up in his palace in the "wilderness" of Brasília, was being badly advised by a "group of palace greenhorns." He offered to help the president achieve legitimate reforms legally.

No doubt many listeners had tuned in expecting to hear another Lacerda attack on the Quadros foreign policy in light of the honor bestowed on Guevara. It came as a shock to hear instead that their president was involved in a conspiracy to end the experiment in democracy after only fifteen years. Lacerda mentioned his distaste for the new foreign policy only in passing. He suggested, in fact, that the proneutralist, pro-Cuban stance of the administration was merely a temporary tactic. Perhaps the leftists were at the moment being encouraged only to make them more outspoken, more visible. Then the claim that dictatorship was necessary to crush the communists could be advanced. The leftists would be well advised not to celebrate prematurely.[14]

From the foregoing it must be clear that Lacerda was a somewhat unstable politician, very much wrapped up in his own ego, and convinced that his personal political mishaps mattered to the world. There would be little point to detailing his petty adventure vis-à-vis Quadros except for two reasons: (1) It did lead to Quadros's resignation, which in turn destabilized the country that had seemed to be one of the most stable in Latin America. (2) The story highlights the personality of the governor most pleasing to American officials, a governor who would be showered with American aid and consulted regularly by the American ambassador. In short, the incident contributes to our understanding of how American foreign policy decisions are reached.

In Brazil, Lacerda's broadside was not taken very seriously by those who had always tended to oppose him. The *Correio da Manha*, for example, devoted only a few inches on an inside page to the story. Justice Minister Horta immediately denied that he was involved in any type of conspiracy and gave his version of the Lacerda trek to Brasília. The governor's primary purpose in begging for an audience with the president had been to solicit funds for his newspaper, Horta suggested; Lacerda's

41

most recent television appearance was merely "another act in the personal soap opera that the country has witnessed for the last week."[15]

But in some quarters, especially among members of Lacerda's own party, the speech created a sensation. Members of Congress who had listened to it were understandably upset: under the reported plot, they were to be sent into permanent recess. Party leaders met in the early morning hours to discuss a congressional response. They agreed that the Chamber of Deputies ought to summon the justice minister to appear before it to answer Lacerda's charges. The leaders' decision was debated in the Chamber's morning session. Some deputies suggested that the charges of conspiracy should be simply dismissed, since the information came from "a man who has injured the most honored figures of the Republic, including those of his own party."[16] Others, such as Senate president Auro Moura Andrade (an opponent of Quadros in São Paulo state politics), insisted that Lacerda's charge ought to be carefully investigated.[17] In the end, a motion to summon Horta passed the Chamber. Then, believing that their principal business was finished, most of the Congress prepared to leave the "wilderness" for the weekend. Only thirty-four were present for the opening of the afternoon session at two o'clock. Routine speeches commemorating Soldiers' Day (that day) were on the agenda. At exactly 3:00 P.M., the routine was interrupted. Congressman Dirceu Cardoso rushed into the Chamber with the news that President Quadros had just committed political suicide: he had resigned.[18]

Quadros was one of those suicides who do not intend the act to be fatal or in any way final. His resignation was partially impulsive, partially carefully calculated. While listening to Lacerda's speech, he had become enraged. Here was a politician who, after threatening to resign for weeks, lacked the courage to do so. Therefore he had concocted this television show to justify staying on as governor. He, Quadros, would show Lacerda how it was done. He would show everyone that he did not have to put up with such insults, such insidious attacks on his character. He was a man of courage and honor before he was a president.

On the other hand, Quadros was probably aware of the tremendous political advantages that an abrupt resignation might bring. Modesty was not among his virtues. He was supremely confident that he was the only person in the country capable of leading the nation during this time of economic crisis. He was indispensable. At least six million Brazilians, those who had voted for him, must share that point of view. They would clamor for him to return to his post and demand that he be given the tools to do the job.

Lacerda had spoken of a plot to fundamentally alter the existing constitution. It seems clear that Quadros would have endorsed such a move. He had thrown out hints to intimates that he felt something must be done about the uncooperative Congress.[19] But as of August 24, the idea of a coup or any other move to change the existing constitution had still not gone beyond idle talk over the whiskey glasses. Not a single general had yet been approached. Lacerda was apprently the only governor favored with a preview of presidential coup yearnings.

Now it suddenly appeared to Quadros that an opportunity to effect such a coup was being handed to him on a platter obviating the protracted plotting and negotiating otherwise needed for any major change of regime. His constitutional successor was Vice President João Goulart. In the eyes of the more conservative military and civilian officials, Goulart was either a Communist, or an admirer of Argentine dictator Juan Peron, or possibly both. At that very moment, as if to underline his supposed communistic leanings, Goulart was in Red China. People would be likely to lose sight of the fact that it was President Quadros who had asked him to head a trade mission there. In addition, Goulart's name was anathema to the Vargas-haters in the UDN. He had entered national politics as a Vargas protégé. Finally, the middle-class groups that had opposed the Kubitschek administration because of its profilgate economic policies and corruption could be expected to oppose Goulart. He had been Kubitschek's vice president also. Kubitschek had turned matters that concerned labor over to his vice president, since Goulart was head of the PTB, the Brazilian Labor Party. Through one of the special presidential committees to investigate corruption, Quadros had already done his best to link the vice president's name to corruption in labor pension funds.

In any case, there was nothing in Goulart's background or training that suggested he would be capable of administering the country at a time of financial crisis. Nothing, Quadros concluded, would make Jango (Goulart's nickname) acceptable to the governing elite. With his constitutional successor thus disqualified and with the public clamoring for Jânio's return to the presidential palace, he would be in a position to dictate conditions. Perhaps his one and only condition would be that Congress be sent on a paid recess while he, Quadros, was given emergency powers to set the country straight.[20]

Quadros calculated that his military ministers would act as a junta to administer the country until his own triumphant return to power. In fact, to make sure that they thought of doing this, he suggested it to them at the morning conference when he informed them that he was resigning.[21] Although he told the top military officials of his plans early the next morning, he requested that Congress not be informed or anything be made public until three in the afternoon. That should give the ministers time to organize a junta. By three, most Congressmen would have left town, and Congress would be unable to take any steps to counter a move by the military ministers.

In an effort to ensure that the public would in fact clamor for his return, Jânio dashed off a farewell letter to the Brazilian people modeled on the one attributed to Vargas exactly seven years previously.[22] In it, Quadros, like Vargas, mentioned unspecified foreign and domestic forces that had conspired against him as he labored tirelessly to liberate Brazil. Unlike Vargas, who had been ousted by the military and omitted any reference to them in his last testament, Quadros put in a favorable reference, thus tacitly endorsing an interim military junta:

> I was defeated by the reaction, and therefore I leave the government. In these seven months I fulfilled my duty. I have fulfilled it day and night, working indefatigably without prejudice and without animosity. But I have been frustrated in my efforts to take the nation on the road of its true political and economic freedom, the only one which can bring about the effective progress and the social justice to which her generous people have a right.

> I wanted Brazil for the Brazilians, but in pursuit of this dream I faced corruption, lies, and cowardice which subordinated the general interests to the appetites and ambitions of individual groups, including foreign ones.

> Therefore I find myself crushed. Terrible forces rose against me and plotted against me or maligned me, even while pretending to collaborate. Were I to remain, it would not be possible to maintain the confidence and tranquility... indispensable for exercising my authority. I also believe that public peace itself cannot be maintained.

> Therefore, with my thoughts turned to our people, to the students and to the workers, to the large family of Brazil, I close this page of my life and of the national life. As for me, I do not lack the courage for resigning.

> I leave with thanks and with an appeal. The thanks go to the companions who struggled along with me and sustained me in and out of government, and in a special form they go to the Armed Forces, whose exemplary conduct, in all moments, I take this opportunity to proclaim.

> The appeal is on behalf of order, harmony, respect, and esteem by each of my fellow countrymen for all; and by all for each.

Only in this way will we be worthy of this country and the world. Only in this way will we be worthy of our heritage and our Christian predestination.

I return now to my work as lawyer and teacher. Let us work, all of us. There are many ways of serving our Fatherland.[23]

In addition to that farewell message to the people, Quadros had written a shorter note:

To the National Congress:

On this date and by this instrument, leaving with the Justice Minister the reasons for my act, I resign the office of President of the Republic.

Brasília, 25 August 1961
Jânio Quadros[24]

Both messages were read to the astonished thirty-four deputies present in the Chamber of Deputies at three o'clock in the afternoon. While they debated the meaning of the farewell message (what exactly were the terrible forces that Quadros referred to?), the congressional leaders sent taxis to the airport to collect congressmen preparing to board departing flights. A joint session of the Senate and the Chamber of Deputies was held in the evening. A few congressmen urged that the resignation be refused, but the majority were of the opinion that Congress lacked the power either to accept or reject resignations of the chief executive. Its duty was to take cognizance of the fact that the office was now vacant and to act to fill the vacancy. The vice president was outside the country; in which case the constitution specified that the president of the Chamber of Deputies should serve as the acting chief executive. Accordingly, the president of the Senate, Auro Moura Andrade, administered the oath of office to Ranieri Mazzilli, the president of the Chamber of Deputies.

Quadros had left Brasília at eleven that morning, four hours before his decision to resign was made public. He flew to his home state of São Paulo and secluded himself at Cumbiça Air Force Base. Late in the afternoon he received a delegation of governors, headed by his former advisor and political ally, São Paulo Governor Carlos Alberto Carvalho Pinto. The governors begged Quadros to reconsider and withdraw his resignation. Quadros assured them that his decision was final. Fearing a possibly violent public reaction, the governors hurried back to their state capitals to prepare riot controls. Another former Quadros political ally, Carlos Castilho Cabral, attempted unsuccessfully to see Quadros that afternoon. During the presidential campaign it had been Cabral who organized and led the Movimento Popular Jânio Quadros. After the election, Cabral had urged Jânio to transform the MPJQ into a new political party to provide continuing support, but Quadros had not acted on the suggestion. He had had little time for Cabral after the election,[25] and on this afternoon he also somehow could not manage to see him. Instead, he sent Cabral a message telling him to use his own judgment as to whether or not the MPJQ should be mobilized. "I do not want to assume the responsibility for setting the nation on fire," Jânio told the minister of labor, who asked for instructions regarding possible labor union action to protest the resignation.[26] But, clearly, he hoped and expected that some sort of conflagration would happen.

It did not. That night in Rio de Janeiro several hundred students demonstrated in front of the American Embassy. Like the Kennedy administration, the Brazilian students thought that somehow the new independent foreign policy and American opposition to it must be behind the resignation—not the bruised egos of two politicians and an evicted suitcase. A railroad union declared a strike and called for a general strike by all unions. Using his own discretion, Castilho Cabral then decided against trying to revive the MDPQ; he did not want an organization associated with him to "act with rowdies or as the auxilliaries of Communists."[27] All student demonstrations were soon dispersed by the Rio police. The railroad strike lasted only a few hours. In the other major cities—São Paulo, Belo Horizonte, Recife, Porto Alegre—total calm prevailed, mixed only with indignation that Quadros had tried it again. "In reality, Mr. Jânio Quadros wasn't defeated. In reality, he ran away," editorialized the *Correio da Manha* on August 26. The newspaper had ardently supported the new foreign policy but dismissed Jânio's farewell message about terrible forces, some foreign, plotting against him as "demagogic." A joke (apparently started by São Paulo politician Adhemar de Barros) soon circulated: those "terrible forces" were named Vat 69, Dewars, and White Horse.

As Quadros waited, first at the air base and then, the next day, at the residence of a friend, a popular uproar did begin to swell. But it was not about him. Everyone was discussing Vice President João Goulart and whether or not he should be permitted to take office as specified by the constitution. Two days later, virtually unnoticed, Quadros and his family sailed to Europe.

Meanwhile, in Washington the initial CIA suggestion that Quadros was simply imitating Fidel Castro was discarded. The embassy pointed out that he had resigned once before. American analysts now thought that "the peculiar temperament of Quadros himself" as well as the coup conspiracy charges made by Governor Lacerda might have something to do with the president's resignation.[28] Nevertheless, Americans remained convinced that the departure of Quadros had somehow been precipitated by his procommunist foreign policy and his decoration of Che Guevara. The Kennedy administration was glad to see him go and worried that he might make a comeback.

Other concerns were more pressing, however. Wasn't the "strongly leftist" vice president even less acceptable? The day after the resignation, the embassy reported that the "military leadership, predominant element of which headed by War Minister Odílio Denys, strongly against allowing Goulart [to] become president."[29] Was there any possibility of armed conflict between the group headed by Denys and the supporters of Goulart? Or perhaps a period of unrest short of open warfare? It was an article of faith in Washington that communists knew how to take advantage of any sort of unrest, while the West, in its innocence, did not. So, what could the United States do to head off conflict and stabilize the situation? Shouldn't President Kennedy reiterate his already-stated opposition to military takeovers and his commitment to democratic processes and constitutional procedures?

Some presidential advisors quickly cautioned against any such declaration. "Although statement supporting constitutional processes might appear [to] be mere reiteration traditional U.S. position," the chargé d'affaires in Rio cautioned, "in present situation in Brazil it would constitute clear endorsement Goulart cause which would be deeply resented by those of our friends who support effort of military to exclude Goulart from presidency on ground his known Communist sympathies." Someone scribbled "Pres agrees" on top of the National Security Committee copy of the chargé's cable.[30] Even this early, some seven months after taking office, Kennedy made it clear that he intended to be "pragmatic" about democracy and U.S. opposition to military coups in Latin America.

The embassy at first held out the faint hope that the man with "known Communist sympathies" might be excluded "constitutionally." The Brazilian constitution—not quite fifteen years old—was still both fragile and flexible. It could easily be changed by amendment. If two-thirds of the Congress could be persuaded to stand together and vote an amendment, Congress could give itself the power to choose the successor to Quadros, and Goulart could be legally kept out, despite prior constitutional provisions for succession by the vice president.[31] But even if Congress should fail to amend the constitution, the CIA was confident that the Brazilian military would prevent the inauguration of Goulart. "On the whole, it now appears to us," noted CIA director Allen Dulles, "that Marshal Denys is in a very strong position, and stands a fair chance of achieving his aims in one way or another. He enjoys great prestige with the military, and the military will almost certainly be the dominating element in the immediate situation."[32]

Kennedy opted for a policy of strict noninterference in this Brazilian crisis. He hoped that the Dulles prediction would prove true, but if it did not, the United States could at least gain moral points with other Latin American countries, all of which opposed U.S. interference in internal affairs. In any case, the United States had little other choice. Since the Quadros resignation had been totally unanticipated, the activist administration was caught without any plan of action. No contingency plans to aid pro-American politicians and the conservative military had been prepared.[33]

Nor did the opponents of Goulart within the Brazilian military have a plan ready to prevent him from assuming office. Divisions within the armed forces became obvious within twenty-four hours. Former War Minister Marshal Henrique Lott was quick to produce a manifesto:

### To My Comrades in the Armed Forces and
### to the Brazilian People

I noted today the decision of War Minister Marshal Odílio Denys...not to permit the present President of the Republic, Dr. João Goulart, to take office and, moreover, to detain him the moment he steps on national territory.... I feel it is my unshirkable duty to make clear my repudiation of the abnormal and arbitrary solution...I urge all the living forces of the Nation ...to take a decisive and energetic position for respecting the Constitution and for the integral preservation of the Brazilian democratic regime, certain...that my noble comrades in the Armed Forces will know how to conduct themselves in view of the legalist traditions that mark their history.[34]

Marshal Denys attempted to stem defections by arresting Lott and other officers who made known their support for the constitution. But state governors who controlled state militia forces began declaring their opposition to tampering with the constitutional succession. The first to do so was the governor of Rio Grande do Sul, Leonel Brizola, Goulart's brother-in-law. He was soon joined by Mauro Borges, governor of Goias.

Other governors, such as Ney Braga of Parana, insisted that it was up to the Congress, not the military ministers, to decide the succession. When General José Machado Lopes, in command of the Third Army stationed in Rio Grande do Sul, announced that he supported the "legality" movement (as the pro-Goulart forces were known), civil war seemed inevitable. A general who was in actual command of troops was opposing the war minister. Other high-ranking officers began announcing their opposition to Marshal Denys. Some journeyed to Rio Grande do Sul to assist Lopes.

Denys appealed to the public for support. The burden of his manifesto was that Goulart had, over the past decade, demonstrated dangerous "ideological tendencies." As labor minister in 1953 he had, Denys charged, not only provoked political strikes but allowed "the wholesale infiltration...of active and known agents of international communism" into the labor ministry and unions. As vice president since 1957 he had continued "to animate and support" strikes. "And, just a little while ago, as an official representative on a trip to the Soviet Union and Communist China, he made clear and plain his unrestrained admiration for the regime of those countries, exalting the success of popular communes." Denys concluded:

> In the presidency of the Republic, in a regime that gives full authority and personal power to the Head of the Government, Mr. João Goulart would constitute, without the slightest doubt, the most evident incentive to all those who wish to see the country drowning in chaos, in anarchy, in civil war. The Armed Forces themselves, infiltrated and tamed, would be transformed into simple communist militias, as has happened in other countries.... The Armed Forces are certain of the understanding of the Christian, orderly, and patriotic people of Brazil. And they remain, serene and determined, occupied in maintaining public order.[35]

But the public disappointed the military ministers. Although the red flag had been dropped, there was no rally round the green and yellow. Without prior mobilization, without proper indoctrination, Brazilians— no matter how Christian, orderly, and patriotic—could not see the quarreling military brass as the last-ditch defenders of democratic institutions. "DICTATORSHIP!" screamed the headline of a front-page editorial in the *Correio da Manha*. "We have read the military manifesto. It abolishes the republican regime of Brazil. It is military dictatorship."[36]

With a few exceptions (such as Lacerda's *Tribuna da Imprensa*) the other major newspapers also defended the vice president's right to be installed as president. In his capacity as governor, Lacerda attempted press censorship in Guanabara, but Brizola took the lead in organizing a radio network, dubbed the Voice of Legality, that reached Rio as well as the other population centers of central and southern Brazil. Several labor unions and the National Students Union announced strikes in defense of Goulart and democracy. Excitement tinged with apprehension suffused the cities of the region. To the north all was much calmer. Details of the crisis in the south was slow to reach areas such as the hinterlands of the Northeast, Pará, or Amazonas. In 1961, television service in Brazil was very limited. It was in fact nonexistent in the north, except in the capital cities. Even radio service was limited, and there were no newspapers at all outside the larger cities.

Goulart cautiously delayed his return from the Far East. He stopped in Paris, then New York. Taking flights that avoided crossing any part of Brazil, he flew to Buenos Aires, and finally to Montevideo, across the border from his home state of Rio Grande do Sul.

As the Third Army and the militia forces of Rio Grande do Sul prepared to fight for Goulart, Marshal Denys named General Oswaldo Cordeiro de Farias the new commander of the Third Army and ordered him to arrest his predecessor, Machado Lopes. Farias tried to do this by telephone and telegraph, as he remained in the safety of Rio de Janeiro. His orders were ignored in Rio Grande do Sul. The task of putting down such an insurrection would necessarily fall to the Second Army, stationed in São Paulo. But the commander of that army now joined the governor of São Paulo in calling for some sort of compromise settlement.

It was the Congress, which refused to yield to the military ministers' demand that it legislate a ban on Goulart, that found a formula for a face-saving compromise. A parliamentary system was introduced via an amendment to the constitution. Goulart would be installed as president, but the military ministers could argue that they had succeeded in establishing checks on a potentially dangerous politician. Under the new system the president would nominate a prime minister and all cabinet ministers. Congress would accept or reject the nominees. The ministers were to be responsible to the Congress and to serve as long as Congress wished. In theory, virtually every act of the president would need the approval of the prime minister and the cabinet minister responsible for the area affected.

On the other hand, the president was more than a ceremonial figurehead. He—not the prime minister—was to preside over the Council of

Ministers. He had the power to approve and promulgate or to veto legislation. He was to represent Brazil abroad and to have the ultimate authority in managing foreign relations. And, since the amendment establishing the parliamentary system did not provide otherwise, the president would continue to have the power to appoint and dismiss the heads of federal agencies such as Petrobrás or SUDENE.

The role of the prime minister was somewhat ambiguous. Was he to be the chief executive officer or merely a special assistant to the president? It was the president, not he, who nominated the other ministers, and, once approved by Congress, a new minister was answerable neither to the prime minister nor to the president. In theory, basic government policy was to be determined by a majority vote in the Council of Ministers, but who had the responsibility for bringing policy matters to the Council? Would each minister strike out independently within his own fief, merely coming to the Council for rubber-stamp approval? No one was sure how the new system would work, and a provision for an automatic review was included in the amendment. In early 1965, a few months before Goulart's term would expire, there was to be a plebiscite on continuing the parliamentary system or returning to the presidential.

Neither Goulart nor his opponents really accepted the compromise settlement. Goulart would devote a great deal of time and energy to trying to move up the date of the plebiscite, to hold it earlier than the end of his term. His opponents began scheming to remove him from office almost before he was installed. Within a month, for example, ex-Navy Minister Sílvio Heck, one of the trio who had tried to bar Goulart, was placed under disciplinary arrest by the new navy minister for involvement in coup plotting.[17]

The plotters soon discovered that a coup was not feasible for the time being. The serious split in the armed forces and the mood of the country dictated that Goulart must be given some sort of chance to prove that he was a competent, safe, and conservative president. His opponents were confident that he would fail the test. So was the American chargé d'affaires, Niles Bond. He cabled Washington:

> While political antecedents of Goulart himself could scarcely be less promising from U.S. point of view, there are many Brazilians who think (perhaps wishfully) that responsibilities of Presidency, even as circumscribed by new constitutional amendment, will have moderating and sobering effect on him. Until we have opportunity [to] judge whether and to what extent Goulart may in fact wish to live down his fellow-traveling past and establish amicable basis

51

for continuing US-Brazilian relations, believe we should be prepared to give him reasonable benefit of doubt.[38]

The tone of Bond's telegram suggested that he had already judged Goulart, though willing to go through the forms of giving him a chance. It was no secret, Bond remarked in a 1976 interview, that "I didn't like the sonuvabitch."[39]

Bond, like General Denys, suggested that Goulart had a procommunist past that was well known and thoroughly documented. In fact, however, that was simply not true. João Goulart was a wealthy rancher from Rio Grande do Sul, who was quite free from commitments to any ideology. Abstract concepts held no appeal for him, either emotionally or intellectually. He thought of himself as a practical businessman, always ready to negotiate a deal. It was easier to negotiate, he remarked, when there were only concrete interests, not intangible attitudes, at stake.[40] He kept his own concrete interests in mind. "A careful man," ex-President Kubitschek assured Kennedy, "and not a Communist."[41]

Jango made no pretensions to intellectual prowess. Renato Archer, who served in the ministry of foreign affairs during Goulart's presidency, felt that Goulart never understood social problems or even administrative ones. According to Archer, he did not even try to understand. "He was always preoccupied with political problems," said Archer.[42] "Jango was a man of the center, dead center [*centrissimo*]," said Abelardo Jurema, who served Goulart as justice minister.[43] But Jurema thought Goulart lacked "the virile personality capable of resisting pressure." Jango always moved to conciliate.[44] "He has few ideas and even less education," wrote Jean-Jacques Faust. "He is slow to make decisions and irresolute in spirit. Therefore he frequently accepts the judgment of somebody else. His nature leads him to postpone decisions and, if he makes one, to change it at the last moment. It is his conviction...that there is always a *jeito*, a conciliation."[45] "Jango never did half the things he agreed to," sourly commented João Pinheiro, head of the agency planning land reform. He thought Goulart had agreed to sign and promulgate a land reform decree in a private ceremony, only to find him flourishing it at a public rally in Rio.[46]

Yet those who knew him personally also thought Jango had many good qualities. Everyone thought he was intelligent, however poorly educated and indecisive. He had "an enormous capacity to listen and also to speak," Jurema observed.[47] Writer Moniz Bandeira noted that the "timidity of his manner disappeared in contact with a crowd at a

52

rally, when he forgot himself, abandoned the prepared text, and improvised his speech."[48] Jango's personal life seems to have been exemplary. "In his private life, the best man in the world," reported Faust. "Simple, generous, loyal to his friends, no matter who they are. He has no arrogant attitudes. Quite the contrary."[49] Renato Archer used to find the president at his official residence in his shirt-sleeves, without tie or coat, drinking gin and tonic. If it was lunchtime (the major meal of the day in Brazil), he would invite the acting foreign minister to share his meal—strips of raw beef to be eaten with a toothpick.[50] Goulart provided none of the lofty palace atmosphere that Brazilians expect of a president. He was a family man who took the time on his trips abroad to buy toys for his two young children, João Vicente and Denise. "Jango was very much in love with Maria Teresa [his wife]," Jurema observed. The justice minister found the phenomenon a little strange. Possibly it explained some of the things Jango did, since "a man in love is likely to be very disturbed."[51] Jango was also fond of his sister, Neusa, and concerned about hurting her, but he disliked Neusa's husband, Leonel Brizola, the governor of Rio Grande do Sul in 1961. Although Brizola and he were to come close to physically fighting, Jango would never publicly repudiate his brother-in-law. Not only was Brizola "family," but Jango felt obligated to him, since it was he who had initiated the "legality" movement that brought Goulart into the presidency.

Perhaps Goulart's indecisiveness and diffidence was related to a deep sense of inferiority. "When you spoke to Jango, he never looked at you," recalled Archer. "He looked at the ground eternally. An obviously anxious person."[52] According to writer Antonio Callado, Jango told a friend that when he had been informed that Quadros had resigned, his first thought had been that he was not prepared to be president of the republic.[53]

Yet, although at age forty-three a year younger than Quadros, Goulart was in some respects better prepared. He already had years of political experience at the federal level. His career in politics had begun when he became active in state politics at the age of twenty-seven. Jango, busy managing the family ranch, might never have gotten deeper in government than the local level had he not been given a push. The push came from his elderly neighbor, Getúlio Vargas. Vargas had retired to his ranch in Rio Grande do Sul after being deposed by the military in 1945, but he had not retired from politics. When he wished to tighten his control over state politics, he picked young Jango to run for the state legislature against Protasio Vargas, Getúlio's own brother. After serving in the state legislature, Jango ran for Congress with Getúlio's blessing. He went to Rio in 1951, the same year that Vargas returned to the capital as president, after winning the election of 1950.

Goulart came to be identified with organized labor, but that identification had developed somewhat accidentally. He had not joined the PTB (Brazilian Labor Party) because he had any strong convictions about labor rights. His reasons were purely political: since Protasio Vargas was running as the PSD (Social Democratic Party) candidate, he would have to run on the PTB ticket. Both parties had been founded by Vargas. Jango's rise to the top party leadership position in 1952 was also, to a large extent, happenstance. A factional dispute within the PTB leadership that year led to the resignation of the party's national chairman. The new faction in power selected Jango as the new chairman primarily because he was seen as the protégé of Vargas. PTB strategists hoped that the move would inspire Vargas to give the party greater support. He had been displaying indifference during his first year and a half in office as president and, in fact, appeared to be courting members of the main opposition party, the UDN.[54]

By the end of 1952, Vargas had abandoned the effort to broaden his support among conservative elite groups and had decided instead to stake more on urban workers and their leftist allies. A maritime strike in June 1953 provided a turning point. Labor Minister Segada Viana proposed breaking that strike by drafting the strikers into the military reserves, thus placing them under military discipline. Labor leaders and the new PTB chairman, Goulart, warned Vargas that Viana's plan would be costly in terms of labor support. Vargas rejected the plan and accepted Viana's resignation. He named Goulart, now age thirty-seven, the new labor minister. Thus a cattle rancher with no personal urban labor experience reached the top position in organized labor in the country.[55]

Under the corporatist labor union structure that Vargas had established in the 1930s, unions were controlled by the Labor Ministry, not by the workers or by an independent labor bureaucracy. The ministry collected a compulsary union tax from all employees and distributed these funds to the unions it recognized. Union elections and union accounts were supervised by the ministry. All labor disputes with management were supposed to be settled by the special labor courts maintained by the ministry, not by collective bargaining. Since the labor minister controlled many patronage positions within his department and within the social security institutes, career labor leaders naturally looked to the minister for guidance, not to the rank and file workers. Labor ministers ordinarily had little difficulty placing loyal henchmen *(pelegos)* in the key positions in the unions.[56]

As labor minister, Goulart made no effort to change the basic structure of this corporatist system. But he introduced a clear change in style and tone. He began appealing directly to the rank and file workers, attempting to mobilize their support for Vargas. In order to do this, Goulart adopted a sympathetic, supportive attitude toward some strikes and to worker demands for wage increases. He also accepted the assistance of left-wing labor leaders who seemed to have rapport with the rank and file. The present or past political affiliations of such leaders did not seem very important under the government-controlled labor structure.

Even if he had not been willing to work with communist labor leaders, Goulart would have been suspected of being some sort of closet Red. Any labor minister who appeared ready to coddle workers and to support strikes would have been suspected of communist leanings. Conservatives in Brazil—not unlike some in the United States—still considered labor unions immoral and all strikes a form of treason. Mentally, the Right had not gotten beyond the thinking of the turn of the century, when labor problems were termed police matters. They firmly believed that Brazilian workers would never turn against their patrons unless they had been hoodwinked into doing so by outside agitators. At the turn of the century such outside agitators were thought to be anarchists. Now they were called communists.

In addition to suspected softness on communism, Goulart appeared to pose another type of threat. He, like Vargas, came from a state that bordered Argentina and shared a cattle-ranching culture with that country. Might not political ideas also be shared? In 1953 the fear of Juan Peron's example was probably even stronger than the fear of communism among Brazilian conservatives. What frightened them was not so much that Peron was a dictator or anti-American but the fact that he was basing his power on the working classes, especially on organized labor, instead of on the military and on the traditional elite, as Latin caudillos usually did. Peron seemed to be out of the control of the military; the labor unions seemed more powerful than the generals. The image of anything like Peron's "syndicalist republic" sent shivers down every proper conservative spine. For the remainder of his political career Goulart would periodically be accused of trying to set one up.

In 1953–54, he was presumably acting on behalf of Vargas rather than himself. His every act as labor minister was scrutinized closely for signs that a Vargas-Goulart move toward a syndicalist republic was imminent.

When Goulart recommended that the minimum wage rates in major urban areas be doubled, the officer corps closed ranks and demanded his ouster from the cabinet. Under the new wage rates skilled workers might end up earning more than junior officers, thus exalting workers above the military. Goulart submitted his resignation as minister of labor on February 22, 1954, but the conservative victory was a hollow one. Jango continued to reside in the presidential palace, his successor continued his policies, and when Vargas announced the new minimum wage on May 1, he followed Goulart's 100 percent recommendation.

The spector of Peron and a syndicalist republic continued to be associated with the name of Goulart in the minds of Brazilian conservatives even after Peron was finally ousted by the Argentinian military. Thus, on the eve of the election of 1955, in a last-ditch effort to prevent the election of Goulart as vice president, a document was produced that supposedly proved that Goulart had negotiated with Peron for arms and advice on how to organize "worker shock brigades." The document, published by Lacerda, was not proven to be a forgery until after the election.[57]

The syndicalist republic charge meant little or nothing to American foreign policy analysts. What interested them was the alternate notion that Goulart, first as labor minister and then as vice president, "fellow-traveled" with the Brazilian Communist Party.[58] Goulart's eight-month stint as labor minister coincided with the peak of the McCarthy era in the United States. At that point most Americans had still not tired of the hunt for Soviet agents within their most cherished institutions, but they were equally prepared to thrill to tales of communist penetration abroad. Sam Pope Brewer, a *New York Times* reporter in Brazil in 1953 and 1954, regularly filed stories about widespread communist activity in Brazil. In August 1953 some Brazilian congressmen suggested that Brewer ought to be expelled from the country for his sensational reporting, but Brewer was unchastened. "There is daily evidence of the Communists' intensified efforts to penetrate all organized groups," he was still reporting a year later.[59]

Leading representatives of the American labor movement, flushed with success in identifying communist sympathizers in American unions, were eager to joust with Red agents in foreign unions. An International Confederation of Free Trade Unions was established in 1949 to combat the Soviet-supported World Federation of Trade Unions. Regional labor organizations were set up under the International. The one for Latin

May 1956. Vice President João Goulart meets with President Eisenhower on his first official visit to the United States. American labor leaders were already worried that Goulart, also head of the Brazilian Labor Party, was procommunist. (Courtesy Dwight D. Eisenhower Library.)

America was known as ORIT (Inter-American Regional Labor Organization). In the 1950s and 1960s the director of ORIT was Serafino Romualdi, who was serving both as AFL representative for Latin America and as CIA agent for labor operations in Latin America.[60] Romualdi, who made frequent trips to Brazil, became one of the Washington "experts" on Goulart as head of the Brazilian Labor Party. He accepted all of the charges against Goulart quite uncritically: Goulart's tactics as labor minister were "reminiscent of Juan Domingo Peron"; communists boring from within, received "indirect support" from Goulart; the victory of Kubitschek and Goulart in the election of 1955 indicated the "growing influence and danger" of communism in Brazil. Even so, Romualdi was more temperate than some other American labor leaders; Jay Lovestone, for example, opposed even AFL-CIO participation in an official reception for the new vice president who played ball with communists.[61]

In a country such as the McCarthy-era USA, where a single association with a "card-carrying" Communist tainted absolutely, it would have been unthinkable to suggest that playing ball with communists might often make political sense. But in postwar Brazil the idea did not seem so shocking. In fact, most politicians routinely accepted PCB (Brazilian Communist Party) help if it was offered.[62] The PCB might have little money to contribute, but it could usually turn out people for political rallies, and well-attended rallies suggested important momentum. Of course, the entire political party setup in Brazil was sharply different from that in the United States. Instead of two fairly stable major parties, in Brazil there were from fifteen to twenty parties with some pretensions to a national status. Most of them, not even organized until late 1945, were only to a minimal degree concerned with political issues, and they evinced strong tendencies to splinter along lines of internal rivalries. During campaigns for local and state offices, parties would typically work out alliances or coalitions, with agreements on patronage distribution in the event of electoral victory. At some point after the election, the coalition would dissolve, usually in disputes over the patronage agreement. The Brazilian Communist Party fitted into the picture as one of the many small parties. It differed from the others in being barred by law from fielding candidates for office under its own banner. It was not barred from supporting other parties or from working out arrangements so that its members could run as members of other parties.

Thus, pragmatic politics in Brazil dictated playing ball with communists. In addition, sometimes personal ties transcended ideological barriers. "Agildo [Barata Ribeiro] was my friend until his death," observed the conservative anticommunist Juracy Magalhães, speaking of a prominent PCB leader.

> I helped him when I could during the time he was in exile. When he returned I was governor of Bahia. I went on board to meet him and bring him to lunch with me. Later, I visited him in detention. Some people even began to suspect that I was a Communist because I wouldn't let go of those ties of affection. When Agildo died, I was one of the friends who conducted the coffin to the grave.[63]

In passing judgment on Brazilian politicians, American intelligence specialists tended to ignore the context of Brazilian politics. The charges made by the embittered foes of Vargas and his political heirs were simply accepted, passed along from one tour of duty group to the next, creating their own historical record. By September 1961, Chargé Bond could state that "Goulart's past associations with Communists and his anti-US positions are matter of public record" and the CIA could report "President João Goulart has a long history of working with Communists in an effort to increase his political strength, particularly in labor groups."[64] Neither analyst felt obliged to offer any supporting evidence.

If the Kennedy administration was as eager to promote democratic reform governments as its spokesmen claimed, in September 1961 it should have warmly embraced Goulart and congratulated his supporters. They had just averted a right-wing military coup. Instead, the administration's first reaction was to hunker down grimly while assessing the extent of losses to communism in Brazil and pondering what might be done to minimize the damage. The embassy advised against any new U.S. aid commitment to Brazil, arguing that haste in offering such aid "in absence convincing disavowal" by Goulart of his past associations with communists "would undoubtedly weaken political strength of U.S. friends throughout hemisphere."[65] On the other hand, analysts at the State Department felt that it was important to maintain a helpful, friendly posture, whether or not any new aid were offered. "The fiasco of the Quadros resignation and the ensuing crisis has been a bitter blow to Brazil's pride and pretensions to be taken seriously as a contender for great power status. We feel that the Brazilian nation is, under the circumstances, entitled to receive a full measure of comprehension and friendship from us."[66]

There spoke the voice of the losers. The American analysts accepted it as the voice of the nation. No doubt those Brazilians who had tried and failed to block the constitutional successor felt that sort of shame and chagrin. But they were a minority. Euphoria and elation marked the postcrisis mood of most Brazilians.[67] For once a military coup had been thwarted with civilians taking the lead. There was a joyous feeling that the young democracy was working. The might of an aroused people was greater than that of misguided generals, perennial conspirators such as Lacerda, and hostile forces such as foreign-owned conglomerates. There was certainly no sense that Brazilian pretensions to great power status had been set back. On the contrary, the inauguration of Goulart was a guarantee that the independent foreign policy would continue. So would development. A democratic revolution was underway and could not be stopped. Brazil, the sleeping giant, was waking up.

To say the least, the joy was premature, the exhuberant conclusions erroneous. In this crisis not only had the *golpistas* (coup plotters) been unusually disorganized, but the United States had not weighed in at all. All of that would change in the next two and a half years.

# 4

# Nation Building: I

---

*Let us once again transform the American continent into a vast crucible of revolutionary ideas and efforts—a tribute to the power of the creative energies of free men and women, an example to all the world that liberty and progress walk hand in hand. Let us once again awaken our American revolution until it guides the struggle of people everywhere—not with an imperialism of force or fear, but the rule of courage and freedom and hope for the future of man.*

*John F. Kennedy, March 13, 1961*

The soaring rhetoric, the call to revolution—how fresh and surprising it was, coming out of the stodgy political center of one of the most conservative nations in the world. Kennedy was quite deliberately attempting to launch a new American foreign policy for Latin America. During the 1950s a number of liberal pundits contributed to the development of the concept of "nation building." It was conceived as an exciting new activist policy that aimed at solving the problems of the underdeveloped world. The seminal text, published in 1957, was *A Proposal: Key to an Effective Foreign Policy*, by MIT professors Max F. Millikan and Walt W. Rostow. Of the two, Rostow had the greater impact on administration policy in the next decade. He served in various posts as a foreign policy advisor under Presidents Kennedy and Johnson, ending up as Johnson's national security advisor after McGeorge Bundy had resigned.

In 1958 Rostow was one of "a large group of academics interested in problems of public policy who were purposefully recruited by Kennedy." At their very first meeting, according to Rostow, he realized that he and Kennedy shared a similar outlook. Both were concerned about new perils in the Cold War, and both "sensed that the domestic agenda was shifting beyond the then familiar categories of conventional liberalism."[1] They believed, in fact, that the domestic issues that had formerly engrossed the energies of American liberals had been pretty much solved.

The farm problem, the status of big business in a democratic society, the status and responsibilities of organized labor, the avoidance of extreme cyclical unemployment, social equity for the Negro, the provision of equal educational opportunity, the equitable distribution of income—none of all these great issues is fully resolved but a national consensus on them exists within which we are clearly moving forward as a nation. The achievement of this consensus absorbed much of the nation's creativeness and idealism over the past ninety years. If we continue to devote our attention in the same proportion to domestic issues as in the past, we run the danger of becoming a bore to ourselves and the world.

To avoid boredom and to keep alive "those basic spiritual qualities which have been historically linked to the nation's sense of world mission," Rostow, like Kennedy, believed the United States must turn its attention to "the great revolutionary transformations going forward in the underdeveloped countries."[2]

The proponents of nation building saw the underdeveloped world as floundering, in a state of flux and uncertainty. Independence from colonial status had been achieved, but the new nations were uncertain of their next moves. They badly needed new direction, new leadership; traditional American diplomacy, as practiced by the Eisenhower administration, had provided neither. Traditional diplomacy concentrated on (1) building military alliances along a containment line and (2) promoting the interests of American business abroad. To a much more incidental degree, it also provided humanitarian relief and limited technical assistance to the underdeveloped countries.

Liberal academics such as Rostow believed that money spent procuring and supplying Third World countries as military allies was money wasted. An underdeveloped country could not really contribute anything to modern warfare. Defense was something that would have to be left up to the United States and NATO.[3]

In addition, Rostow believed that humanitarian relief did little to solve fundamental economic problems or the political problems that they gave rise to. Relief aid did little to stave off revolution, for example. Revolutions were not made by the chronically hungry, the destitute, the homeless. Revolutions were most likely to occur when the living conditions of people were improving somewhat, but not fast enough, when people's expectations about life were raised but not met. That was exactly what was happening in the underdeveloped nations. They were being swept by "a revolution of rising expectations." The expectations were for rapid economic development, education, social and political betterment. If they were not shown the way to achieve these things democratically, they might renounce democratic institutions and seek change through violence. The underdeveloped nations might degenerate into chronic trouble spots, places in constant turmoil. Even worse for the United States, they might turn to communism, "not because of any authentic attractions in its ideology but because the Communists have recognized their opportunities to exploit the revolution of rising expectations by picturing Communism as the road to social opportunity or economic improvement or individual dignity and achievement or national self-respect, whichever fitted a given situation."[4]

Clearly it was in the American interest to learn how to do those things also. Millikan and Rostow recommended that America immediately "take the leadership in a new international partnership program for world economic growth."[5] The United States must engage the attention and enthusiasm of Third World activists and channel their energies into an exciting national development program. "We welcome the revolution of rising expectations among our peoples," said Secretary of Treasury Dillon a few years later, "and we intend to transform it into a revolution of rising satisfactions."[6] To do that, the United States promised to provide planning know-how and expertise in identifying and overcoming obstacles in the development track, as well as much of the necessary capital.

The nation builders were confident that they understood the dynamics of development. Every developing country necessarily went through an evolutionary three-stage cycle: (1) establishing preconditions, (2) the take-off, and (3) self-sustained growth.[7] The American experts could take a look at the economy of any underdeveloped country and determine which stage it was in, what was holding it back, and what remedies should be tried to push the economy forward a notch.

Such a cool activist approach appealed to Senator Kennedy. He was campaigning against complacent inaction and promising to get the nation moving off dead center both at home and abroad. After the 1960 election he made nation building the cornerstone of his foreign policy for the Third World. He also liked the nation builders' insistence that they were pragmatic social engineers, not starry-eyed do-gooders. They were aware of the lack of popular and congressional support for foreign aid programs; Americans in general shared a secret fear that wily foreigners would take advantage of their generosity and play Uncle Sugar for a sucker. As had happened in the past, American taxpayers' dollars might simply line the pockets of the recipient country's elite and/or end up in numbered Swiss bank accounts. To avoid that, the advocates of nation building stressed the importance of allocating funds "according to a banking concept of credit worthiness and technical absorptive capacity." The would-be recipient country must be able to demonstrate that it could absorb and use American aid in actual development. It must prepare a detailed development plan, provide proof that it had the skilled personnel and the available facilities to implement the plan, and indicate the ways in which it would mobilize its own resources and encourage the investment of domestic savings in development projects.[8]

In fact, the proposed prerequisites for receiving American aid were so strict that it was unlikely that any underdeveloped country would ever be able to meet them. Had a country been capable of producing a detailed development plan, providing the technicians needed to carry it out, and dredging up most its own capital from domestic savings, it probably would not have needed American aid at all. But the emphasis on strict banker's rules was modified from the start by political considerations. Foremost in the minds of the liberal academics who were trying to devise an effective foreign policy for America was the realization that the Soviet Union was the major competitor of the United States in world affairs. The communists were attempting to capture the hearts and minds of people in the ex-colonial world. The United States must do likewise. An underdeveloped country did not live by the hope of bread alone. An inspiring democratic ideology was needed. The apathy and inertia of a stagnant society must be overcome. Somehow the masses must be made to feel that they had a stake in their country's future. Enthusiasm must be mobilized and a spirit of hard work and self-sacrifice instilled. Western-style development, with mixed private and public enterprise, clearly needed its own mystique to counter the appeal of communism. To encourage the appearance of such a mystique, the United States must begin by promoting basic social reforms in recipient countries, reforms that would make each country more democratic, with increased social, economic, and political opportunities for all of its classes and regions.[9]

American officials in Brazil began pushing reform ideas even before details of a Latin American nation-building assistance plan were worked out. Thus, on April 17, 1961, a symposium on agrarian reform opened in Rio, with several American professors participating. The conference hoped to develop suggestions on how to implant agrarian reform and create a rural middle class. It was not unusual that American professors who specialized in Latin American studies should be invited to participate in a Brazilian conference. What was unusual about this conference was that it was sponsored by IBAD (Brazilian Institute for Democratic Action), and IBAD was a CIA front.

IBAD had been set up by the CIA's Rio Station in 1959 to provide cover for American involvement in the Brazilian presidential election of 1960. (IBAD supported Quadros.) Its ostensible purpose was to defend democracy, and its ostensible founders were a group of Brazilian businessmen and military officers. It quickly established close relations with a number of like-minded anticommunist organizations such as the Ação Democrática Parlamentar (Congressional Democratic Action), the American Chamber of Commerce in Brazil, the Confederação Nacional do Comercio (the Brazilian Chamber of Commerce), and CONCLAP (Conference of Productive Classes, another business group). In addition, it began spawning new organizations such as ADEP (Popular Democratic Action) and an advertising agency, Incrementadora de Vendas Promotion. It was also active as a welfare agency in the Northeast, distributing food and medical services along with propaganda.[10]

IBAD's early preoccupation with the Northeast and with agrarian reform betrayed its origin as an American organization. In 1961 most Brazilians, unlike the Americans, simply did not consider the solution of the problems of the drought-stricken, agrarian Northeast as the most pressing set of problems facing their country.

IBAD was to become much more active in both its networking and electioneering in 1962. Formal aid agreements between the United States and Brazil might mark the public thrust of the New Frontier's nation building, but there was to be a covert side as well. The CIA was expected to play an important part in nation building. Behind-the-scenes American pressure on the Brazilians could be regarded as preferable to open American preaching about Brazilian shortcomings and what should be done to overcome them. When a CIA front such as IBAD did the preaching, it seemed to come from progressive Brazilians. Rostow recommended that to minimize the natural resentment of the dependent recipients, Americans should minimize their own role as donors. They should stand ready to give the fullest possible credit for whatever contributions the Third World country might make to the nation-building program.[11]

Rostow did not for a moment consider the possibility that American nation-building activity could be seen as American imperialism. He thought of imperialism as a matter of establishing territorial colonies, with full political control vested in the mother country. Western colonial imperialism was, Rostow believed, a thing of the past. Western Europe and America had given their colonies independence. The only country seeking that kind of political control over additional territory was the Soviet Union.[12] Most American academics were agreed on this point. Although ready to concede that the costly nation-building program was actually in the American national interest and not entirely sheer altruism, American pundits were puzzled and pained by the insistence of Latin intellectuals that imperialism should be understood as the economic penetration of another country, that economic, not political, control was really the issue. Fortunately for their own peace of mind, the Americans could dismiss such arguments as Soviet-inspired propaganda. In any case, the nation builders felt, the American objective was to build and strengthen the Latin economies, not to take them over. Adolf Berle, for example, argued that the United States was far from wishing to control Brazil's economy. America did not really need anything at all from Brazil; whatever it supplied could be obtained elsewhere; all of American investment there could be confiscated without even being missed.[13] It is of course unlikely that the American corporations with investments in Brazil were inclined to agree with ex-Ambassador Berle.

The initial Brazilian reaction to news of American interest in a crash program for Brazilian development had been skepticism. The first Kennedy mission to Brazil—that of McGovern and Schlesinger—came offering food relief for the Northeast. That was hardly the type of assistance the Brazilians wanted. Such aid was merely palliative, not aimed at solving any fundamental economic problem. SUDENE chief Celso Furtado told Schlesinger as much. Even middle-of-the-road newspapers such as *Correio da Manha* ran stories reporting that other countries (Argentina, Mexico) were turning down such relief assistance. The implication was that if Brazil had any self-respect, it would do likewise.[14] Then came Adolf Berle with his offer of $100,000,000 in exchange for Brazilian support against Castro. Of course that type of assistance was even worse than food relief. It was an affront to the national honor.

Six weeks after Berle's visit, the Bay of Pigs episode unfolded. It made a deep impression on Brazilian nationalists.

If the United States wants reforms to be carried out, it should help us carry out our national revolutions.

Can we wait for that help?

The Americans showed sympathy for Cuba when Fidel Castro overthrew Batista. But when Cuba carried out agrarian and urban reform, nationalized imperialist enterprises and the monopolies, and initiated the operation emancipating the Cuban economy and liberating all of the productive forces of the country—what did the United States do?

They exported Counter-Revolution to Cuba.[15]

For the leftists, the Bay of Pigs effort revealed the true counterrevolutionary nature of Kennedy's foreign policy. But for most Brazilians, the impression produced by the clumsy and unsuccessful intervention was rather fleeting. Cuba was a small country and the American attempt to interfere with its right of self-determination was clearly wrong, but it had not succeeded, and perhaps the new and inexperienced administration had stumbled into it by mistake. The successful negotiation of the American aid package for Brazil just a month after the Bay of Pigs suggested American repentance for the Bay of Pigs venture. Despite Brazil's public opposition to intervention in Cuba, the American officials offered an impressive package of new loans and a rescheduling of old debt. The "extraordinary" amount of aid, editorialized the pro-American newspaper, *Estado do São Paulo*, should "sweep away all doubts about the new American administration's desire to help."[16] True, most of the $648 million package of new loans was not to be disbursed immediately, but rather to be released over the next few years. But with the formal launching of the Alliance for Progress, the prospects for additional sums seemed bright.

The Alliance for Progress was to be the major nation-building effort of the Kennedy administration. In March 1961, Kennedy had sounded the call for "a vast cooperative effort, unparalleled in magnitude and nobility of purpose, to satisfy the basic needs of the American people for homes, work and land, health and schools."[17] Before making that speech, Kennedy asked José Antonio Mayobre, Venezuela's ambassador to the United States for suggestions. Mayobre quickly set up an ad hoc committee of eminent Latin economists to draw up a statement of the Latin position on development.[18] The suggestions that came out of the committee did not fundamentally conflict with the recommendations made earlier by Millikan and Rostow, and, on the whole, the Alliance for Progress plan followed their nation-building script. Thus, there was to be an American financial commitment for at least a ten-year period, but the United States would try to keep a low profile about its contribution. "Comprehensive and well-conceived national programs of economic and social development" were emphasized as a basic requirement for assistance. Self-help efforts, such as educational reform, agrarian reform, tax reform, and the increased exploitation of natural resources, must be a part of each recipient's national program. Such self-help reforms ought to increase opportunities for all classes and regions and improve the ability of the recipient nation to absorb aid. In addition to the emphasis on development and on social reform, there would be a call for political democracy. Political freedom would obviously be an essential element in the counter-mystique to communism that was to be created.

After task forces established by the Organization of American States had completed preliminary position papers and arrangements, the Inter-American Economic and Social Council met at Punta del Este, Uruguay, from August 5 to 17, 1961, to draft a charter for the new alliance and to work out operational details. The American delegation was headed by Secretary of the Treasury C. Douglas Dillon, who had favored something like the Alliance for Progress when serving as assistant secretary of state for economic affairs in the Eisenhower administration.

The conference was highlighted in part by the contrast between Dillon and Che Guevara, the head of the Cuban delegation. The press sensed confrontation from the outset. When Dillon arrived at Punta del Este, clad in a "banker's" gray herringbone overcoat, he was welcomed by Urguay's foreign minister. When Guevara arrived in his black beret, open-neck shirt, and combat boots, he was greeted by 2,000 student admirers as well as by Uruguayan officials.[19]

Although cooperative in working sessions, in public Guevara appeared to seek confrontation. When Dillon announced that the United States would contribute $20 billion over a ten-year period, Guevara challenged him to prove that the sum represented a "concrete" figure that had been "ratified" by the U.S. Congress. It had not. In fact, Dillon had no authorization to mention any figure other than the $1 billion for the first year that President Kennedy had already pledged.[20]

Dillon did not respond to Guevara's taunts until the final session, much to the disgust of some of the Americans present, such as the American Federation of Labor official Serafino Romualdi. Romualdi, attending as a member of a delegation of labor observers, felt that Dillon's failure to debate or to lash out in a direct, manly fashion meant a serious loss of face for the United States among nations that prized machismo. He attributed Dillon's tendency to turn the other cheek to the baleful influence of White House advisor Richard Goodwin.[21] Actually, the entire delegation had discussed the matter and, fearing that replies would dignify Guevara's jibes, had decided that he should be ignored rather than answered. The Americans followed the somewhat childish tactics of refusing to recognize the existence of the Cuban delegates. If accidentally meeting Cubans in the corridor or caught in the same room at some function, all of the Americans looked icily in some other direction.

Richard Goodwin broke ranks on the last day of the conference when he met Guevara at a birthday party in the apartment of a Brazilian delegate. Guevara urged that all points of difference between Havana and Washington be settled by negotiations. Goodwin promised to convey the offer to Washington. He may have done that, but of course Kennedy would never consider such a politically risky move. Even had the President himself been less paranoid about Castro, too many members of Congress were more so. Goodwin was roundly denounced by OAS Ambassador Morrison for sending up the wrong signal and giving the presidents of Brazil and Argentina the idea that the United States was ready to take a softer line on Castro. Under this impression, both presidents received Che Guevara after the conference.[22] Shortly thereafter, Goodwin was transferred from his free wheeling White House staff post to a desk in the State Department.

As far as the Brazilian delegation was concerned, the Americans had followed a wise strategy. Quadros had expected some sort of confrontation between the United States and Cuba. He had called in the Brazilian delegation just before they left for Punta del Este and instructed them to walk out if the United States tried to make the conference an instrument of the Cold War or if the Americans insisted on taking up political problems instead of sticking to the economic. The American behavior made a walkout unnecessary. Only one member of the Brazilian delegation, Governor Leonel Brizola, left early, and he did so primarily because the rest of the Brazilian delegation was ignoring him. Since he was eager to defend Cuba against the North American Colossus, no doubt Brizola was also disappointed that no opportunity to do so developed.[23]

The other members of the Brazilian delegation were pleased with the conference and agreed with the sentiments expressed by Brazilian finance minister Clemente Mariani when he made the closing speech at Punta del Este:

In a gesture of political vision the United States has placed at our disposal the resources which, in conjunction with those of other sources and those we can mobilize ourselves, will be the mainspring of our economic and social development. . . . This economic revolution is to be carried forward with equally needed social reforms. . . . Development is not enough. We need development with social justice.[24]

It appeared that the Kennedy administration's try at nation building in Latin America was getting off to an excellent start. In Brazil, the Quadros resignation crisis immediately followed the Punta del Este conference and distracted everyone's attention for a time. But by November governors and mayors were happily drawing up lists of projects they would like to have funded by the Alliance for Progress. It took some time before the realization dawned: it would take a very long time to get any American money at all. By "planning," the Kennedy administration meant something other than drawing up a ranked list of needs. It wanted detailed project descriptions backed by feasibility studies, cost analyses, impact statements, and preferably some sort of indication that the project fitted into some overall national development plan, one which managed to reconcile monetary stabilization with economic expansion while simultaneously pushing forward basic social reforms.

Of course it was too much. Even America's friend Carlos Lacerda was soon complaining about the American "mania for sending technicians to make reports" when concrete assistance was urgently needed.[25] Only in the Northeast region, where a competent planning agency, SUDENE, was already functioning, could any plans approaching the American requirements be produced in the short term.

Given the American preoccupation with the Northeast, one would think that here at least the Alliance for Progess would have been put to work quickly. But it did not turn out that way. Instead of accepting the plans that SUDENE had developed, the Kennedy administration dispatched its own team of economists under Merwin L. Bohan to suggest projects. Bohan did work with SUDENE and incorporated many of that agency's proposals in the report he submitted in February 1962. But neither the Bohan Report nor the SUDENE master plan was followed by the AID agency that was set up in Recife. Politics, not development, determined what projects would be financed.[26]

"I feel that we should do something of a favorable nature for Brazil before the election this fall, which is going to be crucial," Kennedy wrote to AID director Fowler Hamilton. "Perhaps a food, water, or some other project could be proposed. Would you talk to Ted Moscoso about this and then discuss with me."[27] A food, water, or other immediate impact project might help pro-American candidates in the October 1962 elections, but it would contribute little to basic development. Even worse, the rush project would undermine SUDENE, which was struggling to retain some overall, apolitical, nonpartisan authority, above the short-term political needs of the state governors of the region.

Even immediate impact projects were hard to launch. Deciding that the governor's race in Pernambuco was the most critical one for American interests, AID decided on a crash elementary school building project in that state. Drawing up the plans, determining sites, selecting contractors, and securing the agreement of SUDENE and of the current governor took so long that little was actually finished by the October election. In any case, the anti-American candidate won the election and took steps to terminate the agreements signed by his predecessor. Governor Miguel Arraes argued (apparently correctly) that under the constitution only the federal government had the power to negotiate such a contract with a foreign power.

A school building program did proceed in other Northeastern states, but progress was slow. Inflation steadily eroded the funds allocated for this and other AID projects in the area. The technicians of SUDENE were not only noncooperative but hostile to the arriving American technicians. The Americans, usually unable to speak Portuguese and quite unprepared for the bleak quality of life in the rural hinterlands, had expected to be gratefully welcomed by the people they had come to help.

One AID technician later reported his discouraging experience:

In looking for a new post after completing my Panama assignment, I sought out Northeast Brazil, believing that this program would offer a challenge of great interest. Upon arrival Recife in June, 1963, however, I found a group of demoralized technicians in the Agricultural Branch. For over a year these men had done their utmost to achieve a working relationship with SUDENE, without success. For the first six months of my tour, I maintained hopes of breaking this impasse. Finally, in December of 1963, the Agricultural Division Chief in SUDENE was frank enough to tell us that the help of the United States would not be requested in the field of rural development....An attempt was made to work with the various NE states, all of which were eager for USAID assistance. Technical help in planning was accorded several states which then presented projects to SUDENE for approval and transmittal to USAID. None of these emerged from the SUDENE morass. With the door closed in our faces, it was decided to reduce the RD staff, maintaining a small nucleus to work on natural resources planning.[28]

Sensing that public enthusiasm for the Alliance for Progress was somehow failing to ignite, one agency decided to do something about it. On

71

Sunday, March 25, 1962, a special supplement entitled *Primer for Progress (Cartilha Para O Progresso)* was inserted in the major Brazilian newspapers. The subtitle was "How to Make a Revolution without Blood." Copies of this supplement had been distributed to the newspapers by a virtually unknown organization calling itself IPES (Institute of Research and Social Studies). The supplement identified IPES as a nonpartisan civic organization of business and professional men who met to discuss economic and social problems. Its activities were supposedly funded by voluntary contributions of individuals and business firms.

By March 25, 1962, IPES had been in existence for four months. In late 1960 a small group of Brazilian businessmen had organized a political discussion group. They met in each other's homes to discuss the communist menace and the problems facing the country. A year later, on November 29, 1961, after the resignation of Quadros and the failure of the attempt to bar Goulart, the informal discussion group was suddenly transformed into an organized research institute named IPES with a suite of offices in downtown Rio and eighty charter members. At about this time the CIA was setting up similarly named organizations of business and professional people in other Latin countries. In Equador it was the Center for Economic and Social Reform Studies, in Colombia, the Center of Studies and Social Action. "Civic organizations of this sort," wrote former CIA agent Philip Agee, "have been established by other stations and have been effective for propaganda and as funding mechanisms for elections and other political action operations." The coincidence is too great to be entirely fortuitous.[29] It was undoubtedly the CIA that contacted the businessmen's discussion group and suggested a somewhat more ambitious undertaking. It was the CIA that provided seed money for the new institute. The seed money probably came through IBAD. Relations between IBAD and IPES were close. The director of IBAD, Ivan Hasslocher, was a member of IPES.

Once established, IPES probably took off on its own. It is unlikely that the CIA played much of a continuing role in running the institute or in determining its policies. There was sufficient local anticommunist talent to do that. No doubt, the United States government continued to contribute financially; American-owned firms also contributed. But IPES was not dependent on American subsidies since Brazilian businessmen, anxious to do their bit to fight communism, readily donated funds. "They didn't need our money. São Paulo was full of money," recalled Ambassador Lincoln Gordon, years later, denying that a great deal of American money had been invested in anti-Goulart activities. Just a dollar here and there, he suggested.[30] American officials continued to supply anti-communist inspirational materials and to set up international forums at which the Brazilian and American business executives might meet and exchange Cold War thoughts. Thus, the month before their *Primer for Progress* circular appeared, the leaders of IPES attended an international convention of similar "civic" groups in Nassau. From Nassau they were flown to Washington, where they met with Department of Commerce officials and with Teodoro Moscoso, the director of the Alliance for Progress.[31] No doubt they were urged to proceed with the project of selling the Alliance via a newspaper insert.

Actually, the *Primer for Progress* illustrated some of the difficulties in the way of creating and putting over a mystique. It contained many photographs and had an attractive layout. It listed the goals of the Alliance for Progress, quoted the preamble of the Alliance's charter in its entirety, and promised benefits for the poor: "The farm worker will have land and the means to work it, the illiterate will have schools, the sick, hospital beds, those who want to work, work." "Work, shelter, land, schools, and health" were listed as the basic social needs that would be satisfied at the same time as political democracy and liberty were "definitively consolidated." The "elites" were advised to be altruistic and to eliminate "conditions that benefit the few and are detrimental to the many." The government was warned against compromising the prompt execution of Alliance projects by bureaucratic red tape and unnecessary delays. But IPES seemed unable to suggest any immediate, specific action that required the participation or involvement of individual volunteers. The image projected was rather of the Brazilian masses waiting passively for a shower of benefits. There was nothing for activists to do. Statements such as "Every country must promote conditions that stimulate the influx of foreign investment, which helps augment the capital resources of participating countries," were hardly calculated to arouse patriotic enthusiasm. The "Revolution without Blood" also promised to be one without sweat, tears, or nationalism. It did not, in fact, sound much like a revolution, but more like a reform package that would be handed down from on high at some indeterminate future date.

Although Alliance for Progress rhetoric frequently mentioned and promised revolution, there was another, decidedly counterrevolutionary side to the nation-building effort: the counterinsurgency campaign. It was a campaign close to Kennedy's heart. Having interpreted Khrushchev's January 6 speech as a pledge to support anti-American guerrillas in the underdeveloped world, Kennedy decided that Americans must develop the necessary skills to fight guerrillas on their own terrain. Only twelve days after his inauguration, Kennedy requested Secretary of Defense McNamara to examine ways of "placing more emphasis on the development of counter-guerrilla forces."[32]

The military establishment, geared to fight modern wars with modern high-tech weaponry, was not thrilled with the prospect of returning to training men to fight with rifles, hand grenades, and bayonets. Kennedy personally had to give the orders for the expansion of the Special Warfare Center at Fort Bragg.[33] Before Kennedy stepped in, only a small number of troops were being trained there to operate behind the lines of a conventional war theater. But in guerrilla warfare there would be no clear lines at all. The president felt that American or allied troops must learn all of the tactics that guerrillas used in order to combat them. They must learn how to live off the land, patrol the jungle, infiltrate enemy-held areas, carry out sabotage operations, win over or terrorize the village people. In urban areas they must be prepared to identify and maintain surveillance over potential subversives as well as to control rioting mobs or to crush Communist-led labor strikes. In addition to training more American Special Forces, the Fort Bragg Special Warfare Center was ordered to train selected troops coming from the underdeveloped nations that America was protecting.

By June 1961, Kennedy had set up a committee called "Special Group (CI)." The CI stood for counterinsurgency: the Special Group, under General Maxwell Taylor, was to coordinate and further develop the counterinsurgency effort. It was made up of representatives from the Departments of State, Defense, and Justice, the Joint Chiefs of Staff, AID, CIA, USIA, and the White House. Walt W. Rostow, as a member of the Special Group, chaired a subcommittee to develop training programs and to establish a Modernization Institute which would be dedicated to economic development planning as well as to counterinsurgency training. One of the institute's principal objectives "would be to integrate, further develop, and disseminate a common U.S. doctrine to guide instruction and operations in the non-technical components of countering subversion and insurgency in the less developed world."[34] Presumably "non-technical" included everything beyond the actual techniques of fighting guerrillas in jungles, controlling mobs in cities, or assassinating leaders. For example, the ability to identify possible subversives and to spot the Communist "line" in print or speech would be included. So would the ability to transmit to the people of the underdeveloped country a sense of abhorrence for such subversion. Ideally, the American trained in counterinsurgency would also be able to communicate an appreciation for the American way of life. All of this would require the study of the history of communist revolutions and of Soviet tactics, as well as a study of American institutions and ideals.

Even before Rostow's subcommittee had time to fully develop an outline of counterinsurgency doctrine, steps were taken "to assist the Latin American countries in preserving internal security." Classes in riot control and counterguerrilla operations, designed specifically for Latin Americans, were set up at Fort Gulick in the Panama Canal Zone as well as at Fort Bragg. American military personnel stationed in Latin countries were assigned an additional duty: "In May [1961], a joint State-Defense message directed that U.S. military personnel in Latin America seize every opportunity to acquaint their host country counterpart with the danger of Castro-Communism."[35]

By mid-August 1962 a policy statement of the American Counterinsurgency Doctrine was ready and dispatched to "all departments and agencies concerned with internal defense of the less developed world." It was to guide them in "countering subversive insurgency where it exists" or preventing it "in those countries not yet threatened, yet having weak and vulnerable societies." The document defined subversive insurgency as any "communist inspired, supported or directed insurgency." As a result of "many years of experience with the techniques of subversion and insurgency," the communists were credited with possessing "a comprehensive, tested doctrine for conquest from within." Four different "classic" models of such "indirect aggression" were identified and described (Czechoslovakia, China, North Vietnam, Cuba). "Social patterns and institutions in most underdeveloped nations are extremely malleable," the Special Group confidently ruled. That meant that the United States as well as the Soviet Union could penetrate, manipulate, and shape them. The ambassadors and "country teams" in all underdeveloped countries were directed to work with local governments and their military forces to get them "to see the relation of insurgency to socio-economic development, and the blend of political and military measures required for an adequate internal defense." "Sound land reform, expanded communications and transportation facilities, and community development programs" should all be emphasized along with the redirection of the country's military from defense against external threats to concentration on the enemy within.[36] Since counterinsurgency required a "blend" of political and military measures, all American foreign service personnel were eventually required to take some courses in it.

The Agency for International Development became responsible for instilling counterinsurgency readiness in Latin American police forces. "As you know," President Kennedy wrote to AID director Fowler Hamilton on February 19, 1962,

> I desire the appropriate agencies of this Government to give utmost attention and emphasis to programs designed to counter Communist indirect aggression, which I regard as a grave threat during the 1960s. I have already written the Secretary of Defense "to move to a new level of increased activity across the board" in the counter-insurgency field.
>
> Police assistance programs, including those under the aegis of your agency, are also a crucial element in our response to this challenge. I understand that there has been some tendency toward de-emphasizing them under the new aid criteria developed by your agency. I recognize that such programs may seem marginal in terms of focussing our energies on those key sectors which will contribute most to sustained economic growth. But I regard them as justified on a different though related basis, i.e., that of contributing to internal security and resisting Communist-supported insurgency.[37]

The AID director responded by focusing new attention on the police training program, especially the one in Brazil. Initially, the police specialists then on duty there were not enthusiastic about adding counter-insurgency to their courses of instruction. It seemed to them that police forces that were unable to control traffic were not prime material for training in techniques of riot control and subversive spotting. "The State Police...are notorious for their inadequacies, inefficiencies, and venality," one specialist pointed out; he recommended that internal security be left to the armed forces.[38] But within a few months, obeying the laws of bureaucratic growth, the police technicians in Brazil were dutifully arguing that police assistance programs should be expanded immediately in view of the increased threat to Brazilian security from Castro-Communist influences.[39]

Most of the Kennedy aides entered into the counterinsurgency fantasies of their chief with greater or less enthusiasm. But there was at least one sour note. It came on September 30, 1961, from Undersecretary of State Chester Bowles in a letter to the president:

> I am concerned that we are failing to build into our training programs for foreign military personnel an understanding of the values and practices of a

democratic society. As you pointed out in your memorandum, recent events in Brazil demonstrated again what a strategic position the military hold in most underdeveloped countries. Through our military aid programs we are creating trained armed forces capable of seizing power and using it for good or evil. Are we preparing them to use their power to foster, however slowly, the institutions of self-government?

It seems to me that we can do much to include in our training programs for foreign military personnel a better appreciation of their role as builders, as well as defenders, of the emerging democratic societies.[40]

Bowles was obviously lacking in appreciation of the need for training in hand-to-hand combat, sabotage, and techniques for interrogation of suspects. He actually seemed to feel the military might be a greater threat to an underdeveloped country than the communists. Perhaps he was too idealistic, not pragmatic enough for the Kennedy State Department. He was having difficulty asserting authority over his subordinates.[41] He was shifted to an advisor post in the White House and then returned to India to serve another hitch as ambassador.

It is possible that Kennedy considered the civic action program a partial response to Bowles's criticism. "The appeal to the village people," General Taylor called it.[42] Civic action was a part of the counterinsurgency program and was designed to give the military and the police some experience as builders—of roads, wells, schools. It meant doing something positive for the community and was supposed to win hearts and minds. The military would be contributing to development, President Kennedy suggested, as they "identified themselves with the aspirations of the people."[43] Unfortunately, in the real world of Brazil, "the police are not generally considered as giving service but instead as an oppressive force," the deputy chief public safety advisor in Rio de Janeiro observed.[44] That was after several years of U.S.-assisted training. Civic action had not caught on in Rio.

On January 8, 1962 a bomb blast damaged the headquarters building in Rio of the UNE (National Students Union). Most of the students active in the organization professed to be Marxists. On the same day three young men wearing hoods attempted to take over a radio station in Porto Alegre in order to broadcast an anticommunist manifesto. Both assaults were the work of right-wing paramilitary terrorist squads. The MAC, Movimento Anti-Communista, took credit for the bombing of the UNE offices; the young men arrested in Porto Alegre belonged to the União dos Patriotas Anticommunistas.

No communist or leftist bombings or assaults had occurred in either city. The United States was giving counterinsurgency training to the wrong people. The rightists already knew how.

# 5

# The Business of America

*My father always told me that all businessmen
were sons of bitches.*

*John F. Kennedy, April 22, 1962*

I f the American Chamber of Commerce or any other business group
in America had been asked to grade President Kennedy at the end of
his first year in office, they would have given him very low marks.[1]
Business did not feel that Kennedy was receptive to its opinions or
sensitive to its needs. True, he had named a Republican investment
banker, C. Douglas Dillon, secretary of the treasury and made a corporate executive, Robert McNamara, secretary of defense, but other
members of the administration seemed pointedly antibusiness. For example, there was Harvard professor Arthur Schlesinger, Jr., ensconced in
the White House as a presidential assistant, sending out memos that
argued against the appointment of businessmen to government posts.[2]

Even worse was the behavior of Secretary of Commerce Luther
Hodges. Instead of serving as the business community's surrogate in the
Cabinet, Hodges lectured businessmen on their ethics and set up a Business Ethics Advisory Council to draw up a specific code for corporate
behavior. In addition, he tangled with and tried to downgrade the Business Advisory Council. The BAC was a self-selected group of top corporate executives who liked to think that the advice they dispensed helped
the government run the country. This advice was dispensed during tax-
deductible, semiannual "work and play" sessions held at plush resorts
and during somewhat more austere business meetings held in Washington
four times a year. All of the BAC meetings were secret, with reporters
banned from the premises. Hodges felt that not only was the advice

tendered superficial and generally useless, but it was wrong for a semi-official agency of government such as the BAC to be entirely self-selected and totally secret. He requested that the BAC broaden its membership to include small business, some representatives of which he, as secretary of commerce, would name. In addition, he asked that the BAC keep minutes and open some of its sessions to reporters. Rather than comply and thus given up their exclusive fraternity, the BAC huffily changed its name to Business Council, vacated its office space in the Department of Commerce building, and stopped inviting selected government officials to speak at its meetings.[3]

During that first year Kennedy was actually not so much antibusiness as somewhat oblivious to it. Never having had to endure the business grind himself or worry about earning a living, no doubt he found the company of sober, money-grubbing businessmen somewhat heavy going. He preferred the company of journalists or politicians or jet-set swingers. Philosophically, he was far from being antibusiness. Not only did he believe that the place of big business in America was a settled issue, he considered that place rightfully dominant in the economy. To promote economic growth, he believed that the government must promote further growth of the biggest corporations. Neither he nor his brother, the attorney general, had any interest in probing the antitrust nerve.[4]

Much of the business community's hostility to Kennedy was based on the irrational fear that any Democratic administration was bound to be antibusiness, especially one that promised increased government activism, which might translate into "more government on our backs." In fact, however, the New Frontier's activism was going to translate into greatly improved corporate profits via tax cuts on corporate income, investment tax credits, and more and bigger defense contracts. But there was one area in which the administration did at first slight, rather than solicit, business goodwill and participation. That was the nation-building effort in Latin America, and the oversight was deliberate.

In their book proposing the nation-building policy, Millikan and Rostow had warned against using foreign assistance programs to promote private enterprise over government-owned and operated companies. In the long run, they believed, private enterprise would promote self-sustaining growth better than public enterprise, but often private enterprise could not prosper until there had been a period of heavy capital formation under government auspices. In addition, to the peoples of the underdeveloped world, the word "capitalism" often stood for "exploitation." It would take time to reeducate them as to the true meaning.[5]

In 1961 those involved in planning for the Alliance for Progress were aware of the Latin American suspicion that the Alliance would be merely a device to increase the profits and Latin American holdings of North American corporations. To allay that suspicion, the New Frontiersmen made a point of emphasizing that the American contribution to the Alliance would primarily come from public funds. In addition, corporate executives were pretty much excluded from a role in drawing up the Alliance charter. "It did not occur to us to invite U.S. businessmen to Punta del Este in August 1961 until a week before the meeting, and they came as observers," reported Arthur Schlesinger. "Nor did we follow up on their recommendation that a permanent private enterprise committee be established to promote investment."[6] The corporate executives who did accept the last-minute invitation found themselves ignored at the conference. "We were called 'consultants' to the delegation, and we might just as well have been in Peoria as to have been in Punta del Este," John Moore, vice-president of W. R. Grace Company complained later. "We were not consulted, not in any meetings at all, and we were left strictly alone."[7]

The deliberate exclusion of business from policy-making on Latin America represented a sharp departure from procedures under the Eisenhower administration. That was what especially pleased White House aides such as Schlesinger who were convinced that the Latin American policy of the previous administration had failed dismally.[8] The basic Eisenhower policy had stressed pressuring Latin governments to improve the climate for private investment. "Improving the climate" was a code phrase, meaning (1) cutting government spending in order to get greater monetary stability, and (2) protecting and welcoming foreign corporate investment. Eisenhower and the businessmen who advised him were convinced that sufficient American private capital to develop all of Latin America was available and would flow south if only American business would be made to feel welcome and secure. As late as his 1960 South American goodwill tour, Eisenhower was still "hammering" away on this theme.[9]

Deeply shocked by the Cuban Revolution and horrified that Castro had been able to expropriate American companies in Cuba without compensation, the American business community turned bearish on all of Latin America. Most businessmen felt, as did Eisenhower, that before any new money could be committed to any country in that region there must be a clear repudiation of Castroism by the government of the would-be recipient country. The Kennedy rhetoric about a "vast new ten-year plan for the Americas, a plan to transform the 1960s into a historic decade of democractic progress''[10] failed to thrill them. All of the New Frontier's talk of revolution made business leaders nervous. They disliked the whole idea of long-range economic planning by governments: it sounded like Russian Five Year Plans, communistic. Similarly the very notion of government-to-government aid for economic development was abhorrent to them. State-owned enterprises, established with American tax dollars, would compete with and drive out private firms, especially the foreign-owned ones. In addition, the call for basic reforms such as tax and land reforms would probably serve as an excuse for the Latin communist-nationalists to confiscate foreign firms via taxation or to take over their land under the pretext of land reform.[11]

Business remained pretty much excluded from policy-making on Latin America until late February 1962. In that month a relatively minor incident in Brazil triggered a massive reaction in the American business community and in Congress. The incident was the expropriation of a small ITT subsidiary by the state government of Rio Grande do Sul on February 16.

The uproar over this expropriation took place just at a time when it appeared that relations between the Kennedy administration and the Goulart government were warming significantly. At first American officials had treated the new Brazilian president with deep suspicion. The CIA had, for example, carefully scrutinized the lists of Goulart's cabinet and staff appointments, checking for dangerous leftists. It was able to report that Goulart had appointed one Communist Party member, Raul Ryff, to his staff as private secretary. Several other appointees—the justice minister, the chief of police in Brasília, a general in command of the Vila Militar (a strategic garrison near Rio de Janeiro)—were put down as procommunists, and the ministers of industry, mining, and health were all marked down as ultranationalists and opportunists.[12]

Actually, the scrutiny of Goulart's first batch of appointments could not have been a very rewarding anticommunist exercise. The appointees were so uniformily from the ranks of centrist politicians. The lone Communist Party member unmasked by the CIA was no longer active in the party. Apparently, Ryff had belonged to the party only briefly during his youth. With the perspective of distance, State Department intelligence specialists in Washington could see that the new parliamentary government set up in Brasília tended "to the conservative side" with "the generally conservative PSD (Social Democractic Party) predominant."[13] But, reluctant to acknowledge the obvious, CIA analysts joined the political analysts of the embassy in Rio in arguing that the "emerging pattern" of Goulart's appointments was "significantly weighted in favor of the Communists." In addition, they cautioned that "we may be witnessing the early stages of an attempted slow-motion coup in which Goulart, wittingly or unwittingly, is paving the way for effective Communist infiltration designed as a prelude to an eventual takeover."[14]

In mid-October of 1961 a type of diplomatic intermezzo was played out that illustrated American coolness toward the new Brazilian president. When Carlos Lacerda, "the only governor who has not recognized President Goulart,"[15] traveled to the United States to address the Inter-American Press Association and an anti-Castro Cuban group in Miami, he was honored with a personal White House interview with President Kennedy. In recommending the reception, the State Department acknowledged that "more than any other single individual," Lacerda was responsible for the political tensions in Brazil that had culminated in the

March 26, 1962. Governor Carlos Lacerda, an outspoken opponent of Goulart, was welcomed to the Oval Office for an interview with President Kennedy. (Courtesy John F. Kennedy Library.)

resignation of Quadros and that he had alienated many in Brazil by his general "disregard for contitutionalism." But it was feared that a failure to receive him might be construed as "evidence of United States ingratitude toward its real friends."[16] Ready to act without all such diplomatic hesitation, the White House staff had scheduled a Kennedy appointment with Lacerda even before receiving the State Department recommendation.

At the same time as Lacerda was being received with such alacrity, the question of whether or not Goulart should be invited to make an official visit was being carefully debated. Such a visit would bolster Goulart's prestige and tend to strengthen his political position. Was that desirable? Chargé d'Affaires Niles Bond still believed that "Goulart is involved in [a] cynical political relationship of 'use and be used' with Communists." But he believed that an invitation to visit might be advisable since it would make possible a "President-to-President understanding on basic ground rules" of U.S. aid to Brazil, and it would enable Kennedy to explain to Goulart the "dangers of ending up inside [the] Communist tiger."[17] Kennedy, attracted by "the royal cousins approach to diplomacy,"[18] had great confidence in his ability to persuade Third World leaders during face-to-face meetings. The invitation to Goulart was duly extended. The date of April 3 was agreed upon as mutually satisfactory.

After Lincoln Gordon, the new ambassador to Brazil, took up his post in late October 1961, American relations with Goulart improved. Gordon was clearly impressed by the cordiality with which Goulart received him. The new ambassador was invited to the presidential palace in Rio on October 21 and treated to a private, informal hearing of Goulart's views on the current political crisis in Brazil, the situation in Cuba, Soviet interest in Latin America, and the state of U.S.-Brazilian relations. It was the type of exclusive, initial contact with a head of state that ambassadors must dream of, providing material for lengthy reports back to the home office.[19] Jango's efforts to win over the new ambassador were at least partially successful. Four days later, Gordon was informing Washington that Goulart would not "knowingly pave way for Communist takeover." Unlike Niles Bond, Gordon saw Goulart's basic problem as economic, not political. "Goulart government's chances of survival depend primarily ability stem inflation," reported Gordon.[20]

In fact, inflation in Brazil was again accelerating. The most common topic of conversation in the streets in late 1961 and 1962 was the latest price of everything, not politics, not the weather, and certainly not the danger of communism. Gordon, formerly a professor of economics at Harvard Business School, was sensitive to economic conditions. But he had more than academic experience and was perhaps better prepared for his post than is usually the case with ambassadorial appointees. He had carried out a variety of diplomatic assignments. His most recent had been as part of the American delegation to the OAS conference at Punta del Este. Before that he had accompanied UN Ambassador Adlai Stevenson on his tour of Latin America, trying to repair Bay of Pigs damage. Still earlier, he had served on the two special task forces on Latin America that were headed by Adolf Berle. Since he had done some academic research on Brazil and written a book—*United States Manufacturing Investment in Brazil, 1946–1960*—published in 1962, Gordon already had some familiarity with Portuguese and was soon to become fluent in it. Prior to taking this post, Gordon did not know President Kennedy personally. Because of Kennedy's interest in Brazil, they were to become better acquainted. Whenever Gordon returned to Washington for consultations (about four times a year), he was scheduled for a White House interview with the president.[21]

The ambassador was involved in planning for Goulart's official visit to the United States when he was called upon to play a major role in quelling the uproar that followed the expropriation of the ITT subsidiary. Prior to taking over the telephone company, the governor of Rio Grande do Sul, Leonel Brizola, deposited $400,000 in an escrow account as the state's estimate of the value of the property. Brizola had arrived at this figure by taking the valuation placed on the ITT subsidiary by an arbitration panel and then deducting from that sum such things as the value of land that had been donated to the company and "profits illegally exported."[22] Although at one point ITT had agreed to the arbitration and named one of the three arbitrators, two months after the panel's report the company had suddenly rejected the arbitration decision and suggested new negotiations. ITT officials now claimed their property was worth between seven and eight million.

In February 1962, ITT was not yet the giant conglomerate it came to be in the course of the decade. It ranked forty-seventh in the *Fortune* list of the top 500 corporations.[23] Ten years later it ranked eighth. The company's rapid growth would be attributed to the hard work and the acquisitions policy of its president, Harold S. Geneen, appointed head of ITT in mid-1959.[24]

The dispute between ITT and Rio Grande do Sul dated back before Governor Brizola and Geneen attained their respective positions. The company's concession to operate a telephone service had expired in 1953. It was not renewed because of public dissatisfaction with the quality of the service. ITT argued that without substantial rate increases it could not improve or expand service, while state authorities and the public felt that in view of the poor service the company deserved no increases.[25]

When Geneen took over ITT in 1959, the Rio Grande subsidiary was operating in the red, without a concession contract. The company offered to invest $40 million in new facilities in exchange for a contract and rate increases. The state government, now under Brizola, countered with a proposal for a mixed state-private telephone company. It proposed that ITT participate in the new enterprise with shares awarded according to the currrent value of its properties. The state would match that figure, and then twice that number of shares would be sold to the public. ITT would thus be limited to a 25 percent share. Initially the company indicated that such a solution might be satisfactory, but it is doubtful that Geneen was seriously interested in a joint venture that ITT would not control. Negotiations dragged on until ITT rejected the arbitration panel's valuation. Brizola then took it upon himself to exclude ITT from the new state telephone company he was setting up.[26] Until the courts ruled on the validity of his proposed compensation, nothing would be paid to ITT.

Geneen had the option of presenting his company's version of the value of their property to the court, but he was unwilling to wait for a protracted judicial decision. In 1960, the year after he had become head of the company, he had been taken by surprise by Castro's expropriation of ITT property in Cuba. The Cuban operation had been profitable, and although the Brazilian concession was not, ITT's telephone business in Chile was a big money-maker, contributing 12 percent of the company's net profits. Unchallenged, the example of nationalization might spread further in Latin America.

On February 17, the day after the takeover, Geneen sent "urgent and confidential" telegrams to both President Kennedy and Secretary of State Rusk. He demanded that the U.S. government act immediately to force the Brazilian government to rescind the governor's expropriation order. Sensing that he had some leverage, since foreign aid appropriations had not yet been considered by Congress, Geneen suggested that unless there was immediate action, public and congressional opinion would "harden" and the whole Alliance for Progress and foreign aid program would suffer.[27]

Other ITT officials alerted the press and some members of Congress that "another blatant instance of irresponsible seizure of American-owned property" had occurred. As befitted a company involved in communications, ITT was adept at getting its version of events before the public. The response exceeded expectations. A year later (after ITT had safely pocketed proceeds of the settlement) Geneen remarked that the expropriation in Brazil had been "exaggerated out of all proportion to what was seized—a $7.3 million company that was running in the red."[28] He did not mention his own role in that exaggeration, but he was apparently surprised that it should have evoked so massive a response. ITT was not considering the welfare of any other company, but there were other corporations that had suffered expropriation in Cuba and were fearful for their remaining investments in Latin America. Geneen had touched a raw nerve. A flood of telephone calls, telegrams, and letters from business executives poured into the White House and State Department. All demanded government action on behalf of ITT.[29] Congress hastened to join the fray. On February 20, four days after Brizola's action, the "confiscation" and the laggard State Department reaction to it were being berated on the floor of the House.[30] Within the next few weeks, the ITT version of events in the Rio Grande do Sul dispute was entered into the records of both the House and the Senate.[31]

No doubt the way in which ITT presented its case helped arouse congressional alarm. What was stressed in the ITT "Fact Sheet" was not the long-standing dispute over telephone service but rather the political orientation of Governor Brizola. Brizola was presented as a pro-communist, scheming to expropriate and expel all American companies while he replaced American equipment and capital with technology and funds from Iron Curtain countries. It was Brizola, the "Fact Sheet" pointed out, who had led the movement to install Goulart as president despite the vice president's "extreme leftist leanings." Other crimes attributed to Brizola included the distribution of a Che Guevara pamphlet on guerilla war, a call for a National Liberation Front, and support of federal legislation controlling profit remittances to foreign countries. In short, according to the ITT interpretation, the dispute was not an ordinary commercial disagreement but an incident in the Cold War.

State Department officials had been quick to denounce the expropriation but at first resisted interpreting the incident as having political overtones. In fact, the department was inclined to regard ITT's demands as somewhat unreasonable. From Rio, Ambassador Gordon pointed out that it was "an absolute impossibility" for the federal government of

Brazil to rescind a state government's expropriation order.[32] After discussion with Brazilian authorities, Gordon concluded that the entire takeover operation had been done in accordance with Brazilian law. The amount deposited in escrow did not necessarily correspond to the definitive value of the property or the final compensation. The sum to be paid ITT would be determined by the courts unless the state of Rio Grande do Sul agreed to extrajudicial negotiations. Geneen's position that there could be no negotiations with the state government but only with the federal government of Brazil was "unsound, impracticable and perhaps impossible for [both] the government of Brazil and Rio Grande do Sul," reported the ambassador.[33] Two months later, in April, Secretary of State Rusk was still inclined to stress the fact that the quality of the service ITT provided was an important aspect of the dispute. He also suggested that state or municipal takeovers of utilities were not unknown in the United States in cases of great public dissatisfaction with a public service.[34]

President Kennedy, however, was ready to shift to a more probusiness position. At his news conference of March 7, in response to a planted question on the expropriation,[35] he remarked that "the telephone company was seized by the governor of a province who has not always been identified particularly as a friend of the United States, and we have been attempting to work out an equitable solution with the Brazilian Government."[36] Kennedy thus accepted ITT's interpretation of the incident as a political act of anti-Americanism; he did not utilize the opportunity to suggest that the case was an ordinary commercial dispute for which there was a judicial remedy. In addition, he accepted Geneen's argument that a solution must be negotiated by the U.S. government with the Brazilian government, not by the company with the state government.

On the same day as the President's news conference, Ambassador Gordon was given more specific instructions.

> You are requested to give fullest possible support to company's efforts [to] obtain prompt and adequate compensation utilizing in this regard full weight [and] influence US Government. In particular you are instructed to request from GOB [government of Brazil] commitment it will assure faithful execution such agreement as is reached for fixing compensation and prompt payment of compensation so fixed.[37]

Following his instructions, the ambassador pressed Goulart to resolve a dispute that was beyond his constitutional power to resolve—as Gordon had at first pointed out.[38]

Taken by surprise with the uproar in the United States over the ITT expropriation, Goulart and his advisors came to the conclusion that ITT, perhaps acting in conjunction with Goulart's domestic political foes, was cleverly orchestrating an anti-Brazil press campaign in order to undermine his official visit in April. An openly hostile reception in the United States would further damage the already weak president's standing in his own country.

Other Brazilians, impatient with the inferior service offered by ITT and other foreign concession holders, were also dumbfounded by the American protest. The ITT must be a different kind of company than had been thought, suggested the *Correio da Manha*. It must be owned primarily by widows and orphans, with the remaining shares held by members of Congress. There was no other way to explain the astonishing American reaction.[39]

Protests by the Brazilian government over the negative press it was getting in the United States were countered with suggestions that Goulart undertake some "constructive" action during the weeks remaining before his visit in order to generate more favorable publicity. Suggested constructive action included "replacement of profits remittance bill by alternative measure satisfactory to Brazilian and foreign business elements," starting on a monetary stabilization program, or, of course, settlement of the ITT case. If the Goulart government felt that foreign ownership of public utilities "cannot be tolerated longer for domestic political reasons, it might well give more serious consideration to proposal AMFORP, for example, to accept valuation by neutral party, take payment over period years, and reinvest equivalent amount in economic development enterprises in Brazil."[40]

AMFORP stood for American and Foreign Power, an electric utility holding company, 51 percent owned by the investment company Electric Bond and Share. Neither company is in existence today. In 1967 AMFORP merged with its parent company under the new name Ebasco Industries. Two years later Ebasco was acquired by Boise Cascade. In the early 1960s, AMFORP was one of the larger utility companies, ranking twenty-fourth in the *Fortune* list of the top fifty utilities in 1962.[41] All of its investment was in Latin America, and the total value of its holdings put AMFORP second only to Standard Oil in the area.[42] Most of the investments had been made in the 1920s, when British and Canadian utilities were purchased. In Brazil, AMFORP's acquisitions were made in 1927. Just as in the case of the ITT telephone subsidiary, the rates allowed by public authorities did not keep pace with inflation.

Private utilities managed to stay afloat during this inflationary period via the mechanism of "additionals," surcharges for fuel and wage price increases, and via a preferential foreign exchange rate.[43] Service deteriorated, however, as equipment was overloaded to meet increased demand, and public hostility to the electric companies grew.

By the late 1950s, AMFORP management had decided on a strategy for getting out of the unprofitable Latin utility business without losing its capital investment. The pattern was established in Argentina in 1958, when AMFORP negotiated the sale of all of its assets to the Argentinian government for a percentage down, payable in dollars, with the remainder payable over a long period with interest. As part of the sale contract, AMFORP bound itself to reinvest much of the proceeds in other Argentinian enterprises. From the company's viewpoint, such an arrangement was eminently satisfactory. The 6 percent interest that the Argentinian government would pay on the balance was greater than the earnings from operating the utilities. As the balance was paid off, AMFORP could invest in the much more profitable manufacturing sector of the economy. Similar contracts were subsequently negotiated with Mexico (1959) and Colombia (1961).[44]

In Brazil, AMFORP owned ten separate subsidiaries, each with its own concession contract with ten different state governments. The contracts had different expiration dates. Most of AMFORP property in the state of Rio Grande do Sul had been taken over by Brizola in 1959, a year after the subsidiary's contract had expired. The question of compensation was still before the courts in 1962. That takeover had attracted little attention in the United States at the time. Now, in the wake of the furor over the ITT takeover, AMFORP lobbyists drew attention to Brizola's earlier action against their company. They urged some State Department action on their behalf. Rather than have to negotiate with each of the ten state governments involved, AMFORP naturally preferred that the federal government of Brazil negotiate purchase as a "global" solution, along the same lines as had been worked out for Argentina, Mexico, and Colombia. In November 1961, three months before the ITT flap, AMFORP had formally proposed negotiations on the sale of its subsidiaries to the Brazilian government. But no action had been taken on the proposal by the recently installed parliamentary government in Brasília.[45]

It was this AMFORP proposal that the Kennedy administration now urged on Goulart as constructive action that would generate favorable publicity for himself and for Brazil. It is not clear just why Goulart decided to adopt it, although from his viewpoint the proposal had certain attractive features. For one thing, nationalization of foreign-owned utilities would please Brazilian nationalists and strengthen Goulart's standing in left-wing circles. Second, the arrangement should cost Brazil little or nothing during Goulart's own term as president. Since the American government was pushing the proposal, adoption of it would probably mean the release of suspended credits and loans and possibly additional American financial aid.[46] Third, government acquisition of the utilities would lay the groundwork for publicly financed expansion of energy and communications networks, clearly needed for industrial development. That would be permanently credited to Goulart. Finally, with minor alterations, Goulart could present the proposal as his own idea. He would thus not be going to Washington empty-handed but with a grand global solution to a long-festering problem that had reached the point of troubling U.S.-Brazilian relations.

Both his foreign minister, Francisco San Tiago Dantas, and the Brazilian ambassador to the United States, Roberto Campos, urged him to take action along these lines. The advice of Dantas, a member of Goulart's own party with a reputation as a respected intellectual, was probably the deciding factor for Goulart. Complex financial arrangements of this type were not the type of problem for which Goulart had developed any expertise. No doubt he felt that if the plan to nationalize foreign-owned utilities did not work out, it could be gently discarded after the official visit or buried in some committee appointed to study it further. As a politician, Goulart typically looked for short-term advantages rather than long-term solutions.

Thus Goulart came to propose the AMFORP plan as his own invention, little thinking that the Americans might consider the proposal a sacred and binding commitment. It was, Ambassador Gordon later observed, "the most specific single thing which came out of the meetings."[47] This "commitment" would haunt Goulart for the remainder of his time as president, and, in the end, was to be bequeathed as a solemn Brazilian obligation to the next regime.

Even in the short run, Goulart did not quite reap the benefits he or his foreign minister had anticipated. Right-wing Brazilian economists ridiculed the idea of a near-bankrupt government purchasing unprofitable utilities.[48] Left-wing groups liked the idea of nationalization but disliked the plan to require the hated foreign capitalists to reinvest in the manufacturing sector.[49] In the United States the favorable publicity Goulart had hoped for did not materialize. Instead, congressmen (unaware that

AMFORP had initially suggested the arrangement) criticized the "Goulart Plan" on the grounds that it sounded like the 1960 Cuban decree of expropriation.[50]

This negative congressional reaction was spurred by alert ITT lobbyists.[51] Geneen opposed the whole idea of a global solution. He wanted the ITT expropriation case in Rio Grande do Sul handled separately and immediately, apart from the question of other ITT property in Brazil or consideration of the problems of other foreign-owned utilities. ITT had worked out its own proposal for a settlement: the Bank of Brazil should immediately grant a "loan" to Standard Electric, an ITT manufacturing subsidiary in Rio. The loan total would correspond to the value that ITT placed on the expropriated telephone company in Rio Grande do Sul and would be repaid when and if the state paid the compensation that ITT wanted.

President Kennedy was informed of ITT's objections to the Goulart-AMFORP plan on the eve of Goulart's arrival in Washington.[52] When the two presidents met on April 4, Kennedy urged that the ITT settlement be "speeded up," apart from consideration of the other utilities, although he thought the Brazilian proposals "generally sound."[53] Later, when ITT loudly objected to any American government endorsement of any Brazilian plan to nationalize foreign-owned private enterprise, the State Department hastened to "clarify" the administration's position: the United States neither approved nor disapproved of the Goulart Plan since it was not an intergovernmental arrangement, but a matter of voluntary negotiation between the Brazilian government and the private companies.[54] Inasmuch as President Kennedy had personally expressed strong approval[55] and since representatives of the government of Brazil were then almost daily being urged by representatives of the government of the United States to get on with the plan, the "clarification" might seem confusing. But Brazilian diplomats well understood the signal. Publicly, the Kennedy administration would have nothing whatever to do with any takeover of American private enterprises.[56] Privately, however, the White House would continue to push for whatever the companies involved wanted, and in the cases of ITT and AMFORP, they wanted to unload their unprofitable enterprises.

Kennedy had other reasons for following the lead of ITT and AMFORP at this time. Governor Brizola had rapidly emerged as the bête noire in administration thinking on Brazil. It was Brizola who had carried out both expropriations. He appeared to be building his political career by consciously appealing to anti-American nationalist sentiment.[57] Kennedy felt that Goulart must be persuaded not only to free himself from his brother-in-law's influence but to work to discredit Brizola. By promptly paying for property that Brizola had confiscated, Goulart would serve notice on the communists and communo-nationalists (a new political hybrid discovered at this time) that his administration was definitely in the anticommunist camp and Brizola had no influence in it. Concern over the political opportunism of Goulart, not concern over the fate of ITT and AMFORP, marked the thinking of the administration during Goulart's visit. Considerably more time was spent lecturing the visitor on the dangers of communist infiltration in labor unions than on discussion of the utility purchase plan. But to Kennedy, the expropriations and communist infiltration were aspects of the same problem.

In addition, domestic political considerations dictated strong administration support for the threatened companies. Now in his second year in office, President Kennedy was becoming more acutely aware that a president is not really free to determine foreign policy by himself. Congress had more power than he thought it had when he was in Congress.[58] Goulart's visit to the United States coincided with the opening of hearings on foreign aid by the Senate Foreign Relations Committee. Prompted by the public reaction to the ITT expropriation, several members of Congress had already introduced bills providing for mandatory termination of American aid to any country in which American-owned property was expropriated without prompt payment of compensation. Unappeased by the Goulart visit and dubious about the AMFORP plan, Senator Bourke Hickenlooper, ranking Republican member of the Foreign Relations Committee, got such a termination provision attached as an amendment to the foreign aid bill.

Kennedy indicated disapproval of the idea of mandatory termination of aid when it was first suggested[59] but took no public stand against the Hickenlooper Amendment when it was introduced on the floor of the Senate in early June 1962. None of the Senate liberals opposed it, and the amendment passed with virtually no debate. At the time, the White House and the liberals concentrated on opposing another amendment that would have barred aid to Yugoslavia and Poland. The House version of the Hickenlooper Amendment, introduced by Representative E. Ross Adair, also passed with little discussion.

The State Department did make an effort to block the amendment. Secretary Rusk sent the Senate Foreign Relations Committee a lengthy memorandum detailing reasons why a mandatory cutoff of aid should be rejected. He argued that in effect it would put U.S. policy in the hands of any one intransigent citizen (or corporation) whose actions provoked expropriation and prevented reasonable settlement. The amendment could conceivably block some of the structural reforms sought under the Alliance for Progress. Land reform, for example, would require expropriation of large estates, some of which might be owned by Americans. In addition, if such a provision were put in an aid bill, it would appear that U.S. aid programs were in fact motivated by a desire to protect this country's private investment and to facilitate capitalist exploitation, as communist propaganda charged. The State Department memorandum was printed as an appendix to the Senate Foreign Relations Committee hearings on the foreign aid bill.[60] Few, if any, senators read it.

By the time the Hickenlooper Amendment was adopted, the administration had embarked on a campaign to win the support of the business community for U.S. policy in Latin America. As part of the campaign, the role of the private sector was now to be stressed. Throughout 1961, New Frontier spokesmen had rarely mentioned the need for private investment in Latin America. Only in the wake of the ITT expropriation was "the great energizing effort from the private field" officially recognized.[61]

In May 1962 President Kennedy appointed a committee of twenty-five business leaders from companies involved in Latin America to COMAP (Commerce Committee for the Alliance for Progess). The committee was to suggest ways in which the contribution of the private sector might be "accelerated."[62] In September, a few months after the passage of the Hickenlooper Amendment, a new position of special assistant for international business was created in the office of the undersecretary of state, with the specific assignment of assisting corporations threatened with expropriation, discriminatory taxation, or profit remittance problems.[63] The special assistant was later also assigned the task of serving as executive secretary of an Advisory Committee on International Business Problems, a committee made up of representatives of multinational corporations and Department of Commerce officials.[64]

The business group that would prove to be the most influential in U.S.-Latin American policy-making emerged the next year, with the support of President Kennedy. This was the Business Group for Latin America, organized in September 1963 by David Rockefeller, president of Chase Manhattan. It was designed as an advisory group composed of "business leaders with long experience in Latin America who represent companies with substantial commitments in that area." Both Henry B. Sargent, president of AMFORP, and Harold S. Geneen of ITT were

May 9, 1962. In the wake of the uproar over the expropriation in Brazil of an ITT subsidiary, President Kennedy named a group of business executives to a committee to recommend changes in the Alliance for Progress. COMAP members met with the president shortly after their appointment. (Courtesy John F. Kennedy Library.)

included on the list of business leaders who were to meet with "appropriate top level government officials" several times a year.[65] In a letter to Rockefeller, dated November 19, 1963, a few days before his death, Kennedy applauded the formation of the group and assured Rockefeller that federal agencies such as the Departments of State, Treasury, and Commerce, AID, and the Export-Import Bank would all "welcome the opportunity to draw on the Committee's vast background of knowledge and experienced views."[66]

The Business Group for Latin America thrived. President Johnson, determined from the first to win over the business community, made a point of inviting members of the group to the White House for periodic briefings. A few years later the group was renamed Council for Latin America, and still later it assumed its present name of Council of the

Americas. President Johnson was much better at charming business executives than was President Kennedy, but it is clear that by April 1962 Kennedy was making a deliberate effort to change the antibusiness image of the New Frontier.[67]

It was thus Goulart's misfortune to visit Washington and draw public attention to Brazil just at the time that Kennedy had decided to push the interests of the multinationals in Brazil. Ambassador Gordon returned to Brazil a short time after Goulart did and was soon hard at work trying to secure a settlement satisfactory to ITT and to get the negotiations for purchase of AMFORP started. The American position was that Goulart could easily produce the settlement and the purchase if only he would "use the great influence of the presidential office."[68] Although becoming more aware of congressional restraints on his own actions, Kennedy chose to ignore the congressional restraints on the

April 3, 1962. President João Goulart arriving at the White House for a luncheon hosted by President Kennedy. In the background are Secretary of State Dean Rusk and, directly behind Goulart, Vice President Lyndon Johnson. (Courtesy John F. Kennedy Library.)

Goulart government. The parliamentary compromise that enabled Goulart to succeed Quadros had reduced the powers of the president, and, in theory, accordingly increased the powers of the Congress. But, since nothing had been done to impart dynamism or direction to the legislative branch, the new powers it exercised were chiefly those compatible with lethargy: it rejected Goulart's legislative initiatives without ever producing its own agenda for action.

Throughout 1962 Goulart was maneuvering to gain political support for an early plebiscite on the question of ending the parliamentary system and returning to the system of full presidential powers. Had he pushed for resolution of either the ITT or the AMFORP case, he would have alienated the Left that was most inclined to support him, without gaining approval of either the Center or the Right. Virtually no group in Brazil favored the proposed settlements. Guided by Brizola on the ITT issue, the Left objected to the proposed Bank of Brazil special "loan" to the corporation as an unconstitutional way of bypassing the judiciary. On the other hand, right-wing governors saw the proposed ITT solution as unwarranted federal abrogation of states' rights. America's friend, Carlos Lacerda, attempted to expropriate the Canadian-owned telephone company in his state as a way of forestalling federal takeover.[69] For their part, Brazilian bank officials questioned the legality of making such a large loan without the customary collateral or a fixed repayment schedule.

The proposed purchase of AMFORP was even more controversial. As noted above, at the time Goulart announced his plan to nationalize foreign-owned utilities, one of the ten AMFORP subsidiaries was already being operated by state authorities. In July 1962 a second subsidiary was expropriated by a governor. In this case the state involved was Pernambuco and the governor was the conservative Cid Sampaio, high in U.S. favor since he supported João Cleofas, the American-backed gubernatorial candidate in the upcoming October elections. Embassy officials attempted to persuade the governor to desist from the seizure. He argued, however, that the takeover was not an act of expropriation since the AMFORP concession expired on July 17, 1962, and the concession contract included a clause providing for the reversion of the properties to the state upon expiration. The company had ostensibly already been compensated for its investment via a special users' tax over the life of the contract. State takeover of the subsidiary was politically so popular in Pernambuco that Sampaio refused to back down.[70] The next month a third expropriation, in the state of Espirito Santo, was prevented only by federal intervention. The intervention had been urgently solicited by the State Department in consultation with AMFORP officials.[71]

The Pernambuco case underlined the legal complexities and the political costs for Goulart in the way of carrying out the purchase of all AMFORP property. The company's concession contracts with several other states included similar "free reversion" clauses.[72] In addition, there were the troublesome problems of determining the value of the properties. Were historic costs, adjusted for inflation, replacement costs, or present value to be used as the basis for compensation? Because of the unfavorable rate structure, AMFORP had invested as little as possible in maintenance and replacement. Much of the equipment had been allowed to deteriorate. When Brazilian politicians referred to AMFORP property as so much scrap iron, in many cases they were not far wrong. An AMFORP official later admitted that, even with the new 1964 rate increases, it would have cost a fortune to put the company's facilities back in order.[73]

In view of the difficulties, Goulart did about as much, or as little, as he could safely do. He submitted his proposal to nationalize utilities to his cabinet, the Council of Ministers. On May 30 the Council approved the proposal and created a special commission to plan and negotiate nationalization. The commission did not get around to a formal hearing of the AMFORP sale proposal until August 23.[74] Negotiations about how the sale price should be computed then proceeded at a snail's pace. No progress had been made by the end of the year.

While the settlements of ITT and AMFORP cases stalled in the summer of 1962, a third American company faced the threat of expropriation. On June 14 the minister of mines, Gabriel Passos, issued an order cancelling the mining rights on certain properties belonging to a number of foreign companies. Included in his order were three properties, rich in high-grade iron ore, belonging to Hanna Mining Company. Passos belonged to the UDN, the party of Lacerda, favored by American officials. Goulart personally had no hand in the minister's action but did nothing to oppose the move. Nationalists of all parties warmly endorsed Passos's action. National control of the country's rich iron ore deposits had long been at the top of the nationalist priority list.

Antipathy to Hanna was especially marked. The company had acquired its Brazilian properties in late 1957, shortly after its president, George Humphrey, resigned as Eisenhower's first secretary of the treasury. Brazilian nationalists felt that undue American political pressure had led Brazilian President Kubitschek to welcome the company to Brazil and to endorse Hanna's plans to invest $40 million in expansion of mining and transportation facilities in order to export the ore.[75] Clumsy public relations did not improve the company's image. The suggestion that Hanna invest part of its export profits in the construction of a steel mill in Brazil was summarily dismissed by a company official with the remark, "We are not a philanthropic organization."[76] To Brazilian nationalists, Hanna symbolized American imperialism at its most predatory, bent on plundering Brazil without putting anything into it. The nationalists' campaign against Hanna was joined and abetted by the government-owned iron ore company, CVRD (Rio Doce Valley Company), which saw Hanna as a competitor, and by the state government of Minas Gerais, which would become the owner of the iron reserves if the property rights of foreign corporations could be cancelled.

For Hanna Mining, the Brazilian government's moves against its mining rights could hardly have come at a more inopportune time if it wished to enlist the aid of the State Department and the sympathy of Congress and the American public. In April 1962 a subcommittee of the Senate Armed Services Committee had begun an investigation of the nation's stockpile of strategic materials, heeding President Kennedy's call for such an inquiry.[77] One of the principal objectives of the investigation was to determine whether there had been corruption and "unconscionable profits" on the part of stockpile suppliers. Among the suppliers to be investigated was the Hanna Mining Company, which reportedly had made a profit of over 400 percent supplying ferronickel. Ex-Secretary Humphrey's turn to testify came in August. The Senate investigation and the subsequent government suit to recover $1.8 million from Hanna naturally strengthened opposition to the company in Brazil. At the same time, Humphrey's charges that the whole investigation was a Democratic "personal vendetta" and "a stab in the back" really aimed at Eisenhower did not endear him to the Kennedy administration.[78]

Although the embassy in Brazil was early contacted for assistance,[79] the company did not press vigorously for State Department aid until January 1963. On January 24 an official of Hanna visited the department to urge that the United States provide "no further financial assistance to Brazil until all of Hanna's problems were resolved." Not only was the request denied, but the department also rejected the idea of assuming "an attitude similar to that we took in IT&T and AMFORP cases" on the grounds that no actual expropriation had yet occurred.[80] The Hanna situation did differ from that of the other two corporations in that Hanna wanted to expand, not sell, its Brazilian operations. However, it seems likely that the political position of Hanna vis-à-vis the administration was a factor in the official coolness to the company's cause. "Increased iron ore exports" was added to the "nag" list of self-help measures that Brazil must take to qualify for continued Alliance for Progress aid, but the State Department did not champion Hanna's interests more directly during the remainder of the Kennedy administration. More direct support came during the Johnson administration.[81]

In addition to the expropriation of utilities and the cancellation of Hanna's mining rights, one additional issue upset the American business community. That was the question of limitations on the export of profits earned in Brazil by foreign-owned firms. Brazilian nationalists felt that most of such profits should remain in the country, providing capital for further development. Legislation limiting profit remission to 10 percent of the investment had been passed in 1952.[82] It had never been enforced. Just as in the case of determining the current value of the electric utilities, it was difficult to decide the basis of investment. How did one adjust for inflation? Were reinvested profits to be added to the basis? There was also the difficulty of identifying what was a profit remission. Did the sums paid by a Brazilian subsidiary to an American parent company for consultation, licenses, or technology represent profit remission? These payments were usually made with dollars purchased at an official and artificially low (or subsidized) price.

On November 29, 1962, the Chamber of Deputies made a fresh attempt to limit profit remittance by passing the much more restrictive Celso Brant bill, which specifically excluded reinvested profits from the investment basis and provided no system of correction for inflation since the original investment. The acquisition of a Brazilian firm by a foreign company was prohibited by the bill, and Brazilian banks were barred from making loans to foreign-owned firms. The more conservative Brazilian press immediately denounced the Celso Brant legislation. "Why sacrifice reality for chauvinism?" asked the *Correio de Manha*. Brazil needed more foreign investment, not less; the bill would inspire panic among all investors. The editorial called on the Brazilian Senate to reject or substantially modify the measure.[83] The Senate did finally modify the bill, but, exercising its prerogative, the Chamber of Deputies reinstated the original terms.

The American embassy openly joined in the debate against the provisions of Celso Brant. Ambassador Gordon, for example, spoke out publicly against the measure in a speech in Belém on August 31, 1962.[84] In private he urged Goulart to veto the bill outright, or at least to veto

100

the most objectionable sections of it.[85] Goulart, typically, hesitated, not wishing to offend either side. He ended by signing the measure but promising to support a new Senate bill that would amend the provision on reinvested profits. When the new bill finally reached the Chamber, however, Goulart's promised support was not in evidence, and the bill failed to pass. But, in yet another gesture to those opposed to the stringent restrictions on profit remittance, throughout 1963 Goulart delayed signing the enabling act that would set up machinery to enforce the new law.

Liberal White House aides such as Arthur Schlesinger were surprised and distressed to find that Kennedy had abandoned the attempt to maintain some distance in Latin America between the New Frontier and the business community.[86] The development did not particularly surprise Brazilians, who had assumed all along that the interests of big business came first with any American government. "I notice," President Kennedy told a group of visiting Brazilian students on July 31, 1962, "that some of you felt that this country, from a story I saw in the paper a couple of days ago, was dominated by the business community and that the Government was dominated by business. That will come as a great shock and a source of pleasure to the business community here in the United States."[87]

That was possible. Business leaders were slow to relinquish their deep distrust of Democratic administrations. In July 1962 they perhaps had still not realized that Kennedy was now respectfully soliciting the advice of business on foreign policy. As far as Brazil was concerned, the State Department was now pressing Goulart for the satisfaction of businessmen's grievances. For all intents and purposes, Kennedy's goals in Brazil were now identical to those of the Eisenhower administration: fiscal stability and greater protection and encouragement for foreign private investment. There was still a great deal of oratory within Brazil about the basic Alliance for Progress goals of land reform, income redistribution, and rapid development, but by mid-1962 little of that oratory came from the Americans. The loudest talk about those goals came from leaders of the Brazilian Left. Their efforts were routinely dismissed as "demagogic" and "insincere" by American officials. Key concepts of the Alliance—government-to-government assistance, long-term economic development plans—made little sense anyway when the United States did not trust the government in power.

The anti-American component of Brazilian nationalism, the country's intractable fiscal problems, the unpredictability of foreign leaders, the

101

power of the American Congress over foreign aid, the skill of American firms in whipping up public opinion—all exacted a toll from New Frontier idealism. Whatever ideas he had entertained before about fighting communist revolution with democratic revolution, Kennedy had been brought back to American political basics: it was not the business of an American government to promote social reform in foreign lands if such reform might in any way hurt American private enterprise. As far as Congress and the public were concerned, the business of America was still business.

# 6

# Convincing Lincoln Gordon

---

I t is important to convince Lincoln Gordon," concluded one report
to the Executive Committee of IPES.[1] During his first year as ambassador, Gordon was not yet convinced that Goulart must go. "We have
no choice but to work to strengthen this government," Gordon wrote
on January 7, 1962, "since there appears no viable alternative."[2] He saw
Goulart as lacking in leadership, weak and irresolute, but at this time
the ambassador was as inclined to fault the Brazilian Congress and the
new prime minister as to blame Goulart. He condemned the Congress
for "irresponsibility" and Prime Minister Tancredo Neves for "disinterest" in exercising the powers of his office.[3] Furthermore, whatever
Goulart's personal limitations, he was easier to deal with than Quadros.

The intelligence bureaucracy in Washington agreed with Gordon. "The
present government," it concluded, "will continue to emphasize the 'independent' character of its foreign policy, but the need for U.S. financing,
as well as domestic political considerations, will probably render it less
truculent toward the U.S. than was the Quadros administration."[4]

During the first six months of his administration, Goulart was not
personally held responsible for pursuing anti-American policies. When
diplomatic relations with the Soviet Union were reestablished in November 1961, the American analysts still held Quadros to blame for the
outrage. Nor was Goulart condemned for the position that Brazil took
during the second OAS conference, held at Punta del Este from January

22 to 31, 1962. Foreign Minister Francisco San Tiago Dantas was held responsible instead.

This conference of foreign ministers of member states was held at the request of the United States specifically to deal with the Cuban "threat" to the hemisphere. Initially, Kennedy hoped that the OAS would unanimously, or with near unanimity, vote sanctions against Cuba, perhaps even authorizing the formation of an inter-American military force to overthrow Castro. But as the opening date of the conference approached, it became obvious that the larger Latin states—Brazil, Argentina, Mexico—would oppose the imposition of any sanctions at all. It was Brazilian Foreign Minister Dantas who took the lead in organizing opposition to sanctions. He proclaimed Brazil's unconditional loyalty to the international principles of self-determination and nonintervention in the internal affairs of a sovereign state, principles that had been reaffirmed in the OAS charter. If the United States persisted in the effort to get tough with Castro, there would be a public clash with Brazil at the conference, perhaps followed by a split of the OAS.

During the weeks before the conference Kennedy presided over a debate among his advisors. One faction, headed by OAS Ambassador deLesseps Morrison wanted the United States to press for "the most stringent action," no matter what the Brazilians or Argentinians or Mexicans thought. If enough American pressure was applied, the Latins would fall in line. It was outrageous to suggest that the United States follow the lead of Brazil. "Why should our policy be dictated by a country suffering from internal confusion, and whose foreign minister was pro-Castro?" asked Morrison.[5]

The other faction (principally Goodwin, Schlesinger, and Rostow) felt it would be a serious error to try to browbeat Brazil or to ignore the Brazilian position. Not only would such a course risk splitting the OAS, but there might be negative repercussions within Brazil. For example, it might somehow provide an opening for a return of Quadros, the author of the pro-Cuban, neutralist policies that the United States found so distasteful. Brazil was, after all, more important than Cuba. It would be better to work with Dantas, Goodwin argued, and try to come up with some sort of resolution that Brazil, along with Argentina and Mexico, could support.

Although like Morrison he may have yearned for some sort of decisive action against Castro, Kennedy decided in favor of the soft line. It was just as well. Latin opposition to sanctions against Cuba was stronger than the Americans had thought. In the end it was necessary to bribe

Haiti just to get the bare two-thirds majority needed to expel Cuba from the OAS. Brazil and five other states abstained from that vote on the grounds that the OAS charter made no provision for the expulsion of a member state.

Leftists in Brazil took pride in the fact that their foreign minister had resisted all of the "blackmail, corruption, and threats" of the United States and thwarted intervention in Cuba.[6] Many Brazilian conservatives, who were usually pro-American, felt that in this case American policy was wrong and Dantas was pursuing an evenhanded, wise policy.[7] Both leftists and conservatives were offended by American pressure at the conference, especially by the arm-twisting of Secretary of State Rusk, who argued that for the United States the sacred principle of nonintervention was really meaningless. Even when the United States took absolutely no action at all—as during the Quadros resignation crisis—that in effect also amounted to intervention, said Rusk. The Brazilians promptly interpreted this as a veiled threat to intervene in their country's internal affairs. Ambassador Gordon was called in later to receive an official complaint about Secretary Rusk's remarks.[8]

The American delegation to Punta del Este put the best face possible on the results and declared themselves delighted with the expulsion of Cuba from the OAS and the resolution stating that communism was incompatible with the American system. These achievements were declared to be a great triumph for American diplomacy. But privately the Americans were convinced that they would have gotten more—perhaps mandatory breaking of diplomatic relations with Cuba by all OAS members—if it had not been for the opposition of the Brazilian foreign minister, dubbed Santiago de Cuba Dantas by the Americans at the conference.

Thus, the New Frontier team set itself up to miss an opportunity that it had been searching for. Back in December 1961, Ambassador Gordon had expressed the American longing that a "prominent figure" who enjoyed "national status" would somehow materialize and mobilize the "centrist forces which continue [to] represent large majority electorate and Congress."[9] Such a figure had emerged. His name was San Tiago Dantas.

Dantas's true position in Brazilian politics was not, at the time, apparent to American analysts. A wealthy lawyer from Minas Gerais, with good social connections and a reputation as an intellectual, Dantas was acceptable to centrists in the UDN and the PSD as well as to those in his own party, the PTB. In his youth he had been a member of the Integralistas, the Brazilian variety of fascists. But not even the Communists seemed to hold that against him. Left-wing nationalists were much more likely to object to his current business connections with foreign-owned firms. However, since Dantas had joined the Brazilian Labor Party (obviously not under the influence of foreign firms) and had vigorously defended the new independent foreign policy, he had, at least for a time, won over the Left as well as the Center. Had he been given support, he might have done just what the ambassador hoped for and mobilized the majority of Congress and the public behind the Goulart government. "He was the one man who might have gotten a government of national unity working," said UDN leader Afonso Arinos de Melo Franco. "A man you could talk to," commented Communist Party head Luis Carlos Prestes. "As long as San Tiago was Minister, destabilization did not succeed," insisted Renato Archer, who served under him in the foreign office.[10]

The American embassy was not unaware of Dantas's abilities. "A man of extraordinary vanity as well as talent," commented Ambassador Gordon.[11] But instead of giving Dantas some quiet behind-the-scenes support, the United States lent its support and funds to the right-wing Brazilians who worked to undermine the foreign minister's position. The American failure at Punta del Este was thus avenged—at a cost to long-term American goals.

The downfall of Dantas came after Goulart's official visit to the United States in April 1962. As foreign minister, Dantas had accompanied Goulart on the visit and participated in the discussions with President Kennedy and State Department officials in the White House and with American labor leaders at Blair House.[12] He remained in Washington after Goulart left in order to work out final details on an Alliance for Progress aid package for Northeast Brazil. The aid agreement, signed on April 13, stipulated that over the next two years the United States would provide $131 million in loans for Northeast development, while the federal government of Brazil invested $145 million in the area.[13]

The Kennedy administration released $33 million of the promised $131 million immediately, and Goulart was thus able to return home with concrete evidence of accomplishment. He was on the whole quite pleased with the visit, especially cheered by the warm and friendly reception he had received; he had anticipated a much more hostile one.[14] But the euphoria engendered by the visit did not last long. Back in Brazil, Goulart was soon engulfed by a rising tide of criticism of his performance as president. Even newspapers (such as the *Correio da Manha*) that had strongly defended his right to succeed Quadros in August 1961 were criticizing his leadership by early May 1962.[15] The American State Department joined in that criticism. The Goulart visit to the United States did mark a turning point: from this time on, American officials focused on Goulart as personally responsible for everything that happened in Brazil. No longer was blame divided among the Congress, the prime minister, the president, and the previous administration.

Few good things were happening in Brazil that spring of 1962. Inflation continued at a rate of more than 40 percent. Shortages of basic foods, such as rice, beans, meat, and coffee, developed, due in large part to price controls that diverted foods to a black market. Urban unemployment continued at high levels while the steady migration from country to city continued. Landless peasants mounted invasions of large estates in the Northeast and in the state of Goias. The would-be squatters were driven off by the police or by the armed bands of thugs *(capangas)* maintained as private security forces by many landowners. In the Northeastern states that had Peasant Leagues there were assorted other violent clashes between peasants and plantation owners.[16] Right-wing terrorists set off more bombs in Rio and Porto Alegre. In cities throughout Brazil there were strikes or calls for strikes. Although communist agitators were usually blamed for the strikes, the fact that wage increases lagged behind price increases probably did much more to fuel labor unrest. To the annoyance of American officials looking for evidence of Goulart government resolve to fight inflation, on May 25 the Brazilian Congress approved a 40 percent salary increase for federal employees. State and municipal employees were not as fortunate; in many states (such as Pará) not even their inflation-eroded salaries were being paid. Payless paydays continued for months as state and city governments ran into financial difficulties. And, relentlessly, prices kept rising.[17]

After eight months in office Goulart had still not made known any agenda for his government. True, in his May Day speech to labor he had called for basic structural reforms. But many voices were calling for the same thing in the same nonspecific way—media pundits, nationalist politicians, the Marxists, the centrist-conservative state governors attending a conference in June 1962. No one suggested any specific procedure for achieving any specific reform. Nor was it immediately clear how a fundamental structural reform such as land reform could solve an immediate problem such as inflation. But some obvious problems lay within the scope of presidential powers—e.g., the corruption and gross inefficiency in government agencies such as the state-owned oil and steel companies, Petrobrás and CVRD. Even for the problems requiring congressional cooperation, it was incumbent on the chief executive to present specific plans pointing to possible solutions. But Goulart excused himself from these difficult tasks on the grounds that the new parliamentary system deprived him of the powers he needed to lead a reform effort. He divided his energies between his campaign for an early plebiscite on the parliamentary system and his effort to strengthen his position within his own party and the Congress.

In late May attention was diverted from the president to the foreign minister. A UDN congressman introduced a motion to censure Dantas for following policies that weakened resistance to communism in Brazil. A phalanx of Congressmen, members of Ação Democratica Parlamentar (funded by IBAD) lined up to give speeches attacking the foreign minister. Dantas was blasted for a number of things: the defense of Castro's Cuba at the second Punta del Este conference, the resumption of diplomatic relations with the Soviet Union, the appearance in Brazil of a "large" number of Russians in connection with a Soviet trade fair that opened in Rio on May 3. All these developments were attributed to Dantas, and all were interpreted as indications that the communists were rapidly gaining strength in Brazil. Dantas was charged with mounting a sneak campaign to undermine democracy in Brazil in order to promote a communist takeover.[18]

At the same time as Dantas was being berated in Congress, Cardinal Jaime de Barros of Rio de Janeiro began his own campaign against an imagined communist threat in Brazil. He held press conferences to denounce something he called "bi-frontism," presumably meaning that Dantas was trying to maintain a position on both the communist and the Western fronts. He also cautioned against rushing into reforms that might change the fundamentals of Brazilian civilization and announced the formation of an Electoral Alliance for the Family as a political pressure group to "educate" voters in those fundamentals.[19]

Major newspapers in Rio and São Paulo and the Chateaubriand newspaper chain throughout Brazil gave extensive coverage to the congressional attacks on Dantas and to the cardinal's new crusade. The sudden uproar over foreign policy had the earmarks of a coordinated attack. No doubt it was. It represented the first salvo in the secret war of IBAD/IPES against the government of João Goulart.

The attack was not immediately successful. At first, other congressmen found it hard to take the charges against Dantas seriously enough to refute, but after Dantas returned from a trip abroad and spoke in defense of the independent foreign policy, nationalists in Congress rallied to his defense. The censure motion was voted down decisively on May 30 by a vote of 131 to 44.[20]

But the principal IPES effort against Dantas was to come the next month. The constitution provided that all government officials who intended to run for elective office must resign their offices at least three months before the October election. Since that provision was incompatible with the new parliamentary system that Congress had just set up, Congress might have passed legislation exempting cabinet ministers from this requirement. But the majority of legislators were displeased with the apparent ineffectiveness of the existing cabinet and refused to exempt them.[21] Prime Minister Tancredo Neves planned to run for Congress. He and the entire cabinet therefore resigned on June 26. Goulart let it be known that he planned to designate Dantas as Neves's replacement. The foreign minister had in fact dominated the Neves cabinet. Tancredo Neves, who held the dual post of prime minister and justice minister, had devoted his attention to the justice minister's duties: tending to patronage matters, trying to keep important politicians happy and in support of the government, generally acting as liaison between the executive branch and the political parties.

A national furor over the nomination of Dantas erupted even before the nomination was formally submitted on June 19. Congressmen and governors gave speeches advising against the nomination. The press, even the more moderate newspapers such as the *Correio da Manha*, carried daily attacks on the foreign minister and his handling of foreign affairs.[22]

"Yesterday forty-two ladies started a movement to organize the women of the city to protest against the increasing Communist propaganda and to make known the desire of the people that Dantas not be named Prime Minister," the *Correio da Manha* reported on June 16. The ladies had a long list of complaints about Dantas's behavior. He had allowed two dozen agents of international communism into the country, after promising to restrict the number of Soviet employees at the newly opened embassy. He prevented "clean-up operations" against the subversive activities of the Cuban ambassador. He humiliated the country by acting as lawyer for Fidel Castro at Punta del Este. He did everything he could to undermine the Alliance for Progress. Perhaps his greatest crime was the one the women listed last: Dantas had brazenly gone to visit union halls, flattering the labor leaders and seeking their support.

Quite unaware that the forty-two ladies had been put up to it by IPES, the reporter thus reported the birth of CAMDE (Women's Campaign for Democracy). The group was destined to play an important role in the battle against Goulart and to provide a model for the way in which middle-class women might be used in anticommunist causes in Latin America. It had been set up by three (male) IPES members, who felt the need for "an effective 'popular chorus' to prevent the inauguration of San Tiago Dantas as Prime Minister."[23] They recruited female relatives of IPES members as the charter members of the group. The CAMDE women entered into their new political role with enthusiasm, promptly organizing a Caravan to Brasília to urge Congress to reject the nomination.

To the horror of CAMDE and its IPES sponsors, Dantas had apparently welcomed the politicization of the working class. Labor leaders were becoming more and more active politically. That same June, pro-Goulart leaders in various unions announced the formation of an inter-union committee, the Comando Geral de Greve (General Strike Command). On Dantas's behalf, perhaps in imitation of CAMDE, this new organization sent its own caravan—busloads of workers—to the capital to make Congress aware of "the wishes and aspirations" of the people they represented. The Comando Geral also threatened to call a general strike if the Dantas nomination was rejected.

The popular chorus that Congress chose to consider legitimate was that of the middle-class *senhoras*. The Dantas nomination was rejected 174 to 110. In place of the capable Dantas, Congress ended up accepting and installing the relatively inexperienced Francisco Brochado da Rocha as prime minister, thus ensuring a further period of political drift and stagnation. Rocha, virtually unknown nationally, was a Rio Grande do Sul law professor who had been serving as state secretary of the interior in the administration of Governor Brizola.

Instead of criticizing the Brazilian Right for immobilizing the government, American embassy analysts decided to blame Goulart for the entire hullabaloo. From the start, said Ambassador Gordon, the nomination of Dantas was a "political power play" ultimately aimed at strengthening Goulart's own position.[24] Never intending to see Dantas made prime minister, Goulart all along aimed at the installation of a puppet prime minister and a more docile cabinet, suggested political counselor Philip Raine. To do this, he had developed "a plan with widespread ramifications," a plan so "devious and secretive as almost to justify use of the word 'plot' rather than 'plan.'"[25]

No doubt the more obvious plotters in IPES gained valuable experience in use of the media and mobilization of public opinion during this campaign against Dantas. By mid-1962, IPES had developed its organization and expanded from its Rio–São Paulo base to other capital cities.[26] To a degree, the society's organization and tactics seemed modeled on those of its arch-enemy, the Communist Party. Like the Communists, IPES operated shrouded in semisecrecy behind a variety of "fronts" that it set up and funded. Like the Communists, IPES attempted to infiltrate other organizations in the hope of influencing them or taking them over. Like the Communists, IPES never tired of trying to persuade the public to accept its philosophy. Polemical tracts, special seminars, media advertising, subsidized books, propaganda films were all employed. Trips to the United States were awarded to promising converts. Of course, again like the Communists, IPES got some of its funding for such expensive proselytizing from a foreign power.

Structurally, IPES was set up as a hierarchy of committees. An executive committee (five to eight members) met daily to check on the various ongoing initiatives of the society and to carry out the latest directives of the larger Directing Committee. The Directing Committee met once a week to discuss and decide on actions to be taken the following week. A step down the organizational pyramid was the Orienting Council, which met several times a year to ratify the decisions taken by the Directing Committee. Operating somewhat independently was the Fiscal Council, in charge of overseeing the society's substantial income and expenditures. To coordinate the work of the two central IPES chapters in Rio and São Paulo, a Regional Executive Committee was established, composed of ten members from Rio and ten from São Paulo, selected by each city's Directing Committee. The Regional Committee met once a week. Contact with the IPES chapters in other cities was maintained by frequent visits of IPES officials and by correspondence. In addition, a National Orientation Council was established to provide for formal conferences of representatives of all chapters.

Membership in IPES had grown to 500 by the end of 1962. Of course, not all members were active in the organization. "São Paulo and Rio have few men for a lot of work. Just as in businessmen's groups, material effort is also from just a few. Most only give money." So read one problem to be discussed by the Rio/São Paulo Executive Committee on April 8, 1963.[27] Those members who wished to play an active role in saving their country from communism could join one of the study groups or task forces that served as the society's operational units. There were units specializing in congressional liaison, publicity, publications, labor relations, student affairs, agrarian reform, and membership.

Perhaps the most important unit in the Rio IPES was the one known as the Situation Analysis Group (Grupo de Levantamento da Conjuntura). Headed by retired General Golbery do Couto e Silva, this group served as the basic intelligence unit of IPES, gathering and evaluating information about social and political developments in all sectors, projecting the likely future impact of those developments, and drawing up plans to influence the emerging situation. To obtain information, the Situation Analysis Group not only established a network of informants within the military, the government agencies, business and professional associations, student groups, and the church, but also illegally tapped telephones. Weekly reports of its activities and those of the other study groups, along with a summary of the current political situation, were sent to key military and civilian officials. In addition, the Situation Analysis Group distributed a biweekly, mimeographed circular—without attribution—among all military officers. The circular described the ongoing "communist" activity in the country.

It was in connection with this intelligence gathering that General Golbery began his dossiers on all known or suspected communist groups and individuals in the country, as well as lists of everyone suspected of being soft on communism or otherwise possibly inclined to be subversive. After the coup, these dossiers would provide the military government with the information it needed to arrest and imprison individuals or to dismiss citizens from their government jobs without a hearing or appeal. In fact, the Situation Analysis Group of IPES became the nucleus of the post-coup National Intelligence Service, with Golbery still in charge.

In the IPES of São Paulo, the equivalent intelligence unit was called the Special Situation Group (Grupo Especial da Conjuntura). It was headed by another general, Agostinho Cortes. The São Paulo Situation Group tended to be more oriented toward action than toward intelligence gathering. It assumed responsibility for coordinating the various anti-Goulart conspiracies brewing within military ranks. It also mounted the efforts to infiltrate labor unions, student organizations, peasant leagues, and the Church.

Beyond a militant anticommunism, there were few doctrines shared by all IPES members. Most of the business executives who were members apparently believed the society was dedicated to promoting private enterprise with less government intervention in the economy. However, most of the economists who were members (both military and civilian) saw more government intervention as essential in order to obtain monetary stabilization as well as planned development. Military officers in general were perhaps less enthusiastic about promoting private enterprise than in promoting a bigger military-industrial complex. However, there was general agreement among IPES members that Brazil was backward and that some sort of reforms, including land reform, were necessary to modernize the country. This IBAD/IPES commitment to the idea of agrarian reform, however limited, made it difficult for the society to recruit members among the arch-conservative rural oligarchs, especially those in the Northeast.

There were other doctrinal differences, as well as personal and factional conflicts within IPES, but the divisive effect of such differences was minimized by the semisecret way in which the leadership operated and by the division into autonomous chapters and many distinct study groups. Seeing their society as an umbrella organization for a variety of elite groups that were all fighting a communist takeover, the IPES top leadership saw no need to press for ideological consistency or absolute unity. There can be no doubt about IPES's success in tying together an imposing coalition of military officers, business executives, professional men and women, church leaders, middle-class housewives, politicians, and technocrats. "IPES was certainly not, as it is frequently described, an amateur movement of businessmen with romantic notions," concluded René Armand Dreifuss, after a careful study of IPES archives. "Nor was it a mere disseminator of limited anticommunist propoganda. On the contrary, it was a sophisticated action group, well equipped and prepared."[28]

The United States contributed to that equipment and preparation. Funding flowed from the CIA through IBAD and from American firms in Brazil. Through its Book Program, the American Embassy provided money to publish some of the anticommunist literature promoted by the society.[29] Most of the anticommunist pamphlets, films, and comic strips that were distributed free of charge by IPES had been supplied by the United States Information Agency. At the Escola Superior de Guerra (Superior War College) American instructors and Brazilian officers trained in America belabored international communism as a godless movement aimed at total world conquest. Members of both the civilian and military elite were invited to take the ESG courses. Many of them were affiliated with IPES.

While IPES was successfully pulling together a coalition on the right, on the opposite end of the political spectrum, the Left was doing what came naturally—splintering. It is perhaps significant that in Brazil at this time, the term "the Left" was given as a plural, "as Esquerdas" (the Lefts). The leftists found it difficult to work together for any length

113

of time. Disagreements over rather obscure doctrinal issues or personality clashes led to constant divisions.

The oldest and best-organized group on the left, the Brazilian Communist Party, had just undergone one of its periodic schisms in early 1962. In January the party announced the expulsion of a (Stalinist) faction that rejected the Khrushchev policy of peaceful coexistence and looked to China for revolutionary inspiration. The next month those expelled organized themselves as the Communist Party of Brazil.[30] There were now two Communist parties, bitterly hostile to each other, although often found on the same side on national issues.

The peasant movement in the Northeast was also fracturing. Francisco Julião, the organizer of the Peasant Leagues, who admired Fidel Castro and frightened Tad Szulc, was already politically on the downgrade. Early in 1961, Luis Carlos Prestes, head of the Brazilian Communist Party, had offered Julião his support. He proposed that the Peasant Leagues merge with a Communist-controlled peasant union in São Paulo state, thus taking a major step toward becoming a national rather than strictly regional force. The catch was that Julião would have to accept ultimate Communist Party control. In November of the same year President Goulart offered Julião the resources of the federal government if he would sign on as a Goulart supporter, either as a subchieftan in the PTB or as leader of an affiliated party. Julião turned down both offers. Dreaming of creating a National Peasant Party with himself as the top leader, Julião was not interested in accepting a subsidiary role within an existing party. Thereafter, the Communist Party dismissed Julião as an opportunist on an ego trip, and Goulart worked to undermine his popular appeal by providing federal benefits to peasants who were *not* members of Julião's Leagues. In addition to his problems with these more powerful political leaders, Julião had increasing difficulty controlling his own subordinates in the Leagues. He also faced growing competition in the field as the Catholic church became active in forming new rural unions. The Church-sponsored unions were in part funded by the CIA. A new rural cooperative movement was entirely initiated and funded by the Americans. Church-led unions and rural co-ops both gained some ground among the peasants.[31]

Left-wing university student activists, who already had a functioning umbrella organization, the UNE (National Students Union), were perhaps in a better position to combat right-wing machinations than were the newly organized peasants. But in mid-1962, UNE energies were deflected from national problems to internal university politics; the UNE demanded one-third student representation on all university administrative councils. Failing to get it, they declared a strike. The strike succeeded for a time in paralyzing most of the universities. It also succeeded in alienating the passive majority of students, the faculty, and the public.[32]

During his visit to Washington, Goulart spoke of his party, the PTB, as though it were a united political force representing a substantial segment of the Brazilian public.[33] In fact, however, the PTB, like other Brazilian political parties represented a loose coalition of politicians, with virtually no grass-roots organization. The politicians acted together as a party to share out the spoils of office and to exchange political favors. Beyond an avowed interest in receiving the votes of the working classes, PTB members shared few ideas on social or political problems. Most vocal were the PTB congressmen on the Left known as the Compact Group, but they were outnumbered in the PTB congressional delegation by moderates. Goulart was the titular head of the party, but that position did not translate into automatic party support when he became president. Control of patronage should have been his best weapon to maintain the loyalty of the moderate rank and file members, but, inexplicably, Goulart very early lost control of the patronage machinery, when he put it in the hands of local PTB units or turned it over to the heads of government agencies.[34] At the same time, Goulart's relationship with the party militants on the Left was usually a strained one. They saw Goulart as too timorous, too ready to compromise, and preferred the flamboyant style and fiery oratory of his brother-in-law, Brizola.

Goulart's critics on the Right never took cognizance of the internecine conflict on the Left. Jango was constantly struggling to stay ahead of Brizola, hold the Compact Group in check, and maintain some influence over increasingly restive labor unions. But his opponents saw him as the wily manipulator of those sinister labor-Left forces, scheming to use them to set up a syndicalist republic with himself as dictator.

The general strike that was called for July 5 by the newly organized CGG (Comando Geral do Greve) intensified the fears about Goulart's ultimate intentions. The strike had purely political objectives: the CGG, in light of the rejection of Dantas, wanted to pressure Congress into accepting a cabinet that would be dedicated to structural reform. On July 4 Goulart did make one attempt to persuade the labor leaders to call off their strike, but it went forward the next day as planned. Nationwide, the strike was far from being "general," but it did disrupt life in some urban areas where transport sector workers heeded the strike call. Airline, maritime, dockworkers, railroad and bus employees stopped work. In Rio de Janeiro some industrial and commercial unions also walked out. There had been food shortages in Rio just prior to the strike, and, without transportation facilities, the markets were emptier than usual. Violent food riots and looting of food warehouses and other stores broke out in several working-class suburbs, with the high toll of 40 dead and 700 injured. Governor Lacerda, under criticism for having taken no steps whatever to prepare for a shutdown of transportation or possible riots and looting, relieved his feelings by sending Goulart a telegram, informing him that communist elements trained in Moscow, Prague, and/or Havana were leading the strike.[35] But many believed that it was Goulart himself who had ordered the strike and the rioting in order to soften up the country for his own devious purposes.[36]

The Americans were as upset by the news of the strike and the riots as were conservative Brazilians. President Kennedy was scheduled to visit Brazil on July 20. Administration officials were soon in a dither about signals. What sort of signal would be sent up by a trip at this time? Would it be interpreted as a Kennedy endorsement of Goulart's recent behavior? Wouldn't it suggest that the United States found nothing unusual in the food riots or the general strike? The Kennedy trip was abruptly called off a week before it was to begin. A date in November was suggested instead. The excuse offered was that Kennedy had urgent matters to get through Congress before the November congressional elections. Heavy in the air, but left unstated, was the suggestion that President Goulart would do well to apply himself in like fashion before the Brazilian October elections.[37]

In the wake of the bloodshed and political general strike, analysts at the embassy rehashed the possibility of direct ties between Goulart and the communists and speculated about his long-range plans for a "syndicalist republic" or some other revolutionary reconstruction.[38] One analyst was shocked to discover that Goulart took Kennedy rhetoric at face value. "One interesting aspect of this situation," he wrote,

> is the belief within the Goulart Administration and among some of its confidants that the Kennedy Administration approves or even encourages revolutionary objectives. The Embassy can find no other explanation for the openness with which the subject was discussed with Professor Kissinger who was heralded in Brazil as one of President Kennedy's principal advisors. President Goulart himself made much in a recent conversation with the Ambassador of the fact that Kennedy Administration spokesmen as well as labor unions in the United States insisted that Brazil would have to have agrarian reform if it were to receive Alliance for Progress funds.[39]

Ambassador Gordon himself seemed more preoccupied with immediate economic issues than with ultimate political designs. He was still not convinced that Goulart must go. But he was very upset over the lack of any progress on the ITT compensation claim. Strictly interpreted, the Hickenlooper Amendment mandated the suspension of all aid to Brazil on August 16, 1962, the date marking six months after the expropriation of the ITT subsidiary in Rio Grande do Sul. Dantas had promised Gordon that he would see to it before he left office, but now Dantas had gone without doing so. Therefore it would be necessary to persuade Goulart to meet ITT's demands. Believing that Goulart would respond to direct personal pressure from Kennedy, the ambassador urged the president to send Goulart a lengthy letter outlining the history of the ITT claim (in case Goulart had forgotten) and dwelling on past promises to settle the matter. Goulart should be reminded, for example, that "on the airplane from New York to Omaha, on April 7...it was indicated that a loan to Standard Electric [the ITT manufacturing subsidiary] would be negotiated within a few days after the return of your party from Mexico."[40]

Other economic matters troubling the ambassador that summer were the continuing inflation, the obvious collapse of all attempts at stabilization, the unresolved matter of amending the profit remittance law, the recent cancellation of the Hanna mining concession, and new expropriation threats to the AMFORP properties that had not yet been taken over by state governments.[41] In the absence of a foreign minister, Gordon hounded Acting Foreign Minister Renato Archer about the apparent threats to American companies.[42]

There is no indication that White House or State Department analysts paid any attention to the revealing survey of Brazilian public opinion carried out that summer. From late June through early August, a Washington-based research firm, Operations and Policy Research, Institute for the Comparative Study of Political Systems, studied the political attitudes of a national sample of urban voters in Brazil. The study demonstrated that Brazilians placed primary emphasis on economic issues. Inflation and the high cost of living were considered the overriding domestic problems, with 45 percent listing the high cost of living and another 26 percent listing inflation (as distinct from price increases) as serious problems. More clearly political issues, such as corruption and incompetence in government, were ranked even below the need for agrarian reform as national problems.[43]

In foreign relations, the need to find new markets abroad—not subversion from Cuba—was seen as the major problem. Forty-seven percent of the sample listed the need to find new markets abroad; only 8 percent were concerned about subversion from Cuba. Overdependence on American aid (rather than on markets) was listed as a serious problem by 25 percent.[44] Noting the willingness to find new markets in the Communist bloc countries plus the concern about overdependence on United States aid, the researchers concluded that the Quadros-Dantas independent foreign policy was favored by the majority of Brazilian voters, who apparently saw it as "a balanced accommodation to Cold War pressures" that enabled Brazil to concentrate on economic problems. Nor was there much comfort in the study for the State Department's campaigns about ITT, AMFORP, Hanna, and profit remittance. The need to control foreign investors was listed as a major problem by 23 percent of the sample.

When the researchers attempted to rank the political standing of Brazilian leaders, they discovered that former President Kubitschek was the most popular figure, with 62 percent ranking him first in some leadership quality. At 26 percent, the embassy favorite, right-wing Governor Lacerda, was ranked just behind left-wing Governor Brizola, at 28 percent. Goulart still enjoyed some support if not enthusiasm; 40 percent ranked him first in some leadership quality, and 72 percent favored a return to the presidential system, which would give him more power. The great majority of those interviewed (70 percent) were unable to even identify Peasant League leader Francisco Julião.[45]

The survey suggests that as the campaign for the congressional and state elections got underway in the summer of 1962, the Red Scare had not yet really caught on. Nevertheless, under the guidance of IPES, pressure groups on the right did their best to make the elections a referendum on communism versus democracy. CAMDE, for example, filled Rio with posters bearing the legend, "Dad, vote for a democrat so that tomorrow I may continue to be free!"[46] Almost every week some previously unknown group held a rally to announce its intention to fight communism. Thus, on August 1, a group with the less-than-catchy name of Movement of Fatherland Volunteers for a Democratic and Christian Brazil held a rally in Niteroi to pledge battle against communist infiltration. The message was sometimes indirect and understated; a billboard went up in Rio asking one question: "What if there were a wall here as in Berlin?"[47] Some organizations invested in paid newspaper advertisements of their anticommunist principles.[48] Cardinal Jaime de Barros used his radio program, "The Pastor's Voice," to urge action against communism and to remind his listeners that the pressure group he had set up, the Electoral Alliance for the Family, was prepared to tell them how to vote.[49] A University of Brazil professor, Gondim Neto, gave a series of lectures, open to the public, denouncing a supposed plot by Goulart to transform Brazil into a syndicalist republic.[50]

For their part, candidates on the Left divided their energies between calling for immediate structural reform and attacking the United States. According to them, American big business was not content with simply plundering the Brazilian economy; it was now intervening in Brazilian domestic politics in a concerted effort to buy the election. The U.S. corporations were doing this with the connivance and encouragement of American diplomatic personnel stationed in Brazil. One left-wing journalist charged that the American Embassy was using the Wheat Fund to finance the campaigns of right-wing candidates.[51]

One of the most outspoken critics of the American embassy was Goulart's brother-in-law, Leonel Brizola, running for a Congressional seat from Rio de Janeiro in this election. During an interview with a reporter from the *Diário de Notícias* on May 8, 1962, Brizola charged:

> The United States Embassy is moving around funds that are at its disposal in the Bank of Brazil and entering into direct understandings with Brazilian politicians. The Embassy is being transformed into a type of Mecca towards which mayors, public and private groups, all move directly, looking for the recommendations and the stamp of approval of the Ambassador and American officials. In a short time, if these strange customs continue, we will have the American Embassy transformed into a super-ministry, eclipsing the Cabinet itself, becoming the sole center for the distribution of funds in the nation.[52]

Ambassador Gordon was highly incensed with the "increasingly violent statements from Goulart-San Tiago Dantas-Brizola camp...the burden of which are that economic power...is seeking to pervert will of people by electing reactionaries and *entreguistas* to Congress."[53] It is not clear why Gordon was so upset. Brizola's charges happened to be true. If anything, in 1962 the leftists erred on the side of underestimating American interference in the Brazilian election. The U.S. intervention in this election exceeded any prior American involvement in Brazilian politics. Honing skills already partially tried out in other underdeveloped countries, the CIA, with assistance from the State Department, developed a model that could be used a little later in Chile.

At this time the public knew little about the CIA and its undercover operations. The American role in staging coups in countries such as

Guatemala or Iran had not yet been publicized. "Destabilization" was not yet a part of the vocabulary of international relations. Neither the anti-American groups abroad nor the American public at home knew that labor leaders, student leaders, journalists, and university professors were systematically recruited to carry out special assignments for the CIA or that the CIA routinely intervened in "democratic" elections abroad in an unending effort to pervert the will of the people who might want to elect communists. "The CIA ordinarily had political funds," Gordon observed fifteen years later. "It all started in Italy in 1948, when American money aided the strengthening of the Christian Democratic Party."

In Brazil, Gordon estimated that probably about $5 million (of U.S. taxpayers' money) was spent on the 1962 election. "Not an enormous sum," he said. But he conceded that since the CIA "uses real companies and some imaginary firms to channel their operations," it was possible "that I didn't know all of the details, although I was aware of the general nature of the operation....I won't try to deny that there was American money. But if you analyze it, it wasn't much per Congressman. Basically, it was money to buy radio time, have posters printed, that type of thing. And you can be certain that there were many more requests for help than were met."[54]

The funds that the ambassador more or less knew about were the ones dispensed by IBAD. An investigation by the Brazilian Congress the next year revealed IBAD expenditures of 400,000,000 cruzeiros during the five-month period before the elections—a sum greater than the annual budgets of some Brazilian states.[55] Eight candidates in state governor races, 250 running for federal deputy, 600 candidates for state legislatures, and an undetermined number running for the federal senate received some funds from IBAD. All of the organization's records were burned before the complete list of names could be revealed. In addition to providing direct money grants to approved candidates, IBAD financed a monthly magazine, *Ação Democrática*, which was distributed free of charge, and half-hour television programs to play on thirteen stations. IBAD also paid for the translation and publication of a book by a Czech writer, Jan Kossak, *Assalto ao Parlemento*, describing the communist takeover in Czechoslovakia by means of parliamentary manuevers. Presumably, Brazil faced the same threat.

Although Brazilian leftists were convinced that the source of IBAD's funds must be the corporate treasuries of American multinationals, most of the money came from the CIA.[56] The Bank of Boston, the First

National City Bank of New York, and the Royal Bank of Canada served as the conduits of CIA funds.[57] Both American and Brazilian firms made supplementary contributions, either to IBAD itself, to its electoral front organization, Ação Democrática Popular (Democratic Popular Action), or to its sister organization, IPES. "Business groups and producers organizations... are quite openly mobilizing their resources to support their kind of candidates and to combat the extreme leftists," reported State Department intelligence analyst Roger Hilsman. "Most of this direct action is taking place through newly-formed 'fronts' such as the Institute of Political and Social Studies."[58]

Money was not the only thing the United States dispensed in the effort to influence the October elections. There was also a flow of advice, perhaps best illustrated in the effort to elect João Cleofas governor of Pernambuco. The Kennedy administration ardently hoped to defeat the "Communist" mayor of Recife, Miguel Arraes, who was running for the governor's post with a leftist, nationalist, anti-American campaign. Arraes was in the process of replacing Peasant League leader Julião as the politician the White House feared the most in the Northeast. Although Cleofas was not a very attractive candidate, the American consul in Recife, Eugene Delgado-Arias, did what he could to steer him through the campaign. Since Cleofas stated that he did not get along with the local IBAD representatives (whom he described as a "bunch of radicals"), the American consul took it upon himself to provide him with anticommunist films, comic books, and pamphlets from the USIA stock. In addition he urged that Cleofas be given "first-rate professional help in field [of] publicity."[59] Similar aid was probably provided to other approved candidates by other American consuls.

In light of such extensive American interference in an election process, one wonders whether American diplomatic personnel experienced twinges of conscience when they lectured Latins on the importance of holding clean, free elections. The American activity in Brazil in 1962 can only be described as a brazen attempt to manipulate the October elections in an effort to twist the will of the Brazilian people according to the will of the White House. Years later Ambassador Gordon expressed his regret that in 1962 he had not opposed the expenditure of American public funds in the effort to influence the Brazilian election.[60] But at the time State Department officials apparently shared the view of White House advisor Ralph Dungan: in the Cold War the end justified the means. Making suggestions for a speech that the president was to deliver to a CIA gathering, Dungan suggested the argument that the basic justification for clandestine operations, "dirty" or otherwise, was self-defense. In order to survive, the United States must adopt the same techniques used by the enemy.[61]

It was, in any case, President Kennedy personally who was responsible for the decision to use USAID funds in the election campaign. As indicated earlier, he had pressed AID director Fowler Hamilton as early as February 1962 for a "food, water, or some other project" that could produce a favorable impact on the October elections. By June $1,000,000 in USAID funds was committed to an emergency school building program in Pernambuco. The construction agreement, negotiated with Governor Sampaio the previous September, was signed on June 6. The hope was that it would bolster the campaign of the candidate supported by Sampaio as his successor—Cleofas.[62] In an even more questionable ploy, generous American loans were provided for a synthetic rubber plant in which Sampaio had interests. The plant was supposed to provide employment and a model for industrialization in the Northeast, but the venture was a disaster.[63]

Despite the lavish expenditure (from the Brazilian point of view) of U.S. taxpayer funds, as the campaign wound down, American analysts realized that the election was not likely to be as decisive as originally thought. In fact, the new Congress was likely to look much like the old one. While the Americans hoped that there would be "increasing crystalization of opinion against Communist infiltration in the Government and the neutralist overtones of Brazil's 'independent foreign policy,'" they had to concede that it was "not clear to what extent the anti-Communist activities of lay Catholic and business organizations have been successful in this regard." In fact, it appeared that purely local issues and personalities would decide the outcome.[64]

Goulart himself played little part in the election campaign. He was engrossed in his own campaign to get an early referendum on the restoration of full presidential powers. In course of maneuvering to get this through Congress, a new "crisis" developed in mid-September. Prime Minister Brochado da Rocha resigned on September 14 after the refusal of Congress to set a date for an early referendum. Again the interunion organization of labor leaders, now named General Workers Command (CGT) rather than the earler General Strike Command (CGG), proclaimed a nationwide general strike. The strike call was heeded by more unions in more cities than the one called in July but again was far from being a truly general strike. Although there was no looting or violence associated with this strike, friction developed within the military between the generals who supported an early plebiscite and felt the strike was a legitimate way to pressure the Congress and the generals who felt that any political strike was too dangerous to be allowed at all.[65] The public, becoming accustomed to strikes and rumors of strikes, did not react to the strike with as much alarm as in June. Nevertheless, Congress again capitulated, set January 6, 1963, as the date for the plebiscite and authorized Goulart to appoint a provisional "technical" cabinet to run the country until the plebiscite. Congress thus gave up its right to confirm or reject the cabinet members in exchange for the freedom to return to the campaign hustings.[66]

The American reaction was more alarmist than the reaction in Brazil. On the same day as Brochado da Rocha resigned, a CIA Information Report was being circulated at the White House. It warned that Goulart had initiated a correspondence with Nikita Khrushchev and had suggested that Russia implement

> several spectacular investment projects in Brazil, such as building a metro or hydroelectric plant. Khrushchev replied that the socialist bloc was short of foreign exchange and normally gave aid only in the form of machinery and services of Soviet technicians. However, he said, in the case of Brazil and in view of its special importance, he would do his best to make foreign exchange available as well.[67]

The CIA suggested that Goulart was sure to regain full presidential powers and, as an unprincipled opportunist, would accept Soviet aid. Then Khrushchev might move to establish ties of obligation between Brazil and the Soviet Union. He might establish something like an Aswan Dam position in Latin America.

Concern over this possibility, as well as concern about the deteriorating economic situation and awareness that the elections were unlikely to end the political stalemate, led the Kennedy adminstration to undertake two new initiatives. First, on September 17, it was decided to appeal to American allies in Europe and to Japan to collaborate with the United States in a new effort to influence the Brazilian government's "actions and policies to extent feasible in ways our common interest would seem to dictate." It was hoped that Britain, France, Germany, Italy, and Japan had enough trade and investment interests in Brazil to induce them to accept the American argument that an effort must be made to halt the "increased influence of extreme leftists, some communist-oriented, who advocate extremist solutions to Brazil's critical problems and in various ways attack democratic processes, foreign private capital, and international cooperation within free world."[68] But nothing concrete came from this initiative; the American allies failed to respond.

Kennedy's second initiative was to dispatch a counterinsurgency (Special Group [CI]) assessment team to Brazil. On September 21 Ambassador Gordon was informed that an interdepartmental team would be arriving in Brazil in early October to review the performance of the country team and to take a fresh look at the situation. Secretary of State Rusk told him that "the technique of interdepartmental team visits" had been first tried out in Vietnam a year before. The basic goal was "the effective acceleration of our programs in developing countries." One team was then visiting Venezuela and Guatemala. Brazil was to be next. Rusk stressed the fact that the idea of these visits was President Kennedy's. The head of the Brazil team would be William H. Draper, Jr., a Republican investment banker and corporation executive who had served in the Eisenhower administration as chairman of the President's Committee on Foreign Aid.[69] Representatives of the CIA, AID, USIA, and Defense Department were included on the mission.

The Draper team arrived in Brazil on October 8, the day after the elections. The elections turned out to be as inconclusive as predicted, with moderates and conservatives maintaining their predominance in the Congress, but without any one party in control. To the chagrin of the American Embassy and the CIA, the two leading anti-American nationalist candidates—Miguel Arraes and Leonel Brizola—won their respective races for governor and congressman. Candidates backed by Lacerda for vice governor of Guanabara and senator lost badly. IBAD-backed candidates for the governor's races in Sergipe and Rio Grande do Sul also lost. And enough left-wing nationalists had been elected or reelected to Congress to ensure the continuation of noisy pressure for radical reform and a great deal of anti-imperialist rhetoric.

During its fifteen-day stay in the country, the Draper team met with State Department personnel, certain Brazilian officials, resident American business leaders, and selected Brazilian bankers and businessmen. Leaders of IPES were prominent among the Brazilian businessmen entertained and consulted by the mission.[70] The group had no contact with left-of-center intellectuals, politicians, or labor leaders. The Brazilian press was apparently unaware of the presence of a counterinsurgency fact-finding mission.

Not surprisingly, the team's report to the president reflected a right-wing perspective of the Goulart government and of Brazil's immediate future. Goulart was seen as an unprincipled opportunist with a career record of bestowing favor and patronage on Communists. If he thought it would pay politically, he "would have no personal conviction or inhibition against turning to the Soviet Bloc." Brazil was right then on the brink of financial collapse. Only "massive external help" could stave off catastrophe. So great was the projected budgetary deficit that, even if it wanted to, the United States alone could not bridge the gap; European countries, Japan, and the International Monetary Fund would have to be brought into the picture. Participation of the IMF, which would insist on a rigid austerity program and the postponement of development in the interest of monetary stabilization, would admittedly "be difficult to sell politically to the Brazilians."

The team pointed out some things that the Brazilian government might do immediately to reduce the budgetary deficit, such as eliminating the subsidies to railroads and other state-owned enterprises, raising taxes, improving tax collection, restricting bank credit, cutting "unnecessary and unproductive personnel" from the government payrolls. Their two-week cram course on Brazil had not taught the interdepartmental group much about the political pressures on either the Kennedy administration or the Goulart government. Thus, apparently ignorant of the congressional and business-community pressures that had led the administration to press Goulart to purchase all foreign-owned utilities in Brazil, Draper observed:

> Brazil's decision to take over all telephone, electricity and gas companies one of worst economic mistakes. Private companies concerned quite ready [to] sell as inadequate rates have prevented keeping pace with inflation or providing needed expansion services. Take-over will, however, involve about one billion dollars (assuming fair settlement) addition to Brazil's internal debt, with large interest and principal payments added to annual budget and balance of payment.

Draper felt that the Brazilian government had been pursuing other "illogical and wasteful policies" that prevented "sound development and balanced growth." The examples he cited ignored the strength of nationalism in Brazil. He casually mentioned two of the most sacred nationalist causes: the obstacles thrown in the way of the export of iron and manganese and the preservation of the Petrobrás monopoly on oil exploration and production. He expressed the hope that "sympathetic discussion and quiet persuasion on our part" might help the Brazilians reverse such

125

illogical policies and open up their economy more to foreign private enterprise.

The mission made two major recommendations for immediate American action. First, President Kennedy should again postpone his trip to Brazil, now scheduled for mid-November. A Kennedy visit would be interpreted as an endorsement of Goulart and would simply encourage the Brazilians to request more money. Second, the United States should adopt a "hard line" and refuse emergency balance of payments assistance, debt postponement, or any new financing unless and until a stabilization plan satisfactory to the IMF was put in effect. Of course, Draper observed, Goulart and his associates were unlikely to adopt and enforce such a plan. If the United States held to its hard line, "the developing financial crisis will soon begin to hurt seriously the general population and thus threaten the stability of the Goulart administration." Goulart would try to shift the blame to the United States. "The likely result would be the final commitment of Goulart to the radical left, an intensification of anti-American sentiment, and the polarization of domestic political forces." Goulart might fall in the confusion, and a more radical government might temporarily take over, but in the end a stronger right-wing military regime, "better oriented toward the U.S.," would triumph.[71]

The sequence of events projected in the Draper report reflected the opinions of American businessmen resident in Brazil. For example, John Richards, an RCA executive and president of the São Paulo American Chamber of Commerce, "suggested that the United States Government should force the economic collapse of Brazil by cutting off all aid to the Goulart administration and thereby bringing about the downfall of Goulart himself. At this point the military would hopefully step in and 'correct the existing conditions.' "[72]

Judging from the declassified material in the Kennedy Library, the Draper report was the closest anyone came to making a "destabilization" recommendation for Brazil. Events the next year were to begin to follow the Draper-Richards scenario. In October 1962, however, Ambassador Gordon strongly disagreed with the counterinsurgency team's conclusions and persuaded the administration to shelve Draper's most drastic recommendations. As an economist, he foresaw no immediate collapse should the United States withhold aid. On the contrary, the Brazilian government "might muddle along for [a] substantial time." Nor did he agree that a crash stabilization program would soon restore prosperity and halt inflation. The Brazilian economy, he felt, was too backward, inflexible, and poorly integrated to respond rapidly to monetary stimuli. As a political observer, Gordon cautioned that a military takeover was far from being a sure thing. The military had failed to exclude Goulart when Quadros resigned. Goulart might in fact emerge stronger than ever in the wave of anti-Americanism that would follow publicity about the U.S. "hard line," and the Brazilian government might then embark on "mass expropriations" of American corporations. Conceivably, the Soviet Union could extend emergency aid to meet Brazil's oil needs, thus gaining a foothold in the country. The ambassador suggested that the United States adjust to "another few months of temporizing" until the scheduled January 6 plebiscite on a return to the presidential system. During this period some aid should be continued, but at the same time the United States could "press for rapid action on ITT case, profits bill, utility negotiations, iron ore export promotion, other elements related [to] investor confidence."[73]

Although the ambassador thus spoke out forcefully against adopting the destabilization policies advocated by Draper, it is clear that his opinion of the Goulart government had changed considerably since January. Then he had spoken of the need to strengthen Goulart since there was no viable alternative. Now he was not concerned about keeping Goulart in office; he was worried that he could not easily be ousted.

The previous July, when Gordon was in Washington for consultations, President Kennedy questioned him about the proficiency of the American military attachés posted to Brazil. Kennedy felt that, the way things were going in Brazil, the military probably represented the key to the future; it was important that the United States be kept abreast of military plots, plans, and opinions. When the ambassador expressed dissatisfaction with the performance of the army attaché then on duty in Brazil, Kennedy asked him for suggestions about a replacement. Gordon suggested a Colonel Vernon Walters as the ideal man for the job and left the Oval Office with a personal presidential authorization to have whatever officer he wanted posted to Brazil. Colonel Vernon Walters was then serving as attaché in Italy. Bound by its own arcane rules, the Army bureaucracy at first resisted carrying out a "lateral transfer" and suggested other officers. When Gordon became convinced that the alternate attachés suggested were not as good as Walters, he pressed his authorization from the commander-in-chief. In mid-October Walters arrived in Brazil to take over the post of army attaché.[74]

Gordon had come to know Walters when the two men served on the committee working on the Marshall Plan. Walters, a linguist fluent in

Portuguese, had developed close friendships with a number of Brazilian officers when he served as combat liaison officer with the Brazilian Expeditionary Army in Italy in World War II. Earlier he had served as interpreter on various U.S. missions to Brazil and Brazilian missions to the United States. From the ambassador's viewpoint, Walters was an invaluable addition to the embassy staff, coming as he did with such excellent personal contacts with the top brass in the Brazilian military. As Walters took over his new duties, Gordon told him he wanted three things: (1) to know what was going on in the Brazilian armed forces, (2) to be able to influence what was going on through the attaché, and (3) to be spared surprises.[75]

The ambassador expected that the military would move sooner or later to oust Goulart. He did not regret that. He worried that it would move prematurely and fail again. Lincoln Gordon had been convinced.

# 7

## Shortening the Leash

---

*It is recommended that support be given to a technically satisfactory Brazilian program for economic stabilization and development, but on a "short-leash" basis permitting periodic review.*

*Lincoln Gordon, March 7, 1963*

For Kennedy, the high point in New Frontier international relations came in October 1962. After obtaining photographic proof that Soviet medium-range missile launching sites were under construction in Cuba, the president announced the development as a crisis and seized the opportunity to confront the Soviet Union—a worthy adversary, not little Cuba—directly. Threatening to plunge the world into nuclear war, Kennedy forced Khrushchev to back down. Years later, critics would condemn Kennedy's actions as "irresponsible," "reckless to a supreme degree," "totally unnecessary," "a puerile act of folly."[1] But at the time the American public hailed the episode as an exhilarating victory for America and a personal triumph for a coolly courageous president. Kennedy's popularity soared.

Though the administration savored its victory and rejoiced in having forced the withdrawal of Soviet missiles, it did not immediately derive any sense of greater security on the Latin American front. Cuba might be less of a threat, but were other Latin countries securely in line? Khrushchev's retreat was not at the time interpreted as a Soviet admission that Latin America belonged to the American sphere of influence. New anxieties about Brazil replaced the fretting over Cuba.

Apprehension about the political future of Brazil had mounted steadily after the elections of October 7. At first the White House focused on the imminent financial collapse forecast by the Draper mission. Heeding the advice of Ambassador Gordon, Kennedy did not act on Draper's recommendation that there be an immediate cutoff of all American aid in order to speed the predicted financial collapse and the subsequent fall of Goulart. Draper's suggestion that the Kennedy trip to Brazil be canceled a second time was accepted, using the Cuban missile crisis as the excuse. In addition, as the Draper committee had urged, Ambassador Gordon was instructed to immediately contact President Goulart to tell him that his country faced financial catastrophe.

The ambassador opposed such a demarche, arguing that the Brazilian officials responsible for finances understood the problems, and it would be better to let them instruct their president, "since Goulart probably more responsive concerted advice from own intimates and preferable to have them rather than us take initiative."[2] Gordon was overruled. Kennedy felt there was no substitute for direct American pressure. The Brazilians might be counting on an American bailout and needed the shock treatment of being told there would be none.[3]

Gordon met with Goulart on November 16. As instructed, he told Goulart that Brazil's financial problems, especially its shortage of foreign exchange, were so serious and of such a magnitude that the United States alone could not help it out. Brazil would have to seek help from the West European countries and Japan as well as from the IMF. In fact, unless the Brazilian government took some positive steps toward working out a sound development program and a stabilization plan before the January 6 plebiscite, Gordon could not even recommend emergency balance of payments assistance. He listed some possible positive steps: paying off ITT, amending the profit remittance law, ending restrictions on iron ore export.

Taken by surprise, Goulart was highly irritated by the threats. He told Gordon that although he had until then refrained from looking to the Soviet bloc for assistance, he might have to do so in the future. At first the State Department was ready to dismiss such a remark as a type of blackmail designed to "exert pressure on U.S. for aid on Brazil's terms."[4] But disdain gave way to alarm: Brazil did seem to be turning to the Soviet bloc. First, there was the rumor (false) that Arraes, the governor-elect of Pernambuco, had negotiated a billion-dollar aid package from the Soviets for his state.[5] Then came news of a barter deal worked out by the Goulart cabinet and Poland, trading coffee for helicopters. This was followed by the signing of an aid agreement with Poland. Poland pledged a loan of $26 million and technical assistance in building a coal-burning power plant in the state of Rio Grande do Sul.[6]

While embassy analysts warned Washington that they saw the beginning "of an all-out drive by Communist forces and their allies to commit Brazil to a course of development fundamentally inimical to United States interests,"[7] stories about a possible open break with the United States surfaced:

> Goulart...keeps talking about possible denunciation of U.S. We are told that when he saw Kubitschek November 28 he said he was getting fed up with repeated delays by U.S. in assisting Brazil and was thinking of telling Brazilian people about recent Soviet aid offers and showing how U.S. was responsible for economic ills of Brazil. Some of things our AID people are hearing seem to indicate that SUDENE is preparing specific case against us on northeast.[8]

Was it possible that the Soviets were actually willing to take on Brazil as a client? Khrushchev could be looking for a way to strike back for the humiliation over the Cuban missile launch sites. Losing Brazil would be like losing China, the White House advisors reminded themselves.

To a certain extent the heightened American fears about imminent communist revolution in Brazil reflected the Red Scare hype being churned out by IBAD-IPES forces in November and December 1962. Their renewed anticommunist, anti-Goulart campaign began as a protest against the arrest of Admiral Sílvio Heck. Heck, one of the three military ministers who had tried to bar Goulart from the presidency in August 1961, was a perennial coup-plotter.[9] He was arrested on October 30, 1962, by order of the minister of the navy for violating a navy rule that prohibited officers from speaking out publicly on foreign policy matters. Heck had just gone public via press interviews to charge that Goulart was following a procommunist policy at home and abroad and therefore a communist coup was merely a question of time. He was sentenced to twenty days of disciplinary detention, to be served in ten-day stints in November and December.

When he was jailed on November 13, a large delegation from the São Paulo state police and various anticommunist organizations staged a mass visit to his prison to dramatize their support for his position. In the days following, the conservative press featured a flurry of front page reports about new manifestos and petitions that protested the arrest of Heck and the "bolshevization" of Brazil. The manifestos came from IPES-funded labor unions, women's clubs, high school student groups and from Church-sponsored family organizations.[10]

In the last week of November the UDN took up the campaign, issuing its own manifestos urging the public to pressure public officials to weed out the "Marxist minority" from the government agencies. On December 1, the UDN president, Congressman Herbert Levy, used the floor of the Chamber of Deputies to announce that Brazil was poised on the brink of a revolution because those who should defend democracy supported labor unions that were working overtime to undermine it.

On November 27 the crash of a Brazilian commercial plane near Lima, Peru, provided Brazilian anticommunists with some concrete evidence of a leftist conspiracy. Among the crash victims was the president of the National Bank of Cuba, on his way home from a conference in Rio. A pouch belonging to him, found in the wreckage, contained documents that linked Francisco Julião's Peasant Leagues with an effort to train a peasant guerrilla force on ranches in the state of Goias. The documents also referred to financial assistance to Julião from the Cuban government. A subsequent Brazilian army raid on the suspected ranches turned up small arms and ammunition but no trained peasant army. Most of the students running the ill-planned venture had already departed, and no local peasants had been persuaded to sign on. But, no matter how half-baked the scheme, the discovery served to confirm the worst fears of the Brazilian Right: not only were Communist union leaders at work organizing illegal strikes, but the peasants were also running amok, arming and rehearsing revolution, aided by international communism.[11]

On the other hand, it was readily apparent that the Brazilian Communist Party was engrossed in its own squabbles rather than in finalizing preparations to take over the government at this time. Far from having worked out any power-sharing arrangement with Goulart, at its December 1962 meeting the PCB underlined its opposition to the president:

> Instead of striving for the realization of the promised structural reforms, the Brazilian government is drawing up economic plans based on the Alliance for Progress, making concessions to the financial policy dictated by the International Monetary Fund, and negotiating an Investment Guarantee Accord that aims at assuring new privileges to imperialist capital....Communists place themselves in opposition to the policy of conciliation with imperialism and reaction being carried out by the government of Mr. João Goulart.[12]

There was little overt reaction from the Brazilian public to the renewed attempt to set off a Red Scare. Perhaps the charges were being subliminally registered in the public consciousness. But they were not taken very seriously at the time. Neither Goulart nor Prime Minister Hermes Lima bothered to respond. "We know that...Communism poses no serious threat to Brazil," concluded an editorial in the *Correio da Manha* on December 19, 1962. "It is simply not true that Brazil is on the brink of a Communist Revolution." If one of the objectives of IPES in this particular campaign was to influence the plebiscite scheduled for January 6, it was clearly a failure. In the plebiscite a record 9,457,448 votes were cast in favor of returning full powers to Goulart, compared to 2,073,582 opposed.[13]

The Brazilian public might not worry; Washington did. In addition to concern about the precarious financial position of Brazil and the fear that Goulart might take his country into the Soviet bloc, there was a third American anxiety—the Alliance for Progress and how to justify it to the American Congress and tax-paying public. By December 1962, it was more than a year old. That is not very long in any bureaucratic time frame, but, since miracles had been promised within a decade, it had to be rated a very slow starter. In 1961 there had been some idea that Brazil, especially the Northeast, would serve as a showcase of the new American revolutionary crusade to strike off the bonds of poverty and ignorance in Latin America. But after one year there was little to show for the money and attention lavished. There was not a glimmer of an Alliance for Progress mystique taking hold. Those Brazilians who did not consider the Alliance a new form of American imperialism thought it was a new name for the old American Point Four aid program. In the United States, the program was under almost continuous attack. At virtually every news conference some reporter questioned the president on its progress. Foreign aid, always unpopular with the American public, was routinely subjected to bursts of critical oratory in Congress.

Neither the congressional opposition nor the business community were aware, at that point, that the New Frontiersmen had already quietly dropped the original emphasis on basic economic and social reform in Latin America, on "broader social justice within the framework of personal dignity and political liberty."[14] Business leaders continued to complain that the Alliance for Progress tended to "export socialistic ideas to Latin America," ideas such as agrarian reform, state-owned and operated enterprise, higher taxes on business and the wealthy.[15] They pointed to the flight of private capital from Latin America (and especially from Brazil) as proof that something was seriously wrong with the Alliance as then conceived and operating. "The encouragement of private enterprise, local and foreign, must become the main thrust of the Alliance," urged one report coming out of the Commerce Committee for the Alliance for Progress.[16] Actually, as indicated above, insofar as Brazil was concerned, as early as April 1962 the administration had switched to emphasizing improvement of the investment climate as the most important "reform" to be undertaken.

Frustrated and puzzled by their failure to generate "Marshall Plan" momentum in the Alliance for Progress program, Kennedy's advisors found some solace in putting the blame on the recipient. "Our failures in Brazil...are fundamentally Brazilian failures," noted White House aide Ralph Dungan.[17] Goulart had failed to publicly support the Alliance. He had also failed to produce the kind of fiscal stability that might promote development. Other Brazilian governmental agencies were actually trying to sabotage the Alliance. SUDENE was becoming "an almost total bottleneck," complained embassy analyst John Keppel, "and is, in addition, threatening our ability to deal directly with states in the Northeast on 'impact' programs....Much the same thing can be said of BNDE [National Economic Development Bank] which has (apparently systematically) been blocking our efforts to use the PL480 wheat fund to aid in the AFP efforts here."

Still, Keppel felt that the United States had a chance to turn the situation around.

> Even though the process of subverting democratic Brazil from top down... has already progressed to a dangerous point, we believe that, if resisted now, anti-American and pro-Communist forces here may find they have gotten ahead of the game and are overextended. We cannot read the Communist mind nor do we know what Communist plans for the hemisphere were prior to our calling the Soviet hand through the Cuban quarantine. In any event, it seems to us that we may be seeing beginnings of all-out mobilization of Communist assets here somewhat ahead of what would have been a well-thought-out time schedule.[18]

The administration carefully reconsidered its options. Ambassador Gordon returned to Washington for consultations. A meeting of the National Security Council Executive Committee was scheduled for 10:00 A.M. on December 11 to discuss all three problems—possible Communist advances in Brazil, the precarious financial position of the country, and the future of the Alliance for Progress.

When the executive committee met that morning, it decided to send Attorney General Robert Kennedy to Brazil to confront Goulart. The attorney general would be acting as a stand-in for the president and would spell out "certain significant positive steps" that Goulart must take to qualify for "any further large-scale assistance." He was to make it clear that specific preconditions included "satisfactory settlement of the IT&T case, a clear Brazilian position on remedying the defects in the present profits remittance law, and a public posture of collaboration in the Alliance for Progress, in addition to the necessary measures for economic stabilization." The State Department Latin American specialists felt that Bobby Kennedy should stage the confrontation within a week. "We need to present our views on the political front immediately," it was argued, "so that we can bring our influence to bear on important near-future political decisions (e.g., appointments to the new cabinet)."

The executive committee considered possible alternatives. "If President Goulart's initial reaction to these discussions should be favorable and he should begin to change accordingly the orientation of his government, the U.S. should avoid ostentatious favoritism toward those elements in Brazil friendly to us but hostile to President Goulart." On the other hand, should he fail to come up to scratch, obviously ostentatious favoritism toward those elements would be in order.[19]

The tactic of deliberately bypassing the central government of Brazil to grant American funds to the armed forces and to state and municipal governments "who advocate democratic and foreign policies we can support" was decided upon at this National Security meeting.[20] The tactic was later dubbed the Islands of Sanity policy. As Ambassador Gordon recalls the policy, its basic purpose was not to destabilize the central government but rather to keep some Alliance for Progress funds coming into the country even though the central government had failed to meet the administrative standards required by the Alliance.[21] However, Brazilian officials saw the policy as a threat to the sovereignty of the central government; it was bitterly criticized in Brazil. "Public controversy raged over whether governors like Lacerda and Aluisio Alves had a right to treat directly with a foreign power and to incur obligations," an AID consultant noted a few years later. "The constitution of 1946 rather clearly stated that they did not; and that was the Goulart position."[22]

The December 11 Security Council meeting also approved the idea of having President Kennedy speak out publicly about Brazil in order to apply some pressure on Goulart prior to his confrontation with brother Bobby. The president did this on two occasions in the next few days. First, there was a complicated, rather obviously planted question at his news conference on December 12.

[Q.] Mr. President, Brazil has not fully carried out the anti-inflation measures which she pledged herself to carry out last year when she got large new loans

135

and rescheduling of old loans. And now she is in very deep economic trouble. What effect do you think this has upon the other nations in Latin America who are trying to meet the demands of the Alliance for Progress program, and what is the possible effect upon members of Congress in their attitude towards aid and the Alliance?

[The President.] Well, I think the situation is most painful to the Brazilians themselves, with inflation of 50 percent. . . . So that I think that this is a matter which the Brazilians must deal with. There is nothing, really, that the United States can do that can possibly benefit the people of Brazil if you have a situation which is so unstable as the fiscal and monetary situation within Brazil.

So this is of concern to the Government. It must be and it certainly is of concern to us. . . . and I think that the Brazilian Government is aware of the strong concern that we have for this inflation which eats up our aid and which, of course, contributes to a flight of capital and, therefore, diminishes rather than increases the stability of the state.[23]

Two days later, during a question-and-answer period following a presidential speech at the Economic Club of New York, Kennedy worked in another attack on the Goulart government, referring to Brazil as "bankrupt" and citing it as the prime example of the problems the United States was facing in trying to implement the Alliance for Progress.[24]

Kennedy's public attacks on their country's solvency shocked Brazilian diplomats and government officials, engaged just then in negotiating with their European creditors for debt rescheduling.[25] Such irresponsible and undiplomatic charges might have been expected from a rival or unsophisticated Third World nation, but not from the president of a friendly superpower that was ostensibly committed to the economic development of the entire hemisphere.

Even more upsetting to the Brazilians was the sudden appearance of Robert Kennedy the following Monday, December 17. The attorney general's visit had all the earmarks of the descent of a trusted lieutenant of the reigning monarch, come to lay down the law to a wayward satellite chieftan. Bobby omitted most of the customary diplomatic niceties. He went directly from the Brasília airport to the presidential palace and was closeted with President Goulart for three hours. Then after a luncheon with a few Brazilian officials and the Americans traveling in his retinue, Kennedy spoke briefly with the press and left Brasília five hours after he had landed.

Only Ambassador Gordon and an interpreter were present during the three-hour interview. Without much of a preamble, Bobby laid it on the line: President Kennedy was seriously concerned about the infiltration of "Communists and anti-American nationalist leftists" into the Brazilian government, the military, labor unions, and student groups. He was equally concerned about the tendency of the "independent" foreign policy to be systematically anti-American. Goulart had failed to support the Alliance for Progress or to take a public stand in opposition to the anti-American statements of other officials. He had also failed to halt rampant inflation or to do anything about the "ill treatment [of] American and other foreign private investors." A critical time was approaching. Goulart was about to appoint a new cabinet. "We want to aid and cooperate, but need personnel not hostile to us," said the attorney general.

Bobby then listened impatiently to Goulart's "rambling one hour reply." At one point during it he passed a note to Ambassador Gordon: "We seem to be getting no place." Goulart went on and on about how the ambassador and the American government were getting all their information about Brazil exclusively from the hostile Brazilian press and American businesses in Brazil. He droned on about how difficult it was to settle the ITT case when it was in the hands of the judiciary of a state and when the public was up in arms over the poor service of foreign-owned utilities. He made excuses about the failure to attack inflation or to develop a coherent economic program. He talked about his need of the support of the Left in order to counter the opposition of the Right.

When Goulart had finally run down, Kennedy "sharpened presentation in rebuttal." He brushed aside the satellite chieftan's "verbiage." He said he was afraid "that President Goulart had not fully understood the nature of President Kennedy's concern. . . . If all officials in Brazil are either attacking the United States or being silent in the face of such attacks, cooperation will not be possible." What really disturbed the American president was that Goulart had not publicly denounced Brizola or the other politicians making anti-American statements. "When there are people in authority in Brazil who follow the Communist line, it can not be expected that we will work with them effectively." If Goulart wanted American assistance he must do two things: (1) see to it that "personnel in key Brazilian positions" were pro-American and (2) begin "effective measures to control the runaway inflation."

Goulart now understood. President Kennedy had sent his brother to get certain men purged from the Brazilian government and to get others appointed. He controlled his irritation and tried to get Bobby or Ambassador Gordon to name names. Just who were the "elements" in his

137

administration that were anti-American or pro-Communist? Suddenly coy, the attorney general said he did not think it appropriate to debate names. The ambassador named federal agencies in which there were "serious" problems: Petrobrás, SUDENE, the Ministry of Mines and Energy, BNDE. There were also some recent military appointments displeasing to the United States, he suggested. Goulart then talked for a while about projected personnel changes in the Ministry of Mines and Energy and how he hoped that Hanna Mining Company would come around to investing in steel manufacturing as one European concern already had. He also promised that future appointments would be more satisfactory to the United States and emphasized his personal pro-American feelings.[26]

In the United States, the Kennedy administration's new "toughness" toward Brazil received high marks from the media and the public.[27] But, though he managed to end the interview with Robert Kennedy on a cordial note, the visit left Goulart furious. So were other Brazilian officials. San Tiago Dantas (back in Goulart's cabinet, this time as finance minister instead of foreign minister) feared the visit indicated that some kind of "tough line" group had won control of American policy towards Brazil.[28] Roberto Campos, Brazilian ambassador to the United States, was indignant that he had to learn of Bobby's trip from the newspapers. Normal diplomatic practice dictated prior discussion of official visits with the target country's diplomatic representatives. Had he been consulted, Campos would have politely pointed out that a trip to influence the composition of the next Brazilian government was "quite inappropriate."[29]

But satellite chieftans have limited options. When the Americans had decided to stage the confrontation, they had calculated that there was an outside chance that the ploy might backfire: Goulart might reject the conditions for renewed aid, break off all economic and commercial relations with the United States, and turn completely to the Soviet bloc for assistance.[30] In fact, however, Goulart did not have that outside chance. The Soviet bloc was offering very little assistance. Perhaps a few more barter-trade agreements might be reached with East European countries, but that would scarcely make up for the loss of markets in the West or provide the hard currency needed to finance essential imports. In addition, Goulart knew that any move on his part toward open dependence on the Soviet Union would undoubtedly lead to his overthrow by the Brazilian military. Therefore, he controlled his anger and assuaged his pride by immediately granting a press interview in which he announced that Robert Kennedy had come to Brazil at his (Goulart's) express invitation. Hearing that the attorney general was on an inspection trip in the Panama Canal Zone, he had decided to invite him to come in order to clarify for him the true financial situation of Brazil. Conditions within Brazil had been misrepresented by "certain Brazilian information media with access to American President and to Department of State." The informal talk with Robert Kennedy had been a great success, said Goulart. By the time he left, the brother of the American president had lost "all negative impressions he had formed on Brazil."[31]

The Kennedy administration took this face-saving maneuver by Goulart with rather bad grace. Presumably, it had expected some sort of mea culpa declaration, followed by immediate criticism of Brizola and other "Communists." Ambassador Campos was chided about Goulart's remarks when he called at the State Department to press a request for emergency balance of payments assistance.[32] The next month the department rather churlishly refused to recommend that President Kennedy send a formal letter of congratulations to Goulart on his overwhelming victory at the January 6 plebiscite, despite Ambassador Gordon's urging that one be sent. Washington officials fell back on the surprising argument that congratulations would amount to American interference in an "internal Brazilian political problem."[33] For a government that had just tried interfering in order to influence the appointment of key officials, such delicate scruples can only astonish.

On the whole, looking back now at the episode, the arrogance of Bobby Kennedy's descent on Brasília stands out most clearly: the democratically elected chief of a sovereign state was called on the carpet and told to shape up or else. But there is also a touch of naiveté about the incident. Kennedy and his staff really appear to have believed that the three-hour mission might "work"—that, confronted by a Kennedy who was acting as the personal representative of the president of the United States, Goulart would instantly face up to his errors and promptly turn things around in his country.

After his victory in the plebiscite, Goulart did make an effort to halt the deterioration of the Brazilian economy. Many of the International Monetary Fund and American government recommendations were undertaken. A tax reform bill that increased federal revenues got through the Congress. The subsidies on imported wheat and petroleum were again eliminated.[34] Passenger and freight rates on the government-owned railroads were increased. The banks were ordered to limit credit to the private sector. All of these deficit-reduction measures were included in a Three

139

Year Plan drawn up by Planning Minister Celso Furtado. The plan further called for limiting wage increases for public employees to 40 percent, below the 50 percent inflation rate of the preceding year. The need for "productive, private investment" as well as the assistance of foreign governments was stressed in the plan. Economic development, social reform, and reduction in the rate of inflation were all to be pursued simultaneously since all were seen as integrally connected.[35]

When he announced his administration's new plan, Goulart called attention to the fact that the charter of the Alliance for Progress called for just such comprehensive long-term plans. As the Kennedy administration had demanded, he thus went on public record as supporting the Alliance for Progress and seeking to comply with its requirements.[36]

With some reluctance, the State Department rewarded these efforts with the concession of an emergency $30 million loan, repayable in ninety days, to finance Brazilian purchases from U.S. firms.[37] Reservations were still expressed about Goulart's determination to really pursue a pro-American, pro–private enterprise policy. His appointments to the post-plebiscite cabinet were scrutinized with care. Although grudgingly conceding that the new cabinet was "better" than the previous one, the State Department remained dissatisfied because it included a few men with "leftist proclivities," a few others who could be branded "extreme leftist, ultranationalist," and one "suspected Communist" (labor minister Almino Afonso). "In short, the new cabinet encourages neither optimism nor despair, but rather watchful waiting," concluded the State Department.[38]

The watchful waiting, tinged with apprehension, continued until a mission headed by Finance Minister San Tiago Dantas arrived in Washington in March 1963 to negotiate further U.S. assistance. Dantas's visit, talked about as early as November 1962, had been repeatedly postponed. Dantas hoped to get some sort of handle on chaotic Brazilian finances before making the trip. He felt three steps were necessary to get his country's economy in order. First, debt rescheduling and a long-term aid package would have to be negotiated with Brazil's major creditor, the United States. Second, similar negotiations would be undertaken with West European countries and Japan. Third, more trade and/or barter arrangements would be worked out with East European countries.[39] The United States would have to be approached first, but Dantas was reluctant to make the trip. He was aware of the increasing anti-Brazil sentiment in the United States and worried that any new American aid would be tied to International Monetary Fund approval. The IMF was generally unpopular in Brazil since in effect it favored fighting inflation with recession and valued price stability above all other economic goods.[40] It was hard enough to try to build support for the austerity measures in the Three Year Plan, without introducing the IMF factor. At one point Dantas suggested that Brazil request only a rescheduling of its foreign debts from the United States but otherwise go it alone. Other officials, however, felt that the probable political fallout from the rigorous austerity program that would be necessary made such a course too risky.[41]

In preparation for his trip to Washington, Dantas pushed through a settlement of the ITT case. The settlement reached in late January provided for a Bank of Brazil advance of $7.3 million to ITT, one-half in dollars to be remitted to the company's American headquarters, one-half in cruzeiros for investment in the ITT's Brazilian manufacturing subsidiary. The Bank of Brazil agreement was phrased in such subtle jargon that ITT could call it "compensation pending final agreement," and Brazilian officials could deny that it represented an illegal advance payment by the federal government in a case still pending in a state court.[42] Dantas also made an effort to speed up the negotiations to purchase AMFORP, but the effort had bogged down again before his departure for Washington.[43] Brazilian officials believed, however, that since at least the ITT case had been resolved, the American Congress would be appeased and therefore the expropriation issue now took second place to foreign policy differences. Dantas felt that the refusal of Brazil to break relations with Cuba was more likely to obstruct full U.S. support for the Three Year Plan.[44]

From the viewpoint of the Brazilians, the entire Dantas mission was a disaster. The timing was extremely unlucky. As Dantas left Brazil, final preparations were being concluded for a Continental Congress for Solidarity with Cuba to be held in Brazil from March 28 through March 30. Although Foreign Minister Hermes Lima had attempted to discourage the organizers (Society of Friends of Cuba) from holding the congress, and Governor Lacerda had barred it from Rio de Janeiro, it was held anyway across the bay in Niteroi.[45] The image of Brazil hospitably hosting a pro-Castro gathering while seeking more American aid did not sit well with the American Congress or public. In addition, as Dantas arrived in the United States, a somewhat garbled version of his three-step economic plans was circulating. As some members of Congress and American reporters understood it, Dantas planned to take the money he got from the United States to finance purchases of goods from the Soviet bloc. It took repeated denials by the Brazilian finance minister before the Americans understood that the American funds were for the most part "tied" to American purchases. Finally, to compound Dantas's bad luck in timing, he arrived just as a subcommittee of the House of Representatives Committee on Foreign Affairs was concluding hearings on Castro-Communist subversion in the Western Hemisphere. At these hearings Ambassador Gordon indiscreetly testified that communists had infiltrated Brazilian labor unions, the student movement, and even the government itself. Gordon was saying no more than Kennedy administration officials had been saying in secret memorandums for some time, but some classification error allowed his testimony to be released and published. The American and Brazilian publics heard it for the first time as an official assessment.[46]

The publication of Gordon's testimony touched off a furor in Brazil. Nationalists called for a halt to negotiations, the recall of Dantas, and a declaration that Gordon was persona non grata. After days of hesitation, Goulart (who had of course heard the ambassador's opinions before) merely demanded an official clarification.[47]

In the United States, fears that Brazil was slowly slipping into the communist camp were exacerbated. Was it right to throw any more of the American taxpayers' money at the Goulart government? "In light of the State Department's charges of Communist infiltration in the government of Brazil," orated Congressman William C. Cramer on 18 March, "I am asking that no further U.S. loans be made to Señor Goulart's government until the Communists are cleaned out of it, until we receive assurances that our aid dollars will not be used to finance Brazilian trade with Russia, and until Brazil follows the lead of the majority of the Latin American nations and withdraws recognition of Castro's Cuba."[48]

Although Dantas had expected that political problems would play an important part in his mission's negotiations, he was probably not prepared for the intensity of the American obsession with an imagined Communist threat. Questions about communist infiltration and about developments within the Brazilian Communist Party—not about Brazil's Three Year Plan—dominated Dantas's two interviews with President Kennedy. When he met with top State Department officials, Secretary of State Rusk quizzed him and his aides on Cuba and possible Cuban links with the Brazilian Left. The Brazilians repeatedly protested that communism posed no clear threat in Brazil and that officials identified in the United States as communist were not so in fact.[49]

March 11, 1963. From Brazil's perspective, the mission of Finance Minister San Tiago Dantas to obtain more American aid was a disaster. From left to right: Alliance for Progress Director Teodoro Moscoso, Brazil's Ambassador Roberto Campos, Dantas, President Kennedy, Ambassador Lincoln Gordon, and Assistant Secretary of State Edwin Martin. (Courtesy John F. Kennedy Library.)

During the more technical negotiations with AID and Treasury officials, the American and Brazilian negotiators disagreed sharply on the question of whether American assistance should be conditional to IMF review of Brazilian performance. In the end, Dantas had to accept such a condition for the bulk of the proposed aid. Another area of disagreement was over the duration of assistance, with the Brazilians arguing that long-term planning was extremely difficult if not impossible when the United States refused to commit itself for longer than a one-year period. Since the Kennedy administration had decided on a "short-leash" strategy, of course it refused to make any longer commitment. A third area of disagreeement was over the question of private foreign investment in Brazil. The Three Year Plan mentioned the importance of private investment but included no specifics. Dantas was therefore pressed to

143

commit himself and Brazil to specific plans for encouraging more foreign private investment. The need to diversify exports by increasing the export of iron ore was also emphasized. Of course, everyone understood that the Americans were promoting the interests of Hanna Mining, although the company was not specifically mentioned.[50]

Government purchase of the utilities was apparently not discussed. However, the AMFORP case came to play an important part in the failure of the Dantas mission and in the collapse of his effort to launch the Three Year Plan. At the time of his first interview with President Kennedy, on March 11, Dantas delivered a letter from Goulart announcing the settlement of the ITT case and regretting the delay in the AMFORP negotiations. The letter included the statement, *"Dentro de poucos dias*, as the National Congress resumes its work and public opinion becomes better informed, I hope that the case of 'American Foreign Power' may also be resolved."[51] Obviously, phrased in this way, *"dentro de poucos dias"* would best be translated as "eventually." However, the Kennedy administration decided to take the phrase literally, as meaning "within a few days." Resolution of the AMFORP case was made a secret condition of the release of any funds in the new aid package, much to the surprise of Dantas and the anger of Goulart.[52]

The aid package in itself was a bitter disappointment to the Brazilians. The total sum that might possibly be provided by the United States during the following year was a substantial $398.5 million, but the amount definitely scheduled for disbursement—as soon as an agreement with AMFORP was signed—was only $84 million, the remaining credits of the loan package promised Quadros in 1961. Of this sum, $30 million would be retained by the U.S. Treasury in repayment of the emergency ninety-day credit granted in January.[53] Both Dantas and Ambassador Campos argued that for political reasons they badly needed more than the release of the credits promised Quadros. The Dantas mission and the anti-inflation struggle were under heavy attack within Brazil. Dantas wanted to go back with a concrete demonstration of American support by returning with new funds and an explicit American endorsement of the Three Year Plan via some sort of commitment through 1965. Instead, there was no definite commitment for even one year. The release of any credits beyond the $84 million was tied to a favorable IMF review, successful negotiations with European creditors, and the completion of more explicit plans for development investment, export promotion, and the stimulation of foreign private investment.

The published portion of the new aid agreement omitted any hint of the American demand that an agreement to purchase AMFORP be concluded immediately, perhaps because there was no way such a step could be presented as an anti-inflationary move. However, Ambassador Gordon made it clear to Goulart personally that no money would be forthcoming until such an agreement was signed. In a telegram dated April 9, 1963, Gordon reported an interview with Goulart in which he had pointed out that the due date for repayment of the $30 million emergency loan had been extended to April 19, but this was the "extreme limit, in view close Congressional interest in Washington in public utility negotiations." Failing to pay by the nineteenth, Brazil would be in open default, which "would undermine completely European confidence and prospect negotiation with IMF." The Brazilian economy would be brought to the "brink of abyss."

> I said worst aspect of AMFORP problem was that it raised question of personal good faith of President. Idea of public utility purchases was his initiative last March and April. We had every expectation signature of this very fair agreement, on which company had made many concessions, before Dantas came to Washington. I reread paragraph from his second letter to President Kennedy looking toward signature "within a few days." Said if no compliance on this, no basis for confidence that other aspect program would be complied with.[54]

Goulart apparently bore the Gordon lecture with remarkable self-restraint. April 19 arrived, however, without an AMFORP agreement and without release of the promised $84 million. In desperation, Finance Minister Dantas then took it upon himself to conclude the negotiations with that company. He called together an ad hoc Interministerial Committee that had been appointed by Goulart to consider the purchase of AMFORP. Meeting on Saturday afternoon, April 20, in War Minister Amaury Kruel's office, the committee unanimously voted to authorize Ambassador Campos to sign a Memorandum of Understanding with William Nydorf, vice president of AMFORP. On April 22, Dantas transmitted the authorization to Ambassador Campos in Washington.[55] On April 24, the $84 million was credited to the Brazilian government.

The terms of that memorandum did not become publicly known in Brazil until late May, when it provided the coup de grace for the Dantas ministry.[56] Even without the complication of so controversial a purchase agreement, Dantas had faced tremendous odds in attempting to implement the Three Year Plan. Initially, he had managed to persuade centrist

145

politicians from all political parties and spokesmen for business groups to voice support for the plan.[57] But as the necessary austerity measures began to be felt, that support dwindled. Business, which had pledged not to raise prices, now faced credit restrictions and began to cut back on production, laying off employees. When large employers such as the automobile companies threatened to close down completely unless credit was eased, even Dantas suggested that part of the plan needed to be reconsidered. Workers became more restive; not only was unemployment increasing, so was the cost of living. The removal of subsidies on oil and wheat of course led to immediate price increases in consumer goods. From the perspective of the workers, the plan that was supposed to halt inflation but still provide economic growth and more jobs was not working. Government employees, both civilian and military, lobbied hard against the plan's goal of holding their salary increase to 40 percent. Members of Congress were importuned to legislate at least a 70 percent increase. A strike of all government employees was discussed. Union leaders who were members of the CGT had from the start let it be known that they would not cooperate in holding down wage demands to a 40 percent level. There was much talk of strike plans in various industries.[58]

The most vitriolic attacks on the Three Year Plan and abuse of Dantas came from the Left. Now in Congress as deputy for Guanabara, Leonel Brizola outdid himself in attacking the plan as capitulation to North American imperialism. He called for the firing of Dantas as a lackey of American monopolists. Brizola and the radical nationalists he represented opposed any kind of accommodation with Washington or agreement with the IMF.[59] They wanted no financial aid from America, believing that Brazil's economic problems would better be solved by defaulting on the country's international debt, nationalizing certain foreign-owned enterprises, and the carrying out of unspecified basic structural reforms. These sentiments were echoed by the Brazilian Communist Party, but Brizola denied any collusion.

> I am not a communist, I have no contact with communists, and I do not believe, since Russia is so distant, that we ought to concern ourselves with it. Our problem, the one we feel within our own house, is that of American exploitation.[60]

In response to the increasing public dissatisfaction with austerity, other members of the cabinet began to criticize the Three Year Plan. Such a rigorous plan really required a superminister with authority over the other ministers and the power to silence them. Dantas had no such authority, and Goulart never felt strong enough to play that role himself. Goulart's political style was to always leave open "a flank for possible strategic retreat"; he never committed himself irrevocably to anything.[61] However, until mid-May Goulart's support of Dantas was firm enough to disconcert the Brazilian Left and to impress foreign observers.[62]

Then came the strategic retreat. In effect Goulart abandoned the Three Year Plan. First, his cabinet voted in favor of a 70 percent pay increase for federal employees, not the 40 percent allowed in the plan. Then, to placate business interests, credit restrictions were eased. The IMF mission then visiting Brazil started giving negative signals. It would apparently refuse to issue the favorable report needed to obtain new American aid; it was perhaps useless to try so hard to placate Washington. The deciding factor for Goulart was the national reaction to publicity about the AMFORP Memorandum of Understanding.

Brizola publicized details of the agreement when he launched a scathing attack on it in a radio-TV broadcast on May 28. Even though no actual inventory of company assets had been completed, the memorandum fixed the price of all AMFORP property at $135 million, with a downpayment of $10 million payable on July 1, when a formal contract was to be signed. In addition, the Brazilian government was to assume all of the company's debts, amounting to another $7.7 million. Brizola denounced the agreement as worse than a giveaway; it was a crime of *"lèse patria."* He demanded that his brother-in-law dismiss Dantas and warned that if Goulart stood by that agreement, the breach between them would be irreparable.[63]

Most of Brizola's major speeches touched off angry protests from the Right. But this one evoked editorials of approval from newspapers normally opposed to anything he said.[64] Conservative politicians, including Lacerda, hastened to charge that Dantas and Goulart were plotting a perfidious giveaway of scarce national resources for a lot of "scrap metal." Sensing scandal, Congress began a formal parliamentary inquiry into the circumstances of the agreement.[65]

Although conceding that Goulart faced "real" political problems in this matter, the U.S. embassy campaigned hard for implementation of the memorandum. Embassy officials chose to ignore the attacks on it from the Right and concentrated on the fact that Brizola was violently opposed and had promised an irreparable breach with Goulart if he stuck with it. "For these reasons," concluded Gordon, "AMFORP case, although not inherently [the] most important issue of U.S.-Brazilian relations, has become a test of Goulart good faith and capacity to resist Brizola in [the] interest of future collaboration with U.S."[66] Although the financial interests of the company and the goodwill of the business community generally were of concern to the administration, apparently the primary interest in AMFORP was political—it provided a clear-cut test of whether Goulart had absorbed the lesson Bobby Kennedy had been sent to give.

But Goulart was not prepared to irreparably jeopardize the support of the Brazilian Left for the uncertain support of the White House— particularly not when not a single political faction in Brazil was prepared to endorse the terms of the AMFORP agreement. He did the only sensible thing. He announced that he had not seen or approved of the Memorandum of Understanding and would never agree to any such disadvantageous proceeding. Then he fired Dantas.

# 8

# Looking for His Hat

---

I'm like a man looking for his hat in the dark," Goulart confided
to a friend.[1] He never managed to find it. The optimistic projections of
the Three Year Plan faded in the reality of rapidly rising prices, declining
production, increasing unemployment, and a negative hard currency flow.
Neither Goulart nor his ministers was able to come up with any coherent
scheme to replace the plan. During his last year in office Goulart followed
a policy of fumble and grope, shifts to the Right, gestures toward the
Left. He was attempting to deal with three distinct sets of problems
simultaneously: (1) maintaining a political position as leader of a Center-
Left coalition, (2) finding some handle on the financial-economic crisis,
and (3) getting agrarian reform started.

Goulart may have been vague on ideology. He did not understand
international finance. Economics was something of a mystery to him.
But he knew his craft. Maneuvering within the contorted channels of
Brazilian clientelistic politics was his forte. "Trust me," he urged Ambassador Gordon. "Complex political maneuvers" were a necessity, he
explained. For tactical reasons he might at times side with the Left. That
did not mean he was endorsing a communist takeover.[2] Dispensing
favors, alternating threats with promises, blandly reversing loftily proclaimed irreversible principles—all of that Goulart knew how to do. It
was part of the Brazilian "system."

Jango's major political problem in 1963 was to hold the Center and
Left together at a time when the pull of polarization was growing stronger.

Just as spokesmen on the Right were louder, shriller, more hysterical in their cries about an international communist conspiracy, so was the rhetoric on the Left noisier, more impatient. Leftists clamored for an immediate radical restructuring of Brazilian society, for completion of the revolution they believed was already underway.

Three leaders on the Left emerged as Goulart's rivals for the support of the masses: Brizola, Almino Afonso, and Miguel Arraes. None of the three was a communist, although in American documents of the time, all three were routinely identified as either communist or procommunist. Brizola represented Goulart's biggest headache, a persistent thorn in the flesh. *"Manda brasa*, Brizola!"* chanted his admirers at rallies. ("Give 'em hell, Brizola!") No one cheered like that when Goulart spoke. As a federal deputy, Brizola was much more visible than he had been as governor. He flew around the country giving fiery speeches. He was a flamboyant orator. His speeches grew increasingly violent. He progressed from attacking American aid, the Alliance for Progress, American firms in Brazil, and pro-American Brazilian politicians, to attacking "gorillas" (right-wing officers) in the Brazilian armed forces who were plotting to overthrow the Goulart government. He also lit into the PSD-dominated Congress for blocking reform, calling it a political club that was out of touch with the real needs of the people. He suggested that a way around the Congress would have to be found in order to move the revolution forward. Brizola alarmed and angered centrist politicians and thoroughly enraged the top ranks of the military.[3] Undeterred by remonstrances from Goulart and the condemnation of most of the media, Brizola proceeded to establish connections with a network of radio stations, the better to broadcast himself. He believed that he was in direct communication with the "people," as opposed to the privileged, who listened to his critics. In May 1963 he urged the underclasses in the Northeast to organize themselves into "groups of five"—revolutionary cells that would prepare to resist the "gorillas."[4] By November he was calling for the organization of "groups of eleven comrades" throughout the country. The groups were to act as "nationalist commandos" to press for agrarian reform and to work "to free Brazil from international plundering." They were to train themselves in the use of arms and prepare to resist any coup attempt.[5]

Although conservatives believed that these Groups of Eleven represented trained communist terrorists, or, in other words, armed paramilitary units similar to the many being organized by rightist leaders, in fact Brizola's activities represented revolutionary theater more than

150

anything else. Other than collect lists of names of men who formed Groups of Eleven, neither Brizola nor his henchmen nor anyone affiliated with the Brazilian Communist Party did anything to prepare the groups for combat.[6]

Brizola was much more the promoter than the serious organizer. He was best at promoting himself in the image of the fearless macho leader, ready to fight for his cause. He demonstrated his personal qualifications on one occasion by engaging in a fist fight with a hostile journalist when the two happened to encounter each other in an airport.[7] No doubt Brizola, in the paternalistic tradition of Brazilian populism, sincerely wished to do something for the underprivileged masses, and perhaps he did have some serious commitments to the socialist ideology he referred to rather vaguely. But there is even less doubt that he was ambitious. The constitution of 1946 barred relatives of sitting presidents from running for the presidency. Unless the constitution could be changed, Brizola could not become a presidential candidate in the 1965 election. But he was still a young man, and there were other high posts in government that he might have held. He wanted, for example, to be named finance minister. "Never!" exclaimed Goulart when a delegation of labor leaders proposed such a nomination. "That would provoke a revolution within forty-eight hours."[8] At the very least Brizola hoped to take over control of the PTB, replacing Goulart as its national chairman. He was confident that he could revitalize the party, turning it into the majority party in the country.

Relations between the brothers-in-law became especially strained after Brizola began attacking the Three Year Plan and Dantas. But, though Goulart criticized Brizola frequently in private conversations with his ministers and intimates, he stopped short of publicly condemning him. Brizola exercised similar restraint. He attacked the "government" in general and Goulart's ministers in particular, but did not directly attack the president. On the one occasion when Brizola was considering a public break with his brother-in-law, Goulart telephoned instructions to Justice Minister Jurema to close down the radio station Brizola was using as soon as he launched a personal attack. Jurema took it upon himself to warn Brizola, who then refrained.[9]

Though also rivals, neither Almino Afonso nor Miguel Arraes was as troublesome as Brizola. As a congressman, Almino was spokesman for the left wing of the PTB, the faction dubbed the Compact Group. In the judgment of another Congressman who often had to listen to him, Almino was "brilliant, a fluent speaker, one of the most verbose

151

Congressmen...enchanted with his own oratory.''[10] He was also ideal-istic; like other socialists, he believed that the hope for a brave new world lay with the working classes. He thought that the Brazilian Labor Party (which he had recently joined) might be the instrument to organize and lead the workers, provided it became a different kind of party. Instead of being a party of ward heelers and job seekers who manipulated the unions and working masses for their own crassly political ends, the PTB should become an ideological party, committed to the goals of radical nationalism. It should work for restructuring Brazilian society, not for merely improving its position within the status quo.

In January 1963, when he reorganized his cabinet after the plebiscite, Goulart made Almino the minister of labor. He clearly wanted someone who had the confidence of the left wing of the PTB and of labor union leaders to sell the Three Year Plan. Union leaders needed to be persuaded to keep wage increase demands within the 40 percent ceiling the plan recommended. The Left generally had to be convinced that the short term hardships of austerity were essential to check the spiraling cost of living. Only when that was accomplished could development and reform proceed.

At first the young labor minister (thirty-four years old in 1963) was cooperative.[11] He urged union leaders to moderate wage demands and counseled all of the Left to have confidence in President Goulart. But by early April, Almino was suggesting that the Three Year Plan needed to be modified, since there was a need to press for basic structural reform at once. Instead of saying nice things about the Alliance for Progress in order to please the Americans and improve Brazil's chances of obtain-ing assistance, Almino publicly criticized the Alliance as ineffective when he spoke at an Inter-American Conference of Labor Ministers meeting in Bogotá in late April. Instead of seconding Goulart's efforts to restrain the CGT, Almino appeared to be egging it on. Goulart was responding to fears expressed by his minister of war and by centrists generally when he tried to discourage the federation from holding rallies and threatening general strikes in April. But Almino chose that moment to announce that he believed the labor code should be amended specifically to make federations such as the CGT legal entities. The next month the labor minister further endeared himself to union activists by publicly siding with the union involved in an airline strike.

In addition to breaking cabinet ranks by criticizing government policy, Almino angered Goulart by his efforts to change the PTB. The staff Almino brought into the Labor Ministry was recruited exclusively from the radical nationalist group, the left wing of the PTB. Party moderates were excluded instead of being accommodated with a share of the patronage. Installed in office, Almino lost no time in announcing a campaign to root out corruption and inefficiency from the Social Security Institutes. He proceeded to oust directors involved in scandals. They were replaced with men loyal to Almino. The ousted officials all had ties to the PTB Old Guard moderates, who thus lost control of more patronage. Losing control of patronage meant losing political power, since it was primarily the traffic in positions and favors that tied party workers to any particular political boss. Of course the Old Guard took their complaints about Almino to Goulart, the party chairman. In effect they threatened the president with the loss of their support unless he did something to halt the erosion of theirs.

The obvious way to stop Almino from replacing appointed officials with his own men was to remove him from the position that gave him the power to do that. Goulart was ready to replace him as minister of labor in April but had to postpone the move when the radical nationalists and union leaders loudly declared their opposition to Almino's ouster. Not until June 17, when he dismissed the entire cabinet, did Goulart manage to strip Almino of his post and power.[12] Almino resumed his position in Congress as one of the more outspoken radical nationalists, but, without the powers of a minister, he no longer represented a serious rival for the leadership of the PTB.

Unlike Almino Afonso, Miguel Arraes had no established clientele in the PTB or in any of the major political parties. He had won election as mayor of Recife and then as governor of Pernambuco as a member of the small Partido Social Trabalhista (Social Labor Party), supported by a coalition of other parties including the PTB. However, as Jânio Quadros had demonstrated, party identifications were easily shed or shifted in Brazilian politics at that time, and even though Goulart did not want to see Arraes join the PTB, the governor might still end up as the PTB nominee for president in the 1965 election. Certainly for the Brazilian Left, Arraes had emerged as the new Northeast star, replacing Francisco Julião as the best hope for a new order in that region. The radical nationalists rejoiced in Arraes's outspoken anti-Americanism. Leftists generally were impressed by his determination to enforce legislation that was beneficial to agricultural workers. Church activists as well as leftists applauded his decision to launch a literacy program throughout the state, a program that employed a method designed to teach basic skills in forty hours.[13] As a governor, Arraes was preoccupied more with local and regional problems than with the national scene. But since the Kennedy administration had identified the Northeast as *the* critical area of Brazil, Arraes enjoyed more importance than a governor of Pernambuco normally had. The fact that he had won election despite the concentrated hostility and the money of the Americans enhanced his reputation as a winner—or as a demagogue, depending on the point of view.

Of course the name of Arraes was anathema to conservatives throughout the country. Rumors circulated that Arraes and/or his communist mentors were training a guerrilla army of peasants somewhere in the state's backlands. It was widely believed that it was the new governor who was behind the land invasions, strikes, and canefield fires that seemed to sweep Pernambuco in 1963. Actually, right-wing terrorists, probably CIA-affiliated, were staging a number of these violent incidents. Arraes personally was a cautious man, criticized by some for being far too willing to compromise. He was keenly aware that he had no military force at his disposal. The state had no militia force. The capital city, Recife, was also the headquarters for the federal Fourth Army. Fourth Army commanders needed no prompting to keep a close watch on the ''communist'' governor. Arraes well understood that his only hope to stay in office or to advance to a higher post depended upon strict adherence to democratic procedures. Instead of encouraging confrontation between the dispossessed and the possessors, Arraes labored to promote negotiation and dialogue. He had remarkable success in bringing about peaceful settlements in several potentially violent disputes.[14]

To Goulart, Arraes represented more of a possible future rival than a present challenger. But there was one way in which the governor complicated his administration. Each time Goulart considered—or was rumored to be considering—federal intervention in Guanabara in order to silence Carlos Lacerda and eliminate one of the centers for subversive conspiracy, Arraes and his supporters loudly protested. Arraes was sure that federal intervention in Guanabara and the removal of Lacerda from office would be followed by federal intervention in Pernambuco followed by his own removal. General Amaury Kruel, Goulart's war minister from September 1962 to June 1963, was known to favor such a trade-off—a simultaneous strike against the extremes of both Left and Right. Goulart, however, denied that he ever even considered a move against Arraes.[15] Whatever the case, without the support of the major factions on the Left, he was unwilling to have a showdown with Lacerda and his supporters.

154

Analysts at the American Embassy rejoiced in every hint of conflict between Goulart and Brizola, Almino, or Arraes. They speculated at length about whether apparent divergences were for real or merely a ruse, "a staged show of estrangement between Goulart and the extreme Left."[16] For the American analysts, the important truth about the three leftist leaders was that the Brazilian Communist Party supported them, either because the three were themselves "crypto-Communists" or at least "pro-Communist." If Goulart were to make a "clean break" with such leaders, he might become more acceptable to the American Embassy and, the Americans thought, to the Brazilian Right.[17]

Goulart knew better. He knew the Right could never forgive him for having been (1) Vargas's protégé and (2) a labor minister who had encouraged the political aspirations of organized workers. A Center-Right coalition could never be organized to support him. It would have to be Center-Left, and for that he needed the cooperation of the leftists who admired Brizola, Almino, or Arraes. Those leftists tended to be the political activists, much more willing than people in the Center to invest time, effort, and money in political causes.

As national chairman of the labor party, Goulart also deemed it essential that organized labor be a part of the coalition standing behind his administration. But the type of organized labor that Goulart was accustomed to dealing with was the type that was subsidized and controlled by the government. The most militant new labor organization, the CGT, was a clearly independent force that might exert itself on his behalf or might work against him. Goulart's relations with the CGT followed an on-again, off-again zigzag that illustrates both his personal indecisiveness and his troubled relations with the Left during his last year in office.

No group on the left aroused more antipathy and horror in the hearts of conservatives than the CGT. The press never tired of pointing out that the organization was illegal: existing labor legislation prohibited such a "horizontal" interunion organization. In addition, though the constitution guaranteed freedom of association, it specified that association must be for legal purposes. Since the CGT promoted work stoppages to achieve political (not bread-and-butter) objectives, its purposes were illicit.[18] The elite's double standard was clearly intact. No one thought it illegal for businessmen's groups such as CONCLAP to lobby continuously for political objectives or to use economic weapons for political ends, such as, for example, blacklisting labor activists or removing advertising from offending media outlets. But when the CGT attempted to use the weapons at its disposal for such ends, it was regarded as symbolizing "communism, atheism, anarchy, and subversion."[19] It is true that some of the CGT directors were active Communist Party members,[20] but probably more upsetting to conservatives was the spectacle of lower-class workers demanding a share in political decision making.

When the CGG (the General Strike Command, the first name for the interunion group) was set up in June 1962, it was on Goulart's side, defending his nomination of Dantas as the next prime minister. Whatever misgivings Goulart may have had about the group at the time gave way to his need for some evidence of popular support as he mounted his campaign for an early plebiscite on a return to a full presidential system. There is no question that the labor group was helpful to him. Their two general strikes in July and September 1962 may have been far from "general," but they had the desired effect on the Congress: an early date for the plebiscite was set. Goulart responded by arranging conferences with CGT directors, soliciting their opinions on cabinet choices and listening to their demands for higher minimum wages, price controls, and the right to organize rural workers.[21] The CGT then labored to get the vote out on the day of the plebiscite. Without their efforts the total might not have been as impressive.

After the plebiscite and the introduction of the Three Year Plan, relations between the president and the CGT cooled. A delegation met with him on February 5 to present a manifesto listing labor's complaints about the plan and suggesting alternative economic policies. Goulart rejected all of their arguments, point by point.[22] Figuratively patting the union leaders on the head as he dismissed their arguments, Goulart observed that "it was natural for the working class to struggle democratically for the modification of certain structures which do not permit greater development of the country," but he warned that such structural modification could not be accomplished in forty-eight hours or by "strike movements."[23]

Rebuffed, the CGT directors retreated to the sidelines to applaud Brizola's diatribes against Dantas, the Americans, and the Three Year Plan. Then, during the last week of March 1963, a quarrel between the CGT and Governor Lacerda led to new friction with the president. A municipal transit strike for a pay raise began in Rio de Janeiro at the same time as the pro-Castro Cuban Solidarity conference got underway across the bay in Niteroi. At first the Guanabara police were busy hunting for foreign Communist agents who might be trespassing in Guanabara, but they were soon diverted into harassing the strikers. The CGT directors attending the Solidarity conference threatened to call a general strike if the harassment did not stop. Lacerda responded by going on television on April 1 to blame Goulart for everything—for the pro-Castro conference, the transit strike, and for a CGT plot to "implant a red fascist dictatorship and reign of terror." He called the president a perjurer who was in the service of foreign communist interests. The CGT demanded that Goulart give Lacerda an ultimatum to take it all back or face federal intervention in his state and removal from office.[24]

Unwilling to be put in the position of following the orders of the CGT, Goulart decided to simply have his foreign minister go on television to answer Lacerda. An anti-Lacerda demonstration staged just before Foreign Minister Hermes Lima's speech would attract wider media coverage. Goulart sent some of his aides to Rio to arrange it. The aides decided against inviting the CGT to the rally. But their proposed media event was a dismal failure. The few people who were prepared to demonstrate at the request of the government were turned back by Lacerda's police before they reached the proposed site.

To show the president that if he wanted to fill up his rallies he must turn to them, the CGT directors decided to stage their own anti-Lacerda demonstration on April 10. The commander of the First Army, General Osvino Alves, promptly promised the CGT military protection for their event, something he had failed to do for the president's rally. War Minister Kruel then threatened to resign unless he was permitted to reprimand Alves for a breach of discipline in taking sides in a political dispute without authorization. In the hope that everyone would cool down, Goulart tried to persuade the CGT leaders to cancel their rally. Brizola also urged the CGT to at least postpone the demonstration. Although expressing distrust of the president and accusing him of being controlled by a right-wing military clique, the CGT chairman did finally announce the indefinite postponement of the demonstration.[25]

It was at this point that Goulart decided that the CGT was getting too hard to handle and must be humbled. He found a rival central labor organization that he could support—the UST (Union of Organized Workers).[26] The UST had been organized in Sao Paulo only six months previously. Although it endorsed the call for basic structural reform, it was more interested in labor issues than in radical nationalist ideology. Its leaders announced their opposition to the inclusion of Communist Party members in leadership positions. Believing that the American government would be pleased that he was backing a non-Communist central labor organization, Goulart made sure that the ambassador had noticed.

During a meeting with Gordon on July 17, Goulart initiated a "brief discussion of labor union situation noting this had been central preoccupation President Kennedy and our Attorney General. Said UST was going well, easily outweighing CGT now in total influence."[27]

In spite of Jango's optimism, the UST failed to win over very many of the nation's labor leaders. The anticommunist union leaders who distrusted the IPES-sponsored anticommunist Movimento Sindical Democrático as an employer or company union tended to also distrust the UST as a vehicle of the government. The CGT included Communist Party members among its directors, but there was no question about its independence or its militancy. By mid-August Goulart recognized that the UST cause was hopeless. He asked the labor minister to halt the flow of special funds to the UST and to ignore UST requests for patronage appointments in the Ministry of Labor bureaucracy.[28]

Goulart returned to a policy of wary dialogue with the CGT. It was a relationship of "cordial enemies," thought one observer, enemies who regarded each other with "reciprocal distrust."[29] In October, when Goulart asked Congress for a declaration of state of siege in order to intervene against Lacerda, (his initiative this time), the CGT failed to back him. Instead it joined other groups on the Left in denouncing the request as a ploy to intervene in Pernambuco, remove Arraes, and possibly set up a military dictatorship. In December, when elections for labor positions on the governing boards of the Social Security Institutes were held, Goulart worked to defeat CGT candidates. Still, the president and the labor group continued the dialogue. The CGT never tired of urging Goulart to move more decisively for basic reforms and to stop trying to placate the United States. "If you pressure me too much," Jango warned one delegation, "I'll be ousted. But remember, I will have time to catch an airplane out, while all of you will be left here."[30]

In January 1964 the largest, most powerful union in the country, the CNTI (National Confederation of Industrial Workers) held elections for officers. Half of all organized workers in the country belonged to this union. Initially, Goulart appeared to be still following a policy of trying to keep the CGT in check. His personal labor advisor was detailed to try to defeat the CGT-endorsed slate. A slate of moderates was put up and assured of presidential support. Shortly before the election (apparently at the request of Minister of Labor Silva, who needed CGT support in his personal campaign for elective office) Goulart reversed himself, disavowed the moderates, and endorsed the CGT slate.[31]

Some observers thought the endorsement marked some sort of final commitment of the president to a communist-dominated Left. It is unlikely that Goulart so perceived it. For the time being he supported the CGT. In the future he might again back away. "Talk to the leftists, converse with Miguel Arraes, encourage discussion," Jango told Justice Minister Jurema. "But," he added, "don't *give* the Left anything!"[32]

Goulart clearly preferred centrist politicians like himself. In none of the five different cabinets he appointed was there more than one or two men who clearly stood left of center. All of his cabinets included stalwarts from the center-right PSD. Vargas, in his time, had orchestrated a PSD-PTB alliance to control Congress. Goulart kept trying to revitalize it by appointing PSD members to high posts and by conferring with the PSD leadership. Some politicians felt that the quickest way for Jango to revitalize that alliance would be for him to endorse the presidential candidacy of the best-known PSD leader, ex-President Juscelino Kubitschek. Such an endorsement would not only rally the PSD to support his administration but might quiet fears that, like Vargas in 1937, Jango would stage a coup in order to stay in office. But, up to the time he was ousted, Goulart had failed to endorse any of the known candidates.

There were actually sound political reasons for him to delay an endorsement as long as possible. The election was not scheduled until October 1965. By committing himself early to any one candidate, he would reduce his slender stock of political influence. The prospect of endorsement by an incumbent carried with it the suggestion of government patronage, helpful in a campaign. If there was any chance of getting it, a politician might be cooperative, but there was no need to be nice if the president had already spoken his piece. Goulart needed the cooperation of Governor José Magalhães Pinto as well as the cooperation of Kubitschek and his supporters. Pinto, who represented the *"bossa nova"* or moderate wing of the UDN, was also a candidate for the presidency. An early endorsement of the PSD candidate would needlessly offend the governor and the UDN moderates who sometimes supported the president. In addition, the candidacy of Kubitschek posed problems for Goulart within his own party. The left wing of the PTB would refuse to accept the former president as the party-endorsed candidate. Radical nationalists blamed Kubitschek for not only opening the country to foreign investment but actually working to encourage such investment. The nationalists found such "denationalization" of the economy unforgivable. If Goulart was able to persuade the moderate majority of the PTB to endorse Kubitschek, the Compact Group would no doubt split

159

the party and endorse their own candidate, probably Arraes. It therefore seemed safest to make no decision at all about his possible successor. Delay was something that came naturally to Goulart.

To the American observers, such dilatory tactics in making a political decision were evidence of crafty, ulterior motives on Goulart's part. In other areas of administration, presidential delay might be put down to simple incompetence rather than to cunning. An economist before he turned diplomat, Lincoln Gordon was frequently annoyed by Goulart's lack of interest in or understanding of the Brazilian economic crisis. The subject was certainly a dismal one. The inflation rate of 55 percent in 1962 rose to 81 percent in 1963 and topped 100 percent in early 1964. Since the budget deficit for 1963 was more than one-third of total government expenditures, there was little prospect of checking the money-printing process. Brazil's foreign debt was over $3 billion. It would take 43 percent of export earnings to meet the interest and amortization payments due from late 1963 to 1965. Since that would not leave enough to finance essential imports, further increases in the foreign debt seemed inevitable.[33] The domestic economy stagnated, failing to keep pace with population growth. There was little new foreign direct investment.

Given the level of tension and discord in the country, it was difficult to see how the crisis could be surmounted without considerable help and understanding from the nation's creditors. However, it was at this juncture that the radical nationalists noisily urged that the Goulart government dictate terms to the creditors, no matter what the consequences. They saw two alternatives: (1) Brazil could unilaterally declare a debt moratorium, announcing that no further payments of interest or principal would be made for a stated period, or (2) Brazil could unilaterally announce that it was defaulting on selected parts of its debt. Should there be reprisals by the creditor nations, the Brazilian government could proceed to seize the Brazilian assets of the creditor. The government would then utilize those assets plus the money saved by not repaying debt to develop the Brazilian economy and reduce dependence on international capitalism. In the eyes of the radical nationalists such harsh treatment of creditors was historically justified because it was exploitation by those monopolistic interests that had made Brazil poor and dependent in the first place.

The economic arguments of the radical nationalists had the advantage of stark oversimplification, but Goulart was never persuaded to adopt them as policy. The finance ministers he selected were all fiscal conservatives who pointed out the probable consequences of either repudiation or a declaration of a moratorium. The immediate result would be a demand from commercial suppliers for prior payment in cash for all imports. There would be no balance of payments assistance, i.e., no short-term credit to finance imports pending export earnings. Brazil was chronically several months in arrears on its debt to oil suppliers. A cutoff of oil imports would have an immediate, drastic impact on all transportation and domestic industry. Periodic food shortages in urban markets already produced riots and mob attacks on food warehouses. What would happen if the entire system of distribution shut down because of lack of fuel? Would the military establishment stand idly by as chaos spread? Would it acquiesce in the drying up of its own oil supplies?

There was no real alternative to seeking accommodation with the creditors. The Soviet Union, burdened with the support of Cuba, gave no hint of readiness to supply another Latin client with oil in exchange for tropical products.[34] Therefore, though Brazil might fail to make payments on its debt on due dates, the government carefully avoided any hint that payment would not be forthcoming sooner or later. In addition, Goulart labored to keep open the channels of communication with the largest creditor, the United States.

It was not an easy thing to do. Evidence mounted that the Kennedy administration was hostile to him personally and disinclined to do anything to help him stay in office. After the International Monetary Fund mission that had visited Brazil in May turned in a negative report in early June 1963, further American aid disbursements were halted. The Islands of Sanity strategy was put into effect: all Alliance for Progress assistance was to be channeled exclusively to "those places where ability, stability, and democratic convictions presented sufficient dimension upon which cooperative ventures could be undertaken."[35] That meant to states headed by conservative governors who were hostile to Goulart. Especially favored with Alliance for Progress funds was Goulart's archenemy, Governor Lacerda.

A Brazilian congressional investigation of the role of IBAD in the 1962 election got underway in May 1963. It uncovered evidence that millions of U.S. dollars had been invested in the campaigns of anti-Goulart politicians. What was the source of those funds? The Brazilian Left was convinced that the giant corporations with investments in Brazil had put up the money. Perhaps Goulart realized that the CIA, and ultimately the White House itself, was the more likely source. It was something he did not want to know for sure. Instead of encouraging the radical nationalists in Congress to press on with the probe and further

161

damage relations with the United States, Goulart did what he could to cut it short. As soon as the federal Supreme Court ruled that IBAD was an illegal organization, Goulart ordered it dissolved. All of IBAD's records were then hastily destroyed.[36]

Although Goulart tried to keep lines of negotiation open, the question of the purchase of AMFORP continued to plug them. For the American embassy, the premier performance test for Goulart was now fulfillment of the terms in the Memorandum of Understanding signed by Ambassador Campos and AMFORP officials on April 22. The other "performance standards" mentioned in the Dantas agreement with AID Administrator David E. Bell[37] might be overlooked if Goulart would demonstrate his willingness to defy Brazilian public opinion as well as the logic of austerity in the interest of placating an American firm. Ambassador Gordon and other embassy officials brought up the case as often as possible in their contacts with Brazilian officials. The Memorandum of Understanding specified that Brazil would make a $10,770,000 down payment on July 1, when a final purchase agreement would be signed. Before leaving office in mid-June, Finance Minister Dantas warned AMFORP officials that, in light of the public outcry, the government was not prepared to proceed with the down payment or to sign a purchase contract on the agreed-upon date.[38] A formal inventory of AMFORP assets by Brazilian authorities would have to be completed before any formal contract could be signed. The next finance minister, Carlos Alberto Carvalho Pinto (the ex-governor of São Paulo), announced his opposition to the purchase of utilities and refused to get involved. He suggested that the foreign minister or the minister of mines and energy might be more appropriate officials for the American diplomats and company officials to see if they wished to discuss purchase. But the Americans found neither of those ministers any more anxious to take up the case.[39]

As the July 1 deadline approached, Goulart prepared to take a hand in the matter himself. He and President Kennedy would both be in Rome on that date, attending the coronation of Pope Paul VI. Goulart decided to seek an audience with Kennedy in order to make a personal appeal for shelving the AMFORP case temporarily so that more of the promised American aid could be released. Anticipating such a move by Goulart, White House and State Department advisors went into a flurry of activity, rushing cables to the presidential party in Europe to prepare and brief the president. Should Goulart fail to mention the fact that a payment to AMFORP was due that very day, Kennedy should bring it up, urged his advisors. He should offer Goulart sympathy, but nothing else.

> Appropriate presidential posture would therefore be renewed expression our deep interest in Brazil's successful passage through current economic and financial difficulties and achievement solid basis continued economic and social development.... but gravest difficulties posed for US congressional and public opinion if GOB [government of Brazil] withdraws from fulfillment of commitment to purchase on fair and reasonable terms under policy initiated by Goulart himself and repeatedly confirmed by him, most recently in March 11 letter to President delivered by Dantas....[40]

Kennedy was simultaneously cautioned not to overemphasize the AMFORP case even while he emphasized it:

> In making this presentation the President should be aware of the dangers of giving Goulart the impression that Brizola is right. Brizola's line of course is that the interest of the USG [U.S. government] in Brazil is only to protect the commercial concern of U.S. businessmen. Presentation on AMFORP should be such as to avoid any Goulart reaction on Brizola line.[41]

Goulart did bring up the case, without prompting, during his brief interview with Kennedy on July 1. He suggested a two- or three-month postponement in implementation of the Memorandum of Understanding, during which time he and his cabinet would work to win public acceptance of the purchase. In response, Kennedy followed the script suggested by his advisors. He made it clear that he considered the memorandum a firm commitment; the terms must be carried out exactly before there could be any resumption of American aid to the Brazilian government. Of course, Goulart might negotiate with the company to change the starting date. He could also go on with his inventories of AMFORP assets. But the price to be paid had already been fixed; the government of Brazil had indicated its acceptance when it signed the memorandum. To justify his rigidity, Kennedy spoke vaguely of the Hickenlooper Amendment and possible problems with Congress over foreign aid if there were "negative developments" in Brazil. He did not mention the State Department's doubts that the Hickenlooper Amendment applied to the AMFORP case at all.[42]

The embassy in Rio continued to press the cause of AMFORP until the campaign was temporarily halted by Assistant Secretary of State Edwin Martin on August 15:

In reviewing recent developments in Brazil. . .I am increasingly concerned that US image in Brazil, rightly or wrongly. . ., is dominated by three things: (1) pressure for financial austerity in support of IMF; (2) protection of US investments especially in public utilities; and (3) support for Governor Lacerda in his opposition to Goulart. . . .

While I accept the impossibility of a public repudiation of Lacerda, I continue to feel that his general approach is too far on the right and too fanatically anti-Goulart to be accepted as a useful contribution to US objectives, and his tactics are equally irresponsible and unacceptable.

Regardless of the reasons, however, this is a false picture of US policy both in Brazil and in the Hemisphere. Its continuation can damage our position not only in Brazil but in other countries. It seems to me that we must seek means for impressing on Brazilian people and Government a better rounded picture of our objectives for Brazil. . . .

We should find additional means for emphasizing more clearly and widely by word, and insofar as possible by action, that we favor social and economic reform and development just as strongly as we favor financial stability and protection of foreign investment.[43]

Ambassador Gordon was thoroughly shocked by Martin's cable, especially "surprised that idea of 'direct repudiation' of Lacerda should even arise." His response to the assistant secretary made it clear that he had been completely won over to the Lacerda-IPES view of Goulart and believed any new American emphasis on reform and development was wasted effort as long as Goulart was president.[44] Nevertheless, Gordon complied with Martin's instructions and stopped mentioning AMFORP each time that he talked to a Brazilian official.

Within the next few months, as U.S. contingency planning for a coup in Brazil got underway, it was clear that Gordon's view of Lacerda and Goulart, rather than Martin's, had prevailed in Washington.[45] No new means for emphasizing an American commitment to basic reform had been found. There had been one more effort to revitalize the faltering Alliance for Progress as an instrument for reform and development. The Economic and Social Council of the Organization of American States met in São Paulo in November 1963 to consider ways to do this. But the Brazilian delegation to the conference was composed of men who believed the Alliance was doomed to collapse completely within a year.[46] Other Latin delegations may have shared that view. As chief of state of the host country, Goulart delivered the opening address. In it, he ignored the stated purpose of the conference and devoted his time to calling for

164

Latin unity on world trade policy at a U.N. Conference on Trade and Development scheduled for Geneva in March 1964. After the conference had ended, at a dinner for Averell Harriman (head of the American delegation), Goulart directly criticized the Alliance, referring to it as an American "error."[47] In the end, the São Paulo conference dutifully voted the administrative changes in the Alliance that the United States wanted. The changes failed to revitalize the crusade, but the Americans could comfort themselves with the thought that Goulart and other left-leaning Latin chiefs were to blame.

The assassination of President Kennedy, a few days after the close of the conference, had the effect of arresting a further deterioration of Brazilian-American relations. In Brazil, the tragedy transformed the American president into an instant popular hero. The media covered the story in depth. Prior to the assassination not even the name of the American president had been well known outside elite circles. Afterward, even the Brazilian politicians who had consistently criticized the American president as the captive of Wall Street, remembered him fondly. Crowds lined up in Rio de Janeiro to sign the book of condolences at the American Embassy. In the outpouring of sympathy for the young president's family, there was mixed an undercurrent of sympathy for his country and all of its people.

Either Goulart himself or his advisors saw the opportunity to reestablish a dialogue with the United States. "Then there suddenly appeared in the presidential palace in Brazil a kind of grey eminence," Gordon recalled, "an extraordinary man, apparently exerting quite a lot of influence on Goulart, who was basically moderate in his view and with whom I developed quite a close relationship."[48] The grey eminence was a Brazilian business executive, Jorge Serpa. He and Gordon worked out an exchange of "good will" letters between President Goulart and President Johnson. The letters were followed by new negotiations about rescheduling the Brazilian foreign debt and about the protection of foreign investment. By January 15, 1964, the purchase of AMFORP was again being discussed at length.[49] Goulart personally received AMFORP president Henry B. Sargent, accompanied by the ambassador, to express regret at the long delays in completing the purchase.[50] In addition he went so far as to secretly receive lawyer John J. McCloy, who had left government service and was now representing Hanna Mining. McCloy presented Hanna's case for expanding the export of iron ore. He left believing that he had made a "strong impression" on the Brazilian president.[51]

Characteristically, Goulart tried to balance these new overtures to the United States with reassuring signals to the Brazilian Left. On January 23, 1964, he finally signed the enabling act that established procedures for administering the law on profit remittances that had been passed by Congress in September 1962.[52] If actually enforced, the law would sharply curtail the export of hard currency by both businesses and private citizens. Leftists hailed Goulart's action, refraining from pointing out how belated it was.

"Def-i-ni-tion!" chanted university student audiences when Goulart spoke to them. They felt the president spoke constantly of structural reforms without ever actually defining any.

"Stand for something!" outgoing Finance Minister Dantas had urged Goulart in June 1963. He knew that the president was absorbed in political manuevers, in backroom wheeling and dealing, in trying to patch together a congressional majority. He also knew that was not enough. To restore "a spirit of initiative" to the administration, to regain momentum and public confidence, Goulart must take a public stand for a concrete reform measure, one which would have "a serious impact," something "profound, not palliative."[53]

What Goulart decided to stand for was agrarian reform. On the face of it, this was a wise decision, a stand for a measure that would be both "profound" and popular. Calls for agrarian reform came from across the political spectrum, the *Jornal do Brasil* noted in July 1961. "The impression one gets is that the country is ripe for agrarian reform, since the conservatives, the Communists, the *fidelistas*, the clergy, industry, the Brazilian authorities, and the Americans are all demanding it."[54]

That was in 1961, while Quadros was still in office. Even then, those who called for agrarian reform were not necessarily in agreement about what it was. To many conservatives, reform meant simply government intercession to bring certain social benefits to peasants—better schools, housing, medical care—as well as government technical assistance to landowners to improve farming methods and productivity.[55] But to most Brazilians agrarian reform meant land redistribution. Some of the mammoth landed estates would be acquired by the government and redistributed to the landless. No doubt few were willing to go so far in land redistribution as were the peasant leaders who attended the First National Congress of Agricultural Workers and Farmers in November 1961. The

Declaration of Belo Horizonte, drawn up at this congress called for the "radical transformation of the current agrarian structure of the country, with the liquidation of the monopoly of ownership of land exercised by the *latifundiarios*. The federal government should expropriate the large estates and substitute peasant ownership for monopolistic ownership of property."[56]

President Goulart had endorsed the convocation of that convention. He attended it himself, bringing with him several cabinet ministers and a bevy of other politicians. But he did not endorse the Declaration of Belo Horizonte nor the slogan adopted by the group: Radical Agrarian Reform, by Law or by Force! He was the owner of large estates himself and hardly anxious to see their liquidation. "Was Goulart's reform oratory sincere?" mused journalist Maia Netto, a supporter of Brizola in 1963. "God knows...he probably ended up believing in his own speeches."[57] Ambassador Gordon thought he knew. "It is, I fear, simply wishful thinking for you to assume that there is any relation between Goulart's reformist preaching and truly constructive democratic reforms," Gordon cabled Assistant Secretary Martin. "His handling of agrarian reform has been calculated to prevent Congress from passing either an ordinary law or constitutional amendment, with apparent singleminded purpose of discrediting Congress."[58]

Gordon's views reflected the arguments of the Brazilian Right. But Goulart's actions were never *that* carefully calculated, nor was he ever that "singleminded." Like the majority of Brazilians at the time, he undoubtedly believed some land redistribution was necessary from the standpoint of social justice, as well as to increase agricultural productivity. Far from using his position to exempt his own properties, Goulart made a point of including one of his ranches on the first expropriation list.[59]

Expropriation should logically begin with the underutilized, oversized properties in accessible areas. To begin even such limited land redistribution, two obstacles had to be overcome. First, the constitution specifically stated that the federal government could not expropriate property without paying the owner "prior indemnification, at a fair price, and in cash." Since such payment was impossible for the near-bankrupt treasury, a constitutional amendment was needed before orderly redistribution could begin.[60] The amendment that Goulart and his advisors favored would allow payment in twenty-year bonds paying 6 to 10 percent interest, with the face value adjustable for inflation to a limited degree.

To amend the constitution, a two-thirds majority vote in Congress was needed, and this led Goulart to face his second obstacle. In theory, the

PSD was one of the mainstays of his governing coalition. Goulart needed the support of most PSD congressmen to get anywhere near the necessary two-thirds majority. But the PSD, preeminently the party of the rural establishment, was the party most opposed to any form of agrarian reform that involved land redistribution.

Goulart was later criticized for not pushing hard enough, not even trying to unite his own party behind a PSD compromise amendment that would have permitted token, limited expropriation and redistribution.[61] During the period from April to August 1963 he did make some effort to line up dissident PSD and *bossa nova* UDN[62] support for the PTB agrarian reform package. Political leaders such as the PSD ex-President Kubitschek and UDN Governor Magalhães Pinto were persuaded to speak up for an agrarian reform bill that would include a constitutional amendment. Both men, however, urged that some compromise be found between the PTB package and those suggested by PSD congressmen. Apparently miscalculating the depth of commitment to reform, Goulart failed to seize the opportunities for compromise. Various suggested substitute bills were rejected by Congress during July and August 1963. In the end, all agrarian reform proposals, including the government's, had been rejected.

At this juncture Goulart might have immediately tried again, resubmitting a modified agrarian reform proposal to the Congress. But opinion was now more sharply polarized, and the middle ground for compromise had narrowed. The Left berated Goulart for a lack of firmness and declared the votes in Congress on these bills proved that it was impossible to achieve any of the needed reforms under the existing constitution. Brizola led a call for a Constituent Assembly to make necessary changes in the constitution, since it was clear the Congress would never do so. Convinced that any change in the constitution would open the way for Goulart to perpetuate himself in power, the Right screamed that a presidential plot to introduce dictatorship was in the making, and the talk of the need for agrarian reform was only a smokescreen. The expropriation of large estates would be followed by the communization of all private property.

The immediate prospect for congressional action on agrarian reform was certainly not promising. There remained the possibility that more might be done for the peasant by using the powers of the executive office more fully. In October 1962, under authority delegated by Congress the previous August, Goulart set up SUPRA (Superintendency of Agrarian Policy)[63] as the coordinating and planning agency for all agrarian policy matters. The next month, Congress passed the Rural Labor Law, which specifically authorized the unionization of agricultural workers, and (at least in theory) extended social security benefits to such workers. Prior to this legislation there had been no law barring the organization of peasants, but there had also been no procedure for the legal recognition and registration of peasant unions with the Ministry of Labor.

A rush to organize rural unions developed after Goulart officially promulgated the statute on March 2, 1963, indicating strong administration support. Left-wing Catholic activists, the Communist Party, and conservative Church groups financed by the CIA and IPES competed to sign up peasants and register unions, unions that each organizing group hoped to control. The SUPRA staff took to the field to supervise the campaign and to register the unions on a first-reported, first-accredited basis. More than a thousand new peasant unions were created in 1963.[64] Some of the new unions actively pressed for immediate improvement in working conditions for the rural laborer. In Pernambuco, for example, in November 1963 a confederation of workers in the sugar industry initiated a general strike when sugar plantation and mill owners rejected their demands for an 80 percent increase in the minimum wage and payment of a year-end bonus that had been just decreed by Congress for all workers. After three days the employer group gave in to the union demands.[65]

There seems little doubt that unionization and collective bargaining held the potential for improving rural conditions much more rapidly than any government program of land redistribution. A new spirit of militancy and aggressive hope stirred the peasants, formerly resigned and apathetic about their lot in life. The number of invasions of large estates by peasant squatters increased, and more violent clashes between peasants and the private armies of landowners took place. Many Brazilians, conservatives and moderates alike, interpreted the violence and unrest in the countryside as communist-inspired, a dangerous breach of social peace that would lead sooner or later to a communist takeover of Brazil. They put the blame on Goulart. Hadn't he actively encouraged the communists to organize rural unions? Who had ordered the Ministry of Labor and SUPRA to give the communist organizers (the Catholic activists were counted as communists) financial and logistic support? Wasn't he brazenly preparing for a coup, utilizing the urban CGT, the new peasant unions, the misguided university youth?

Overlooked at the time was the possibility that in pushing the organization of peasants, Goulart was really just attempting to establish the same kind of government control over rural workers that the state already had over urban workers. Once registered with the Ministry of Labor, the union would collect the state-provided subsidy, the union tax. It would come under the mediation and supervision machinery of the Ministry of Labor. The government would gain the opportunities it already had in the unions of urban workers, the opportunities to co-opt union leaders or to intervene in unions that were too militant.[66] Thus, the organization of the peasants might serve to pacify rather than to incite social unrest. But in the 1963–64 Red Scare, most middle-class Brazilians were unable to see union activity that way.

In addition to encouraging the formation of rural unions, Goulart considered making use of the expropriation powers that the government already had. The federal government, for example, had the power to expropriate and redistribute land located along federally financed, improved highways and irrigation projects.[67] Goulart asked João Pinheiro, the head of SUPRA, to study and report on how such an expropriation-redistribution procedure should be carried out. Pinheiro farmed the study out to a committee of "technicians." Before reporting back to Pinheiro, the committee submitted their study to a prominent jurist, Carlos Medeiros da Silva, to make sure that no part of it was unconstitutional.[68] Pinheiro then prepared an expropriation decree based on the study and formally presented it to the president on March 9, 1964. The decree authorized expropriation of underutilized estates larger than 500 hectares (1,250 acres) that were located along federally financed roads or railroads. Underutilized farms larger than 30 hectares (75 acres) located in an area serviced by a federally financed water project could also be expropriated. The decree attempted to set standards for determining "underutilization." The expropriated land was to be divided into farms no larger than 100 hectares (250 acres) and sold to peasant families at the cost of expropriation. The decree did not get into the problem of how the expropriated land was to be paid for.[69]

Goulart decided to sign the decree and to promulgate it at the first suitable public occasion. It might be a way to rekindle popular support for his leadership.

"Enough of this delivery of the country to Communism!" trumpeted the Rio newspaper, *O Globo*, in a front page editorial on January 18, 1964. "No one in the country has any doubt any more that Goulart is the principal coordinator of coups,'' announced the leading São Paulo paper, *Estado do São Paulo*, the next day. Both newspapers were at the time reporting in detail the sensational charges by UDN president Bilac Pinto to the effect that Goulart was conniving in, if not directing, a "revolutionary war."[70] But during the same week the progovernment newspaper, *Ultima Hora*, tranquilly continued its regular diet of crime stories, reports on Carnaval preparations, terse accounts of the latest outrage committed by Governor Lacerda, all interspersed with glowing reviews of the achievements of the Goulart administration.

It is unlikely that those reviews were read carefully or believed by very many. The Brazilian public might be far from unanimous, in early 1964, about the reality of the Red Menace or the threat of a syndicalist republic. But after two years of economic and political crises, few expected much of Goulart any more. "What made me think that Goulart's ousting might not be such a bad idea," wrote Marcio Moreira Alves (then a vaguely leftist young journalist),

> was his inability to follow a program, to stand by his ministers, to rule. He seemed to be opportunistic, erratic and politically dishonest. He was weak and plainly unfit for the presidency of a nation in crisis that cried out for a strongminded reformer. Some minor personal traits also helped stain Goulart's image: he was seen drunk in public, he let corrupt cronies maneuver him who were capable of sabotaging important reform policies when offered the right price, and he had a gaucho's penchant for whoring. Moreover João Goulart was a prey to deeper contradictions, such as increasing his landholdings while preaching agrarian reform. In short, the man was utterly disordered. Not even his closest aides and allies trusted him, and this attitude was widely shared by the upper and middle classes.[71]

Some observers thought Goulart looked very tired, exhausted, even desperate; others were impressed with the calm sincerity he still displayed as he talked of the reforms he hoped to achieve.[72] Celebrating his forty-sixth birthday on March 7, 1964, in seclusion on one of his country estates with his wife and children, the president gave every appearance of a man who was at peace with himself and hopeful about the future. Falling back on an inbred fund of Latin optimism, Goulart still thought that he might find his hat tomorrow.

# 9

## Friday the Thirteenth

*Haunted by the idea of reforms and knowing that without
them his government would pass into History as empty and
inefficient, the President made a courageous decision: to go
into the streets, call the people together and clearly explain
to them how no one could succeed in freeing the country with
the existing archaic infrastructure....Then Congress would
see itself pressured to vote reforms....a bold plan, but truly
democratic. And the President set the first gathering for Rio
in front of the Ministry of War on the 13th of March, Friday.*
                                                *João de Seixas Doria*

So, aren't you going to the Communist rally?'' residents of Rio's
more prosperous Zona Sul asked one another, half in jest, that Friday
afternoon. Some went, out of curiosity, or because they agreed with the
administration, or because they were violently opposed and wanted to
see the worst for themselves. Those who didn't go watched on television.

In the living room of his apartment in Ipanema, army Chief of Staff
General Humberto Castello Branco watched in the company of his American
friend, Colonel Vernon Walters. President Goulart was the final
speaker. Switching off the set after the president's speech, Castello
remarked, "That man is not going to leave when his term is up."[1]

The remark was not particularly profound or original. It was the sort
of thing people had been saying about Goulart since he assumed the
presidency. It was the sort of thing that had been said about Kubitschek
when he was president. Political observers affiliated with the UDN were
convinced that recent political history would be repeated. Since Vargas
had staged a coup rather than leave office in 1937, surely his political
heirs would do the same. By 1964, Goulart's opponents had been waiting
and watching for more than two years for some sign that Goulart was
preparing to take the plunge. When news of the time and place of the
rally was published, the thrill of alarm swept through their ranks. This
would be it! A new session of the Congress was scheduled to begin on
March 14. Obviously Jango planned to forestall that by decreeing its
closure or an indefinite recess; no doubt he would take advantage of the

brief hiatus between the end of one congressional session and the beginning of the new one. Preparing (as they had on various occasions in the past) to fight such a move by the executive, opposition congressional leaders resolved to remain at their posts in Brasília until the new legislative year actually began.[2]

Also preparing to do their bit to preserve democracy, the women of CAMDE got busy on their telephones. They urged other women of Rio to place lighted candles in their windows on the evening of the thirteenth. They pressed in particular to get the cooperation of women who lived along the route from Laranjeiras Palace (the presidential residence in Rio) to Cristiano Otoni Square (the location of the rally). Candles were symbols of mourning. Goulart, they hoped, would take note and reflect about the meaning as he was driven to the mass meeting. In São Paulo a similar women's group União Civica Feminina, urged its members to go to the cathedral and kneel on its front steps during the hours of the rally, praying for deliverance from communism.[3]

No such qualms troubled the hearts of the labor union members, students, left-wing Catholic activists, and PTB party workers who prepared to attend the Rally for Reform. Passage on the "Reform Trains" running from São Paulo to Rio was free. Buses and trucks transported those who wished to attend from other points in the greater São Paulo area, from Belo Horizonte, and from the working-class suburbs of Guanabara and the state of Rio de Janeiro.

It was a beautiful day in Rio, sparkling clear, with a light breeze. A festive, holiday mood prevailed, "something between Carnaval and Independence Day," wrote one journalist.[4] Governor Lacerda had decreed a holiday, hoping that such a move would reduce attendance at the rally. The streets of central Rio, deserted in the morning, begin to fill up in the afternoon with out-of-town visitors, the various groups planning on going to hear the president. Thousands of army troops took up positions around the rally site. Workers cleaned and rechecked the speakers' platform. Just before dawn, a right-wing terrorist band had attempted to burn it down.[5] Television crews set up their equipment. Then groups of union members, led by bands, marched from the business district to the square. Others were transported in caravans of buses, horns blaring. Student leaders organized a caravan of VW Beetles from the UNE headquarters. Street vendors of sandwiches, cold drinks, and ice cream followed the caravans. By late afternoon, Cristiano Otoni Square was jammed with a crowd estimated between 120,000 and 150,000.

The speeches began about 6:00 P.M. The president of the Guanabara Metal Workers Union spoke first. He was followed by a number of other union leaders, by Governor Arraes of Pernambuco, Governor Seixas Doria of Sergipe, Governor Badger Silveira of the State of Rio de Janeiro, by the vice governor of Guanabara, by a Congressman representing the Nationalist Parliamentary Front, by João Pinheiro, director of SUPRA. As usual at such gatherings, no one said very much that he had not said many times before, but the audience cheered anyway. "This will end up like the doings last August," one cynical *Jornal do Brasil* reporter told his colleagues. "Just a lot of talk."[6]

Brizola gave one of his fiery orations. Reportedly, he had toned down the rhetoric at the insistence of CGT leaders, but his speech still struck many as unusually arrogant. He urged Goulart to end his policy of conciliation and to reorganize his cabinet on strictly reformist, populist lines. He bitterly criticized the Congress and called for a plebiscite on whether Congress should be closed and a constitutional convention held in its place. He suggested that a Congress made up of workers, peasants, nationalist officers, and sergeants ought to be substituted for the existing reactionary Congress. At one point, Brizola asked all those in favor of reforms to raise their hands. The sight of a hundred thousand hands shooting straight up struck television viewers unfavorably. Like Mussolini, like Hitler? "Arms raised en masse just to say 'yes' will always remind us of arms raised en masse ready to go to madness."[7]

Finally, about 8:45, President Goulart began to speak. Those who had decided ahead of time that Goulart was going too far thought the speech he made was violent and threatening. It is hard to find that in the printed text.[8] No doubt his manner was more animated than usual, his delivery more forceful. He was exhilarated by the size of the crowd and perhaps also by the fact that his beautiful young wife was on the platform beside him. Somewhat timid, unsure of herself, bored with politics, Maria Teresa rarely accompanied Jango to public functions. She was reportedly tremendously impressed by her husband's performance at this function and by the enthusiastic reception given him by the crowd.

Whatever Jango's speaking style on this occasion, he did not actually say anything violent or threatening. As was true of other speakers, most of what he said he had said many times before. It had already been announced (and discussed in the press throughout the previous week) that Goulart had signed the SUPRA expropriation decree. Goulart's decision to sign another decree expropriating several small privately owned oil refineries had not been disclosed before, but the president made only a brief reference to this "reform." Most of his speech dealt with the need for agrarian reform. He did announce that he planned to sign a decree setting up rent controls for apartments in the cities, starting with vacant apartments that were advertised for rent. The announcement was warmly applauded by his urban audience.

In spite of the apprehension about Goulart's intentions vis-à-vis the legislative branch, Goulart made no derogatory remarks about Congress, much less threaten to replace it with a peasant-worker soviet. Rather, he politely urged "the gentlemen of Congress," in their "patriotism" to heed and act upon the presidential message that he would send them within forty-eight hours. Nor did he call for the convocation of a constitutional convention to amend the constitution or to write a new one. That was Brizola's pet project, one he had been pushing for some time. The opposition routinely attributed Brizola's views to the president, but in fact the two were so hostile to one another at this time that up to the last moment the CGT organizers of the rally were not sure that they would agree to appear on the same platform.[9]

Contrary to numerous predictions before the rally (and many accounts of events afterward), Goulart did not call for the legalization of the Brazilian Communist Party. And he certainly did not suggest that the constitution should be amended so that either he or Brizola might become presidential candidates in the 1965 election. True, he called the constitution "antiquated," but he was referring to its socioeconomic provisions, not its rules on political succession. The constitution legalized an economic structure "that is already obsolete, unjust, and inhuman," said Goulart. He made it clear that what he most wanted changed in it (via amendments by the existing Congress) was the requirement that expropriated property be paid for in advance in cash. He also suggested that all Brazilians over the age of eighteen should be given the right to vote and to hold elective office. In other words, the constitution should be changed to permit illiterates to vote and enlisted men in the armed forces the right to run for and hold elective offices, as well as to allow agrarian reform to proceed.

Despite the moderate tone of his remarks and the absence of any clear threat to existing institutions, the notion spread rapidly that just by speaking at all at a rally of this sort, Goulart was somehow short-circuiting or bypassing the democratic system. To those already convinced that Brazil represented the next target of the evil empire of international communism, the entire ambience of the rally seemed unequivocally sinister. The "frenzy of the screaming masses," the fiery radical oratory, especially Brizola's—it all thoroughly frightened the people viewing the event from the safety of their living rooms.[10]

Especially shocking was the sight of "card-carrying" Communists sharing the speaker's platform with the president of the republic. One of them could actually be seen whispering in Goulart's ear from time to time, no doubt prompting him. "The 13th of March marked my adherence to the revolutionary ranks," recalled retired General Juracy Magalhães, a former *"tenente,"* a veteran of the revolutionary movement of 1930.

> On that day, when I saw Osvaldo Pacheco on television at the Central rally giving instructions to the President I could not continue on the outside. It was too much! A fellow who had been expelled from Congress for being an admitted Communist militant drawing closer to the President of the Republic and whispering in his ear: 'Mention the refineries.' and Jango immediately turned and said, 'The refineries . . .' Definitely we were witnessing the Communist Party in power, giving orders to the President of the Republic. That I couldn't stomach![11]

It is not clear how Juracy, watching on television, was able to pick up what Pacheco was whispering in Goulart's ear. A journalist at the rally insisted that Pacheco whispered so loudly that the microphone picked up the request: "Ask the people to help keep watch on the landowners." "And," continued the reporter, "Jango, a well-trained student, already without pride, began the following phrase a few seconds later, 'The people must help us keep watch on the landowners.'"[12] The text of Goulart's speech contains no such phrase or request. But no matter. It was the appearance, not the actuality, that mattered when people later attempted to justify their support for a military coup that ousted a civilian, constitutional administration.

Then, too, there were all those placards, thousands of them being waved by the screaming multitude. Some were short identifications: CGT, Guanabara Metalworkers. Others carried rather lengthy historical messages: "On the 13th of May, 1888, blacks got their liberty. On the 13th of March, 1964, workers will get their liberty." Some placards made requests: "Jango, sign the agrarian reform bill. We'll take care of the rest." "Osvino, stick a knife into the trusts!" "Jail for the gorillas!" "Jango, we request jail for the exploiters of the people!" But the banners that attracted most attention were the ones portraying hammers and sickles, or demands for the legalization of the Communist Party, or calls for Jango to continue as president, or legends such as "PCB—Your

Rights Are Sacred," "Yankees, Get Out!" and "Diplomatic Relations With China."[13]

Unknown to the horrified viewers, most, if not all, of the more extreme placards were carried by right-wing opponents of Goulart, who had infiltrated the ranks of his supporters or were simply attending the rally as dirty tricksters. The first influx of suspect placards had been noted by the rally organizers before the speeches began. When Goulart was informed, he ordered the removal of such placards, especially those calling for his reelection. But, after the rally was underway, there was a second influx of people bearing signs with radical messages. The media of course focused on them. In addition, agents provocateurs, mingling in the crowd, instigated the burning and destruction of some banners. The fire touched off one incident of pushing and shoving and panic, during which fifty people were injured, one fatally.[14]

The presence of hostile agents provocateurs at the March 13 rally points up the strength and sophistication that the right-wing subversive movement had achieved by early 1964. Obviously Goulart's inability to cope with the various conspiracies to overthrow him represented his most serious weakness as a chief executive. In part, his problem was due to the fact that the government's intelligence service was rudimentary; he was always poorly informed as to the extent and the current status of the plotting.[15] But much of the preparation to stage a coup to overthrow the government was fairly open, and Goulart's failure to move against the conspirators represented a fatal error of judgment. The president could not help but know, for example, that General Olympio Mourão was spending much of his time preaching to his fellow officers and to any politicians who would listen about the need to stage a coup in order to save the country from communism.[16] True, Goulart considered Mourão something of a crackpot[17] and did not take his activity seriously, but obviously there were a number of more discreet, more effective right-wing military men who might be active conspirators.

Goulart also must have been aware that the number of anticommunist paramilitary bands in the country was growing. Most of such part-time vigilantes were preparing themselves to put down rioting peasants or to do battle against Communist-led workers and students when Armageddon came, but at least one group (connected with the Guanabara political police) aspired to kidnap or murder the president. In early October 1963 a cache of weapons and communications equipment was discovered hidden near the Guanabara summer home that Goulart and his family often used. Goulart sometimes used the house for private meetings, away from

177

the notice of the media, meetings with politically embarrassing individuals such as Communist Party officials, Francisco Julião, AMFORP or Hanna officials. Hoping to catch Goulart with a group of Communist house guests, the vigilantes staked out the house, stored the weapons nearby, and prepared to storm the building at the propitious moment. The federal troops who took charge of the accidentally uncovered cache, noted that some of the equipment bore Alliance for Progress stickers. The embassy quickly determined that it came from "stocks delivered Guanabara police on September 30, 1963," but issued a statement denying the material was "part of any U.S. military or civilian aid package."[18]

On this occasion the embassy denial became "inoperative" rather quickly. The Guanabara secretary for security informed the press that the arms belonged to the state police (who wanted them back) and claimed that they had been deposited in the suburb because the area was threatened by Peasant League groups who were secretly training to be leftist guerrillas in the woods near the resort area.[19]

Incidents such as this reinforced Goulart's tendency to regard Lacerda as the most dangerous of the right-wing extremists. Lacerda had the reputation of being a "destroyer of presidents." He had been involved in intrigues against both Vargas and Kubitschek. He had a long record of hostility to Goulart. He had opposed him as labor minister in 1953, as vice presidential candidate in 1955 and 1960, and as the legal successor to Quadros in 1961. The burden of his attack was that Goulart so longed for the creation of a syndicalist republic that he had sold his soul to the communists and/or devil in the hope of achieving it. Judging from his record, it was reasonable to assume that Lacerda was in the forefront of coup plotting. "But, when the conspiracy to overthrow Jango really began, I don't know," Lacerda said later. "I don't know for a reason that might seem very strange: I did not participate in the conspiracy."[20] Lacerda insisted that all of his acts of opposition to Goulart were public political acts, nothing covert, nothing "under the table." He contacted other governors, several leading newspaper publishers, a few military men. With all of these contacts he conversed about the "unbearable" current situation of the country. "But, conspiracy, no. Nothing was worked out about any move of any army to any place, nor what I would do, nor what that person would do. We only exchanged ideas about something we already agreed upon."[21]

Jango and his advisors believed otherwise. They were convinced that Lacerda was the heart and soul of a conspiracy that involved other governors, certain businessmen, disgruntled retired military men such as

Admiral Heck and Marshal Denys, members of IBAD/IPES, and American businessmen and intelligence agents.[22] Goulart's aides closely monitored the governor's speeches and did their best to harass him and make his administration of Guanabara difficult. Thus, Guanabara state police and firemen were suddenly given the option of choosing to remain state employees or becoming federal employees with superior benefits. At least one-third chose to work for the federal government, leaving the state agencies seriously undermanned.[23]

There was one botched attempt by Goulart loyalists in the army to kidnap Lacerda. The officers, who had imbibed "much whiskey," set out to trap the governor in a building he was inaugurating but were delayed by traffic and an automobile breakdown, giving Lacerda, who had been tipped off by another officer, plenty of time to leave the target area.[24]

Adhemar de Barros, the governor of São Paulo, commanded greater financial resources than Lacerda and controlled much larger, better-trained state police and militia forces. His participation in anti-Jango activities was somewhat less public than Lacerda's, but obvious enough to be noted by the press by April 1963.[25] His imagination was almost as active as Lacerda's. Early in 1963 he confided to a number of intimates that he had learned that Goulart planned to launch the syndicalist republic on Labor Day, May 1, 1963. When nothing of the sort happened—instead, Goulart gave a sober, moderate Labor Day speech—Adhemar updated the prediction by changing the year to 1964 and passed it along to a fresh batch of confidants.[26] On another occasion he announced that he had just learned that, by order of Soviet Premier Khrushchev, the command of the Brazilian Communist Party was being turned over to Pernambuco Governor Miguel Arraes.[27] Despite such public flights of fancy on the part of the governor of São Paulo, Goulart never considered Adhemar as implacable a foe as Lacerda. Adhemar had supported Vargas in the 1950 election and did not have Lacerda's record of intrigue.

There had been one occasion during this troubled year when rumors swept Brazil, the U.S. State Department, and the CIA that Goulart was finally prepared to move decisively against both governors. On October 4, 1963, the president suddenly asked Congress to declare martial law for thirty days. The drastic measure had been urged upon Goulart by his three military ministers and Justice Minister Jurema. The ministers saw the step as necessary to head off the coup they believed that Lacerda and Adhemar were hatching. Lacerda had just told a *Los Angeles Times* reporter that the Goulart government would fall before the end of the year.[28] Lacerda had stipulated that the interview be published only in

November 29, 1962. An interview with President Kennedy was arranged for São Paulo Governor-elect Adhemar de Barros. Adhemar, deeply involved in the right-wing conspiracy, assured Kennedy that the Brazilians would oust the Goulart government in the near future. (Courtesy John F. Kennedy Library.)

the United States, but it was of course promptly published in Brazil as well. Recent speeches by Adhemar suggested collusion. In addition, new strikes were underway or imminent in both Rio and São Paulo. Goulart could request the martial law declaration to deal with the strikes and the general unrest in the country, then move to replace both governors with federal *interventors*. Not only would the immediate coup threat be thwarted, but the government might use its decree powers to introduce needed reforms or to stabilize prices.

The request, however, boomeranged. Before he submitted the request for emergency powers to Congress, Goulart secured the support of Brizola and of congressional leaders of the PTB and PSD. But Brizola and the PTB leadership promptly abandoned the cause as soon as it became clear that any period of martial law, however limited, was vociferously opposed by the media concerned about censorship, labor leaders worried about losing the right to strike, and supporters of Arraes fearful that federal intervention in Guanabara and São Paulo would be followed by intervention in Pernambuco.[29] Deserted by the Left, regarded with heightened suspicion by the Center, and berated as usual by the Right, Goulart rapidly perceived his isolation on this issue. He withdrew his request for martial law three days after he had submitted it. Although his government was to stumble on for another six months, Goulart never completely recovered politically from the humiliation of trying, but failing, to deal decisively with the problem of subversive conspiracy.

Encouraged by these developments, the conspirators accelerated their plotting for a coup. Participation in the subversive movement widened as more of the governors, businessmen, and military officers joined in. "Military leaders hostile to the government of President Goulart are holding meetings daily to plot anti-government actions," the CIA noted with satisfaction on October 7.[30] Although he was aware that the military was doing a certain amount of plotting, neither Goulart nor his advisors seemed especially alarmed by it. As president, Goulart controlled appointments to the top military posts; he controlled promotions and duty assignments as well. He was confident that he could use these powers to maintain the loyalty and support of most members of the armed forces.[31] In addition, he believed that military was really dedicated to "legality" and the defense of the constitution as its orators frequently proclaimed.

Goulart clearly overestimated the extent of that dedication. He was not alone in making this mistake. At the time the Brazilian military was a curiously sacrosanct institution. Not even the more extreme of the groups on the Left criticized it as an institution. Leftist leaders attacked outspoken anti-Goulart generals and admirals as "gorillas," but always made it clear that they were not criticizing the officer corps as a whole

181

or the military as such. Despite the facts that the Brazilian military's support of a constitution and democratic institutions dated back only to 1945 and that it had older traditions of supporting authoritarian regimes and of disrupting the political process via armed intervention, the military was thought to be an "effective bulwark of democracy."[32] Excuses might be found for the American analysts who referred to the Brazilian military in this way. It is harder to explain Goulart's complaisance about the subversive activity of those officers who were meeting daily to plot his demise.

The American embassy was well informed about the extent of military plotting. CIA agents as well as the Defense Department attachés regularly reported it.[33] But, though it was clear in 1963 that plotting against Goulart was widespread within the military, American analysts also noted that it was not well coordinated. Too many generals were planning to become the supreme leader of a glorious revolution.

The best organized of the various coteries of military conspirators was the "Sorbonne" group, operating under the aegis of IPES. The officers of this group, enjoying a reputation as the military's "intellectuals," were all past or present instructors, or recent alumni, of the Escola Superior de Guerra (Superior War College). The ESG, created in 1949, was modeled on the U.S. National War College and regularly had American officers as visiting instructors. Its curriculum was modeled on that of its American counterpart, with heavy emphasis on anticommunism and counterinsurgency.[34]

The Sorbonne clique was not the only military faction conspiring to overthrow the government. There was a "trooper," or line officer, faction, more or less headed by the ranking line officer, General Arturo Costa e Silva. There was a group of "historic" coup plotters who had conspired against Vargas and Kubitschek and tried to bar Goulart from succeeding Quadros. Marshal Odílio Denys and Admiral Sílvio Heck belonged to this clique. There was an extremist faction headed by Air Force Colonel João Paulo Moreira Burnier. However, under the guidance of retired General Golbery de Couto e Silva, the Sorbonne group emerged as the most important coordinator of the various military conspiracies. Until March 31, 1964, the group was even able to keep loose cannon, such as the excitable General Olympio Mourão, in check.[35]

The ESG-affiliated officers were particularly suited to maneuvering within a business-oriented group such as IPES because they had already established personal contacts with prominent business executives. Unlike its American model, the Brazilian War College invited members of the

August 27, 1963. President Kennedy meets a visiting class from the Brazilian Superior War College (ESG). Under American guidance, the ESG course of instruction stressed anticommunism and the American view of the Cold War. (Courtesy John F. Kennedy Library.)

civilian elite to join selected ranking officers in the forty-week Information Course and the Superior War Course. Flattered by the invitation to participate in discussion of their country's national security needs, those invited rarely refused to attend. During the courses, participants were led through "objective" analyses of communist ideology, the Russian Revolution, the history of communist takeovers of other countries, communist techniques of subversion and infiltration, and the nature of "revolutionary war." National development needs and problems were also discussed, primarily in relation to defense against the imagined communist threat. The Kennedy, or "post-Sputnik," theory

183

that underdeveloped countries were currently the special target of international communist imperialism was stressed. Also stressed was the idea that all members of the elite, civilian as well as military, must do what they could to solve national social problems in the interest of strengthening internal security.

The same message of the "civic action" responsibility of the elite was being preached to businessmen in the United States. The concept had been developed as part of Kennedy's counterinsurgency program and initially was boosted as a positive new role in nation building for the Latin military. "Civic action is the use of military forces in projects useful to the populace at all levels in such fields as training, public works, agriculture, transportation, communications, health, sanitation, and others helpful to economic development."[36] Now the business elite was urged to undertake similar tasks in order to win over members of the underclasses to the anticommunist cause. If "revolutionary war" was total warfare, then every civilian, as well as every soldier, had the obligation to do what he could to further the common defense.

Businessmen took up the civic action idea readily. In Brazil, representatives of American corporations had adopted an activist role as early as 1962, when some firms secretly contributed to the campaigns of conservative candidates in the October election. It was resident American corporate executives who had privately urged the visiting Draper mission to recommend a total cutoff of all American aid in order to bring about the fall of Goulart and the establishment of a military government. By mid-1963 the hostility of American business to Goulart was quite open. The *Wall Street Journal* reported on October 25, 1963, that Americans in Brazil saw Goulart as "a desperately devious, totally ambitious figure, whose aim is to seize permanent power and run a fascist state." The businessmen resident in Brazil were not at all reticent about expressing such opinions to the press, visiting congressmen, and foreign service personnel.

Assistant Secretary of State Edwin Martin worried that the businessmen were somewhat too influential with embassy personnel and had led Ambassador Gordon, for example, into his strongly pro-Lacerda position.[37] Later, in turning his job over to his successor in December 1963, Martin listed the activities of "elements in the U.S. business communities abroad" as one of the key problems that an assistant secretary of state for Latin America had to face. These elements were busy attacking presidents such as Goulart, Martin complained, presidents whom the United States government was attempting to keep in office. In addition, the conservative opinions of such business leaders, locally identified with the American government, helped push Latin countries further toward anti-Americanism and the Left.[38]

But other American officials did not agree with Martin that American businessmen abroad ought to be muzzled. There was in fact a feeling in some congressional circles that one of the things wrong with the State Department was that its diplomats abroad paid far too little attention to resident American businessmen, who were likely to have lived in the country longer than the ambassador and who were just as concerned about the success of American policy. After all, Senator Karl Mundt explained to Secretary Rusk, "they have the normal patriotic motivation plus the fact they have a selfish interest. Their whole investment goes down the drain if the government gets to be unfriendly to Uncle Sam and the American people."[39] Congressmen holding hearings on "Winning the Cold War" wondered whether American business might not do more to expose the Communist threat within their Third World host countries, and the Senate debated establishing a Freedom Academy that would give businessmen going abroad some basic Cold War training.[40]

Reflecting the business community's pride in its new activism, *Business Week* reported on March 16, 1963, that American companies in Latin America were mobilizing to combat communist and Castro-inspired subversion by enlisting in a variety of civic action programs. The programs were supposedly designed to promote the image of a democratic society as opposed to a communist model. They were described as ranging from simple anticommunist propaganda to community improvement projects such as school building renovation. Some of the civic action projects involved complex political schemes such as the infiltration of leftist schools or the removal of leftist university administrators. *Business Week* advised American businessmen to remain in the background in the case of the complex political schemes, simply providing support to the Latin businessmen directly involved.

The idea that the American personnel running a corporate subsidiary abroad should become involved in community improvement activities was an accepted public relations dictum. What was new in 1963 were the ideas that civic action should be political action aimed at promoting anticommunism and that it was not only fitting and proper for American businessmen abroad to engage in such activities but almost a sacred Cold War duty. Of course, officially the State Department maintained the position that American businessmen should not become involved in the internal politics of host countries.[41] The CIA ostensibly seconded that

185

position. Kennedy's second CIA director, John McCone, testified in 1973 that it was CIA policy when he headed the agency to not only refuse corporate offers of financial support but also to advise companies not to become involved. His testimony was somewhat clouded by the fact that, as an ITT director in September 1970, he approved of the company's offer of $1 million in support of any U.S. plan to prevent Salvador Allende from becoming president of Chile. McCone argued that the ITT money was being offered for social purposes, for civic not for political, action. Presumably the CIA had made the same murky distinctions in Brazil a decade earlier.[42]

For the most part, American firms operating in Brazil probably assumed civic action tasks without being urged to do so by congressional or adminstration officials. However, there was at least one project (called civic action) in which business participation had to be solicited. This was the AFL-CIO operation known as the American Institute for Free Labor Development (AIFLD). The program set up training institutes for Latin labor leaders in order to spur the organization or the strengthening of noncommmunist labor unions. Corporations doing business in Latin America were invited to participate and contribute funds. It was felt that the anticommunist message could be preached more effectively by a management-labor partnership. Cooperation with management, not confrontation and class struggle, would be the AIFLD message. A contrast with communist labor practices would thus be sharply drawn. "We believe in capitalism," AFL-CIO President George Meany emphasized when testifying before the House committee that was considering ways to win the Cold War.[43]

The idea of a special institute dedicated to instructing Latin labor leaders in anticommunism came from Joseph A. Beirne, head of the Communications Workers of America. In 1959, financed primarily by U.S. foreign aid funds,[44] Beirne had conducted an experiment in the indoctrination of Pervuvian communications workers through special courses and seminars. The next year he was given a grant by the AFL-CIO council to plan a broader and more permanent institute. The AIFLD was chartered as a nonprofit corporation in August 1961. Although American firms with investments in Latin American were urged to make donations, the response was so meager that the new institute might have been stillborn for lack of funds if President Kennedy had not come to the rescue. The President's Emergency Fund transferred $100,000 to it,[45] and Kennedy then backed the idea of having AIFLD funded with Alliance for Progress funds through AID. Some CIA money was also invested in the institute since a number of AIFLD officials were salaried CIA agents.[46] The institute thus became a quasi-governmental agency.

By the end of 1962, the AIFLD was operating two centers in Brazil, one in São Paulo, the other in Recife. The centers served as agencies for the distribution of propaganda as well as locations for training classes. The classes, lasting as long as a month, served the purpose of recruiting future leaders. Those chosen as promising candidates were treated to a paid three-month training program at the São Paulo center. Selected graduates of the three-month program were sent to the United States for another three-month course. After completing this program, the candidates returned to Brazil to practice what they had learned, while remaining on the AIFLD payroll for an additional nine months. Descriptions of the content of the training classes suggest that much more time was spent on the problems of identifying and combating communists in unions than on topics such as collective bargaining, negotiation strategies, or managment of union finances.[47]

It is not entirely clear how much of an impact AIFLD had in Brazil. There was no upsurge in the organization of new anticommunist unions and no apparent turnovers of leadership in the established unions. William Doherty, the AIFLD director in 1964, boasted that Brazilian workers trained by his institute played an important role in the coup against Goulart, but such labor involvement went unnoticed by any other observer.[48] Was the American message of labor's solidarity with management likely to be a congenial theme to workers engaged in a desperate struggle to keep wages in line with runaway inflation during a period of widespread unemployment? One suspects that bread-and-butter issues might have interested workers more than the possible presence of communists in their unions. But American labor leaders were as fervently anticommunist at this time as American corporate executives or the American public in general. To Joseph Beirne or George Meany or Walter Reuther, the struggle against communist domination of trade unions in the Third World was much more important than any struggle to improve wages and working conditions for working men and women in those countries.

Laying plans—in September 1963—"to facilitate the most favorable possible succession in event that there is a crisis of regime," State Department policy planners vowed to "promote and strengthen in all sectors of Brazilian life democratically oriented forces which can restrain undemocratic or anti-democratic excesses by the present government and its extreme leftist or ultranationalist supporters."[49] "Crisis of regime" can be taken as a euphemism for military coup. "Democratically oriented forces" definitely included IPES. In light of the leftist-nationalist bias against foreign-owned business, some officials of the Kennedy administration might be reluctant to encourage American firms in Brazil to take an active part in anti-Goulart activities. Such caution obviously did not apply in the case of organized labor. Nor did it apply to Brazilian business enterprises. The subversive activities of Brazilian businessmen, just like those of the Brazilian military, could be regarded with approval and covertly financed.

IPES stepped up its campaign to alert business to the communist danger and the need for counterrevolutionary action before it was too late. A growing number of business executives overcame their reluctance to become personally involved in politics. More became active members of, or contributors to, IPES. More joined vigilante cells and armed themselves, preparing to fight in the civil war they believed to be inevitable: they were sure that the communists were arming the labor unions and Peasant Leagues.

The business leaders made little attempt to conceal their preparations for civil war. Some were reported in the press. As early as May 24, 1963, at a meeting of the American Chamber of Commerce in São Paulo, the Brazilian vice chairman, D. M. Lobo Rosa, reported plans to organize and arm civilians in a "block control group" that "could be depended upon to support overall action which group as a whole would take against the federal government" and "to counteract communist aggression and subversion in [the] event civil war broke out and São Paulo police and military units were involved elsewhere in large-scale fighting." The timing of the action against Goulart was still indefinite, according to Lobo Rosa, but it should take place before leftist forces seized the intitiative. The American business community and U.S. government officials were urged to understand and support the action.[50] Similar campaigns to arm and train business executives were announced by the Commercial Association of Rio de Janeiro and by CONCLAP.[51]

Leftists were sure that the arms for the businessman-vigilantes were being supplied by the American government. They believed the U.S. military attachés, the CIA, and the U.S. consulate at Recife were all involved in a flow of arms to the vigilantes. In addition, they were sure Americans were providing training in sabotage and guerrilla warfare at secret training camps.[52] They were probably right. President Kennedy certainly approved of such activities. According to the guidelines that his administration laid down for itself:

A paramilitary operation is considered to be one which by its tactics and its requirements in military-type personnel, equipment and training approximates a conventional military operation. It may be taken in support of a rebel group seeking to overthrow a government hostile to us. The U.S. may render assistance to such operations overtly, covertly or by a combination of both methods.[53]

In addition to arming themselves in preparation for a class war, some of the anticommunist activists adopted the practice of disrupting opposition rallies by loud heckling or by physical assaults on speakers and government supporters in the audience. The recently organized upper-middle-class women's clubs proved especially adept at breaking up meetings using such tactics. In one incident that took place two weeks before the March 13 rally, the Women's League for Democracy of Belo Horizonte prevented Brizola from addressing a political gathering. Before most of Brizola's supporters had arrived, the women (with a large contingent of male supporters) packed the auditorium. As people who wanted to hear Brizola got there and tried to take seats, they were attacked with chairs and umbrellas. Fifty people with injuries had to be taken to hospitals, including a congressman whose skull had been fractured. State police were on guard outside the building, but not within. When Brizola arrived, the hostile crowd barred his entrance. Securing a microphone, Brizola attempted to address the people milling about outside. He was drowned out by a phalanx of women rattling their rosaries and praying loudly. In other instances, conservative priests led devout lower-class women and schoolchildren to join in noisy protests against freedom of speech for "communists." To prevent Goulart's cabinet ministers from addressing university audiences, São Paulo Governor Adhemar de Barros had his state police dress as students and sent them to brawl with the real students, barring the entrance for the federal officials.[54]

Whatever hand the CIA might have had in instructing Brazilians in such tactics, American diplomatic personnel warmly applauded their use. "Thousands of Paulistas—most of them armed—were organized into 'democratic-action' groups with ambitious plans," wrote Niles W. Bond, minister consul general at São Paulo, shortly after the coup:

the anti-Communist Paulistas had mastered the technique of disrupting Leftist meetings by force and harassment, of organizing "spontaneous" rallies of their own at a moment's notice, of flooding the Government with telegrams, of putting out manifestos, and of organizing "popular demand" for wanted actions.

189

The importance of the anti-Communist, anti-caudilho movement must not be played down. It may not have had much participation from the lower class—Brazilian political movements seldom have—but it was far more "popular" than anything the Communists could drum up.[55]

By late 1963 the right-wing militants were also much better at infiltrating leftist organizations. They had one striking success in September when anticommunist military activists who had infiltrated a noncommissioned officer organization learned that a group of marine and air force sergeants were planning a nationwide rebellion on September 14 if the Supreme Court proceeded to rule that noncoms could not hold elective office. The Supreme Court ruling came on September 11. One of the infiltrators addressed a mass meeting of the sergeants in Brasília that day and persuaded the group to stage their rebellion at once instead of waiting for the fourteenth. The 600 sergeants, corporals, and enlisted men who did participate in the premature, disorganized rebellion the next morning were easily subdued by army units within a few hours.[56]

The event made a deep impression on the commissioned officer corps. Until then the officers had been confident that the chain of command and discipline was intact and that it was the commissioned officers who controlled actual military force. Traditionally, Brazilian presidents looking for military "cover" had always constructed it from the existing officer corps, carefully respecting rank. Suppose Goulart now decided to base his "cover" on the noncoms? Who would then actually be in control of the enlisted man's firepower? Or the new technology? "We are the technicians," boasted Sergeant Antonio García, a leader of the Sergeants Club. "We handle mechanical problems, meteorology, etc. At the present time we can totally paralyze the Brazilian armed forces."[57]

Officers who had, until then, been wrapped up in their own careers and private lives, indifferent to politics and/or unconvinced about the reality of a communist threat, started attending the lectures and discussion sessions on "revolutionary war" and the military's obligation to combat it. The Brazilian Cold Warriors used the term "revolutionary war" to describe an imagined Soviet master plan for achieving their objective of "implanting Communist tyranny" around the world at a time when conventional warfare was no longer feasible because of the nuclear threat.[58]

Among the experts on the subject was General Humberto Castello Branco, who began delivering lectures on the threat of international Communism as early as December 1961.[59] His audiences were strictly military, and his platforms were usually special seminars or graduation exercises of advanced army training schools. Outside military ranks, few Brazilians had ever heard of Castello Branco before 1964. Aged sixty-six at the time of the coup, Castello had spent his entire life in the rigid, somewhat sterile, world of the Brazilian army. His father had been an army officer before him and had entered his son at age fourteen in the Colégio Militar de Porto Alegre to begin military training.

During the half-century of his military service, Castello had acquired a reputation as a strict "legalist." He had never been involved in any of the military uprisings or plots to overthrow presidents or constitutions—not in the *"tenente"* uprisings of the 1920s, not in the 1930 revolution when the elected president was barred from office and the defeated candidate installed, not in 1937 when a coup was staged to permit Vargas to stay in office, not in 1945 when Vargas was ousted the first time, not in 1954 when he was removed a second time, not in 1955 when War Minister Lott staged a "preventive" coup to check a conspiracy to bar Kubitschek, not in 1961 when War Minister Denys tried to bar Goulart. Castello's refusal to get involved did not mean that he was uninterested in politics. He followed political developments closely. His personal position was definitely right of center. He always voted for UDN candidates. In 1958, in his one major venture into military politics, he ran as the conservative Democratic Crusade candidate for the presidency of the Military Club. He had been trounced.

It was probably Castello's reputation as a strict legalist, as well as his reputation for conscientious attention to duty that kept him moving up the military hierarchy, even during the periods when presidents he opposed were in power. In 1962 Goulart had given Castello the next promotion he was in line for—that of four-star general. In 1963 he appointed the general to the prestigious post of army chief of staff. It was true that in this position Castello did not command any troops, but the post put him in a position to communicate with all other army officers. Since in his opinion he deserved the promotion and the post in the High Command, Castello felt no gratitude to Goulart. In fact, his antagonism increased: Goulart had failed to promote all of Castello's friends.

In January 1964 Castello was persuaded by a group of officers who had been conspiring against Goulart for two years to join them as their leader, as chief of staff of a secret revolutionary command. Castello Branco, Generals Ernesto Geisel, José Ulhoa Cintra, Antoñio Carlos Muricy, Jurandir Mamede, retired generals Ademar de Queiroz and Golbery de Couto e Silva made up the secret command. They began meeting at night, two or three times a week, planning the coup, plotting the coordination of all other conspiratorial factions. Golbery, called the "pope" of ESG, was also a key leader of IPES and probably played the guiding role in these preparations for a revolution. But it was a stroke of luck to get a respected legalist who actually was the chief of staff play that same role in a conspiracy that would be dedicated to hierarchy, discipline, and the maintenance of the social status quo.

Perhaps to salve his conscience, Castello Branco soon developed the argument that he had not abandoned his legalist position since it was necessary to "act offensively on behalf of legality." In other words, the military must overthrow the legally constituted government in order to save it. Castello argued that Goulart was about to destroy Congress, the judiciary, and the electoral process. He was abetting a communist effort to subvert the Brazilian armed forces. "If the Marxist-Leninist Revolutionary War enslaves the nation, who is going to defend the democratic institutions?"[60]

The March 13 rally was taken by the conspirators as the final proof of Goulart's intentions. There was a feverish burst of activity. One of the IPES leaders, Alberto Byington, flew to the United States to arrange the purchase of a shipload of oil that might be needed in the coming civil war. It was believed that communists had firm control over Petrobrás, the government oil monopoly, and would of course deny supplies to the rebels.[61] General Costa e Silva, who outranked Castello Branco in the military hierarchy, having been promoted to the rank of four-star general a half year earlier, now formally declared himself into the conspiracy. UDN congressmen discussed a new try at impeaching Goulart. Minas Gerais governor Magalhães Pinto, until then an apparent supporter of the president, mended fences with his UDN rival, Carlos Lacerda, and began drawing up manifestos. For his part, Lacerda busied himself sending circulars to other governors. Castello Branco's secret revolutionary command stepped up its effort to tie all conspiratorial groups together and to contact all of the important army command posts to gain their cooperation for the coup.

Castello sent a "restricted" memorandum to all staff officers at the command posts on March 20, a week after the rally. He gave them his interpretation of the event. It had underlined two immediate threats to the nation: the convocation of a constituent assembly and increased agitation by the "illegal" CGT. A constituent assembly would mean "the closing of the present Congress and the institution of a dictatorship." The subversive agitation of the CGT would probably lead directly to the subjugation of Brazil to Moscow. It was the duty of the armed forces to defend legality as spelled out in the existing constitution and established laws. If the military allowed itself to be used to defend a constituent assembly or the CGT, it would be betraying the country.[62]

Castello's "confidential" memorandum was widely circulated among both military and civilian conspirators and was soon being discussed by the media. Since Castello had violated the existing laws by not first clearing his memorandum with the minister of war, the president had grounds for dismissing him as army chief of staff. On March 24 Goulart apparently decided to take that step, but he delayed acting on the dismissal until after the Holy Week holidays.[63]

The most dramatic response to the March 13 rally came on March 19 in São Paulo, when more than 200,000 people (variously estimated between 200,000 and 800,000) participated in a demonstration against Goulart. During his address on March 13, Goulart had denounced the "exploitation" of the religious feeling of the Brazilian people by "an anticommunist industry." He indicated his own agreement with "the unforgettable Pope John XXIII" who taught

> that the dignity of the human person requires, ordinarily as the natural foundation for life, the right and the use of the fruits of the earth, corresponding to which is the obligation to grant property to all. It is on this true doctrine that the Brazilian government is attempting to base its social policy, especially with respect to our existing agrarian structure. Christianity never was a shield for the privileged condemned by the Holy Father, nor, Brazilians, can rosaries be raised against the people's will and against their most legitimate aspirations. Nor can the rosaries of faith be raised against people who have faith in a more human social justice and in the dignity of their hopes. Rosaries cannot be lifted up against those who protest discrimination in the ownership of land, today still in the hands of so few.[64]

Goulart was referring to the incident in Belo Horizonte when praying women clicking rosaries had drowned out Brizola.

Calling these remarks an "insult to the rosary," a small group of conservative Paulistas hastily prepared to avenge it.[65] March 19, St. Joseph's Day, the next important date in the religious calendar, was chosen as the day for the demonstration. Since St. Joseph was the patron saint of the family, the march was named "March of the Family with God for Liberty." Most of the women marchers, who outnumbered men, carried rosaries. The men carried Brazilian and state flags as well as placards with messages such as "Down with the Red imperialists!",

"Resignation or Impeachment," "Reforms, yes / With Russians, no." As they marched, participants chanted *"Um, dois, tres / Brizola no xadrez!"* (One, two, three / Brizola to the clink!) and *"Ta chegando a hora / de Jango ir embora"* (It's getting to be time / for Jango to go away.) So large was the number of participants that it took over an hour for the column to pass any given point.

Organizers exulted that whereas Goulart's rally had required weeks of preparation and great expense to the treasury, their march, organized in a few days at no cost to the taxpayer, had attracted many more people. But leaders on the Left dismissed the numbers who marched as middle class and politically insignificant. "Those are not the People," they said, clinging to their faith that the future lay with the proletariat.[66] Nor were liberal Catholic leaders impressed with the supposed defense of the rosary. Catholic leaders in São Paulo and in Belo Horizonte issued manifestos that echoed Goulart's address at the rally. They condemned the political exploitation of religious feeling and reaffirmed their determination to fight for reforms.

Leaders of women's clubs, especially those who had traveled to São Paulo to participate in the march, began to plan similar Marches of the Family with God for Liberty in their own cities. April 2 was selected as the date for such a march in Rio, with CAMDE in charge of preparations. Neusa Goulart Brizola, sister of Jango and wife of Brizola, countered with a plan by two leftist women's groups (the Liga Feminina da Guanabara and the Movimento Nacionalista Feminina) to stage a counterdemonstration to CAMDE's march on April 3. The CGT leadership contacted Goulart's advisors to plan future mass rallies, at each of which the president would announce the signing of an important reform bill.

Brazil appeared to be getting set for a battle of demonstrations. But the preoccupation with body counts at rallies probably did not reach very deep into Brazilian society. The visit of Brigitte Bardot to the beaches of Rio distracted many cariocas. In Brasília and its satellite shanty towns, 7,000 unemployed construction workers rioted off and on for three days, demanding food, jobs, and housing. The attention of bankers, economists, and businessmen involved in the import-export market was turned to Paris, where financial negotiations were under way with Brazil's six major creditors (including the United States) to reschedule debt repayment. President Goulart, speaking at a ceremony marking the signing of a contract with a German firm to export additional iron ore, insisted that Brazil was free of prejudice against foreign capital.[67] Bureaucrats at Itamarati, the Brazilian foreign service, began working on preparations for an official visit by French President Charles de Gaulle. Brazilian parents with sons in the army were concerned with the possibility that Brazil might furnish troops to the U.N. peace-keeping force being sent to Cyprus; there, conflict between Greek and Turkish Cypriots threatened to widen into an international war involving Greece, Turkey, and Great Britain.

Routines of daily life continued. Ticket and travel agencies in the major cities were mobbed—not by people trying to flee the country because of impending revolution—but by middle-class urbanites booking passage to resorts or other locations to spend the Holy Week holidays. Most of Brazil would be on a holiday schedule from Wednesday evening, March 25, through Easter Sunday, March 29. Goulart left Brasília Wednesday afternoon for his ranch in São Borja, Rio Grande do Sul. He hoped to get in some fishing.

"There is a general realization that Goulart has finally 'defined himself,'" reported an American embassy official, a few days after the Friday the 13th rally.[68] "The significance of the March 13 rally was unmistakable," concluded historian Thomas E. Skidmore, a few years later. "Goulart had finally turned to the radical left for his policies."[69]

Had he? True, the Left very much hoped he had, and the Right was convinced that he had made that choice long before March 13. There was talk among leftist leaders of a new Popular Front that would unite all leftist factions in support of the president's new drive for reforms. The leaders were optimistic about the chances of unity, despite the fact that a "Broad Front" that San Tiego Dantas had been attempting to organize had foundered. Goulart, basking in the support denied him at the time of his October state of siege request, thought he was really governing at last.

One must, however, guard against confusing the new outpouring of oratory about revolutionary change by leftist leaders with the oratory of Goulart. His next major address was his Message to Congress on March 15. The address was read to the Congress by Darcy Ribeiro, Goulart's secretary for civil affairs. Darcy had probably written most of it, just as he had prepared much of Goulart's speech at the rally. The message followed the rally script—i.e., it was fairly moderate in tone. It is necessary to make the prior assumption that Goulart definitely planned to subvert existing institutions in order to see his statements in this speech as threats.

195

Goulart claimed repeatedly that he was trying to bring public pressure to bear on Congress in order to get it to act on needed reforms. Such a tactic was not unknown to American presidents or other democratic chiefs of state. Why should he not be taken at his own words? In any case, Goulart made no apparent preparations either to stage a coup or to fend one off. Although CGT leaders worried about the open preparations for civil war by the radical Right, Goulart was satisfied that his own military "cover" was adequate to deal with any rebellion.

# 10

# April Fool!

---

*Future historians may well record the Brazilian revolution as the single most decisive victory for freedom in the mid-20th century.*

*Ambassador Lincoln Gordon*

*I have heard...that all of the members of the Brazilian Congress who advocated the kind of reforms which we have made a prerequisite for Alliance for Progress aid are now in prison.*

*Senator Albert Gore*

On the evening of March 13, Ambassador Gordon watched the first part of President Goulart's speech at the rally on television at the embassy. He had to leave for the airport to catch a plane to Washington and listened to the last part of the speech on the car radio. He thought that he recognized the hand of Darcy Ribeiro in the speech. Darcy, an anthropologist who had served as rector of the University of Brasília and as minister of education, was currently Goulart's secretary for civil affairs. The sight of Darcy standing next to Goulart on the speaker's platform, apparently prompting him from time to time, was enough to damn the entire rally in the eyes of the American ambassador. He regarded the Brazilian professor as some kind of hard-core Communist-liner, an outspoken anti-American nationalist, who, on several occasions, had had the effrontery to accuse the ambassador of meddling in Brazil's internal affairs.[1]

The new presidential decrees announced at the rally also thoroughly alarmed Gordon. Disagreeing with conservative Brazilian constitutional lawyer Carlos Medeiros da Silva, who had reviewed the SUPRA decree, the American ambassador thought it was unconstitutional, "without any legal, without any statutory basis."[2] And, to him the other decree nationalizing the small oil refineries seemed positively ominous. True, no American investment capital was at stake in these expropriations, but the takeover fever could easily spread. Most of the factions of the Left appeared to be uniting in support of the "new Goulart offensive," which embassy officials believed to have been "carefully planned." The American analysts tried to guess the contents of those careful plans. To keep the support of the Left, *perhaps* the plans called for "government encroachment following sectors: pharmaceuticals, petroleum distribution, air transport, foreign public relations firms, newsprint, meat packing, coffee exporting, and commercial banking." U.S. firms were "involved in all above specified industries except aviation and newsprint." *Perhaps* the future of American private corporate investments in Brazil was at stake. "Our contacts with U.S. business community in last few days have shown that most, if not all, view situation with alarm," cabled Chargé d'Affaires Gordon Mein on March 18.[3]

Alarming as these developments were, the embassy staff did not see an anti-Goulart coup as likely in the immediate future. In their opinion, Goulart's opponents had "definitely not effectively coalesced position... efforts to coordinate unified position in face of threat have not materialized." In fact, the embassy worried that the conspirators might become so discouraged that they might never even try to overthrow the government. "We [are] somewhat apprehensive that (1) if rapid deterioration of situation continues and (2) if opposition does not somehow rally, substantial amount of ground may be lost irrevocably. This leads us to wonder what actions...U.S. could take at this time to keep opposition from becoming overly demoralized in face of Goulart drive."[4]

At so critical a time no doubt Ambassador Gordon would have preferred to remain at his post in Rio. However, President Johnson had summoned all of the American ambassadors posted to Latin American countries to return to Washington to be briefed on changes in Latin American policy. Of course Gordon was pleased with the prospect of finally meeting the new president. When he had been in Washington two months previously for one of the routine conferences with State Department officials, he had been surprised that no appointment with President Johnson had been scheduled for him. President Kennedy had always seen him during his Washington visits.[5]

Lyndon Johnson personally shared neither the Kennedy preoccupation with Cuba[6] nor his fear that Brazil and other South American countries might fall victim to international communist intrigue and expansion. The Rostow-Kennedy theories about a post-Sputnik Soviet offensive failed to alarm the new president. Unlike his predecessor, Johnson was much more interested in domestic problems than in foreign affairs. But, in light of his lifelong association with Mexican-Americans in Texas, LBJ considered himself something of an expert on Latin America. He had been prepared to lend Kennedy a hand in this area and had been somewhat miffed to find his expertise ignored by the New Frontier's nation builders in the Kennedy White House. While still vice president, Johnson have privately expressed the opinion that Kennedy's entire Latin American policy had ended up as a "thorough going mess" because the Kennedy approach was too "ideological," too antibusiness, insufficiently "realistic," and not "tough-minded" enough to work in a region such as Latin America. On principle, Johnson believed that U.S. self-interest—not development or ideology—must be the starting point for all negotiations with the Latin republics.[7]

Taking office, Johnson vowed to complete what John Kennedy had set out to do. In foreign affairs, that obviously included the revitalization of his faltering Alliance for Progress. One of Johnson's first appointments was that of Thomas Mann to be assistant secretary of state for Latin America. Mann was simultaneously named special assistant to the president and coordinator of the Alliance for Progress, in an effort to enhance his power and position and enable him to turn things around in the troublesome region. Within a year the president would begin to focus on Vietnam as the most critical area for American interests abroad, but at first Latin America claimed his attention. The first foreign affairs crisis he faced was in Panama. After an incident in which American high school students raised an American flag without also raising a Panamanian flag, full-scale nationalist rioting broke out in January 1964. Panamanian nationalists and government officials demanded that renegotiation of the Panama Canal Treaty begin at once.

Thomas Mann, a career diplomat with a great deal of experience in Latin America, seemed the perfect choice to do the type of job Johnson wanted done. He had turned down President Kennedy's request that he stay on as assistant secretary for Latin America because, right at the outset, he had strong reservations about the whole Alliance for Progress effort. He considered it entirely too visionary, with too much emphasis on "revolution," certain to be misunderstood by the Latins.[8] Mann prided himself on being a "hard-headed, down-to-earth sort of fellow" who made no attempt to conceal his cynicism about the Latin American republics.[9] So skeptical was he about the chances for successful, genuine reforms in the region, that he was unwilling to push for any. Mann was sometimes "a little insensitive to the need for reform," National Security Advisor McGeorge Bundy (a Kennedy appointee) complained to President Johnson.[10]

But the president shared Mann's skepticism and his distaste for Alliance for Progress rhetoric about revolution and structural reform. Hadn't Panamanian nationalism been inflamed by such talk? Johnson authorized Mann to redraw the lines and restate the limits of U.S. policy toward Latin America. Thus, all American ambassadors in Latin America were summoned to Washington in mid-March 1964 to be briefed on the new limits. In his address to the conference on March 18, Mann listed the promotion of economic growth, protection of American investments, anticommunism, and observance of the principle of nonintervention in the internal affairs of sovereign states as the basic objectives of U.S. policy in the hemisphere. Implicit in such a listing, though Mann refrained from even mentioning the Alliance for Progress, was the idea that the Kennedy goals of promoting political democracy and basic social reforms were being dropped. Mann stressed instead the idea of nonintervention and the new administration's policy on the diplomatic recognition of Latin governments that might come to power via armed force rather than through the ballot box. American opposition to right-wing regimes that came in by coups had never succeeded in unseating them, said Mann. Such opposition merely involved the United States in the internal political affairs of Latin nations. Therefore in the future the United States would stop making distinctions among new regimes and recognize any government that was in control.

To the annoyance of the White House, a detailed account of Mann's address was immediately leaked to the press.[11] Media pundits focused on the address as an important policy shift. Dedicated Kennedy partisans, busy developing a Kennedy legend, soon condemned the Mann-Johnson approach to Latin America as the betrayal of a sacred trust.[12] But the fact was that at most Mann was leading a shift in emphasis, not introducing something entirely new. The difference was in style and sound, not in substance. As detailed earlier (see chap. 5), as early as February 1962 when the ITT subsidiary in Brazil was expropriated, Kennedy had backed away from his early coolness toward the American multinationals involved in Latin America. He had become solicitous of their opinion as well as manifestly concerned about their protection. Anticommunism had always been the mainspring of the Kennedy policy toward the Third World. And, though initially Kennedy had established a policy of withholding aid and diplomatic recognition from Latin military governments that came to power by overthrowing civilian, constitutionally elected regimes, he was ready to abandon the effort by late 1963. Assistant Secretary of State for Latin America Edwin Martin signaled the change

200

in an article published in the *New York Herald Tribune* on October 6, 1963.[13] Although the U.S. government deplored military coups, wrote Martin, and although it believed that military men often showed little capacity for government, the United States could hardly do more than accept the fait accompli when the people involved were unwilling to fight for a democratic regime. Martin was paving the way for American recognition of recently established military regimes in the Dominican Republic and Honduras. He formally extended recognition to these two regimes on December 12, 1963, in one of his final acts as assistant secretary. In his address to the ambassadors on March 18, Martin's successor, Mann, was obviously only underlining this new policy, while omitting the verbiage about American dislike for military regimes.

The military coup in Brazil took place fourteen days later. It was almost as though the Brazilian military conspirators had been waiting for some final signal of American approval, the signal supplied by Assistant Secretary Mann. Actually, of course the American blessing of their cause had been made manifest long before mid-March 1964. The signal the conspirators had been waiting for was one from Goulart—he had to take some final outrageous step that would galvanize and unite the opposition. Up to that point the conspirators had been unable to get their own act together.

Coup coordination by the "secret" command in Rio headed by General Castello Branco was complicated by the appearance of a second secret revolutionary command post headed by General Costa e Silva, the director of army production and works. There were, in addition, a number of other active conspiracy centers in other parts of the country and within the other services—the navy and air force. The Castello Branco-IPES group attempted to establish contact with all such centers, as well as with the more important state governors, in order to coordinate plans.[14] It was felt that it would take until at least April 2, and possibly until April 10, to reach understandings with all antigovernment groups.[15]

The basic plan of action called for a march on Rio de Janeiro by the state militia of Minas Gerais plus the federal troops stationed in that state, to be immediately followed by a sweep through the Paraíba Valley and on to Rio by the Second Army stationed in São Paulo. Both forces would confront the First Army in Rio, the army considered the most loyal to Goulart. After the drive toward Rio was well under way, the Fourth Army in Recife and elements of the Third Army in Rio Grande do Sul would attempt to secure those areas.

As far as Castello Branco was concerned, the commander of the Second Army posed the biggest problem for a successful coup. General Amaury Kruel was a personal friend of Goulart and personally hostile to Castello Branco.[16] If Kruel should refuse to join the conspiracy and insist on fulfilling his duty of defending the constitutional government, the military forces of the rebels might be crushed, caught between the First and Second armies. The Fourth Army and the parts of the Third that were ready to join the coup attempt were too distant from the political center of the country to decide the matter. A stream of emissaries from Castello Branco, Costa e Silva, and Governor Magalhães Pinto of Minas Gerais visited Second Army headquarters during the weeks after the March 13 rally, all attempting to persuade Kruel to abandon Goulart. But until the coup was actually underway, Kruel promised only to talk to his friend, the president, to try to convince him to break with the "Communists." However, the conspirators were encouraged by rumors that, in a showdown, Kruel would be arrested by the officers under him should he opt to fulfill his sworn duties to the legal government.[17]

In the end it was these middle-ranking officers—the majors, colonels, and lieutenant generals—who played the key roles in the collapse of the Goulart government. Events during a five-day period from March 26 through March 30 convinced those officers that Goulart must be overthrown. Questions of military discipline—issues that cut closer than communist ideology—seemed to be the central issues. Even those officers who were unconvinced about a communist threat became concerned about their future as officers. The communists, and/or those who had Goulart's ear, hoped to transform the army into a "simple militia," cautioned Army Chief-of-Staff Castello Branco in his March 20 circular, echoing the manifesto issued by War Minister Denys during the failed coup attempt of August 1961.

A dispute between Navy Minister Sílvio Mota and an association of enlisted men triggered the confrontation that led directly to the overthrow of Goulart. The Association of Sailors and Marines had been organized in March 1962 by left-wing university students who had enlisted in the navy to do their compulsory military service—service that was ordinarily waived for university students. The association was deeply distrusted and disliked by navy officers who regarded it as communist dominated. Actually, whatever communist domination there was did not extend very far. The president of the group in March 1964, Corporal José Anselmo dos Santos (dubbed Cabo Anselmo by the media), was later revealed to be an infiltrated right-wing agent, who was probably on the CIA payroll.[18]

As long as the association confined itself to pressing for improvements in living conditions for navy enlisted men, it was tolerated by the navy command. In the wake of the March 13 rally, however, its directors began taking overt political stands in support of Goulart reform initiatives. Pointing out that such political activity violated laws forbidding armed forces personnel from engaging in politics, Navy Minister Mota ordered ten days of disciplinary detention for the eleven directors of the association. The association responded by calling for a giant protest meeting of its members and sympathizers, to be held the evening of March 25 in the Rio headquarters building of the Metallurgical Workers Union.

Goulart proceeded to make a series of mistakes in dealing with this situation. His first mistake was to blame the navy minister for the confrontation, failing to see that Mota was under great pressure from his peers, other navy officers, to do something to reassert discipline. Instead of making some gesture of support for the minister who had served him loyally (to the extent of being regarded as a Goulart toady), the president let it be known that he felt Mota had mishandled the situation and needlessly antagonized the enlisted men. Instead of expressing disapproval of the protest rally, Goulart implied that he personally would be willing to attend the gathering, were it not for the fact that was the day he was leaving to spend the Holy Week holidays in Rio Grande do Sul. He asked Justice Minister Jurema to attend as his representative, telling Jurema that since so few of the admirals supported him, he needed the support of the enlisted men.

After the president had left town, Jurema decided that attendance as presidential surrogate would not be a good idea. He saw the position of his fellow minister, Mota, more clearly than had Goulart. Jurema did feel that the constant breaches of discipline and the open antigovernment activities of senior navy officers had stimulated the sailors to similarly take up political activity. But he realized that any hint of a presidential endorsement of the enlisted men's rally could only undermine the authority of the navy minister and, therefore, of the entire administration. He spent the rest of the day fruitlessly attempting to get the association leaders to call off their meeting. He failed to communicate his concerns to the vacationing president.[19]

Goulart's next series of errors came two days later, on Good Friday, March 27. He flew back from Rio Grande do Sul to handle the confrontation, which had become much worse. Navy Minister Mota had ordered the arrest of forty sailors who had organized the rally. Fired up by the defiant oratory of their president, Cabo Anselmo, about 600 of the sailors attending the rally had then declared themselves in "permanent session" and refused to leave the building when ordered to return to their posts. They demanded the firing of Mota and the release of the association leaders who had turned themselves in earlier to serve their ten days' detention. The navy minister decided to use force if necessary to arrest the mutineers. But the first detachment of marines sent to carry out the order laid down their weapons and joined their comrades inside the building. Mota managed to persuade an army commander to send troops to take up positions around the union building, but the commander was unwilling to order his men to enter without a direct order from the war minister (incommunicado, undergoing surgery in a hospital) or the president. A second detachment of marines also held back awaiting army assistance.

In choosing to try to defuse the confrontation by negotiation instead of firepower, Goulart was being true to his personal style of administration. Probably most Brazilians, especially the sailors themselves, were relieved; only the fiercest of the admirals, holding their own "permanent session" in the Navy Ministry, wanted blood.[20] But it was an error for Goulart to accept mediation by the CGT and to negotiate primarily with the CGT leaders instead of with the admirals and the mutinous sailors themselves. The labor leaders had been brought into the affair by Darcy Ribeiro because the mutiny was taking place in a union building, which Darcy and others considered a type of sanctuary, immune from military intervention. However, since the officer corps was already convinced that the CGT was a communist organization bent on destroying the military institutions, its leaders did not make ideal mediators.

It was also a serious error for Goulart to accept Mota's resignation before the confrontation had been resolved, thus yielding to the key demand of the rebellious enlisted men. Compounding this mistake, without sounding out the admirals and officers at the Navy Ministry, Goulart accepted the suggestion of the CGT mediators (who claimed to be simply relaying a request by the mutineers) that sixty-nine-year-old retired Admiral Paulo Mário da Cunha Rodrigues be named the new navy minister. The appointment was totally unacceptable to the officer corps; not only did Rodrigues appear to be the nominee of the CGT, but he seemed to lack the experience and "force" needed to assert his authority. Another strike against him, in the eyes of his racist brother officers, was the fact that his wife was a black.[21]

Goulart also obviously erred in failing to clearly repudiate the idea of an immediate amnesty for the rebels. Although it was the new navy minister who made the actual decision to free the sailors almost at once, amnesty at some point was part of the agreement negotiated by the CGT leaders before Rodrigues had been named navy minister.[22] The spectacle of the rebellious enlisted men celebrating with a noisy victory parade through downtown Rio infuriated their officers and alarmed the commissioned ranks of the other services. What would the military institution be worth when enlisted men could with impunity organize themselves into labor unions, consort with the CGT, hire and fire the service ministers, and be cheered as heroes when they rejected orders to return to their duty posts and barricaded themselves in a union building? The officer corps was not impressed with Justice Minister Jurema's argument that the sailors had not been in a state of rebellion because they had not been armed. Nor were they much impressed with his suggestion that the grant of amnesty to the enlisted men was analogous to the grant of amnesty to officers who staged rebellions against President Kubitschek.[23] To them, rebellion and conspiracy were part of the perquisites of commissioned rank.

"These lamentable events were the result of a plan directed and perfectly executed by a group already identified by the Brazilian nation as interested in the general subversion of the country, with clearly Communistic characteristics," read a manifesto issued the next day, signed by 220 navy officers. They were referring to the CGT. In his March 20 circular, Castello Branco had hypothesized that the CGT planned first to paralyze the country with strikes, then put forward a "revolutionary scheme." It was the duty of the armed forces, said the army chief of staff, to thwart such a scheme. One group of admirals wanted to use force immediately to seize the Navy Ministry Building, oust the new navy minister, and defy Goulart. But Castello and his co-conspirators, afraid that a premature uprising would be crushed, were unwilling to advance the date of their coup. They gave the admirals no encouragement, despite the naval officers' warning that the damage "cannot be isolated in the naval sector. It is an event with repercussion on the Armed Forces, and the Army and Air Force cannot remain indifferent to it. It clearly involves the infiltration of agents of subversion within the structure of the Armed Forces."[24]

Goulart's final blunder was to appear Monday evening, March 30, at an assembly for noncoms in Rio's Automobile Club. Flanked by most of his cabinet ministers and by Cabo Anselmo, the president delivered the principal address at a ceremony commemorating the fortieth anniversary of the Benevolent Association of Military Police Sergeants.

"That assembly was decisive for the coup," observed Luis Carlos Prestes, head of the Brazilian Communist Party, but a former army officer himself. "What army officer was going to remain tranquil knowing that the President of the Republic addressed the sergeants in that language? The sergeants would feel direct ties with the President and would disobey the officers. The person primarily responsible for that assembly was Darcy Ribeiro, who held the leftist views acceptable to Jango."[25] At the time that Goulart had been debating whether to go to the assembly, he had not solicited Prestes's opinion. Nor had he asked for the opinion of Deputy Tancredo Neves, his former prime minister. Tancredo went out of his way to urge Goulart not to go, not to throw firewood on the fire of possible civil war. The president's appearance at such an assembly, immediately after the crisis of the sailors' mutiny, would, Tancredo felt, be interpreted as a challenge to the military high command.[26]

"Don't fire the first shot, Mr. President. Don't go to the Automobile Club," urged another deputy, Tenório Cavalcanti.

"You talk of shooting, Tenório, but there's no question of that," Jango responded. "Don't be alarmed; everything's going quite well."[27]

Perhaps, as a few observers thought,[28] Goulart might still have saved his position and defused the crisis, had he used the nationally broadcast speech to denounce communism, reassert the need for stricter discipline in the armed forces, and announce punishments for the enlisted men who had mutinied. However, Jango did not even use the carefully vague speech that had been written for him. Clearly upset by that day's editorials (that charged him with preparing to stage his own coup) and by the manifesto of the navy officers (just released that morning), Goulart spoke extemporaneously. He was determined to answer his critics. Interpretations of that answer varied sharply with the listener. "The last view that the country had of its president was of a wounded and ferocious animal, pressed against a wall," said one.[29] Another journalist saw an intensely sincere moralist, not a wild animal, "with the ardor and sincerity of a student making his debut at the podium, he defined himself as a nationalist, never as a communist."[30]

Goulart charged the "privileged minority" conspiring against him with "preaching hate" and with cynically attempting to manipulate the religious faith of the people by calling his administration anti-Catholic and communist.[31] He insisted that the reforms that he was seeking were being sought "strictly in accordance with the law and the Constitution." Of course, all constitutions needed to be modified with time, according to legal procedures, as he was proposing. "In the 1961 crisis, the same

Pharisees who today exhibit bogus zeal for the Constitution wanted to tear it up and bury it under the cold tombstone of fascist dictatorship." Sure that his opponents were the same ones he had faced down in 1961, Goulart tried to sound hopeful that the result would be the same this time. He defended his actions in dealing wth the sailors' mutiny as necessary to prevent needless bloodshed. Denying that he personally was responsible for the amnesty granted (the navy minister had authority over that), Jango insisted that he understood the need for discipline in the armed forces. "But discipline cannot be built on hatred and high irritation. Discipline is built on the mutual respect between those who command and those who are commanded." He concluded his address by charging that greedy foreign and domestic business interests were bankrolling the conspiracy to overthrow the government, "the terrible campaign that at this very moment is in motion throughout the country." It was, he charged, especially the interests hurt by his effort to limit profit remittances, expropriate private oil refineries, and impose some rent controls.[32]

To most Brazilians it did not really matter what Goulart said that night. He was speaking to "an audience that had decided to no longer listen to him, consider him, or believe in him."[33] And for most of the military officer corps, just the fact that the president appeared at such a gathering clinched the argument that he must be ousted.

The impetuous General Olympio Mourão, until then held in check by other conspirators, resolved to wait no longer. Mourão, commander of the Fourth Infantry Division and the Fourth Military Region in Minas Gerais, had a personal reason for being in a hurry. A military coup and/or civil war would provide his last chance to win military glory: he would reach retirement age on May 9. As one of the few senior conspirators who still had actual command of troops, he resented being constantly told to wait by four-star but troopless generals such as Castello Branco, Costa e Silva, or Cordeiro de Farias. Now, in late March, he discovered that a general under his command was as impatient as himself. General Carlos Luís Guedes believed firmly in astrology. He suggested that Mourão and he start the revolution on March 30 since this would be the last day of the full moon.

Both generals had conferred frequently with the governor of Minas Gerais, José Magalhães Pinto. The governor controlled the state's militia forces, larger than the army units controlled by Guedes and Mourão, though less well trained. Pinto had agreed, in private conversations, not only to join in an attempt to overthrow Goulart but to initiate it. Publicly, however, the governor still seemed to be straddling the fence. After the March 13 rally he conferred with anti-Goulart governors Lacerda and Adhemar de Barros, but he also consulted pro-Goulart governors Miguel Arraes and Seixas Doria. He issued manifestos that urged both basic reforms and the preservation of the constitution. Until March 31, Goulart had the impression that Magalhães Pinto was on his side.

Mourão wanted the governor to make it clear to the people of Minas and to Brazil as a whole that he opposed Goulart. The support of the civilian population would be vitally important in a civil war; the general wanted the governor to issue some sort of "strong" manifesto, a clear call for the overthrow of the president, a manifesto that would invite the nation to join that cause. Without some such "cover," Mourão feared his troops might be defeated by troops loyal to the government. The general expected the governor to submit the proposed text of such a manifesto to him for editing before it was published. He fancied himself as something of a writer. He had been the author of the Cohen Plan, a crude forgery detailing an imaginary plan for a communist takeover in 1937; the document had been used to justify the military coup that gave Vargas dictatorial power. In 1964 Mourão had the vague feeling that something similar was needed to legitimize the overthrow of the government. Magalhães Pinto did draft another of his manifestos on March 30. He released it to the press without submitting it to Mourão first. Furious, the general denounced the proclamation as insipid and announced that he would therefore refuse to lead troops against Goulart.[34]

He changed his mind after listening to Goulart's speech to the sergeants at the Automobile Club. In the early morning hours of March 31, Mourão began making telephone calls: to General Guedes requesting the assembly of troops at his headquarters in Juiz da Fora; to other officers in the state ordering the arrest of Catholic activists, student leaders, and union officials;[35] to fellow conspirators in Rio and São Paulo telling them that the revolution had begun.

At 9:00 in the morning, when he learned of Mourão's activities, Castello Branco in Rio telephoned both Magalhães Pinto and Guedes, attempting to convince them that they must somehow stop Mourão from staging so premature a demarche. The work of coordination was still not complete, Castello warned, and an isolated rebellion could easily be crushed. But, hearing that it was too late to stop Mourão, Castello Branco and his secret command staff scrambled to tell all their contacts that the big day had been advanced and the uprising had begun.

Castello Branco was right: the coordinating work had not been completed. Despite the years of plotting, the revolution unfolded in a wildly haphazard, hit-or-miss fashion, with none of the participants sure who was in charge. The two secret command posts of Castello Branco and Costa e Silva both operated at full steam, duplicating each other's efforts to line up support for the coup. American army attaché Vernon Walters, many of the governors, and perhaps the majority of the army officers thought the supreme commander of the revolution was Castello Branco. But other officers were sure that it was Costa e Silva or perhaps retired Marshal Denys who was calling the shots. Vice Admiral Rademaker Grünewald believed that his actions in taking over the Navy Ministry building determined the fall of Goulart, while General Kruel was confident that he controlled the key, and Mourão just knew that he was making a revolution singlehandedly. A number of new proclamations and manifestos were read over the radio, troops were marched here and there, roads were blocked. But the most important action took place on the telephone, as officers throughout the country received calls from one or the other of the command posts (and in some cases by both) and asked to declare themselves "with us" or "for the Communists."[36]

Anxious to prove their valor, the large number of officers who had desk jobs in Rio (still at the time the working capital for most government agencies) or who were enrolled in advanced officer-training classes, strapped on their sidearms and hurried to the Army Staff and Command School to volunteer for action. They were organized into "staffs," each headed by a general, and assigned tasks such as seizing military strongpoints, arresting Justice Minister Jurema, or infiltrating other units to find out what action Goulart was planning. Believing that most of the sergeants and enlisted men in the city had been corrupted by the communists, the officers moved about very cautiously, ready to start firing every time an enlisted man was spotted. Finding that most of the enlisted men either acted "completely unconcerned, as though there were no Revolution unfolding"[37] or were ready to put down their arms as soon as ordered to do so by the clusters of officers, the volunteer revolutionaries were able to congratulate themselves on their courage without slaughtering sergeants or innocent civilian bystanders, as they excitedly fired their pistols.

The steady rain that began in Rio the evening of March 31 and continued most of the next day discouraged demonstrations, either for or against the government, but there were some incidents. A pro-Goulart crowd gathered at the Military Club building in Cinelândia square to jeer the military. Officers inside the club fired into the unarmed crowd when a group of students started to enter the building. In addition, a few shots were exchanged with progovernment sentries at several checkpoints. A number were wounded in these exchanges, and three civilians were killed.[38]

Of all of the displays of bravado enacted this April Fool's day, the stellar performance was turned in by Governor Carlos Lacerda. General Castello Branco at first attempted to persuade Lacerda to abandon the governor's mansion, which was likely to be a prime target for forces loyal to Goulart. But Lacerda refused to leave his post. "Each person, General, must do his duty as best he can," he told Castello. "Civilians also know how to die. Good luck!"[39] Lacerda had prepared his own defenses. To reinforce the 500 state police detailed to guard Palácio Guanabara, he accepted the services of volunteer gunmen, primarily civilians, who began gathering on mansion grounds as soon as news of Mourão's march spread. Air Force Colonel João Paulo Moreira Burnier, a right-wing extremist who had been granted amnesty after attempting to overthrow Kubitschek, was put in charge of the volunteers. He was, in fact, already acquainted with many of them since he had been secretly drilling them as a paramilitary force, using the grounds of a nurses' training school located near Palácio Guanabara.[40]

The defenders of the mansion expected to be attacked by the tanks of the Marine Corps. The Marine commander, Admiral Cândido Aragão, was staunchly pro-Goulart. To try to block the anticipated tank assault, city garbage trucks were driven to the palace and parked across all access streets. Burnier planned to use his volunteers as some sort of antitank shock force. Some of them would man the jeeps he had equipped with bazookas, while the others provided the cover. For his part, Lacerda ordered loudspeakers rigged up outside the perimeter of the mansion so that he could personally address his troops and the neighborhood and tell everyone to be calm but wary. Battle-ready, wearing a leather jacket and lugging around a submachine gun, the governor periodically made rounds of inspection of the defenses. He also spent a lot of time talking to a radio-television audience in Minas Gerais and São Paulo, reaching it via a ham radio network and one of the two functioning telephones in the mansion. The local radio and television stations had been occupied by progovernment forces that morning.

Periodically, rumors swept Palácio Guanabara that the attack was about to begin. One such alarm was flashed while Lacerda was broadcasting via the telephone to Minas Gerais. "My friends of Minas," he had started, "my fellow countrymen, help me, help the government of Guanabara, under siege but undaunted, encircled but ready for all-out resistance. Help me spread, throughout Brazil, information about what the truth is; help me elevate the truth against slander and infamy; help me, all you free Brazilian soldiers, in order that the liberty against which these men conspire can be restored. . . . Brazil doesn't want Cain in the Presidency of the Republic. Cain, what hast thou done with thy brethren? Your brothers who are going to be killed by your Communist accomplices; your brothers who were robbed so that you might transform yourself into the largest landowner and biggest thief in Brazil. Down with João Goulart!"

It was at this moment that Lacerda was told that the marines had arrived. As everyone in the Palácio dove for the floor, Lacerda asked for the microphone that was connected with the loudspeakers rigged up outside. "The Palácio Guanabara is being attacked at this very moment by a band of desperados!" he shouted over the telephone. His spellbound audience in Minas Gerais and Sâo Paulo heard him shouting simultaneously to the imaginary attacking marines. "Brazilians! Put down your arms! You're being deceived by an unscrupulous officer! Aragão, you coward, guilty of incest, leave your soldiers and come settle this farce with me. I want to kill you with my revolver; do you hear, Aragão? Man to man! The soldiers have nothing to do with this."[41]

The marines never came, and their commander, Aragão, never heard the challenge to a personal shootout at ten paces. The communist hordes neither stormed the garbage trucks nor infiltrated through the back garden gate. No forces of any kind approached the Palácio until several tanks that had been guarding the presidential palace made the short trip over to defend the governor instead.

By the time this happened, 4:00 in the afternoon of April 1, Goulart had already left Rio. He was in Brasília, discussing his remaining options with some aides there. His options were limited since he had left behind what was supposed to have been his major military "cover"—the First Army and the marine and air force units stationed in Rio. His former friend, General Kruel, had already made public his betrayal. Few military units were located in the nation's new capital. Goulart's stopover there was intended to be temporary; he had already made arrangements to continue on to his home state of Rio Grande do Sul to make his last stand under the protection of the Third Army.[42]

Justice Minister Jurema, who spent much of March 31 as well as April 1 at the presidential Palácio das Laranjeiras, has described the complete confusion reigning there during those critical early hours after the rebel forces from Minas Gerais began their march on Rio. The previous evening Jurema and the other ministers had left the sergeants' rally in a euphoric state, feeling that "with the people, with the Armed Forces, and with legality, there would be nothing to fear."[43] They were confident that the "people" were really on Goulart's side and that the president's military "cover" must be powerful, or he would never have gone to the rally at all. The phone calls early the next morning about troop movements in Minas Gerais were a rude shock. Even more upsetting was the apparent inability of Goulart and his top military aides to decide on an appropriate military response, even though they conferred throughout the day.

> No one even knew what was happening! Why wasn't the city ostensibly taken over [by the First Army] as on the other occasions? Why did Col. Borges [head of Lacerda's Political and Social Police] seem to be the commander of the First Army in dominating the strategic positions of the city? Why didn't one hear the clatter of a single tank? Why?
>
> Airplanes in Santa Cruz base roaring for battle, well-armed marines with high morale yearning for an order to fight, and very strong units of the army, such as GUE, stayed put, their commanders worn out waiting for a word of the order that never arrived.[44]

Actually Goulart had given the orders, but they never trickled down to the level of the officers, noncoms, and enlisted men inclined to obey them. Those top military officials whom Jango trusted did in fact remain loyal to him (with the crucial exception of Kruel),[45] but when they passed his orders on to the officers beneath them, nothing happened. Their subordinates responded sluggishly, if at all, and manifested readiness to betray the government and join the *golpistas* as soon as it was judged safe—i.e., as soon as the officers were no longer in a position where they might fear retribution by their own subordinates and noncoms. Thus, General Milton Barbosa Guimarães, head of the staff of First Army Commander General Armando Âncora, was in on the conspiracy and effectively sabotaged the efforts of General Luis da Cunha Mello to move rapidly against the Mourão-Guedes forces in Minas Gerais. Guimarães simply refused to turn over armored personnel carriers to Mello, despite a written order from Goulart. Subordinate officers under Cunha Mello's command accompanied their units, ostensibly ready to deal with the insurgency, but actually only waiting to make contact with the Mourão-Guedes forces in order to defect. The air force officers loyal to

Goulart never received any order to bomb or strafe the rebels in Minas Gerais or the Second Army headed by Kruel. The officers charged with arresting Castello Branco never managed to ascend the few floors in the War Ministry to reach him.[46]

Goulart personally seemed to have had a horror of unleashing genuine civil war, with civilians joining the battle. He rejected the request of union leaders for arms to combat Lacerda's police and fight for the government. Perhaps Goulart was too conservative to want to see social upheaval along class lines; perhaps he believed that resistance would be useless since the United States was prepared to intervene militarily and thus internationalize the conflict. According to later reports, San Tiago Dantas (still acting as Goulart's advisor, although no longer in the government) strongly warned him that American recognition of the insurgents in Minas Gerais was imminent and would be followed by open military intervention. In any case, when he disembarked at the Porto Alegre airport at 4:00 A.M. on April 2, Goulart realized that not even the Third Army was loyal to him. No troops were stationed at the airport to receive him. Only one captain and three tanks stood by on guard duty. After quarreling with his brother-in-law, Brizola, over the desirability of making a heroic, macho last stand, Goulart left for one of his ranches in the interior of the state. For the next two days he flew from ranch to ranch, evading army patrols. On April 4 he crossed the border into exile in Uruguay. He was destined to be the first Brazilian president to die in exile.

Goulart's fear of overt American intervention was well founded.

Two or three days after the victorious Revolution, I [Carlos Lacerda] had a visit from Ambassador Lincoln Gordon, a visit of congratulations and jubilation, and he said the following to me (in the presence of Rafael de Almeida Magalhães and other people who were in the room): "You accomplished something wonderful! That Revolution without bloodshed and so rapid! With that a situation was avoided that would have been extremely sad, disagreeable, with unforeseeable consequences on the future of our relations: you averted the need for us to intervene in the conflict!"[47]

American contingency planning for a coup and/or possible civil war began in September 1963 during one of Ambassador Gordon's periodic visits to Washington.[48] When the ambassador met President Johnson for the first time, on March 19, 1964, he was able to assure him that the embassy had continued contingency planning "in view of the civil war possibilities."[49]

The military aspect of the American plan was dubbed Brother Sam when put into operation on March 31. It called for the dispatch of a "fast carrier task group with required support for operations in the South Atlantic" in the "vicinity of Santos."[50] Since the "Communists" were thought to control Brazil's oil refineries, tankers to provide emergency oil supplies to the "democratic forces" were included in the Brother Sam task force. Initially, American direct aid to the insurgents was to be limited to oil. But after Ambassador Gordon warned on March 27 that a Communist takeover of Brazil was an immediate threat, worried contingency planners added a 110-ton "package" of small arms and ammunition as aid that might be turned over to the Brazilian conspirators.[51] Since no armed resistance to the coup materialized, the Brother Sam operation was cancelled on April 3, before the fleet had neared Brazilian waters.

On the political side, contingency planning called for "quick recognition and support to any regime which the Brazilians install to supplant the Goulart regime if it seems reasonably firmly installed and offers prospects of providing a more constructive and friendly administration, but press hard for action to follow constitutional paths insofar as possible."[52] Although the new Brazilian regime was installed by following clearly unconstitutional paths, American officials followed the prepared script. A special interagency task force was set up at the State Department on March 31, almost before the coup began, to consider emergency relief and longer-term economic assistance "to possible and acceptable post-coup Brazilian government."[53]

Of course the post-coup government was deemed acceptable, irrespective of how it was formed. Acting in the dead of night (2:00 A.M., April 2) without a vote by the Congress, at a time when the constitutional president was still in the country, Senate president Auro Moura Andrade declared the presidency vacant and swore in Chamber of Deputies president Ranieri Mazzilli as the acting president of the republic.[54] Mazilli did not, however, get the powers of a president. Instead he served as a figurehead chief of state, dutifully following the instructions given him by General Costa e Silva. This general, without any constitutional path whatever, without as much as a canvass of fellow officers or a vote by the Military Club, had declared himself, first, commander in chief of the National Army and, second, head of a self-appointed military junta that named itself the Revolutionary High Command. Nevertheless, despite the blatant illegality and the makeshift nature of the post-coup regime, Ambassador Gordon strongly urged Washington to have President Johnson immediately recognize and endorse Mazzilli. Gordon prevailed over the objection of Assistant Secretary of State Mann, who thought such action, less than twenty-four hours after Mazzilli was illegally sworn in, was a shade precipitous. The evening of April 2, the White House released a presidential statement extending the "warmest good wishes" to His Excellency Ranieri Mazzilli "on your installation as President of the United States of Brazil."[55]

Publicly the State Department stood by the myth that Secretary of State Rusk put forth at his news conference the next day, that "in the case of Brazil...the succession there occurred as foreseen by the Constitution," and therefore the question of recognition of a new government did not arise.[56] Privately, American officials were troubled by the illegality and the ambiguity of the succession. Ambassador Gordon urged the head of the embassy branch in Brasília to press Brazilian congressional leaders to ratify the swearing in of Mazzilli ex post facto. Official concern was also privately expressed as it became clear that Mazzilli's authority was nominal and that he would be replaced, before the thirty days provided in the constitution, by a general who was ineligible to serve as president. Article 139 of the constitution that the coup makers were supposedly dedicated to defend stated that chiefs of the General Staff (the office that Castello Branco held) were ineligible to run for the office of president or vice president until three months after they had vacated their posts.[57]

The witch-hunt that followed the coup was perhaps the greatest shock of all to the American officials who had cherished the illusion that "democratic forces" had vanquished communist totalitarians. Through the utilization of the lists of "subversives" compiled by IPES and other right-wing organizations, thousands of Brazilians—union officials, students, intellectuals, left-of-center politicians, peasant leaders, Catholic activists—were arrested and held without charges or the right of habeas corpus. Without the formality of search warrants, private homes and offices were ransacked by police and army units in a search for subversive literature or stockpiled weapons.[58] Foreigners as well as Brazilian citizens were suddenly deprived of their rights. The Hungarian Embassy was raided and rifled. Soldiers invaded newspaper offices, including those of the *New York Times* and the Associated Press, rummaged through their files, and imposed censorship.[59] A Chinese diplomatic mission suffered the most. The Guanabara state police imprisoned the nine members of a visiting Chinese trade mission on the grounds that they were really interested in subversion, not trade. Lacerda's police supposedly uncovered a Chinese plot to assassinate Lacerda by flying kites, ingeniously loaded with bombs, over the Palácio Guanabara. The kites were supposed to release their explosive cargo when in the desired position.[60] The Chinese were held in prison for more than a year.

No doubt these early excesses were due at least in part to the natural frustration of the officers who had rushed out, armed to the teeth, to do battle with Cuban-trained, Russian-equipped hordes of sergeants, peasants, workers, and students, only to find themselves charging windmills. There were no trained guerrilla bands, no caches of weapons, no plans by noncoms to murder officers, no crowds of defiant union strikers, no secret, Communist-run drill camps for peasant militants. There was no way to demonstrate valor under fire. Raids on private homes, takeovers of union headquarters, the arrest of potential—if not actual—subversives, all helped to relieve frustration and to justify the war preparations. However, in part the witch-hunt was also due to the deep conviction that the witches existed but were in hiding, biding their time to strike back. Their heads full of information about an international communist offensive in which Brazil was a "target of convenience," the true believers in anticommunism worried that their war—a part of the struggle of Western Christian civilization versus Eastern materialist communism—had not yet been won and that it would be foolhardy to lay down arms without first carrying out a thorough purge. Thus, Rio's anticommunist cardinal, Dom Jaime de Barros, gave his blessing to Operation Clean-Up. He stated that

> victory achieved will be of no value if battle remains incomplete, only suspended....no persecution should take place...but without punishment of guilty, we risk loss of final battle, that is, salvation of fatherland...to punish those who were [guilty] is an act of mercy also.[61]

Although he had never shown any compunction about lecturing President Goulart about his behavior or that of his brother-in-law, Ambassador Gordon appeared reluctant to chide the new Brazilian authorities about their excesses. After Assistant Secretary of State Mann instructed him to "bring influence to bear to check or slow down such developments," the ambassador and the embassy staff did mention the importance of "maintenance [of] constitutional formalities" and of "juridical appearances" to Guanabara Governor Lacerda, to the figurehead president, Mazzilli, and to the real power, War Minister Costa e Silva.[62] The war minister received the ambassador's remarks with very bad grace, professing himself shocked that the United States would attempt to intrude in a matter that touched on Brazilian sovereignty. Instead of fussing in this way, the United States should be happy to see Brazil saved from communism and economic ruin.[63]

Inclined to agree with the general, Gordon was ready to make excuses for the new military regime. "Department should bear in mind," he cabled Washington, "that Brazil had very narrow escape from Communist-dominated dictatorship and is only few days past what could have been civil war type confrontation. I see no way now of pushing this question further without over-straining our credit and producing counter-productive reaction."[64] The next day he discovered that Operation Clean-Up was already being run with "characteristic Brazilian sense of moderation." Citizens might be arrested arbitrarily and detained illegally, but their detention was humane: "most prisoners detained at location where they [are] permitted to take sunbaths, et cetera. We have no information of any physical torture or brutality in connection with operation."[65]

The ambassador's information was curiously incomplete. Although it is true that at this time the regime's apparatus of repression and torture was not yet systematized, incidents of brutality occurred from the start. In Recife, for example, Communist leader Gregório Bezerra was publicly tortured. A rash of peasant "suicides" was reported in the Northeast. The beating of prisoners, including some left-wing reporters, was common knowledge. As early as April 3 the *Correio da Manha* condemned the "terrorist" violence of the security police of Lacerda's DOPS (Department of Political and Social Order). These defenders of the new order were extremely busy arresting and beating up suspects. Two weeks later, on April 18, José de Souza, a metal worker who had been active in his union, threw himself out of a DOPS window to escape further interrogation, thus becoming the first torture victim in the city where the ambassador lived. And, of course, the "sun baths, et cetera," mentioned as prison amenities, meant only that prisoners were allowed to leave their rat-infested, fetid cells for brief periods of time to sit or walk in the prison courtyard.[66]

The American officials were not the only ones fooled by the victors of the April 1 coup. Just as surprised were the Brazilian politicians and officeholders who had enthusiastically supported the military's overthrow of Goulart but who had expected the generals to order a return to the barracks as soon as this task was completed. In their previous interventions in the political process, the military had either turned power over to a new slate of civilian politicians or had reaffirmed the tenure of elected officials. This time they behaved differently. "I am tired of seeing Brazilian revolutions spoiled by politics," announced General Costa e Silva.[67]

Only three days after the coup, Costa e Silva became involved in bitter infighting with his erstwhile civilian allies, the governors who had given the coup their wholehearted support, mobilizing their state militias to back up the federal armies. Governor Carlos Lacerda, worried that the PSD would somehow walk off with all the political plums in the aftermath of the coup, had called all of the governors together on April 4 to consider appropriate political arrangements for the period up to the scheduled election of 1965. Several political leaders suggested that Congress might elect a general as a nonpartisan interim president. Lacerda decided to back General Castello Branco. Costa e Silva attended the meeting in his self-proclaimed role as head of the Revolutionary High Command.

Governor Magalhães Pinto was waiting to ask the general a question:

"General, we are a little concerned about the situation of some of our colleagues. The wife of Governor Seixas Doria, of Sergipe, looked me up because she doesn't know where he is. He was arrested and is in some unknown place." Costa e Silva said, "So, that business has begun! He's in prison and he'll stay in prison! I'm not here to give that kind of information."...then [Governor] Nei Braga said, "Actually there are difficult situations. For example, there's a problem in Parana—" He said, "You're going to start already with stories of Parana? Why haven't you people gotten rid of that thief there— that Moisés Lupion?" Moisés Lupion was the close friend of Ademar de Barros, who was seated next to Nei Braga.[68]

The meeting broke up after the general managed to insult several other governors. The question of an interim government had not been resolved. Costa e Silva made it clear that he did not care for the idea of immediately electing a military man to complete Goulart's term. But, lacking the support of his fellow generals, he was unable to dictate to the governors at that point.

The military, united in their opposition to Goulart and communism, divided over the question of who should get post-coup power and how it should be exercised. Costa e Silva and his "trooper" supporters wanted to continue existing arrangements for an indefinite period, with Costa e Silva wielding the real executive power as war minister and head of the Revolutionary High Command, while Mazzilli or some other tractable civilian occupied the presidential mansion and performed ceremonial chores. On the other hand, the Sorbonne clique, guided by General Golbery, wanted a military man, one of their own, preferably Castello Branco, installed as president as soon as possible. They wanted to see the presidency strengthened, not diminished. Freed of congressional restraints or political party considerations, the general-president could impose the needed reforms that would repair the country's economy, solve the foreign debt crisis, restore close ties with the United States, and with American help build Brazilian hegemony in South America as Brazil guarded the South Atlantic flank of Christian civilization in its struggle with international communism. Fiercely anticommunist younger officers made up a third military faction, soon known as the Hard Line. They believed that the problems the country faced could not be addressed until there had been a more thorough purge, until all Communist-liners, all left-wing elements had been rooted out, until corrupt officeholders had been exposed and punished, until peasants, workers, students, civilians generally, has relearned obedience, discipline, and hard work. Civilians could not be trusted. The military must retain power indefinitely. Like the Sorbonne faction, the Hard Line hoped to see Brazil emerge in the near future as a world-class power, but they were less interested in close cooperation with the United States; they were more likely to identify themselves as nationalists.

Within a remarkably short time, a compromise among the military factions was worked out. (1) Costa e Silva would be allowed to exercise authoritarian powers until a new president was inaugurated on April 15. He would use those powers to purge the Congress and the armed forces. After April 15, he would stay on as war minister and thus would be in a position to look after the interests of his trooper supporters, as well as retaining a voice in the administration. (2) The Sorbonne clique would get the strengthened presidency they wanted, with Castello Branco installed as the interim president on April 15. He would at least temporarily retain the authoritarian powers that Costa e Silva was to exercise until that date. In any case, Congress, purged by Costa e Silva, could be expected to docilely follow the lead of the new president. (3) The Hard Line colonels would get the purge they wanted when first the war minister and then the president enjoyed authoritarian power. In addition, they would get some control over the duration and extent of a purge. The colonels were permitted to set up a little ad hoc Inquisitions, the IPMs (Military Police Investigations), to unmask the communist network in the country. The IPMs rapidly developed into "a parallel judicial system notorious for its disregard for human rights."[69]

Had the generals been unable to compromise their differences so quickly, there might have been some hope for the retention of civilian government and the preservation of the constitutional political system. But the governors and the political leaders of the major parties helped the military compose its internal differences by coming out strongly in favor of the election of a "nonpartisan" military man, i.e., Castello Branco, as the interim president. The politicians were no doubt influenced by the lightning campaign mounted by IPES immediately after the coup to get Castello named president. IPES leaders again called out the women's groups they had created—CAMDE in Rio, UCF in São Paulo, LIMDE in Belo Horizonte—to serve as a "popular" chorus. The women obligingly staged demonstrations and lobbied Congressmen, demanding the "election" of Castello Branco, though some UCF members were apparently troubled by the fact that under the constitution they were supposedly defending, the army chief of staff was ineligible.[70]

In naming Castello as their choice for interim president, the politicians of course expected that such a military interim would last no longer than January 1966. They expected the scheduled October 1965 presidential election to take place on schedule. The leading presidential hopefuls— Lacerda, Kubitschek, Magalhães Pinto, Adhemar de Barros—all explicitly endorsed the installation of Castello Branco and tacitly accepted the "temporary" assumption of authoritarian powers by the military chiefs.

No one thought the military interim might last for twenty-one years.

# 11

# Nation Building: II

---

*We've reached the point at which two industrialists...*
*exchanged the following dialogue: "In Jango's day every time*
*I entered my factory I was afraid of finding a Communist*
*sitting at my desk."*

*"Right. But now every time I enter mine, I'm afraid of finding*
*an American sitting at my desk."*

*Marcio Alves*

At his April 3 news conference Secretary of State Dean Rusk emphatically denied that the United States had been involved in the coup in Brazil "in any way, shape, or form."[1] No doubt most Americans believed him; in 1964 the credibility gap had not yet been discovered. The premature recognition of the new Brazilian government made it clear that the United States intended to be supportive and closely associated with the post-coup regime, whatever it was. "We take as basic premise the absolute necessity that the new government succeed both politically and economically," cabled Ambassador Gordon, even as he admitted "considerable dismay" over the early authoritarian moves of the military junta.[2]

To the Americans, political success would mean the establishment of a stable, "responsible, representative and democratic government."[3] But the way in which the victorious generals brusquely amended the constitution of 1946 did not augur well for the future of democratic government. The junta members had decided that some sort of juridicial underpinning was needed for the thorough "cleansing" (*limpeza*) that they wanted. A constitutional amendment (later called Institutional Act No. 1) authorizing the executive to unilaterally carry out such a purge was drawn up and sent to Congress for its approval. But congressional leaders balked at passing an amendment that drastically reduced the powers of Congress and expanded the powers of the executive. Annoyed, the generals tacked on a preamble to their Institutional Act announcing that by virtue of winning the coup they now held the supreme, sovereign authority. Congressional approval of their amendment was unnecessary. Neither Congress nor the 1946 constitution had any legitimacy beyond that which the junta chose to bestow. "A wordy statement that might makes right," commented Gordon.[4]

Among the new powers assigned to the executive by the Institutional Act was the power to *cassar,* to strip any individual of office and of political rights. The victim had no right of appeal; there was no provision for any type of judicial review. The military junta exercised this power until a new president could be installed and promptly used it to purge forty deputies from Congress and 122 officers from the armed forces. Ambassador Gordon considered the number purged from Congress to be excessive. Perhaps ten or twelve congressmen could be identified as Communists or Communist sympathizers, but not forty.[5] In reply, Assistant Secretary of State Mann suggested that purging 40 out of some 900 legislators did not sound excessive, providing there had in fact been communist infiltration of the government. In other words, a clear and present danger to democracy might justify temporary undemocratic excess. He suggested that the ambassador get the "hard facts" on subversion and then persuade the new Brazilian government to publish the evidence.[6] Although Mann confidently suggested to a congressional committee that evidence of Cuban involvement in subversion in Brazil would soon surface, hard facts on any sort of international communist conspiracy were never produced.[7] Nor was there any concrete evidence that Goulart had conspired to stage his own coup and set up a personal dictatorship.

Despite the embarrassing lack of evidence, American officials continued to believe that there had been a dangerous Red menace. For example, at his confirmation hearings two years later (for the assistant secretary of state position), Gordon still presented a scenario in which the *golpistas* struck in the nick of time to save Brazil from falling under the dictatorship of Goulart.[8] The ambassador's firm belief that "Brazil had a very narrow escape from Communist-dominated dictatorship" helped lessen his concern that there might be innocent victims of the witchhunt.[9] In any case, he seems to have worried much more about the reaction of the American public to news of the excesses of the new regime than about the excesses themselves. A public outcry would probably lead to congressional refusal to vote aid to Brazil. Without "our cordial and generous support" the new government might collapse. He went on to suggest possible press releases on the "depth and breadth of subversive activity," releases that might be used to blunt criticism of the activities of the post-coup regime.[10]

The ambassador need not have worried. News from Vietnam was discouraging. The American public hungered for a Cold War success story. In a special supplement, the *Readers Digest* soon certified the April 1 coup as the "inspiring story of how an aroused Brazilian people stopped the Communists from taking over their nation.[11]

The State Department, then, was free to support the new military dictatorship in Brazil without having to deal with embarrassing questions about human rights from the American public. Officials in Washington did express some concern about basic civil liberties in Brazil when the new president, General Castello Branco, used his arbitrary powers under the Institutional Act to depose several state governors and to deprive the popular ex-president Juscelino Kubitschek of his Senate seat and political rights.[12] But concern faded after one part of the Institutional Act expired on June 15. On this date the president lost his power to *cassar*. Other provisions of the act remained in effect, however. Congress had been transformed by the act into a veto body with limited discussion powers. The president had the exclusive power to initiate money bills and the right to introduce any other legislation. Congress was required to act within thirty days on legislation submitted by the executive. The president also had the power to unilaterally declare a state of seige. In addition, the witch-hunt by the IPMs continued unabated. Nevertheless, American officials were convinced that Brazil had turned a corner and was headed back in the direction of "responsible, representative, and democratic government."

American officials reasoned that by maintaining close ties with the new regime, the United States could nudge the process of democratization along. Conditions appeared optimal for a positive American influence. The new president, Castello Branco, was a personal friend of the American army attaché, Colonel Vernon Walters; many of the military officers now taking over key positions in the government had received part of their training in the United States; a procession of state governors, federal legislators, AIFLD-trained labor leaders, had been treated to tours of the United States; Brazilian business executives had been flooded with pro-American propaganda through groups such as IPES. The new government and its supporting elite were in absolute accord with the American Cold War view of the world. In fact, some of the Brazilian officials seemed almost pathologically pro-American. It would be difficult to find another foreign minister of a sovereign state proclaiming, as did Juracy

Magalhães, that what was good for the United States was good for his own country.[13]

In addition to playing on the pervasive pro-American orientation of the new government, the United States could employ economic leverage. Brazil badly needed bailout assistance. Inflation continued to accelerate while production declined, little new foreign capital was coming in, deficits in the balance of payments soared, interest payments on the outstanding foreign debt could not be met. "The new opportunities which this situation opens for us should be evident," wrote Ambassador Gordon to White House aide Ralph Dungan, "and I gather from both correspondence and Hew Ryan's personal visit that this is well appreciated in Washington. I hope that it will continue to be so, because if there is a failure of policy now, the fault will rest with us and we shall have missed an opportunity which is most unlikely to repeat itself."[14]

If the American nation-building strategy would work anywhere, it should have worked in Brazil. Although the country's economic problems were serious, the potential was great. This was not an overpopulated land with limited resources and an economy geared to a single product. Brazil had rich resources in its vast territory. Its diversified economy was already partially industrialized. Since the "communists" had just been cast out, little energy or funds need be spent on the counterinsurgency aspect of nation building. Moreover, the nation builders still had the support of their own government. President Johnson was determined to not only continue but to improve upon the Alliance for Progress initiative that President Kennedy had begun.[15]

Mindful of the historic opportunity to "turn Brazil into lasting example [of] accomplishments and leadership under AFP [Alliance for Progress],"[16] the policy-planning staff of the State Department debated and drew up a detailed statement of American policy objectives in post-coup Brazil. The promotion of a democratic society in Brazil provided the predominant theme of the sixteen-page statement. Nine objectives were listed, with political democracy placed first:

I. Maximum possible stability, effectiveness and democratic orientation of the Brazilian Government and political system.

II. A substantial reduction in the rate of inflation and the resumption of an adequate rate of economic growth.

III. Betterment—within the context of improved price stability and a growing economy, and subject to priority allocation of available funds—of the economic well-being of urban and rural masses to reduce their susceptibility to extremist demagoguery.

IV. A more favorable climate for private enterprise, both domestic and foreign.

V. A more effective and responsible trade-union movement which is increasingly free of government domination, increasingly democratic in orientation and more broadly representative of urban and rural workers.

VI. A greater orientation toward democratic moderation and away from leftist extremism on the part of students, student groups and youth in general, and a redirection of the energies of these groups into constructive channels.

VII. The maintenance and strengthening of democratic thinking and friendship for the U.S. among the Brazilian military.

VIII. Increased understanding of and friendship toward (a) the U.S. and its democratic, free enterprise system, and (b) the Alliance for Progress.

IX. The continuance and strengthening of the present anti-communist, pro-Western disposition of Brazil's foreign policy.[17]

What is most notably missing in this list of American objectives is any clear call for the basic social reforms that would promote land and income redistribution. Initially, in keeping with themes sounded in the Alliance for Progress charter, the United States had harped on the need for such reforms. The third goal on the list—betterment of the economic well-being of the masses—came the closest to calling for social reform. Judging from the list of changes attached to the position paper, it had touched off the most debate within the policy committee. At first this goal had been placed second on the list, but some committee members feared that "extravagant programs" to benefit the masses would "seriously disrupt stabilization efforts." Feeling that price stability had a higher priority at the moment, the committee moved that goal into second place and added a reference to it as a condition for any improvement in living standards for the masses. The Alliance for Progress charter had barely mentioned price stabilization, instead emphasizing economic growth as well as the basic reforms that would "make the benefits of economic progress available to all citizens of all economic and social groups through a more equitable distribution of national income."[18]

The State Department's policy-planning staff also addressed the problem of how the desired goals were to be achieved. They placed their greatest emphasis on behind-the-scenes persuasion. The operative word was *discreetly.* Thus, under goal 1, U.S. officials were to "press discreetly, as circumstances may require, for mitigation of repressive measures in which some authorities in the post-revolution period have engaged.'' To achieve objective 4, the State Department would "discreetly press for amendment and changes as necessary in administration of the profit remittance law'' and would "press discreetly for the satisfactory elimination of harassments to American enterprise, including the completion of the AMFORP purchase and a satisfactory resolution of the Hanna Company's difficulties. Seek to obtain a final settlement of the IT&T claims.'' Under objective 5, American representatives would "continue to press discreetly for modification of the fascist-type provisions of Brazil's labor code.'' To promote objective 6, the United States would "discreetly oppose the proposed abolition of the National Student Union (UNE).''

In the ensuing months the expansion of the American official presence in Brazil got under way. Increasing numbers of analysts and technicians were dispatched to be discreet about American objectives, until, according to Ambassador Tuthill, by 1966 the "ubiquitous American advisor" could be found in almost every Brazilian government office, not to mention the 510 Peace Corps men and women scattered in city slums and rural areas.[19]

American goals were thus carefully considered, clearly stated, limited and, from the American standpoint, unexceptional, even traditional. Although the United States would no longer talk "revolution," it intended to use its unique position of predominance to nudge Brazil in the direction of a more democratic society at the same time that it promoted price stabilization and private enterprise. Brazil would end up with institutions—political, educational, economic—that would be more like American ones.

From the political standpoint the great nation-building effort can only be seen as a fiasco. During the next four years, while the American "quiet diplomacy" was at its height, Brazil moved steadily toward a more repressive authoritarian state, in which the gap between the elite and the masses widened, inflation rates were reduced by further reducing the standard of living of the lower classes, labor unions were more firmly controlled by the government, and, barred from legal expression of their grievances and opinions, student groups turned to experiments with terrorism.

What went wrong? One difficulty was semantic. The *golpistas* and their civilian supporters had called themselves "the democratic forces.'' American analysts had uncritically accepted that denomination. But if the military plotters who overthrew a constitutional civilian government were "the" champions of democracy, what, exactly, did democracy mean? For most Americans, no doubt, it is a sacred but unexamined ideal. Nevertheless, it is difficult to promote the maximum possible democratic orientation of another country's political system without determining the essential elements of such a system. Was anticommunism coupled with an endorsement of private enterprise sufficient? At the time it seemed to be enough to decide inclusion in the lists of the Free World. Would an anticommunist, pro–private enterprise government qualify as a democracy if it had, in addition, some sort of Congress and some type of elections, no matter how limited the powers of that Congress or how manipulated the elections? Brazilian President Castello Branco thought so; he proclaimed the Institutional acts that reduced the powers of Congress and increased his powers to manipulate elections "powerful instruments of democracy."[20] Must a reasonably free press and an independent judiciary that safeguards civil rights be added to the mix? State Department officials seemed to think so. Does democracy, if its institutions are to function at all, require a basic commitment to the ideal of the essential equality and dignity of all individuals? It was difficult to make such a commitment, even at an abstract level, in a society as fundamentally elitist and paternalistic as that of Brazil.

Another factor hampering the American effort to build a democractic nation in Brazil, or even to perceive what was happening in the country, was the set of fixed ideas American analysts had about the Brazilian military. One idea was that the Brazilian military differed from the military in other Latin countries in that it had no political ambitions, eschewed violence, and would soon return to the barracks. "The armed forces show every indication of refraining from any interference in the governing process," a CIA intelligence memorandum announced confidently on April 3, 1964.[21] A military junta was running the country at the time. On September 22, 1965, a few weeks before new military pressure led to Institutional Act No. 2, which in effect scrapped what remained of the constitution, Ambassador Gordon opined that the Brazilian military had a "strong sense of legality and respect for [the] constitution" and conceived of their role in politics "in passive rather than active terms."[22] It was also firmly believed that the Brazilian military were prodemocracy and pro-America and that additional military aid would preserve that orientation.

Carefully copying one another, guided by this set of ideas, American analysts simply ignored the mounting evidence that the Brazilian military intended not only to participate in but to dominate politics and all other aspects of Brazilian life. In 1961 and 1962, as the Alliance for Progress was launched, a great deal had been said about the need for a "mystique" that would give life to the new crusade by touching people's hearts and minds, inspiring dedication to its lofty democratic ideals. No such ideology ever developed. The only new mystique to appear in Latin America was a militarist one that was inherently elitist and antidemocratic, suspicious of the masses, and contemptuous of civilian leaders. It was called the National Security Doctrine.[23] Introduced to the Brazilian public in November 1964 as *the* philosophy of the revolution, it aroused no discernible popular enthusiasm. On the other hand, some of the military participants in the coup were pleased to discover that their revolution had any philosophy at all.[24]

The National Security Doctrine had developed in the 1950s and early 1960s in the select discussion groups of the Superior War College. It was based squarely on Cold War cosmology, with its assumptions of a bipolar world and the everlasting antagonism of the evil forces of Eastern communist imperialism versus Western Christian civilization. The security of Brazil was in jeopardy because the conflict between the West, led by the United States, and the Communist bloc, led by the Soviet Union, was worldwide. Since a direct nuclear confrontation between the United States and the U.S.S.R. was impossible, the conflict was channeled into peripheral wars such as the limited conventional war in Korea or into the anticolonial "wars of liberation," such as those in Algeria or the Belgian Congo, or into "revolutionary war"—the process of subversion and infiltration as, it was believed, had characterized the Goulart administration. Underdeveloped countries on the periphery are therefore in greater peril than are the developed nations of Western Europe and Japan.

The state was conceived of as an organic entity, independent of and grander than the human population that was settled within its boundaries.[25] The state is the agent that guarantees the survival of the nation and the achievement of national goals. In the climate of worldwide Cold War, the government of the state must be strong, centralized, able to efficiently mobilize the population, capable of rationally maximizing the outputs of the economy, while quickly suppressing displays of disunity on the part of subversive agents or malcontents. In developed countries ordinary civilians might be permitted to run the state. In the underdeveloped world, where the threat of internal subversion is so much greater, the state must be entrusted to a military elite that was disciplined and

228

rigorously trained to think objectively about security problems and national objectives. The military elite would ally itself with a civilian elite of industrialists and technocrats who could be trained in the National Security Doctrine and closely supervised by the military.

Development was linked to security. Brazil needed its own industrial-military complex. Industrial capacity, technological know-how, a modern communications systems, full employment, all would enhance the nation's ability not only to defend itself from external or internal threats but also to achieve great power status. The proponents of the National Security Doctrine took the quest for the status of a great power as the premier national objective. They promised to achieve that objective within one generation, i.e., by the year 2000.

"Security and Development" emerged as the slogan of the new military regime. Significantly, security came first. Development was being pushed because it would promote security; anything that appeared to threaten development—a strike, a mass demonstration, agitation for higher wages—could be seen as a "national security matter." A newspaper editorial or political speech criticizing top officials or deriding the military could also be seen as threatening development and/or security by reducing popular confidence in the government. Of course all national security matters had to be dealt with promptly by military authorities, without recourse to ineffectual civilian judicial procedures.

From the perspective of the National Security Doctrine, governments are obviously instituted to further the security and grandeur of the state, not to secure the natural rights of the governed, not to establish justice, not to promote the general welfare. But American officials at first missed the authoritarian implications of the National Security Doctrine. The military's intellectuals continued to insist on their democratic convictions. "There was not, within the revolutionary leadership of that time, as there is not today, a single discordant voice about the democratic philosophy of the Revolution," said Colonel Carlos de Meira Mattos in 1970, five and a half years after he had published the first explanation of the National Security Doctrine. "Acting with the concept of democratic life, with an existential democratic style, with a democratic morality and ethic, we made the Revolution in order to build a developed society."[26] Convinced that General Castello Branco and the officers of his staff were, as they claimed, all dedicated to democracy, the embassy and the State Department expected that there would be a fairly rapid transition to more democratic political and legal procedures as soon as the dust of revolution settled.

In particular, the Americans pinned their hopes on Castello Branco. The new president made an excellent impression on the American officials who became acquainted with him after he was installed in office. He had been a personal friend of Army attaché Walters for years, but before the coup he was virtually unknown to other American officials. Visiting Brazil in August 1964, Walt Rostow decided Castello was "a remarkable Latin American chief of state"; the same month William D. Rogers, a State Department official, described him as "a man of dignity, knowledge, and courage"; White House advisor Jack Valenti, a year later, assured President Johnson that Castello was honest, strong, a man of "total integrity."[27] Ambassador Gordon, who met the Brazilian president more frequently, soon became his convinced admirer.[28] The one flaw in Castello Branco's character that disturbed the ambassador was his lack of interest in public relations or in any campaign to sell the public on the need for the policies he pursued.[29] In part, no doubt, the general's disdain for any such campaign was due to an exaggerated sense of his personal dignity and of the dignity of his new office, but at the same time his disinterest in the opinion of the general public reflected political realism. The general public did not, after all, matter politically. The only interest group that mattered was the military, as Castello Branco well understood. He must keep the military more or less united in support of his presidency. In practice that meant concessions to the group within military ranks that was most likely to bolt, the Hard Line.

Castello Branco early revealed his tendency to forestall action by the Hard Liners by adopting their policies. He refused to intervene in the IPMs except to try to limit their use of torture. In November 1964 when Hard Liners threatened to take matters in their own hands unless the president intervened unconstitutionally in the state government of Goias to remove the governor (alleged to be soft on communism although he had actively supported the coup), Castello hastily obliged them, all the while protesting his dedication to constitutional government.[30] He followed the same pattern in subsequent showdowns with the Hard Line.

American displeasure over Castello Branco's failure to move toward a restoration of constitutional government was diluted by American pleasure with the economic course taken by his administration. There was, in fact, a fairly rapid shift in American priorities, with the quantifiable "banker's goals"—balanced budgets, lower inflation rates, improved tax collection, better foreign exchange management—replacing the vaguer intangibles of human rights or a democratic orientation of government or even the betterment of the economic well-being of the masses.[31] The administration's Latin American experts believed that a measure of economic progress must precede lasting progress on the political and social fronts.[32]

To the delight of the State Department, Castello Branco tackled and passed the performance tests that Goulart had failed. As has been detailed, by mid-1963 two tests had been imposed on the Goulart government as preconditions for further American aid: the purchase of AMFORP and the imposition of a drastic austerity program to reduce inflation. Despite American satisfaction with the overthrow of Goulart, both tests were promptly reimposed on Castello Branco. An emergency grant of $50 million would not actually be disbursed until a contract with AMFORP was signed, and no long-term aid would be available until a stabilization plan was in place.[33]

Negotiations on the purchase of AMFORP dragged on from mid-April to September. Mauro Thibau, Castello Branco's minister of mines and energy, was a believer in private enterprise and at first tried to persuade AMFORP to continue its operations in Brazil. Henry B. Sargent, the president of the utility, flatly refused. He insisted that his company be expropriated at the price that had been agreed upon in April 1963 plus accrued interest dating back to January 1963.[34] Disagreements followed over the amount and timing of any back interest payment, over the length of time that AMFORP would be required to reinvest proceeds of the sale in Brazil, and over how the value that the company had placed on its assets could be verified. AMFORP was willing to have "third party" appraisal of its properties but apparently expected this to be either a rubber stamp arrangement or grounds for concessions on the reinvestment requirement.[35]

By making the purchase of the utility a precondition for aid, the United States had transformed an ordinary "commercial negotiation" into "de facto intergovernmental commitment."[36] State Department officials and Ambassador Gordon in particular devoted a great deal of time to the commercial negotiation. At his very first meeting with Castello Branco, the ambassador took the time to explain the history of the AMFORP affair to the new president.[37] Thereafter Gordon met frequently—if not daily—with representatives of AMFORP and almost as often with the members of Castello Branco's cabinet who were in charge of the purchase. He relayed information from one party to the other, criticized aspects of offers tendered, made suggestions about compromising differences, and paid a call on Governor Lacerda to try to convince him that Castello Branco was not buying a lot of "scrap iron." Gordon

231

warned the Brazilian negotiators about "possible reactions in U.S." to further delays in the purchase at the same time as he attempted to keep the public in both countries in the dark about the ongoing negotiations. "There should be no rpt [repeat] no publicity," he wired, regretting the fact that *Hanson's Latin American Letter* had discovered and made public the link between the $50 million of emergency aid and the purchase of AMFORP.[38]

Actually, by 1964 few Americans remembered or had ever even heard of AMFORP and its problems. In Brazil, however, the purchase of the utility on AMFORP's terms continued to be extremely unpopular, with both antigovernment leftists and pro-coup rightists emphatically opposed.[39] In view of this opposition, soured by their experience with Goulart, American officials in Washington were at first somewhat skeptical about Castello Branco's ability to deliver either the purchase of AMFORP or a drastic austerity program.[40] They were delighted to discover that the general was determined to ram through both measures, even if it did mean touching off a major recession and even though it was necessary to station troops at the doors of Congress in order to persuade that already-purged body to pay AMFORP the price it wanted. Nor did Castello Branco stop there. Before he had completed a year in office, he had Congress ease restrictions on profit remittances by foreign-owned enterprises, he had signed an investment guarantee agreement with the United States (designed to encourage direct private investment), and he had taken steps to end the dispute that prevented Hanna Mining Company from mining and exporting Brazilian iron ore.[41]

American officials were immensely impressed and pleased by such "courageous economic policy decisions," as President Johnson later characterized Castello Branco's moves.[42] Johnson was working to forge an alliance between his administration and big business. As vice president he had observed with silent disapproval the early noisy squabbles between some of the New Frontiersmen and corporate executives.[43] As president he seized an early opportunity to let the spokesmen for the multinationals know that he valued their advice and support. When David Rockefeller, the president of Chase Manhattan, wrote to offer the assistance of the newly organized Business Group for Latin America, Johnson not only seconded the arrangements that President Kennedy had made for meetings between the businessmen and the heads of various government agencies but asked to meet with the group himself. When he did address the gathering of mostly Republican executives on January 31, 1964, he won them over completely. "Dear Mr. President," wrote John T. Connor, president of Merck & Co.,

> I want you to know that we of the Business Group for Latin America who met with you last Friday afternoon in the White House were deeply impressed by what you said. We, of course, were thoroughly familiar with your views on human rights before that meeting, and it was very reassuring to hear your emphasis on property rights also. It is my impression that attacks on property rights usually go hand in hand, or even precede, attacks on human rights....
>
> Those of us who have worked hard to build up businesses in Latin American countries...will now take heart in knowing that the President of the United States understands what's going on, and will not sit by while the Communists and Castroites make a shamble of what we are trying to do.[44]

The January 1964 meeting with the Business Group for Latin America was only step one of the "Johnson treatment." He began inviting corporate executives to the White House for lunches, for dinner parties, for special commemorative ceremonies of various sorts; he sent the vice president or top cabinet officials to speak at business gatherings in other cities; he found time to personally receive and "debrief" prominent businessmen in the Oval Office when they returned from some overseas trip.[45] He addressed the Business Group for Latin America (renamed Council for Latin America in 1965) every year. Johnson could point to the steps taken by the Brazilian government as proof that he understood the problems the corporations had faced in Latin America and had the State Department working to improve the climate for private enterprise and expand the opportunities for direct foreign investment.

Politically, Johnson's overtures to big business paid off in business community pressure on Congress to pass the president's foreign aid bills and other measures that related to the Alliance for Progress. "I was pleased and impressed with what you had to say yesterday at the more than one-hour meeting with the Council for Latin America," wrote William E. Knox, chairman of Westinghouse Electric International. "I feel fortunate, if not to say privileged, to have been present, and I am determined more than ever to support your foreign policies, particularly including Latin America and Vietnam."[46] When the Alliance for Progress had first been launched, the emphasis had been on government-to-government aid and on long-term planning for self-sustained growth—not on the promotion of the investment interests of American corporations. Liberals had been delighted with the novel approach, while the business community had been distinctly cool. Now, in 1965, convinced that property rights had been restored to their rightful primary position, it was the U.S. corporations involved in Latin America that were the most enthusiastic about the Alliance for Progress.[47]

However, political self-interest on the home front was not President Johnson's only consideration in courting big business. He genuinely believed that if businessmen were free to compete and make money, society as a whole would benefit. Commercial and industrial development, economic growth, that was the business of businessmen, just as politics and social programs were his business. Anxious to make the faltering Alliance for Progress an economic success, Johnson felt strongly that the American private sector must be persuaded to play a more active role in Latin American development. Administration officials were disturbed when American corporations did not respond to the "courageous economic policy decisions" of Castello Branco by rushing to invest capital and expand their operations in Brazil. "U.S. private enterprise cannot properly sit back and behave in the parochial manner typical of Brazilian private enterprise," complained nation-building expert Walt Rostow. "They must lead the way in the modernization of Brazilian industrial attitudes and price policy. The must lead the way in helping create the agricultural revolution which is the key to next phase of Brazilian industrial, as well as national, development.... I therefore believe we must have a heart-to-heart talk with David Rockefeller soon."[48]

In fact, however, it was not so much "parochial" attitudes but the recession in Brazil that discouraged new investment; there was already considerable idle industrial capacity. The heart-to-heart did not help. The American firms that did commit new capital to Brazil tended to invest it in the acquisition of existing Brazilian firms, not in breaking new ground in industry or in leading an agricultural revolution. Brazil continued to export more capital in the form of interest, license and patent fees, and dividends than it received from abroad.[49] Some of the Brazilian businessmen who had supported the coup because they feared that under "communist" Goulart their businesses would be taken over by the government now were taken over by American firms. Others who had thought the ouster of Goulart would mean a return to business prosperity, witnessed instead the drying up of credit and the shrinking of consumer demand as the rigid austerity measures demanded by the International Monetary Fund were imposed. Nor did the American nation builders meet their goal of promoting domestic private enterprise in Brazil. Under the National Security Doctrine it is the state, not private enterprise, that is the organizer and engine of the economy. The growth of the foreign multinationals was to a certain extent balanced by the increase in state enterprise.

Neither the setback to domestic private enterprise in Brazil nor the sharp decline in real wages for Brazilian workers was immediately obvious to the American nation builders. Washington officials had a powerful additional reason to be pleased with Castello Branco: they liked his foreign policy. On the original list of American short-term objectives, maintaining a pro-West orientation of the Brazilian government was ranked last. Brazilian support of American foreign policy was seen as highly desirable, but not crucial, since, with the exception of De Gaulle's France, all American allies supported American policy. However, as Johnson embarked on more controversial foreign policy initiatives, he faced growing criticism from within the United States and within the Western alliance. Therefore, gestures of support from even minor allies such as Brazil assumed greater importance. Castello Branco was quick to express support of the expanded U.S. role in Vietnam. A personal presidential correspondence between Johnson and Castello began in August 1964, when the Brazilian president wrote to congratulate Johnson for the bombing of Vietnamese torpedo boats in the Tonkin Gulf incident.[50] Brazilian solidarity with the United States in Vietnam never extended beyond the donation of medical supplies and coffee, but Johnson remained hopeful that Castello Branco might be persuaded to commit token army or naval forces.[51]

Closer to home, Castello Branco faithfully supported American policies in the Western Hemisphere. A month after the coup, Brazil broke diplomatic relations with Cuba and took the lead in the Organization of American States in an effort to set up a strict economic blockade of Cuba. Castello thus atoned for the diplomacy of his predecessors in 1962, when Brazil had led the Soft Six in opposing harsher measures by the OAS. Even more important to President Johnson was the Brazilian endorsement of American intervention in the Dominican Republic in April 1965. After the president had ordered in the marines, the State Department scrambled to try to legitimize the intervention by broadening it into collective action by the OAS. Most Latin American countries were extremely critical of the marine landing, regarding it as a violation of the OAS charter and of American pledges of nonintervention, pledges so recently renewed by Thomas Mann. Brazilian politicians were also critical, but Castello Branco, with the support of the military high command, supported the action at once as a necessary and justifiable battle against international communist subversion.[52] A decision to commit Brazilian troops soon followed. The first Brazilian troop contingent arrived in the Dominican Republic on May 23. The next week a Brazilian general assumed the top command of the Inter-American Peace Force, and the White House was able to argue that the interference in Dominican affairs represented an OAS, not a United States, effort.

A clear test of American priorities in Brazil came five months later. In October 1965 gubernatorial elections were held in eleven Brazilian states. Despite considerable prior presidential manipulation of the electoral laws, candidates approved by the government failed to win two key states (Guanabara and Minas Gerais). New talk about the need for another coup at once swept the military. Military unrest became worse when the Brazilian Congress balked at passing a "security amendment" that would turn over new arbitrary powers to the president. To top that civilian outrage, the Supreme Court refused to accept presidential dictation on the selection of its presiding officer. The Hard Line demanded action, and Castello saved himself from being deposed by again doing exactly what they wanted. He decreed Institutional Act No. 2, which restored his power to *cassar*, or strip individuals of their offices and political rights by executive fiat. With Act No. 2 Castello also gave himself new powers to pack the Supreme Court, amend the constitution by decreeing new Institutional or Complementary acts, intervene in state governments, and to suspend Congress altogether and rule by decree. In addition, Institutional Act No. 2 dissolved all existing political parties, authorizing the administration to set rules for the creation of two new ones, one pro- and one (more or less) antigovernment. Finally, the jurisdiction of the military courts was extended to include cases in which civilians were charged with crimes against national security.

Ambassador Gordon, shocked by the authoritarian turn of events, urged that the White House or the State Department publicly criticize the new Institutional Act, in the hope of forcing its retraction or amendment. Administration officials in Washington rejected the idea for two reasons: (1) "A statement on Brazilian domestic politics will lay us open to charges of intervention in Brazil," and (2) Castello Branco might be annoyed enough to pull Brazilian troops out of the Dominican Republic.[53] In reply Gordon argued that since "some of the provisions of new institutional act...could raise legitimate questions of conflict with [the] Inter-American Declaration of Human Rights" the United States was "on weak ground in taking line that Brazilian developments are exclusively internal political matters of no legitimate international concern."[54]

He was overruled but authorized to express U.S. concern in private talks with Brazilian officials.[55]

The next month Secretary of State Rusk was in Rio for an OAS meeting and followed the same tactic. He met privately with Castello Branco to voice American fears that Brazil had taken a turn to outright dictatorship. The Brazilian president assured Rusk that the purpose of Institutional Act No. 2 was "to conserve and fortify democratic institutions" and suggested that "in certain types of critical situations, the law must be broken in order to strengthen the legal structure itself." To illustrate his point, he suggested that in order to prevent a communist takeover, the United States had in fact broken the law by unilateral intervention in the Dominican Republic before OAS sanction. He thus adroitly reminded the secretary how important Brazilian cooperation was to U.S. policy in the hemisphere.[56]

In the wake of Institutional Act No. 2, the Johnson administration undertook a nonpublic "fresh look at our assistance to Brazil."[57] Although he opposed any reduction of aid to Brazil, Ambassador Gordon, nettled by the Brazilian "assumption there is no limit to USG [U.S. government] toleration of arbitrary abuse of power by GOB [government of Brazil]," favored some jangling of the purse strings in order to put pressure for moderation on the military. His illusion that the Brazilian officer corps was prodemocracy and uninterested in active participation in government had finally been shattered. He now felt that U.S. "encouragement" was "needed to stimulate especially [the] military to think hard before taking further rash initiatives in political area."[58] CIA analysts also now conceded that the Brazilian military's "respect for hierarchy and for constitutionalism" had "diminished."[59]

No change in the level of assistance came out of the fresh look. For Ambassador Gordon economic considerations still took priority over political objectives. He conceded that the suspension of aid until constitutional democracy was fully reestablished in Brazil "would put us on record throughout the hemisphere in favor of democratic processes." But a cutoff of aid "would make impossible the successful completion of the stabilization effort" and "reverse the healthy trend toward renewed confidence of foreign private investors and the prospects for major World Bank and European support for long-range Brazilian development."[60] For President Johnson it was the foreign policy considerations that were paramount. Under the administrative procedures established by Johnson, all program loans in excess of $5 million were referred to him personally for final approval.[61] Usually, before a proposal was forwarded to Johnson, the bureaucrats involved had reached consensus on it. In the case of the 1966 program loan for Brazil a standoff developed, with some officials favoring a continuation of program funding at the $150 million level, while others held out for a reduction to $100 million.[62] The president decided in favor of $150 million, on condition that here be a new "strong pitch on the Vietnam question." At the time that Castello Branco was informed that Johnson had personally approved the full $150 million, "the need for more flags in Vietnam" was to be stressed. It was Johnson's "strong hope that Castello Branco will contribute forces to Vietnam as rapidly as he can."[63]

By the time the president made the decision on the program loan, U.S. concern over "the arbitrary abuse of power" in Brazil had already faded. American analysts had been easily convinced that Castello Branco had issued Institutional Act No. 2 against his will in order to placate the Hard Line, that he had no intention of using the authoritarian powers he had given himself, and that his basic problems had been poor public relations and the lack of a supportive political party. "Castello Branco and his team now understand that in the next year they must offer their people not merely economic recovery but a realistic vision of what can be built on the foundations they have laid," nation builder Rostow reported to President Johnson after a visit to Brazil in November 1965. In an unwittingly ominous prediction, he went on to suggest that the new political party system decreed unilaterally by Castello would work as well as did the one in Korea.[64] Embassy personnel happily returned to the task of encouraging, rather than criticizing, Castello Branco. It was feared that unless his morale were boosted, he might resign.

In fact, even at the height of alarm over developments in Brazil, American criticism had been so discreet that Brazilian officials had scarcely noticed it. "I talked at length with Secretaries Rusk and [Jack H.] Vaughn, and similarly with a number of the members of Congress who attended the OAS Conference," Juracy Magalhães wrote to Thomas Mann. "All of them seemed to understand our problems and, as good friends, threw no stones at us, a task that remained for the regrettable action of Senator Kennedy." Magalhães, then justice minister and principal political adviser to Castello Branco, was incensed that Robert F. Kennedy, now New York's junior senator, had publicly criticized the Brazilian government during a tour of Brazil.[65]

American faith in Castello Branco's dedication to democracy slowly eroded during the following year, Castello's final year in office. In July 1964, three months after being installed in the presidency, Castello had

had the docile Congress cancel the presidential election of 1965 and extend his own term until March 15, 1967. Instead of proceeding in his final year in office with a public relations campaign to win popular support and make a progovernment political party a viable reality, Castello's use of power became ever more heavy- handed. In January 1966 War Minister Costa e Silva, with the support of the Hard Line and other dissatisfied elements in the military, announced his candidacy for the presidency. After reluctantly accepting the war minister as his heir apparent, Castello Branco devoted his attention to "cleaning up the area," that is, carrying out a new purge in order to guarantee that the succession would be a smooth one and that his own projects would have been carried through far enough to be irreversible.[66]

The leading civilian contenders for the presidency (with the exception of Adhemar de Barros, not *cassado* until June 1966) had already been deprived of their political rights. Now generals who might be tempted to accept the nomination of the offical opposition party were relieved of their commands. Costa e Silva's "election" by Congress in early October 1966 was therefore quite smooth: there were no other candidates, and the opposition party boycotted the proceedings. The gubernatorial elections a month earlier had been manipulated just as high-handedly by the president. After first decreeing that governors were to be elected by the state legislatures, not by the public, Castello Branco then made lavish use of his newly restored authoritarian powers to remove enough opposition state legislators in the states with scheduled elections to insure the election of governors whom he personally approved. In addition to the ever-lengthening list of *cassados,* two additional institutional acts, a stream of "complementary acts," and other decree laws flowed from the presidential palace. After a show of resistance in Congress to any further purging of Congressmen, the president dispatched the army to close it down.[67] While Congress was thus forcibly recessed, Castello had a handpicked committee write a new constitution that incorporated on a permanent basis many of the authoritarian provisions of the first two institutional acts, provisions that had been scheduled to expire in March 1967. Congress was recalled to ratify the document.

Castello had thus done most of the things that João Goulart had been accused of planning to do: he had extended his term of office instead of leaving the post on the date specified in the constitution; he had established a dictatorship, reducing the Congress to rubber stamp functions and destroying the independence of the judiciary; he had canceled direct elections; he had torn up the constitution of 1946 and written one

239

geared to continuation of the dictatorship. But, as far as American analysts have been concerned, Castello seems to have enjoyed some "Teflon" qualities, and the destruction of Brazil's democratic regime has never been charged to his account. Instead, the idea took hold that Castello personally was deeply committed to liberal democratic principles but was forced to compromise them by pressures from the Right.[68] Evidence of that commitment is hard to find; it seems more likely that Castello's understanding of a liberal democratic system was quite limited, flawed by his dedication to the National Security Doctrine.

At the time, in 1966, American embassy officials confessed disappointment with the general-president but did not recommend public condemnation of any of his arbitrary actions. Rather, the State Department clung to the idea that the Brazilian government was not really a dictatorship but merely a "transitional regime" that had found it necessary to take some "extra-constitutional measures" which presumably would be dropped by the next general-president.[69] Nevertheless, a degree of coolness developed in the U.S.-Brazil official relationship during 1966, and when the 1967 program loan to Brazil was reduced to $100 million, no American official argued for the retention of the $150 million level.[70]

The departure of Ambassador Gordon in March 1966 from the post he had held since October 1961 contributed to the cooling of the special relationship. The new ambassador, John Tuthill, did not arrive in Brazil until late May 1966 and developed no personal relationship with Castello Branco during the remaining nine months of Castello's presidency. Nor did much closeness develop during the following year and a half in the ambassador's relationship with the new president, Costa e Silva. At one point, in fact, Costa e Silva even considered declaring Tuthill persona non grata and having him expelled. This surprising denouement came about after Tuthill had the temerity to lunch with Carlos Lacerda! The former favorite governor of the Americans had severed his close ties with the military government when it became clear that neither he nor any other civilian politician was to be permitted to occupy the presidential palace. Lacerda then reversed himself completely: he took the initiative in organizing an alliance (the Broad Front) with his two former arch enemies, Kubitschek and Goulart, both in exile at the time.[71]

Costa e Silva never impressed American officials as favorably as had Castello Branco, but the problem was not primarily one of personality.[72] Costa e Silva had to deal with something his predecessor had been able to ignore: the growing spirit of anti-Americanism, not only in the usual places—among students and intellectuals—but also within the military

May 23, 1966. President Lyndon B. Johnson with newly appointed Ambassador John Tuthill. Tuthill recommended and carried out a sharp reduction in the number of "ubiquitous" American advisors present in Brazil. (Courtesy Lyndon B. Johnson Library.)

and among members of the civilian elite, especially Brazilian business-men hurt by Castello Branco's economic policies. In the interest of survival, Costa e Silva had to maintain some distance from the American embassy.[73]

Dismayed by the size and incoherence of the American official con-tingent, which he was supposed to oversee, and disturbed by the strength of anti-American feeling, Ambassador Tuthill undertook a campaign to reduce substantially the American presence in Brazil. After carefully preparing Washington, Tuthill launched his empire-reducing campaign in the summer of 1967. The campaign, dubbed Operation Topsy, even-tually reduced the number of American advisors by one-third.[74]

The ambassador's drive to cut back antagonized personnel of the other agencies that were nominally under his authority, especially members of the Defense Department's Military Assistance Advisory Group.[75]

However, in spite of his quarrel with this group, Tuthill continued to call for increased military aid to Brazil, as had Gordon before him.[76] This situation underlines one of the inconsistencies in American policy. State Department analysts now appeared thoroughly aware that the Brazilian military posed the greatest threat to any possible transition to a more democratic regime and to any genuine political stability. Thus, embassy analyst Philip Raine warned, just before Costa e Silva took office, that a military coup against the general was likely if he attempted any liberalization. "If in attempting [to] 'humanize' government program he proves too tolerant with recalcitrant civilian elements and unheedful of demands of military hardline and other committed 'revolutionaries,' he could well be removed by military within one or two years or face a completely new set of circumstances such as losing his freedom of action to military while still retaining office," warned Raine. Yet, with the support of the State Department, the nation builders continued to work to improve the Brazilian military's ability to control the Brazilian people. Military aid continued to stress the training of Brazilian officers in counterinsurgency techniques, and AID public safety programs aimed at improving the efficiency of police departments proceeded without interruption. American taxpayers continued to pay nearly half a million dollars annually to make Brazilian police more effective. "This increased effectiveness was applied not only to normal problems of law and order but to repressive activities as well," embassy analyst Raine later conceded.[77]

As Costa e Silva took office in March 1967, American officials still hoped that massive civilian support for the regime might be mobilized, in which case a new military coup might be averted. Castello Branco had failed in this task; perhaps Costa e Silva, with American help, would do better. It was believed that major efforts in the area of social services could make the regime popular. One project that had been strongly recommended for some time was the modernization of the Brazilian educational establishment, with particular attention to increasing educational opportunities at the secondary school level. A month after Costa e Silva was inaugurated, a major AID project agreement on educational modernization was signed. Almost at once the project was denounced by Brazilian students and intellectuals as a new front for American imperialism. Instead of attempting to defend the program, the Costa e Silva administration promptly abandoned it, leaving the U.S. State Department "holding the bag," as one aide later complained.[78] Other American efforts to interest the regime in agricultural and labor reforms

January 25, 1967. President-elect Artur da Costa e Silva on the grounds of the White House with President Johnson. Costa e Silva's "election" was performed by a rump Congress from which all opposition members had either been purged or voluntarily absented themselves. (Courtesy the National Archives.)

that would benefit workers similarly failed to attract the sustained attention of the Brazilian government.

In fact, in spite of all of the American effort and money, there was little that the nation builders could point to with pride in Brazil by the end of 1968. It was already clear by this date that the major initial AID projects must be written off as failures.

April 12, 1967. President Johnson met Costa e Silva at a breakfast meeting during the Punta del Este Economic Development Conference. Johnson was more favorably impressed with the new Brazilian president than were State Department officials. (Courtesy Lyndon B. Johnson Library.)

Housing for slum dwellers in Rio had been one such project. Bypassing the central government, American funds for housing had been channeled into the state headed by Lacerda. Two housing projects, named Vila Kennedy and Vila Aliança, were completed by 1964. Proud of the undertaking, embassy officials had regularly treated visiting Congressmen to on-site inspections to see American foreign aid at work. The shanties in four *favelas* on the steep hillsides of Rio were destroyed, and 6,000 families had been moved to the new projects before the April coup took place.

Ignored at the time were the protests of the "beneficiaries" of American generosity. The slum dwellers forced to move objected to the amount of rent they had to pay in the projects and to the locations of the new Vilas, distant from the urban center, from jobs, schools, churches, and stores. Family income was reduced, not only because of the increased rent, but because women and children who had formerly performed domestic services for upper- and middle-class families living nearby could no longer earn money in this way. Those individuals who did hold full-time jobs were forced to spend up to 20 percent of their income and three or four hours a day on public transportation. In addition, much of the work on the projects had been slipshod, and, since maintenance was negligent, living conditions in the Vilas rapidly deteriorated. Within a year Brazilian newspapers were running human interest stories describing the deplorable conditions in the American-financed projects.[79]

Short-term "impact" programs for Northeast Brazil had been another major thrust of AID. From 1961 to 1964, no other area of Brazil had seemed so critical to the nation builders. To prevent the impoverished people of the Northeast from turning to communism out of the sheer frustration of unrealized rising expectations, projects in education, public health, improvement of community water supplies were rushed through. American funds totalling $131 million were committed to the Northeast in the formal agreement signed in April 1962.

The expansion of elementary educational opportunity had been especially stressed.

> The great emphasis of the program was on physical construction of classrooms. Schools were to be built in as many areas as possible where there were at least 100 primary school age children out of school. Heavy emphasis was also placed on training teachers and on the building or strengthening of normal schools and teacher training centers to provide the expanded teaching corps to be required....the overriding aim was to dot Northeast Brazil—a region about the size of the American South—with schools as symbols of the Alliance for Progress.[80]

But of 15,595 classrooms planned, only 2,941 were completed; only nine of the forty-seven normal schools and only thirteen of the planned fifty-seven industrial arts shops were built; 13,926 teachers and administrators, rather than the projected 23,060, were given some new training.

Other impact projects for the Northeast were no more successful. "There has been little progress in fields such as education, public health, and agricultural modernization," the author of an AID Program Memorandum admitted in August 1967. "In fact, in some cases, the situation may be deteriorating."[81]

Long-term AID projects—development of the regional mineral resources, irrigation projects, construction and maintenance of highways, development of hydroelectric power, development of facilities for agricultural research and marketing—never got beyond the survey and planning stage. Reform of the existing plantation system of land ownership had been one of the long-term basic reforms much emphasized in the early sixties. The American nation builders had dedicated a great deal of time and energy to the in-depth studies of possible land reform and peasant resettlement projects. Although the studies continued, in June 1970 AID officials had to report that "the land reform process in Northeast Brazil has not yet moved, in effect into the 'results' stage..." since "at the very highest levels of government in Brazil, the leadership simply has not yet made up its mind about land reform."[82] The American experts were sadly reduced to drawing "inferences as to their probable results" should meaningful reforms ever be implemented.

By 1969 it was thus clear that not a one of the problems of Northeast Brazil, which had so exercised the Americans in 1960, had been solved. At first it was possible to attribute failure to the lack of cooperation on the part of Goulart, Governor Arraes, and SUDENE. But that explanation wore thin after Goulart was ousted, Arraes imprisoned, and SUDENE cowed by the new military government. The truth was that under an authoritarian regime without genuine elections or popular mobilization, the misery of the Northeast simply did not matter. A Brazilian military-industrial complex, based on the manpower and resources of the Center-South, could be planned and developed no matter how the poor lived and died in the Northeast.

American AID officials were quick to sense the change. "The star of empire had drifted south from Recife to Rio," observed W. Alan Laflin, head of planning for rural development of the Northeast, "taking with it any program authority that we presumed to have had. Projects upon which we had worked hard, along with SUDENE and State Secretaries of Agriculture, were challenged by the Rio Program office, and finally disapproved."[83]

Laflin unconsciously employed the language of old-fashioned colonial imperialism. Perhaps there was not that much difference between the idealistic "technical experts" sent out by AID and the public school–Oxbridge graduates dispatched by the Home Office to govern India or Africa. Aren't many of their End of Tour laments similar? The natives showed shocking little interest in the training the Americans offered. Some even "had a tendency to feel there was nothing they could learn from an outsider."[84] The preparation of the natives for the offices they held was minimal, they showed little initiative, were apathetic about their work, casual about keeping schedules, but opposed to putting in time beyond their official six-hour workdays. "The nature of the Brazilian dictates a lackadaisical attitude towards any project that requires immediate accomplishment through relentless effort," complained one embittered Public Safety advisor.[85] "Because of the culture of the country, and manifested irresponsibility in many police officers, I have found it exceedingly difficult to implant any ideas regarding traffic and traffic enforcement," reported another.[86] A vocational education expert noted more philosophically that in developing countries one must expect to have to struggle with "the relative inefficiency which attends practically every enterprise, the discouraging inertia of traditional practices and viewpoints, the rigidity of behavior patterns which stifle experimentation."[87] A degree of corruption was one such traditional practice; funds allocated for specific projects sometimes seemed to disappear.[88]

In fairness, some of the technical experts were ready to fault their own country's nation-building bureaucracy. A number felt they had been given inadequate Portuguese language training. Some arrived at their posts to find that no interpreters were available. Others complained of the red tape and difficulty in getting Washington to move quickly on funding and supplying projects. One police advisor felt the wrong type of equipment and supplies had been furnished: "an excessive amount of highly technical, laboratory and scientific type equipment" that was bound to be wasted when "the vast majority" of the Brazilian police officers were "untrained, inexperienced and not familiar with basic subjects, such as criminal investigation, collection and preservation of physical evidence, crime scene protection."[89] On the other hand, the failure to receive such sophisticated American equipment incensed the Brazilian chiefs of police and the state secretaries of public safety.

As the American presence continued year after year, friction mounted between the "natives" and the earnest American technicians who had come to uplift and enlighten them. Not even the Peace Corps volunteers, so determined not to be "ugly Americans," were exempt from "irritating demonstrations of [Brazilian] nationalism." In addition to being considered CIA agents, they were accused of teaching sterilization, not birth control, to the peasants of the Amazon area, in a secret attempt to reduce the population of that region in order to facilitate direct American annexation.[90]

By 1968 the military regime no longer stood in critical need of U.S. public funds or American aid in renegotiation of foreign debt. The recession had finally ended in 1967. The inflation rate had been substantially reduced. The Brazilian economy was just beginning a period of rapid growth, a period later dubbed the Brazilian Miracle. Costa e Silva continued Castello Branco's policy of encouraging foreign private investment. American corporations responded by expanding investments in Brazil. Private banks, such as Citicorp and Chase Manhattan, were ready and eager to loan Brazil money. The international lending institutions and some foreign governments were also ready to supply credit, should the American government reduce support.

As Brazilian dependence on U.S. taxpayer funds decreased, new areas of friction surfaced. The Brazilians objected to the "tying" of American aid, especially to the requirement that 50 percent of tonnage financed by the United States be shipped on American vessels, which were considerably more expensive than the Brazilian merchant fleet. On the American side, by early 1967 the Commerce Department was concerned over the decline in the American share of the Brazilian market. American manufacturers were losing ground to Japanese and European.[91] A dispute over instant coffee began in 1967 and dragged on for years. The American coffee industry objected to a Brazilian government subsidy to Brazilian coffee processors as unfair competition; the Brazilian government argued that it was necessary to subsidize infant industries. Responsive to the grievances of American firms, the U.S. Congress withheld support from the International Coffee Agreement that sought to stabilize world coffee supplies and prices.[92]

Costa e Silva's major problem, however, was not friction with the United States but with Brazilian dissidents. A protest movement against the continuing dictatorship had begun in early 1966 and continued sporadically through 1968. In comparison with the antiwar protest movement in the United States during the same period, protest in Brazil was relatively limited and peaceful, consisting primarily of student rallies and marches and a few brief (and unsuccessful) strikes for higher wages by workers. In addition, a growing number of Catholic clergy began to criticize government repression and human rights violations and to speak out in defense of the poor.[93] Despite the muted nature of their protests, the Brazilian dissidents met increasing violence from governmental authorities and from the anticommunist vigilante groups that were recruited largely from military and police ranks. Within the officer corps, the Hard Line renewed demands for a period of more repressive military dictatorship. If CIA analysts were still ready to accept the Brazilian right-wing judgment that the students, clergy, and workers involved in the protests were all either communists or communist dupes, the U.S. press, and perhaps the State Department, were no longer so ready to accept the idea.[94]

As embassy analysts had foreseen, Costa e Silva was unable to resist pressure from the Right. Matters came to a head when the usually docile

Congress defied the administration on the question of lifting the parliamentary immunity of one of its members. Deputy Marcio Moreira Alves had dared to criticize the military, referring to the army as "a nest of torturers." Outraged, the top military brass demanded the deputy be arrested and tried for subversion. After delaying action as long as possible, Congress ended up rejecting the presidential demand that Alves's immunity be lifted. Yielding to an ultimatum from the Hard Liners that he deal decisively with such congressional defiance, on December 13, 1968, Costa e Silva decreed Institutional Act No. 5. Under the act the Brazilian Congress was closed indefinitely, the right of habeus corpus was suspended, and the president was again given the power to dismiss civil service employees, deprive individuals of political rights, and issue decree laws. In addition he could intervene in state governments at will, replacing legislators or governors, and suspending state and local elections. Moreover, the president acquired new powers over private citizens: he could restrict or prohibit the right of any individual to engage in his chosen profession if he judged the individual's professional behavior contrary to national security interests; he could also confiscate the private property of anyone who had once held public office if he felt that it had been illegally acquired. There was to be no appeal or judicial review of any presidential action under the act. Strict media censorship and more rigid controls over education were instituted in the following weeks. Priests who criticized the military government for ignoring the plight of the poor were arrested and charged with subversion. The French and American priests in this group were deported; the Brazilian priests were held in prison for varying periods, or, if not imprisoned, sometimes beaten up or even murdered by the anticommunist vigilantes or by the new Death Squads that dedicated themselves to terrorizing the lower classes. The use of torture against political prisoners became routine. The fiction of a constitutional state operating under a rule of law had been essentially abandoned.[95]

In response, the American government suspended disbursement of the 1968 program loan and postponed discussion of the 1969 aid package.[96] A number of the AID technical assistance projects were already over or being phased out. "Social patterns and institutions in most underdeveloped nations are extremely malleable," Kennedy's Special Group (CI) had asserted in 1962.[97] "It is impossible for the United States to change the basic national goals, priorities, or political philosophy of a foreign country," concluded Ambassador Tuthill in 1969.[98] It sounded like an epitaph for nation building, though the United States was still

249

pursuing that objective in Southeast Asia, under much more unfavorable conditions.

The Johnson administration was in its final month. The Nixon administration soon resumed the payments and the negotiations for additional aid for the next fiscal year. The "limit to USG toleration of arbitrary abuse of power by GOB," which ex-Ambassador Gordon had looked for back in 1965, had not yet been discovered.

# 12

# Retrospect

*"Those bastards," he proclaimed as if he were literally sur-*
*rounded by active historians, "they are always there with their*
*pencils out."*

                                                    *Benjamin C. Bradlee*

By that Friday the thirteenth of December 1968, when Institutional Act No. 5 swept away the last vestiges of a government limited by constitution and law, Brazil had already faded in the American consciousness. The war in Vietnam absorbed the attention of citizenry and government alike. Latin America as a whole seemed much less important to the United States than the small nations on the other side of the vast Pacific Ocean. Awareness of Brazil as a distinct and distinctive Latin country had rapidly dimmed. For most Americans, Brazil was again just another small Latin republic where the people spoke Spanish and grew a lot of coffee. The news that the military there had staged another coup aroused little interest. Weren't Latin generals always staging coups? The American liberals' stock of moral indignation was totally expended on Vietnam war atrocities and the bombing of North Vietnam. It was hard to take Latin generals very seriously, with their dark glasses, rows of medals over pompous chests, carefully tailored uniforms. Somewhat ridiculous, certainly obnoxious, but not very alarming. At least they were pro-American, or, if not, easily bought off. "The gimmee boys," President Johnson had called them.[1]

In fact, American interest in Brazil began to fade shortly after the overthrow of Goulart back in 1964. The military officers and the businessmen who had plotted against Goulart for years, with unwavering American encouragement, had been surprised by the rapid drop-off of American interest, just as they were pained by the definitely negative reaction in other Western countries. Convinced that they had struck a momentous blow for the freedom of Western Civilization and the preservation of Christianity, they were shocked to find their glorious revolution treated as just another Latin military coup. They wanted international credit for their "splendid victory," applause for their success in thwarting "one of the best prepared offensives of the Cold War."[2] Attributing the world's indifference to misinformation disseminated by the media, IPES dispatched a truth squad to the United States and other western countries to better explain just why their revolution must be considered "the greatest victory yet secured by the free world in the Cold War."[3] But their effort bore little fruit. Even White House officials, though delighted with the April Fool's Day revolution, were soon ready to turn to other things. There is more than a hint of impatience in White House aide Robert Sayre's comments about the unfortunate Brazilian "undercurrent" that the United States "owed" Brazil assistance because it had "thrown out" the Communists.[4]

That "undercurrent" was much in evidence during the rest of 1964. "We need billions of dollars in order to develop national production," observed General Olympio Mourão. He regarded himself as an expert in economics as well as an expert in leading revolutions. "Where will that financial stake come from? From the Western Bloc. We gave that bloc a victory as a present. It didn't cost it a cent. We prevented the international security system of the West from falling to its knees. Had we been just a little too late, the United States, in Brazil alone, would be facing twenty-two Cubas all at once."[5]

But, outside the United States, the ungrateful Western bloc was never able to see that communism had posed any kind of threat to Brazil in 1964. The Hard Line colonels running the IPMs never produced the promised evidence of any Castro-trained peasant army, or heavily armed communist guerrilla units within the labor unions, or infiltrated Cuban or Soviet agents in government agencies. So meager was their harvest of evidence, after months of interrogating and reinterrogating likely suspects, that the colonels were forced to advance the charge of corruption as an alternate reason for harassing supporters of the overthrown government. But it was hard for others to see how such an ordinary and perennial a sin of governments justified the retention of the extralegal inquisitorial military courts; wasn't São Paulo governor Adhemar de Barros, famous as the most corrupt politician in Brazil, a member of the winning side?[6] The international credibility of the IPM colonels was further damaged when their nominal commander, Marshal Taurino

Resende, resigned his post in August 1964, after his son was arrested as a subversive. The marshal indignantly insisted that his son was neither corrupt nor subversive but rather "an idealist like his father." How many other idealists were being harassed by the witch-hunting colonels?

Within Brazil and in exile abroad, the losers—left-wing intellectuals, radical nationalists, centrist politicians who had supported Goulart— bitterly debated the significance of their defeat. Whose fault was it? Was Goulart to blame? Or perhaps Brizola? Who was really calling the shots—Lacerda, Lincoln Gordon, Castello Branco, AMFORP, ITT? To what extent was the April Fool Revolution made in Washington? Or was it Wall Street? How soon would the military return to their barracks?

In 1964 leftists were highly incensed over use of the word "revolution" to describe the overthrow of Goulart. "Revolution" was a sacred word to them, an event watched and waited for like the Second Coming. Much ink was at first spilled proving that what had happened was at most a counterrevolutionary setback, a temporary glitch in the inexorable march of the "real" Brazilian revolution. But the months, the years went by, and the "bland" dictatorship (*dita-blanda*) of General Castello Branco tightened into the "harsh" dictatorship (*dita-dura*) of General Médici. Hope for an imminent revolutionary advent waned.

Opposition intellectuals turned to more long-range analyses of the political and economic forces that had led to the collapse of Brazil's "populist" government. Two major types of explanation emerged. One stressed the idea of a political "structural" crisis. For some fifteen years the political system set up in 1946 had been able to defuse conflicts and reduce social tensions while at the same time maintaining the power and privileges of the governing elites. But those conflicts and tensions steadily increased as the pressures of modernization and development mounted. In 1964, unable to moderate the internal contradictions any longer, the political structure simply collapsed, and the military was compelled to intervene in order to prevent chaos.[7]

The other explanation focused on global economic developments. The expansive forces of international capitalism had long required access to the resources and markets of the underdeveloped Third World countries such as Brazil. Now the dynamics of international capitalist growth had reached the point at which the creation of "associated, dependent" manufacturing areas located on the "periphery" of "hegemonic" centers made sense. Such associated, dependent subcenters could take advantage of the plentiful cheap labor as well as of local natural resources. In Brazil in the early 1960s, that type of development was hampered by the growing political mobilization of the urban workers and the peasantry and by the opposition of nationalist politicians who were supported by a petty national bourgeoisie that was not tied to the multinational corporations. From the standpoint of world capitalist development, it was necessary to repress the workers and peasants and sweep aside the nationalist politicians and petty bourgeoisie. Hence, the 1964 revolution, a genuinely revolutionary event in an economic sense, with a new elite group in control of the means of production. The Brazilian economy was soon effectively adapted to modern forms of international capitalism as military bureaucrats, "internationalist" businessmen, and technocrats tied to the multinationals replaced those who had advocated nationalist and "statist" development.[8]

A good argument can be made for either explanation. Both have merit. The theory of structural collapse in 1961–64 elucidates the internal political tensions and enormous domestic problems faced by the Goulart government. Dependency theory helps explain the Brazilian economic "miracle," the direction taken by the economy after 1964. However, both explanations tend to obscure the part played in the revolution by the United States government and by anticommunist ideology.

Of course the dependency explanation does allow a role in the 1964 coup for the large American multinational corporations, if not directly for the American government. It thus retains interpretations advanced by early Marxist critics of the revolution. According to these critics, the Kennedy-Johnson administrations, like all previous American governments, obediently followed the dictates of American big business; it was Hanna Mining Company, Bond and Share, ITT, Exxon, and Chase Manhattan Bank who really determined U.S. foreign policy in Brazil.[9]

The argument is worth considering. We have seen that, in response to heated criticism from the business community and Congress, Kennedy abandoned his initial policy of minimizing the role of American private enterprise in Latin American development. He became extremely solicitous of business opinion and designated officials to listen to and try to solve the grievances of corporate investors in Third World countries. The president never chided American businessmen resident in Brazil who became actively involved in anti-Goulart activities, although some State Department officials privately expressed displeasure. Lyndon Johnson, determined from the first to strike a probusiness note, was even more solicitous of corporate goodwill than Kennedy had been.

However, it must be noted that there is a difference between soliciting the advice of business and actually acting on it. "Superficial" and "generally useless" were the terms that Secretary of Commerce Luther Hodges used to characterize the advice tendered by the top corporate executives who made up the Business Advisory Council. Lyndon Johnson, so successful in winning over big business, was clearly following a "stroking" policy. "He had two meetings and they were back to back," reported Ralph Dungan:

> One was with the Business Council and the other was with the trade union leaders. And I'll never forget it. I sat in on both meetings and I heard practically the same bullshit given to both groups, and they both ate it up! He was phenomenal that way; it was pure blarney, but they really . . .
>
> [QUESTION]: The businessmen are supposed to be super sophisticates.
>
> [DUNGAN]: They're the worse, believe me, they're the worse ever. They go for it like trouts to flies. Fantastic![10]

Though Johnson met with business groups frequently and with individual corporate executives like David Rockefeller regularly, there is no evidence that he ever picked up or acted upon a single suggestion made during those meetings. Communication and influence seems to have generally flowed the other way, with Johnson making use of big business to speed his foreign aid and defense bills through Congress. At least some of the corporate executives recognized that they were being used. United States Steel president Roger Blough, for example, suggested that Johnson derived some sort of personal psychological relief from his long talks to groups of business leaders, when he could "ramble on" about the nation's problems to people "who had no power or authority to deal with them."[11]

"You can never rely on businessmen," a member of the Cold War pressure group Committee on the Present Danger insisted years later. "They operate out of a very narrow frame of reference. Generally speaking the smart ones can think about the balance sheet for the year after next. The ordinary ones can't even think that far."[12] It was liberal academics and bureaucratic ideologues, not businessmen, who worked out the nation-building response to an imagined Soviet threat to the Third World. It was Kennedy himself who added an emphasis on counterinsurgency and a buildup of conventional warfare capability. Nation-building activities in Brazil might directly benefit American corporations, but corporate executives, rightly tending their balance sheets, did not develop the doctrine.

It was true, of course, that the business community set certain limits to presidential foreign policy initiatives and exacted specific concessions from Kennedy in the case of Brazil. The president must not pursue basic reforms abroad that might in any way threaten American private investment there. He must talk up the significance of private foreign investment and press Third World governments to welcome such investment. In Brazil, the administration must try to obtain compensation for ITT for its expropriated subsidiary, permission for Hanna Mining to mine and export iron ore, and the takeover (on AMFORP's terms) of unprofitable public utilities by the Brazilian government.

As long as those limits were observed, the administration was free to carry out whatever policy it could sell to, or conceal from, the American Congress and public. It could pour millions of dollars into an effort to distort a "free" election and defeat left-wing, progovernment candidates. It could promote a crash economic development program but then withhold financing from the central government while channeling it to antigovernment state governors. It could spend large sums drilling soldiers and police in counterinsurgency tactics, tactics aimed at the enemy within—i.e., other Brazilians. It could provide covert financing and guidance to antigovernment business, military, and church groups. It could recruit, fund, and arm right-wing, antigovernment, paramilitary terrorist bands. It could, after the coup, provide millions in bailout assistance that enabled a repressive military dictatorship to tighten its grip on power. It could, finally, dispatch hundreds of eager technical experts and advisors in a futile attempt to redo Brazilian institutions according to American models.

To what end? For what purpose were funds provided by American taxpayers spent so lavishly? Was it all done to enable American multinationals to better penetrate the Brazilian economy? If that was the objective, it was hidden deep in some sort of collective unconscious. At the conscious, decision-making level, the wellspring of action was clearly anticommunism. The administration was gripped by the fear that all of South America, starting with Brazil, would fall to communism, never to emerge again from the Soviet yoke. American political leadership must find a way to prevent such a catastrophe. The United States's own survival would be at stake, were it to be cut off from the markets and resources of the Third World. Any expense, any means was justifiable when it came down to the Survival of the Free World.

Anticommunism had captivated all but a small minority of Americans. It might be a negative ideology, but it provided a comprehensive definition of the Devil, an apocalyptic vision of the future, and a guide to present conduct.[13] It simplified and provided direction for the nation's foreign policy, while forging a national consensus in support of it. Thus, American labor leaders were as eager as corporate executives to do their bit to fight the Red Tide in Latin America. But the maintenance of U.S. hegemony in Brazil held no conscious or unconscious economic advantages to U.S. labor. The establishment of associated, dependent production centers on the periphery would only mean the export of American factory jobs and the decline of American labor unions.

Nor was anticommunist ideology important only for the Americans. In underlining the role of the United States in the 1964 revolution, it is not my intention to suggest that the United States was in any sense a sole or sufficient producer of that event. Whether the New Frontiersmen believed it or not, the limits to American influence operated as strongly in underdeveloped as in developed countries. Had not the Brazilian elites themselves adopted the American Cold War message and made it their own, no amount of American preaching would have borne fruit, as witness the meager results of the more constructive aspects of the nation-building effort.

One strain of anticommunism was already well embedded in Brazil. A supposed Communist threat had, after all, provided the rationalization for the Vargas dictatorship from 1937 to 1945. What the Americans offered in 1961 was an embellished, updated version of the old fear of rampant Bolsheviks, a version that suggested that strategically located Brazil had special cause for alarm and would necessarily play an important role in the coming East-West showdown. Forecasting "revolutionary war" as the thrust of international communist imperialism in the Third World, the new American Cold War message gave the Brazilian military a new raison d'être: counterinsurgency. Although Brazil might face no enemies across its frontiers, there were enemies within—communist dupes, pushy unions, infiltrated Red agents. Anticommunism was especially important for the victorious Brazilian military faction, the ESG, or Sorbonne, faction. They proceeded to weave concepts and the worldview of the new anticommunism into their own national security ideology.

By 1963 anticommunism had also caught on with other Brazilian elite groups, and that is what gave the generals significant civilian support as they seized power. Businessmen, plantation owners, middle-class club women, many members of the clergy, some writers, journalists, and other intelligentsia had come to see communists behind all national problems—behind the strikes, the food shortages, the inflation, the widespread unemployment, the land invasions by landless peasants. It may be true that, at bottom, the elites simply felt their privileges threatened by recently

257

mobilized lower classes, but they cast their bitter antagonism to under-classes in the nobler, less selfish terms of an anticommunist crusade.

History tends to be hard on losers. There is always the strong temptation to suggest that whatever happened, happened because it was right; wrong must lie with the vanquished. At first, Goulart was roundly condemned by Brazilians who supported the coup for encouraging communist penetration of the government, laying the groundwork for the installation of either a Peron-style syndicalist republic or a Castro-Soviet-style regime. Gradually, as the public tired of hearing the few shreds of evidence, opinion shifted to condemning him for incompetence rather than for subversion. American officials were slower to relinquish their belief that the military coup had narrowly averted a coup by Goulart that would have established a procommunist dictatorship. But by 1968 even official American opinion had shifted. "The Goulart regime fell largely from the weight of its own ineptitude," testified the AID director in Brazil. According to his analysis, by March 1964 Goulart's government was on the verge of collapse because it was bankrupt, had exhausted its international credit, and suffered an inflation rate of over 100 percent.[14]

As indicated above, other analysts suggested that long-term problems of modernization and development, not just the short-term fiscal crisis, underlay the 1964 revolution. Goulart, a simple ward heeler, lacked the ability to make the existing institutions work any longer, much less carry the nation through the next stage of modernization. The military government, with its powers of repression, would be able to pick up the pieces and carry out modernization. In the Third World, according to this interpretation, authoritarian repression is one of the cruel dilemmas of development.[15]

Perhaps it is time to reevaluate Goulart. He seems to have been a political leader of modest talents, albeit one who knew his limitations and tried to appoint ministers of proven ability. He inherited a government with staggering economic problems—accelerating inflation, deepening recession, constant balance-of-payments problems, an unrepayable foreign debt load. In addition, political consensus had broken down, and he was caught between the bitter hostility of an implacable right wing and the incessant pressure for immediate reforms from impatient left-wing nationalists. Goulart was unable to make a dent on any of these problems; all continued to worsen during his two and a half years in the presidency.

On the other hand, it would be only fair to conjecture what might have happened if he had not faced the hostility of a superpower, over and above the economic and political burdens that he had inherited. If the United States had not done so much to destabilize his government, might he not at least have been able to stagger on until the end of his term, thus preserving the political institutions of the young democracy? If a portion of the American aid showered on the military dictatorship had been made available to the Goulart government, would his performance record have been better? Were perhaps some of the economic problems he faced essentially insoluble? It might be noted that, in spite of all the powers they possessed and all the aid they received, the generals were unable to solve all problems; returning power to civilians in 1985, the generals also turned over an enormously swollen foreign debt load, a staggering rate of inflation, and a record of widespread corruption by high government-military officials.[16]

Of course, even if the American government had refrained from interfering, Goulart might still have been overthrown by the Brazilian military. "Do I have any knowledge that special North American CIA agents collaborated in the preparation of March 31? I have no such knowledge," said Carlos Lacerda, the confidant of the U.S. ambassador, years later. "If you ask do I believe that perhaps there was some collaboration, I can easily believe it, and I think it normal. But I also believe that it wasn't necessary, because I would not insult the Brazilian armed forces by supposing that they are incapable of staging a coup, for that's something they've done throughout their existence! They have the know-how to teach the American army."[17] As a confirmed *golpista* himself, Lacerda might be presumed to be in a position to know the military's coup capability. But he was probably overly sanguine about the generals' ability to do it all alone in 1964. They had tried, after all, to stage a coup barring Goulart in 1961. Their failure then unnerved them. Without the mobilization of the civilian elite groups and the junior military officer corps behind the anticommunist banner, without the active encouragement of the U.S. government, the military coup plotters might never have tried again.

"For our unfulfilled task," John F. Kennedy told assembled Latin American diplomats in 1961, "is to demonstrate to the entire world that man's unsatisfied aspirations for economic progress and social justice can best be achieved by free men working within a framework of democratic institutions."[18] The task remained unfulfilled in 1971; in fact, it seemed more difficult than ever. As the military regime tightened its grip on Brazil and established a framework of authoritarian institutions and new models of repression for other Latin countries to emulate,[19] many of the American liberals who had at first so enthusiastically endorsed the Alliance for Progress abandoned the nation-building crusade. "Given the magnitude of our effort during the 1960's," said Senator Frank Church in 1970, "we are left to wonder why it produced such disappointing results. We thought we were seeding the resurgence of democratic governments; instead, we have seen a relentless slide toward militarism. We thought we could remodel Latin societies, but the reforms we prescribed have largely eluded us."[20] The next year the senator declared his opposition to the entire foreign aid program:

> Even if we should succeed in purging our minds of the anti-Communist obsession which has driven us into league with military dictatorships and oppressive oligarchies all over the globe, it would still be all but impossible for us to promote radical reform in the countries of the third world. Even indeed if we were a revolutionary society ourselves and were committed to a revolutionary conception of development—as most assuredly we are not—there is still very little we could do to foster social revolution in alien societies. The catalyst of radical change in any society must be an indigenous nationalism giving rise to a sense of community, commitment and shared sacrifice.[21]

A few dedicated Kennedy partisans continued to try to pin the blame for the failure of nation building in Latin American on President Johnson.[22] Johnson refused to accept the onus. "Our dealings with Brazil were based on the recommendations of Linc Gordon, George Ball and Dean Rusk—all Kennedy men," McGeorge Bundy (another Kennedy man) sternly reminded one such partisan.[23]

In any case, Johnson personally probably did not consider American policy in Brazil such a failure; he had never shared the great expectations of the liberals who devised the Alliance for Progress. During his own term of office there were some definite short-term returns from the American investment in the Brazilian military regime. Castello Branco sent Brazilian troops to legitimize the American occupation of the Dominican Republic as an OAS venture, and he sent at least words of praise for American intervention in Vietnam. Since aid to Brazil was "tied" to purchases of American goods, the American economy as a whole benefited, and the balance of trade with Brazil continued to run in America's favor. Just as important for Johnson was the political spinoff: the executives representing the American multinationals were absolutely delighted with the change in the business climate of Brazil. They were more than ready to give Johnson full credit. Liberal "bellyachers" like Senator Church might complain that American aid to Brazil was designed "primarily to serve private business interests at the expense of the American people."[24] President Johnson knew his public: it would be extraordinarily difficult to persuade the American people that what benefited business interests hurt them.

Of course Brazil has changed a great deal over the years since Johnson left office. More armaments than coffee are now exported, and the balance of trade with the United States is definitely in Brazil's favor. Brazilian elite groups enjoy more modern comforts and wealth than ever before. But the social dimensions of Brazil's contemporary problems are little changed from what they were in 1961. One-third of the population is still stalked (in the words of President Harry S. Truman) by "their ancient enemies—hunger, misery, and despair."[25] A new strand of interpersonal violence and violent crime has been woven into the fabric of Brazilian urban culture. Ghosts of the disappeared, spirits of Death Squad victims, echoes from the torture chambers still linger. The military, unchastened and unrepentant, still stands in the wings, ready to resume operations against the civilian population.[26]

The question remains: might Brazilian development have proceeded differently, more humanely, more equitably, with greater social justice, if President Kennedy had never given his "special pledge" to the "sister republics south of our border" to assist them "in casting off the chains of poverty" and to "join with them to oppose aggression or subversion anywhere in the Americas"?[27]

It is too early to put away the pencils.

# Notes

## Abbreviations Used in Notes

All translations were done by the author.

CPDOC      Centro de Pesquisa e Documentação de História Contemporâneo
           do Brasil, Instituto de Direito Público e Ciência Política, Fun-
           dação Getulio Vargas. Rio de Janeiro.
DDEL       Dwight D. Eisenhower Library
Dec.DOS.doc. Declassified Department of State document. Copy in author's
           possession.
Decl.Doc.  Many recently declassified documents are listed in Research Pub-
           lications, Inc., *Declassified Documents Quarterly Catalog* and
           reproduced on microfiche. Available in research libraries.
JFKL       John F. Kennedy Library
    NSF Co-K National Security Files: Country: Brazil
    NSF MM  National Security Files: Meetings & Memos
    NSF Trips National Security Files: Trips and Conferences
    POF Co   President's Office Files: Country: Brazil
    POF Dep  President's Office Files: Departments & Agencies
    POF Staff President's Office Files: Staff
    WHCF-K  White House Central Files

LBJL          Lyndon B. Johnson Library
    NSF Co-J    National Security Files: Country: Brazil
    NSF LA     National Security Files: Country: Latin America
    NSF NSC Staff National Security Files: National Security Council Staff
            File
    WHCF-J    White House Central Files
    Confidential  White House Central Files: Confidential CO 37
    Name File   White House Central Files: Name Files

## Chapter 1

1. In Brazil first names are used more frequently than surnames. Thus, public figures will usually be referred to by their first names: Jânio, Juscelino, Getúlio—not Quadros, Kubitschek, Vargas. But there are exceptions. Some individuals are better known by a nickname (e.g., Jango), or by one of their surnames (e.g., Lacerda), or by a combination of first name and one surname (e.g., Afonso Arinos), or by two surnames (e.g., Moura Andrade).

2. Mário Victor, *Cinco anos que abalaram o Brasil* (Rio de Janeiro, 1965), 80–89; "Quadros Pledges Democratic Rule," *New York Times*, 1 Feb. 1961, p.3, col.5.

3. Cf. Frank Bonilla, *"Jânio Vem Aí:* Brazil Elects a President," American Universities Field Staff Reports Service, East Coast South America Series, vol. 7, no. 2 (Oct. 1960): 23.

4. Editorial, *Correiro da Manha,* 1 Feb. 1961.

5. *Public Papers of the Presidents of the United States: John F. Kennedy, 1961* (Washington, D.C., 1962), 28.

6. See E. Bradford Burns, *Nationalism in Brazil: A Historical Survey* (New York, 1968).

7. Gondin da Fonseca, *A miséria é nossa* (São Paulo, 1961), 51.

8. Cf. Michael Parenti, *The Anti-Communist Impulse* (New York, 1969).

9. E.g., Willard L. Beaulac, *A Diplomat Looks at Aid to Latin America* (Carbondale, 1970), 65.

10. Dwight D. Eisenhower, *Waging Peace, 1956–1961* (Garden City, N.Y., 1965), 522.

11. Walt W. Rostow, *The United States in the World Arena* (New York, 1960), 254.

12. John F. Kennedy, *The Strategy of Peace* (New York, 1960), 132–33.

13. Ibid., 5.

14. Cf. Bruce Miroff, *Pragmatic Illusions: The Presidential Politics of John F. Kennedy* (New York, 1976), 35–63.

15. Nikita S. Khrushchev, "For New Victories of the World Communist Movement: Results of the Meeting of Representatives of the Communist and Workers' Parties," in *Communism—Peace and Happiness for the Peoples* (Moscow, 1963), 1:14.

16. Walt W. Rostow, *The Diffusion of Power, 1957–1972* (New York, 1972), 34–35.

17. Khrushchev, "For New Victories," 53, 55.

18. Arthur M. Schlesinger, Jr., *A Thousand Days: John F. Kennedy in the White House* (Boston, 1965), 303.

19. *Time,* 20 Jan. 1961, "Man Wanted," 35.

20. Milton S. Eisenhower, *The Wine Is Bitter* (New York, 1963), xi.

21. Richard M. Nixon, *Six Crises* (Garden City, N.Y., 1962), xvi.

22. *New York Times,* 7 July 1961, "Birch Society Building Files on 'Leading Liberals,'" 9:5. Welch's principal publication, *The Politician* (Belmont, Mass., 1963), "proved" that Dwight D. Eisenhower had been "planted" in the presidency by the international communist conspiracy, a conspiracy that Eisenhower had been "consciously serving...for all of his adult life" (278–79).

23. See Geoffrey Perrett, *A Dream of Greatness: The American People 1945–1963* (New York, 1979), 266–86, 589–95.

24. DeLesseps S. Morrison, *Latin American Mission* (New York, 1965), 175.

25. Joan Blair and Clay Blair, Jr., *The Search for JFK* (New York, 1976), 524–31; Lewis J. Paper, *The Promise and the Performance: The Leadership of John F. Kennedy* (New York, 1975), 48, 62–66.

26. Schlesinger, *Thousand Days,* 206.

27. Richard J. Walton, *Cold War and Counterrevolution: The Foreign Policy of John F. Kennedy* (New York, 1972), 6.

## Chapter 2

1. Herbert K. May to State Dept., 23 Jan. 1961, POF Co.

2. *Public Papers of the Presidents of the United States. Lyndon B. Johnson, 1963–64* (Washington, D.C., 1965), 1:290.

3. Arthur Schlesinger, Jr., to President, 6 Feb. 1961, POF Staff, Box 65. Not everyone in the White House was impressed by the choice, however. As Schlesinger staked out a claim to the job of "watching" Latin America, longtime Kennedy aide Ralph Dungan transformed himself from expert on Africa to expert on Latin America in part to watch Schlesinger. Ralph Dungan, interview, 6 Apr. 1972, Oral History Collection, LBJL. When he was appointed special assistant to the president, Schlesinger had some difficulty discovering what his duties were supposed to be and had to more or less define them for himself. See John K. Galbraith, *Ambassador's Journal* (New York, 1970), 45.

4. Schlesinger to President, 11 Feb. 1961, POF Staff.

5. Schlesinger, *A Thousand Days: John F. Kennedy in the White House* (Boston, 1965), 180–81.

6. Joseph A. Page, *The Revolution That Never Was* (New York, 1972), 128–29.

7. Communist leader Gregório Bezerra describes one such incident in *Memórias, segunda parte,* 2d ed. (Rio de Janeiro, 1980), 118–20.

8. See Carlos Castilho Cabral, *Tempos de Jânio* (Rio de Janeiro, 1962), 93.

9. For analysis of the campaign, see Vladimir Reisky de Dubnic, *Political Trends in Brazil,* 102–21; and Frank Bonilla, *"Jânio Vem Aí:* Brazil Elects a President," American Universities Field Staff Reports Service, East Coast South America Series, vol. 7, no. 2 (Oct. 1960), 17–32.

10. Party chairman Luis Carlos Prestes also cited a personal affection for Lott, dating back to his childhood days, when both attended the same military school. Dênis de Moraes and Francisco Viana, *Prestes: lutas e autocríticas,* 2d ed. (Petrópolis, 1982), 163–64.

11. Cabral, *Tempos de Jânio,* 173.

12. Mário Victor, *Cinco anos que abalaram o Brasil* (Rio de Janeiro, 1965), 54–65. Juarez Tavora, *Uma vida e muitas lutas* (Rio de Janeiro, 1965), 3:138–39.

13. "Barbara" to Mr. Stephens, memo, 12 and 13 Oct. 1960, Pres. Papers, DDEL.

14. Christian A. Herter to President, 29 Oct. 1960, DDEL.

15. See unsigned White House memos, 5 and 7 Nov. 1960, DDEL.

16. Herter to AmEmbassy, London, 10 Nov. 1960; "H. C." to Mr. Stephens, 18 Nov. 1960, DDEL.

17. See White House memos of 22, 25, 29 Nov. and 2 and 15 Dec. 1960, DDEL; *Time,* "Journey to the East" ("The Hemisphere"), 5 Dec. 1960; *New York Times,* "Quadros Absence Worrying Brazil," 23 Dec. 1960, 7:4; John S. D. Eisenhower, Synopsis of State and Intelligence, 6 Dec. 1960, Decl.Doc. no. 1732, 1986.

18. See *New York Times,* "Quadros Delays Cabinet Choices," 22 Jan. 1961, 31:3.

19. John M. Cabot to SecState, 31 Jan. 1961, NSF Co-K.

20. "Sam" (Samuel E. Belk) to Bundy, 26 Jan. 1961, Co-K.

21. Herbert K. May to Dept. of State, 23 Jan. 1961, POF Co.

22. Rusk to President, undated, and Rusk to AmEmbassy, 3 Feb. 1961, both POF Co.

23. See *Correio da Manha,* 18 Feb. 1961.

24. Beatrice Berle and Travis Jacobs, eds., *Navigating the Rapids 1918–1971: From the Papers of Adolf A. Berle* (New York, 1973), 737. Adolf A. Berle, *The Cold War in Latin America* (Storrs, Conn., 1961), 9–10.

25. See Afonso Arinos de Melo Franco, *Planalto: Memórias* (Rio de Janeiro, 1968), 83–84.

26. Berle, *Navigating the Rapids,* 741–42.

27. Ibid., 725.

28. John M. Cabot, Interview with William W. Moss, 27 Jan. 1971, 4, Oral History Collection, JFKL.

29. Franco, *Planalto,* 83–84.

30. Cabot to SecState, 3 Mar. 1961, NSF Co-K.

31. Berle, *Navigating the Rapids,* 736.

32. Ibid., 737, 739. *New York Times,* "U.S.-Brazil Talks Close in Discord over Cuba Issue," 4 Mar. 1961, 1:4, and "Brazil Leaning to Neutralism," 5 Mar. 1961, IV, 6:1. See also *Correio da Manha,* 4 Mar. 1961 and editorial, 5 Mar. 1961.

33. John W. F. Dulles, *Unrest in Brazil: Political-Military Crises 1955–1964* (Austin, 1970), 119–120.

34. Franco, *Planalto,* 85–86.

35. See L. D. Battle to Ralph A. Dungan, memo, 16 Mar. 1961, NSF Co-K.

36. Rusk to President, memo, 21 Mar. 1961, POF Co.

37. Dillon to President, 12 Apr. 1961, POF Co.

38. See Victor Wallis, "Brazil's Experiment with an Independent Foreign Policy," in *Contemporary Inter-American Relations,* ed. Yale H. Ferguson (Englewood Cliffs, N.J. 1972), 35–50.

39. Franco, *Planalto,* 24–27, 60.

40. Jânio Quadros, "Brazil's New Foreign Policy," *Foreign Affairs* 40 (Oct. 1961): 19–27.

41. Franco, *Planalto,* 84–95.

42. Memorandum of Conversation, 16 May 1961, NSF Co-K.

43. Niles Bond to SecState, 31 May 1961, NSF Co-K.

44. Renato Archer, interview with Lucia Hippolito and Helena Maria Bomeny, interview/ Aug. 1978, 269–70, Oral History Collection, CPDOC. However, the $648 million committed

by the United States was not scheduled for immediate disbursement. It was to be paid in installments over the next few years.

45. Victor, *Cinco anos,* 256.

46. Cabot to SecState, 12 July 1961, NSF Co-K.

47. Leonard G. Wolf to Chester Bowles, memo, 29 Mar. 1961, NSF Co-K.

48. A month earlier, Jânio had cordially received Cabot at the presidential palace, laying it on "not with a trowel, but with a bulldozer." The ambassador was far from mollified, however. He was sure that Quadros's earlier performance represented "a deliberate gesture to leftist nationalists," not a misunderstanding, and believed that Jânio's present cordiality was "engendered in part because of his announcement at morning press conference regarding Russian recognition and because of special courtesies he had extended to Russians before." Cabot to SecState, 25 July 1961, NSF Co-K.

49. One was a proposal to restrict the export of profits by foreign-owned corporations; the other was aimed at restricting the growth of monopolies. See statement by Pedro Aleixo, the leader of the Quadros government in the Chamber of Deputies, in Cabral, *Tempos de Jânio,* 310–12.

50. Victor, *Cinco anos,* 210.

51. Ibid., 139–52.

52. A February 16 decree changing the hours of federal employees and an order on June 6 to shut down a radio station for three days also caused a great outcry. Quadros reversed himself on the work hours on August 8, reinstating the old schedule. The penalty against the radio station was carried out (federal employees carted off part of the station's transmission tower to make sure), but Quadros did much to destroy his image as a defender of a free press in the process. The arbitrary punishment did not seem to fit the crime: the station had merely erroneously reported that Quadros and the president of Argentina had reached a verbal agreement to reduce armaments. See *Correio da Manha,* 7 June 1961; and Victor, *Cinco anos,* 90–99, 189–97.

53. Franco, *Planalto,* 59.

54. From a Lacerda editorial, quoted in Victor, *Cinco anos,* 252. See also Lacerda, *"As quatro mentiras sôbre Cuba,"* in his *O poder das idéias,* 4th ed. (Rio de Janeiro, 1964), 286–306.

55. Franco, *Planalto,* 101. See also Serafino Romualdi, *Presidents and Peons: Recollections of a Labor Ambassador in Latin America* (New York, 1967), 226.

56. See Stoessel to Dungan, 17 Feb. 1961, POF Co; and Schlesinger to Fred Holborn, memo, 9 Mar. 1961, Schlesinger Papers, JFKL. Lacerda had spent much of 1956 in the United States; he had fled Brazil, fearing arrest, after involvement in a plot to prevent the inauguration of Kubitschek and Goulart.

57. Franco, *Planalto,* 157.

58. Misunderstanding was mutual. State Department analysts believed that Afonso Arinos personally was "in full sympathy with our appraisal of Castro as a significant danger to the hemisphere" but that he had been "personally ordered" by Quadros to introduce the independent posture (Battle to Ralph A. Dungan, memo, 16 Mar. 1961, NSF Co-K). Actually, Arinos supported the policy enthusiastically.

59. Quoted in Jerome Levinson and Juan de Onis, *The Alliance That Lost Its Way* (Chicago, 1972), 62.

60. See *New York Times,* "U.S. Seeks to Spur Latins to Joint Action on Cuba," 27 Apr. 1961, 1:6; "Quadros Weighs U.S. Plea on Cuba," 30 Apr. 1961, 19:1; "Brazil Opposes

Censure of Cuba," 11 May 1961, 19:1; "U.S. Hope on Cuba Suffers Setback," 14 May 1961, 23:3.

61. Always worried about sending up the wrong signal of approval by granting the honor of a White House reception, State Department analysts warned that Furtado had been or still was "a Marxist who is still socialistic in his political beliefs and economic orientation" (Battle to Bundy, memo, 7 July 1961, POF Co).

## Chapter 3

1. See Richard J. Barnet, *Intervention and Revolution* (New York, 1968), 237–43, for a succinct summary of Kennedy administration intervention in British Guiana.

2. DeLesseps Morrison, *Latin American Mission* (New York, 1965), 75–76. Secretary of Treasury Dillon, in particular, received the full treatment: "full military honors including national anthem and review of troops." Quadros had then treated Dillon to a soliloquy on his personal philosophy of how to contain communism. Dillon to SecState, 4 Aug. 1961, POF Co.

3. Director CIA to White House, 25 Aug. 1961, POF Co.

4. Afonso Arinos de Melo Franco, *Planalto: Memórias* (Rio de Janeiro, 1968), 101.

5. Mário Victor, *Cinco anos que abalaram o Brasil* (Rio de Janeiro, 1965), 147–51.

6. Lacerda's television address of August 24, when he told all, is reprinted in Carlos Lacerda, *O poder das idéias,* 4th ed., (Rio de Janeiro, 1964), 329–43.

7. See ibid., 338–39.

8. Water shortages were particularly troublesome in 1961. Cf. editorial, *Correio da Manha,* 19 Aug. 1961.

9. Newspaper interview with Eloa Quadros, quoted in John W. F. Dulles, *Unrest in Brazil: Political-Military Crises, 1955–1964* (Austin, 1970), 127.

10. Ibid., 128.

11. Lacerda, *Poder das idéias,* 336.

12. Franco, *Planalto,* 102–3.

13. For example, *Correio da Manha,* 22 and 24 Aug. 1961.

14. Lacerda, *Poder das idéias,* 341–42.

15. *Correio da Manha,* 26 Aug. 1961. Victor, *Cinco anos,* 307.

16. Deputy Oswaldo Lima Filho, quoted in Victor, *Cinco anos,* 304.

17. Auro Moura Andrade, *Um congresso contra o arbítrio* (Rio de Janeiro, 1985), 32–40, 48.

18. The president of the Chamber, Mazzili, had been informed about the resignation by War Minister Denys at noon. He shared the news with other party leaders but waited for the actual letter of resignation before making the news public. Hélio Silva, *1964, golpe ou contragolpe* (Rio de Janeiro, 1975), 39–43.

19. Foreign Minister Afonso Arinos, for example, received his hint at the end of July. See Franco, *Planalto,* 160–62.

20. See Dulles, *Unrest in Brazil,* 133–36, on the resignation story. Some Brazilian politicians, such as Castilho Cabral, thought that Quadros resigned in order to spare his justice minister from humiliation by Congress. See Carlos Castilho Cabral, *Tempos de Jânio e outras tempos* (Rio de Janeiro, 1962), 245–46. However, Quadros had made up his mind to resign hours before the Chamber of Deputies voted to summon Horta. He mentioned his decision to a military aide at 7:00 A.M.

21. Victor, *Cinco anos,* 308–9.

22. The use of Vargas's note as a model was recognized and deeply resented by Vargas admirers such as Moura Andrade. Andrade, *Um congresso contra arbítrio,* 42.

23. *Correio da Manha,* 26 Aug. 1961.

24. Silva, *1964,* 45.

25. Cabral, *Tempos de Jânio,* 219–20, 231.

26. Dulles, *Unrest in Brazil,* 136.

27. Cabral, *Tempos de Jânio,* 235.

28. See Bond to SecState, 26 Aug. 1961, NSF Co-K; and CIA memo, 28 Aug. 1961, POF Co.

29. D/O Situation Room to Col. McHugh, 26 Aug. 1961, POF Co.

30. Bond to White House, 1 Sept. 1961, NSF Co-K.

31. Situation Room to Col. McHugh, 27 Aug. 1961, POF Co.

32. Allen Dulles, memo, 28 Aug. 1961, POF Co.

33. In addition, there was the nagging worry that protracted delay in inaugurating a new president might mean the return of Quadros. At one point, Chargé d'Affaires Niles Bond suggested that a weak Goulart who could be controlled by the military might be preferable to a strong-willed Quadros who could not be. Situation Room to Col. McHugh, 26 Aug. 1962, POF Co.

34. Silva, *1964,* 53.

35. Victor, *Cinco anos,* 347–48.

36. *Correio da Manha,* 31 Aug. 1961.

37. *Correio da Manha,* 3 Oct. 1961.

38. Bond to SecState, 6 Sept. 1961, NSF Co-K.

39. Jan Knippers Black, *United States Penetration of Brazil* (Philadelphia, 1977), 43.

40. Aurelio de Limeira Tejo, *Jango: debate sobre a crise dos nossos tempos* (Rio de Janeiro, 1957), 110.

41. Memorandum of conversation, Kubitschek and Kennedy, 15 Sept. 1961, NSF Co-K.

42. Renato Archer, interview with Lucia Hippolito and Helena Maria Bomeny, Aug. 1978, 272, Oral History Collection, CPDOC.

43. Abelardo Jurema, interview with Aspasia Camargo and Eduardo Raposo, July 1977, 354, Oral History Collection, CPDOC.

44. Ibid., 316.

45. Jean-Jacques Faust, *A revolução devora seus presidentes* (Rio de Janeiro, 1965), 54.

46. João Pinheiro, interview with Aspasia Camargo, Helena Maria Bomeny, and Maria Luíza Heilborn, June 1977, 50, Oral History Collection, CPDOC.

47. Abelardo Jurema, *Sexta-feira, 13,* 3d ed. (Rio de Janeiro, 1964), 26.

48. Luiz Alberto Moniz Bandeira, *O governo João Goulart* (Rio de Janeiro, 1977), 26.

49. Faust, *A revolução,* 54.

50. Archer, interview, 432–33.

51. Jurema, interview, 276.

52. Archer, interview, 273.

53. Antonio Callado, *"Jango, ou o suicídio sem sangue,"* in Alberto Dines et al., *Os idos de março e a queda em abril* (Rio de Janeiro, 1964), 254.

54. See Thomas E. Skidmore, *Politics in Brazil, 1930–1964* (New York, 1967), 112–15.

55. Initially Vargas had considered naming Jango minister of agriculture, a post that would have been more in keeping with his rural background. Abelardo Jurema, *Juscelino e Jango* (Rio de Janeiro, 1979), 164–67.

56. See Kenneth P. Erickson, *The Brazilian Corporative State and Working-Class Politics* (Berkeley, 1977), 34–43.

57. Dulles, *Unrest in Brazil,* 23. Bandeira, *Governo João Goulart,* 31–33.

58. Skidmore, *Politics in Brazil,* 149–50.

59. *New York Times,* "Vargas Reassures Brazil on Charter," 8 Aug. 1953, 5:1, and "Vargas is Victor on Wage Decree," 6 July 1954, 3:7.

60. Philip Agee, *Inside the Company: CIA Diary* (New York, 1976), 68–69.

61. Romualdi, *Presidents and Peons,* 275, 277. Unlike Lovestone, Romualdi thought Goulart should be given a chance to make a "clean break" with the Communists. Goulart visited the United States as vice president in 1956. Romualdi became ecstatic when David Dubinsky, at a meeting in Atlantic City, asked Goulart "some pointed questions, finally succeeding in extracting from him an indirect denunciation of Communism" (280). Romualdi was aware that Goulart had taken the trouble to explicitly condemn communism on April 26, just before his departure for the United States, but apparently for Romualdi once was not enough.

62. E.g., PCB support in Pernambuco first for João Cleofas de Oliveira and then for Cid Sampaio, both conservative candidates for governor. See Paulo Cavalcanti, *O caso eu conto como o caso foi* (Recife, 1980), 1:261, 288–94. In Sergipe the PCB supported the UDN candidate for governor in 1962. See Joel Silveira, *Meninos, eu vi* (Rio de Janeiro, 1967).

63. Juracy Magalhães, *Minhas memórias provisórias* (Rio de Janeiro, 1982), 96.

64. Bond to SecState, 8 Sept. 1961, NSF Co-K, CIA Current Intelligence Memorandum, 27 Sept. 1961, NSF Co-K.

65. Bond to SecState, 8 Sept. 1961, NSF Co-K.

66. Background Paper, Brazil, memo for R. Goodwin, 14 Sept. 1961, NSF Co-K.

67. See José Coelho Pinto, *Um deputado no exilio* (Rio de Janeiro, 1965), for contrast of moods in 1961 and 1964. Franklin de Oliveira, *Revolução e contrarevolução no Brasil,* 2d ed. (Rio de Janeiro, 1962) provides an example of the mood of the Left at this time.

## Chapter 4

1. Walt W. Rostow, *The Diffusion of Power, 1957–1972* (New York, 1972), 125.

2. Max F. Millikan and Walt W. Rostow, *A Proposal: Key to an Effective Foreign Policy* (New York, 1957), 149–51.

3. Ibid., 12.

4. Ibid., 5–6.

5. Ibid., 55.

6. Department of State, *Bulletin* 45 (28 Aug. 1961): 357.

7. Millikan and Rostow, *A Proposal,* 44–48. Rostow expanded on this scheme in *The Stages of Economic Growth: A Non-Communist Manifesto* (New York, 1960).

8. Millikan and Rostow, *A Proposal,* 57–58, 64–65, 70–77.

9. Ibid., 24–32.

10. Philippe C. Schmitter, *Interest Conflict and Political Change in Brazil* (Stanford, Cal., 1971), 218.

11. Millikan and Rostow, *A Proposal,* 10–11.

12. Rostow, *Stages of Economic Growth,* 156. Cf. Bruce Miroff, *Pragmatic Illusions: The Presidential Politics of John F. Kennedy* (New York, 1976), 135–36.

13. Adolf A. Berle, *The Cold War in Latin America* (Storrs, Conn., 1961), 14. Beatrice Berle and Travis Jacobs, *Navigating the Rapids, 1918–1971. From the Papers of Adolf A. Berle* (New York, 1973), 757.

14. Arthur M. Schlesinger, Jr., *A Thousand Days: John F. Kennedy in the White House* (Boston, 1965), 180. *Correio da Manha,* 18 Feb. 1961.

15. Franklin de Oliveira, *Revolução e contrarevolução no Brasil,* 2d ed., (Rio de Janeiro, 1962), 76.

16. *Estado do São Paulo,* editorial, 17 May 1961.

17. White House reception for members of Congress and Latin American diplomats on March 13. Reprinted in Jerome Levinson and Juan de Onis, *The Alliance That Lost Its Way* (Chicago, 1970), 333–39.

18. Ibid., 56–58.

19. *New York Times,* "Dillon and Guevara in Uruguay for Americas Parley," 5 Aug. 1961, 1:7.

20. Levinson and Onis, *The Alliance,* 64–73.

21. Serafino Romualdi, *Presidents and Peons: Recollections of a Labor Ambassador in Latin America* (New York, 1967), 230–32.

22. See DeLesseps Morrison, *Latin American Mission* (New York, 1965), 77–105 for a detailed account of the conference.

23. Renato Archer, interview with Lucia Hippolito and Helena Maria Bomeny, Aug. 1978, 287, Oral History Collection, CPDOC. Oliveira, *Revolução e contrarevolução,* 94–97.

24. Quoted in Levinson and Onis, *The Alliance,* 73.

25. *Correio da Manha,* 24 Nov. 1961.

26. Cf. Riordan Roett, *The Politics of Foreign Aid in the Brazilian Northeast* (Nashville, 1972), 106–15.

27. JFK to Fowler Hamilton, 5 Feb. 1962, POF Co.

28. W. Alan Laflin, End of Tour Report, 30 July 1965, AID Reference Center.

29. Philip Agee, *Inside the Company: CIA Diary* (New York, 1976), 247–48. Even though President Kennedy had ruled that ambassadors were to have the ultimate authority over the rest of the "country team," Ambassador Gordon was poorly informed about the origin and work of IPES. He was under the impression that IPES was a businessmen's organization set up simply to issue publications that would counter the publications produced by the left-wing Instituto Superior de Estudos Brasileiros. Lincoln Gordon, interview with author, Washington, D.C., 19 Oct. 1988.

30. Lincoln Gordon, interview with Roberto Garcia, "Castello perdeu a batalha," *Veja,* 9 Mar. 1977, 6. The best study of IPES is René Armand Dreifuss, *1964: A conquista do estado,* 3d ed. (Petrópolis, 1981). See 162–64 for the founding of the organization. Dreifuss had access to IPES files. See also Philip Siekman, "When Executives Turned Revolutionaries," *Fortune,* Sept. 1964, 147–49, 210–21, and Paulo Ayres Filho, "The Brazilian Revolution" in *Latin America: Politics, Economics and Hemisphere Security,* ed. Norman Bailey (New York, 1965), 239–60.

31. Dreifuss, *1964,* 170–71.

32. Bundy, Memo for the President, 3 Feb. 1961, Box 328–330, NSF MM.

33. Schlesinger, *Thousand Days,* 340–41. See also Miroff, *Pragmatic Illusions,* 18.

34. Rostow, "Talking Paper for Gen. Taylor," pt. 3, NSAM 131 (undated), Box 334–335, NSF MM.

35. Bundy, Memo for the President, 16 Oct. 1961, Box 331–332, NSF MM.

36. Maxwell D. Taylor, Memo for Bundy, 13 Aug. 1962, NSAM 182, Box 335A-338, NSF MM.

37. JFK to Fowler Hamilton, NSAM 132, Box 335A-338, NSF MM.

38. Leonard J. Saccio, Memorandum for the Files, 4 June 1962, AID Decl.Doc. no. 130-C, 1981.

39. USAID/Rio de Janeiro, Airgram A-631 to AID, 17 Sept. 1962, Decl.Doc. no. 132-B, 1981.

40. Chester Bowles to President, 30 Sept. 1961, Box 331-332, NSF MM.

41. John K. Galbraith, *Ambassador's Journal* (New York, 1970), 175–76, 224.

42. Belk, Memo for Bundy, 16 May 1962, Box 334-335, NSF MM.

43. *Public Papers of the Presidents of the United States: John F. Kennedy, 1962* (Washington, D.C., 1963), 535.

44. Jack K. Ellis, End of Tour Report, 29 Jan. 1963, AID Reference Center.

## Chapter 5

1. An earlier version of this chapter appeared in the *Hispanic American Historical Review* 59 (Nov. 1979): 636–73.

2. E.g., Schlesinger to Dungan, 26 Aug. 1961, Schlesinger Papers, Subject Files, JFKL.

3. Hobart Rowen, *The Free Enterprisers: Kennedy, Johnson and the Business Establishment* (New York, 1964), 61–88. Eisenhower had an especially close relationship with the BAC, using it as a recruiting grounds for top positions in his administration.

4. Bruce Miroff, *Pragmatic Illusions: The Presidential Politics of John F. Kennedy* (New York, 1976), 167–222.

5. Max F. Millikan and Walt W. Rostow, *A Proposal: Key to an Effective Foreign Policy* (New York, 1957), 14–19.

6. Arthur Schlesinger, Jr., "The Alliance for Progress: A Retrospective," in *Latin America: The Search for a New International Role,* ed. Ronald G. Hellman and H. Jon Rosenbaum (New York, 1975), 66.

7. House Committee on Foreign Affairs, *Hearings, Winning the Cold War,* 88th Cong., 1st sess., pt. 2, 238. See also Serafino Roumaldi, *Presidents and Peons: Recollections of a Labor Ambassador in Latin America* (New York, 1967), 233.

8. See Schlesinger to Dungan, 15 Oct. 1962, Schlesinger Papers, Subject Files, Box 2, JFKL.

9. Dwight D. Eisenhower, *Waging Peace* (Garden City, N.Y., 1965), 531.

10. *Public Papers of the Presidents of the United States: John F. Kennedy, 1961* (Washington, D.C., 1962), 172.

11. *South Wind Red* (Chicago, 1962), a book written by Philip A. Ray, business executive and secretary of commerce under Eisenhower, provides a typical early business reaction to the Alliance for Progress.

12. CIA Current Intelligence Memorandum, 27 Sept. 1961, NSF Co-K.

13. State Department Background Paper, Brazil, memo for R. Goodwin, 14 Sept. 1961, NSF Co-K.

14. CIA Current Intelligence Memorandum, 27 Sept. 1961, NSF Co-K.

15. Editorial, *Correio da Manha,* 22 Sept. 1961.

16. State Dept. Memo for P. Kenneth O'Donnell, 18 Oct. 1961, POF Co.

17. Bond to SecState, 11 Oct. 1961, NSF Co-K.

18. Arthur M. Schlesinger, Jr., *A Thousand Days: John F. Kennedy in the White House* (Boston, 1965), 305.

19. Gordon to SecState, 21 Oct. 1961, NSF Co-K.

20. Gordon to SecState, 26 Oct. 1961, NSF Co-K.

21. Lincoln Gordon, interview with Paige Mulhollan, 10 July 1969, 21, Oral History Collection, LBJL. It was probably because he was quite well prepared for his post that Gordon was shocked to discover how inadequately trained many of those on his staff in Rio were. See comments by Walt Rostow reported by Sam Belk, Memo for Bundy, 16 May 1962, NSF MM, Box 334-335.

22. Luis Alberto Moniz Bandeira, *Brizola e o trabalhismo* (Rio de Janeiro, 1979), 64.

23. *Fortune,* "The Fortune Directory," July 1962, 172.

24. See *Fortune,* "Now It's Growth from Within for Harold Geneen," Sept. 1971, 33; *Business Week,* "One Man's $1-billion Company," 4 May 1963, 80–88; and Anthony Sampson, *The Sovereign State of ITT* (New York, 1973).

25. Poor telephone service by ITT was not limited to Brazil. The service the company offered in Puerto Rico in the 1960s also left much to be desired, as Alliance for Progress coordinator Teodoro Moscoso hinted. Senate Foreign Relations Committee, *Hearings on Foreign Assistance Act of 1962,* 87th Cong., 2d sess., 1962, 418. Cf. Sampson, *Sovereign State,* 139–42.

26. For a summary of the case from the State Department's point of view, see Senate Foreign Relations Committee, *Hearings on Foreign Assistance Act of 1962,* 417. The Brazilian government's version of the case appears in Airgram A-710, 19 Dec. 1962, 10, NSF Co-K.

27. Geneen to Rusk, and Geneen to President, 17 Feb. 1962; see also Rusk to Geneen, 22 Feb. 1962, and Battle to Bundy, 28 Feb. 1962, all in NSF Co-K.

28. *Business Week,* "One Man's $1-billion Company," 4 May 1963, 87.

29. The large volume of telephone calls, telegrams, and letters received by the State Department is stressed in Rusk to Gordon, 3 Mar. 1962, NSF Co-K.

30. *Congressional Record,* vol. 108, 1962, 2615–16, 2699.

31. Ibid., 3393–95, 4633–34.

32. Gordon to SecState, 24 Feb. 1962, NSF Co-K.

33. Gordon to SecState, 25 Feb. 1962, NSF Co-K.

34. House Committee on Foreign Affairs, *Hearings on Foreign Assistance Act of 1962,* 87th Cong., 2d sess., 1962, pt. 4, 819.

35. Assistant Secretary of State Woodward states that a question will be planted in the press conference. Rusk (Woodward) to Embassy, 3 Mar. 1962, NSF Co-K.

36. *Public Papers of the Presidents of the United States: John F. Kennedy, 1962* (Washington, D.C., 1963), 203.

37. Rusk to Embassy, 7 Mar. 1962, NSF Co-K.

38. Gordon infuriated Brizola during subsequent negotiations by stating that the Brazilian judiciary was "suspect" in judging cases involving American-owned companies. Bandeira, *Brizola,* 65.

39. *Correio da Manha,* 21 Feb. 1962. See also Carlos Castello Branco, *Introdução à revolução de 1964* (Rio de Janeiro, 1975), 1:127.

40. Rusk (Woodward) to Embassy, 3 Mar. 1962, NSF Co-K.

41. *Fortune,* "The Fortune Directory," Aug. 1962, 122.

42. *Revista Brasileira de Politica Internacional* 8 (Sept. 1965): 221. See also H. W. Balgooyen, "Problems of U.S. Investments in Latin America," in *Foreign Investment in Latin America,* ed. Marvin Bernstein (New York, 1966), 212–28.

43. Judith Tendler, *Electric Power in Brazil* (Cambridge, 1968), 43–79.

44. *Fortune,* Feb. 1962, 101–3, 216–20. *Business Week,* "How to Survive Foreign Expropriation," 1 June 1963, 86–88. The parent company, Electric Bond and Share, worked out its own strategy for profiting from adversity. It periodically sold and repurchased large blocs of AMFORP stock, selling stock purchased in the 1920s at much higher prices, and thus taking paper capital losses that could be used to offset other income. All dividends paid out in the 1960s by the firm were tax-free. See *Wall Street Journal,* "Bond and Share to Buy up to 400,000 Shares of Foreign Power," 28 Sept. 1965, 32, and *Forbes,* "So What's New?" 15 June 1965, 46–47.

45. See the review of the history of the negotiations as presented by AMFORP chairman Henry B. Sargent on 5 Mar. 1964, Airgram 1060, AmEmbassy to Department of State, 7 Mar. 1964, Dec.DOS.doc.

46. The availability of "financing arrangements" was incorporated as a condition of the Goulart plan. See point six, p. 3, of Memorandum of Conversation, 4 Apr. 1962, NSF Co-K.

47. Lincoln Gordon, interview with John E. Reilly, 30 May 1964, Rio de Janeiro, 55–56, Oral History Collection, JFKL.

48. E.g., Eugenio Gudin, *Analise de problemas brasileiros* (Rio de Janeiro, 1965), 397–403.

49. See, for example, the statement by Brazilian Communist Party official Jacob Gorender in Irving Horowitz, *Revolution in Brazil* (New York, 1964), 333–34.

50. *Congressional Record,* vol. 108, 1962, 6014, 6106–7, 9940–43.

51. Ibid., 5946.

52. Bond to SecState, 2 Apr. 1962, NSF Co-K. The ITT plan is detailed in the embassy draft of a suggested Kennedy letter to Goulart, Gordon to SecState, 30 June 1962, NSF Co-K.

53. Memorandum of conversation, 4 Apr. 1962, NSF Co-K.

54. Martin to Embassy, 22 June 1962, NSF Co-K.

55. See the Brazilian summary of Kennedy's remarks in *Revista Brasileira de Politica Internacional* 8 (Sept. 1965): 181–82.

56. Roberto Campos, interview with John E. Reilly, 29 May 1964, Rio de Janeiro, 25–26, Oral History Collection, JFKL.

57. For example, in July 1960, Brizola had given a reporter a story about how Point Four technicians had offered him money for microfilms of state police files. He then waited two days before denying the story, saying he had been misquoted, thus giving the press a chance to blast the United States and laud the patriotic nationalism of the governor. Resumé of an Attempt to Discredit the Public Safety Program, 23 Aug. 1960, Decl.Doc. no. 129 B, 1981. However, in the cases of the expropriations, it should be pointed out that the preparatory work for both had been completed by Brizola's UDN predecessor. *Revista Brasileira de Politica Internacional* 8 (Sept. 1965): 163–64.

58. *Public Papers of Presidents: John F. Kennedy, 1962,* 892, 894.

59. Ibid., 203.

60. Senate Foreign Relations Committee, *Hearings on Foreign Assistance Act of 1962,* 555–58.

61. Department of State, *Bulletin* 46 (1962): 460. In 1961 one of the rare occasions when the importance of private investment in Latin America was stressed came when Secretary of Treasury Dillon responded to a reporter's questions on the subject. Department of State, *Bulletin* 45 (1961): 443, 445. On another occasion Ambassador Gordon emphasized the role of private enterprise in a speech to businessmen in Brazil in October 1961. *A New Deal for Latin America* (Cambridge, 1963), 15–16.

62. *Public Papers of Presidents: John F. Kennedy, 1962,* 372. In Brazil the ambassador relayed the news of the organization of COMAP to resident American businessmen, treating it as an important new initiative. Gordon to SecState, 5 June 1962, Airgram, NSF Co-K.

63. Department of State, *Bulletin* 47 (1962): 585.

64. Department of State, *Bulletin* 48 (1963): 296. *Public Papers of Presidents: John F. Kennedy, 1962,* 882.

65. Reuter to Reardon, 23 Sept. 1963, Box 234, WHCF-K.

66. Kennedy to Rockefeller, 19 Nov. 1963, WHCF-J, FO 3-2-1. See also David Rockefeller to President, 29 Nov. 1963, and Johnson to Rockefeller, 11 Dec 1963, ibid.

67. His efforts were not, of course, limited to the foreign policy area. Sorenson reports that a general "be kind to businessmen" campaign was on for the last six months of 1962. Theodore C. Sorenson, *Kennedy* (New York, 1965), 466–68.

68. Martin to Gordon, 29 Nov. 1962, NSF-K.

69. Lacerda also acted in the hope of improving telephone service. Carlos Lacerda, *Depoimento* (Rio de Janeiro, 1977), 385–86. See also editorial, *Correio da Manha,* 22 Feb. 1962.

70. Gordon to SecState, 14 and 18 July 1962, NSF Co-K.

71. Gordon to SecState, 3 Aug. 1962, Rusk to Embassy, 7 Aug. 1962, Gordon to SecState, 10 Aug. 1962; all are in NSF Co-K.

72. Rubem Medina, *Desnacionalização, crime contra o Brasil?* (Rio de Janeiro, 1970), 54–55.

73. Tendler, *Electric Power in Brazil,* 86–87.

74. *Revista Brasileira de Politica Internacional* 8 (Sept. 1965): 182–83.

75. The legal and political problems of Hanna in Brazil are detailed in Raymond F. Mikesell, *Foreign Investment in the Petroleum and Mineral Industries* (Baltimore, 1971), 345–64.

76. *Fortune,* "Immovable Mountains," Apr. 1965, 56.

77. Senate Armed Services Committee, *Stockpile Investigation, Hearings* pt. 6, *Hanna Nickel Contracts,* 87th Cong., 2d sess., 1962.

78. Ibid., 2209. The claim was settled in 1966 for $536,000 (*Wall Street Journal,* "Hanna Mining Agrees to Pay U.S. $473,000 More to Settle Dispute," 7 Apr. 1966).

79. Gordon to SecState, 19 July 1962, NSF Co-K.

80. Rusk to Embassy, 30 Jan. 1963, NSF Co-K.

81. The State Department's attitude toward Hanna did not prevent other officials from directly espousing Hanna's cause. Harold F. Linder, head of Eximbank, for example, reported that he had linked a Brazilian loan request to satisfactory resolution of the Hanna situation. Linder to Embassy, 28 Sept. 1962, NSF Co-K. Humphrey had served on the directorate of the Eximbank while secretary of the Treasury.

82. Thomas E. Skidmore, *Politics in Brazil, 1930–1964* (New York, 1967), 99.

83. *Correio da Manha,* 3 Dec. 1961.

84. *New York Times,* "U.S. Ambassador Warns Brazil of Peril in New Investment Bill," 1 Sept. 1962, 22:2. See also Luiz Alberto Moniz Bandeira, *O governo João Goulart* (Rio de Janeiro, 1977), 110–11.

85. Gordon to SecState, 23 Aug. 1962, NSF Co-K; Skidmore, *Politics in Brazil,* 227.

86. Schlesinger to Dungan, 15 Oct. 1962, Schlesinger Papers, Subject Files, JFKL.

87. *Public Papers of Presidents: John F. Kennedy, 1962,* 584–85.

## Chapter 6

1. Report by Gilbert Huber, Jr., 27 Mar. 1962, quoted in René Armand Dreifuss, *1964: A conquista do estado* (Petrópolis, 1981), 205.

2. Gordon, memorandum, Points Supplementary to R. N. Goodwin draft of January 1, 1962, NSF Co-K.

3. Gordon to SecState, 16 Dec. 1961, NSF Co-K.

4. Special National Intelligence Estimate No. 93-2-61, Short-term Prospects for Brazil under Goulart, 7 Dec. 1961, Schlesinger Papers, Subject File, JFKL.

5. DeLesseps Morrison, *Latin American Mission* (New York, 1965), 170. See also Arthur Schlesinger, Jr., *A Thousand Days: John F. Kennedy in the White House* (Boston, 1965), 780–81.

6. Luiz Alberto Moniz Bandeira, *Presença dos Estados Unidos no Brasil* (Rio de Janeiro, 1973), 420–22; *Ultima Hora* 26 Jan. 1962; Luiz Alberto Moniz Bandeira, *O governo João Goulart* (Rio de Janeiro, 1977), 47–49.

7. Roberto de Oliveira Campos, interview with John E. Reilly, May 29–30, 1964, Rio de Janeiro, 40–41, Oral History Collection, JFKL.

8. Bandeira, *Presença dos Estados Unidos,* 420; Renato Archer, interview with Lucia Hippolito and Helena Maria Bomeny, Aug. 1978, 341–42, Oral History Collection, CPDOC. On the other hand, Schlesinger was especially delighted with Rusk's performance at this conference, praising his "intelligence, command of detail, inexhaustible patience" (*Thousand Days,* 781).

9. Gordon to SecState, 16 Dec. 1961, NSF Co-K. Gordon was still hoping for an "effective coalition of centrist political forces" on March 27, 1962. Gordon to SecState, Schlesinger Papers, Subject File, JFKL.

10. Afonso Arinos de Melo Franco, *Planalto: Memórias* (Rio de Janeiro, 1968), 227. Denis de Moraes and Francisco Viana, *Prestes, lutas e autocríticas,* 2d. ed. (Petrópolis, 1982), 166. Archer, interview, 378. See also Campos, interview, 17.

11. Gordon to SecState, 2 July 1962, NSF Co-K.

12. The AFL/CIO leaders were invited to participate because it was believed that though Goulart was ostensibly in control of organized labor, he was insufficiently alert to communist infiltration in Brazilian unions. See Gordon to SecState, 14 Mar. 1962, Ball to AmEmbassy, 16 Mar. 1962, and Memorandum of Conversation, Blair House, 4 Apr. 1962, NSF Co-K.

13. *Public Papers of the Presidents of the United States: John F. Kennedy, 1962* (Washington, D.C., 1963), 326–27; *Washington Post,* 14 Apr. 1962.

14. Campos, interview, 33.

15. *Correio da Manha,* 3 May 1962.

16. Bandeira, *Governo João Goulart,* 56–57.

17. I was in Pará from July 1962 to April 1963. Salary arrears of up to eight months were common for state and municipal workers.

18. Gordon to SecState, 28 May 1962, NSF Co-K.

19. *Correio da Manha,* 13 and 30 May 1962.

20. The *New York Times* reporter felt the decisive vote against censure represented a vote of confidence in the independent foreign policy. *New York Times,* "Legislators in Brazil Vote Down Motion to Censure Foreign Chief," 31 May 1962.

21. Ambassador Gordon believed that Goulart could easily have had the constitutional provision altered by referring the matter to the courts but did not do so because he wanted an excuse to replace the cabinet (Lincoln Gordon, interview with author, Washington, D.C., 19 Oct. 1988).

22. See *Correio da Manha,* 13 June through 30 June 1962.

23. Dreifuss, *1964,* 296. Solange de Deus Simões reports three different versions of the founding of CAMDE in her study, *Deus, pátria, e família: As mulheres no golpe de 1964* (Petrópolis, 1985), 29–31. All three versions credit male IPES members with initiating the organization. Philippe C. Schmitter, *Interest Conflict and Political Changes in Brazil* (Stanford, Cal., 1971), 220.

24. Gordon to SecState, 2 July 1962, NSF Co-K.

25. Philip Raine to DepState, Airgram A-87, 20 July 1962, NSF Co-K.

26. See Dreifuss, *1964,* 172–209, for a detailed analysis of the IPES organization.

27. Ibid., Appendix Z.

28. Ibid., 185.

29. Norman Blume, "Pressure Groups and Decision Making in Brazil," *Studies in Comparative International Development,* 3, no. 11 (St. Louis, 1968), 215.

30. This name—*Partido Communista do Brasil*—was actually the historic name of the Brazilian Communist Party. The name had been changed in September 1961 in an effort to suggest that the party was Brazilian and not an instrument of the Soviet Union. Ronald A. Chilcote, *The Brazilian Communist Party* (New York, 1974), 72–73. See also John W. F. Dulles, *Unrest in Brazil: Political-Military Crises, 1955–1964* (Austin, 1970), 368–74.

31. Joseph A. Page, *The Revolution That Never Was* (New York, 1972), 77–109, 129, 150–57; Dreifuss, *1964,* 300–304.

32. Arthur José Poerner, *O poder jovem: historia do participação politica dos estudantes brasileiros* (Rio de Janeiro, 1968), 195–97.

33. Memorandum of Conversation, 4 Apr. 1962, NSF Co-K.

34. Kenneth P. Erikson, *The Brazilian Corporative State and Working-Class Politics* (Berkeley, 1977), 92.

35. *O Globo,* 6 July 1962.

36. See, for example, editorial, *Correio da Manha,* 7 July 1962.

37. By canceling, Kennedy probably disappointed America's friends on the Right much more than anyone else in Brazil. IPES members had been hoping for a "visit of J. K. to Brazil, with Jackie and all" *before* the Brazilian election in order to attract votes to their pro-American side. IPES, Executive Committee-Rio, 5 Feb. 1962, quoted in Dreifuss, *1964,* 264–65.

38. See memorandum, Background on Current Situation in Brazil, 28 July 1962, POF Co., 112.

39. Raine to DepState, Airgram A-87, 20 July 1962, NSF Co-K.

40. Gordon to SecState, 30 June 1962, NSF Co-K. See also Gordon to SecState, 19 July 1962, NSF Co-K. An abbreviated version of Gordon's suggested letter was sent on July 11.

41. See Gordon telegrams of 16, 19, and 21 Aug. 1962, NSF Co-K.

42. Archer, interview, 389.

43. Agrarian reform had clearly caught on as a national priority. It was rated as a major problem by 25 percent of the sample. Only 19 percent listed corruption and incompetence in government. Operations and Policy Research, *Brazil 1962, Parties, Issues, and Political Personalities* (Washington, D.C., n.d.), 18.

44. Ibid., 30, 38.

45. Ibid., 50–68.

46. Dulles, *Unrest in Brazil,* 180.

47. *Correio da Manha,* 26 Sept. 1962.

48. E.g., the Ação Democratica Popular's *"Carta de Princípios"* advertisement in *Correio da Manha,* 23 Aug. 1962, or the Ação Democratica attack on Brizola, *Correio da Manha,* 5 Aug. 1962.

49. *O Globo,* 18 Aug. 1962.

50. *Correio da Manha,* 5–8 Aug. 1962.

51. The Wheat Fund was established as the Brazilian government purchased wheat and other surplus commodities from the United States at bargain prices in their own "soft" currency. Forty percent of the proceeds of the sale was turned over to the American embassy for embassy expenses and programs, which presumably might include subsidizing pro-American cultural events or pro-American politicians. A portion of the remaining 60 percent of sale proceeds went to the military assistance program. The Plan of Action for Period to October 7, 1962, Memo for Latin American Policy Committee, mentions use of the Wheat Fund to purchase "internal security equipment and material engineer battalion support and equipment for civic action activities." Schlesinger Papers, Subject File, Brazil. See also Bandeira, *Presença dos Estados Unidos,* 429–30.

52. Quoted in Bandeira, *Governo João Goulart,* 73.

53. Gordon to SecState, 6 Sept. 1962, NSF Co-K.

54. Lincoln Gordon, "Castello perdeu a batalha," interview with Roberto Garcia, *Veja,* 9 Mar. 1977, 3–8. Philip Agee, the CIA spy who came in from the cold, put the total figure spent between twelve and twenty million (*Inside the Company: CIA Diary,* Bantam ed. [New York, 1976], 325).

55. Eloi Dutra, *IBAD, sigla da corrupção* (Rio de Janeiro, 1963), 27.

56. Lincoln Gordon, interview, 19 Oct. 1988.

57. Agee, *Inside the Company,* 326.

58. Roger Hilsman, memorandum, Brazil and the Alliance for Progress, 11 July 1962, Schlesinger Papers, Subject Files, JFKL.

59. Delgado-Arias to SecState, 23 Aug. 1962, NSF. Cleofas's expressed distrust of IBAD in this conversation with the consul may have been a tactical maneuver to get more out of the American consulate, since IBAD openly backed him anyway, according to other reports. See Delgado-Arias to SecState, 28 June 1962, NSF Co-K; and *"As sombras do IBAD,"* Veja, 16 Mar. 1977. On the other hand, not knowing that IBAD was an instrument of the American government, Cleofas may have just been cautiously voicing the accepted opinion of Northeast oligarchs, who considered IBAD communistic because it advocated agrarian reform. Dreifuss, *1964,* 300–301.

60. Gordon, "Castello perdeu a batalha," *Veja,* 9 Mar. 1977, 8.

61. Memo, Dungan to Schlesinger, 7 May 1962, Schlesinger Papers, Subject Files, Box 3.

62. Page, *Revolution That Never Was,* 73–74, 135–40; Riordan Roett, *The Politics of Foreign Aid in the Brazilian Northeast* (Nashville, 1972), 75, 112.

63. Phyllis R. Parker, *Brazil and the Quiet Intervention, 1964* (Austin, 1979), 26–27.

64. Dept. of State, memo, Brazilian Elections of October 7, 1962, NSF Co-K.

65. Dulles, *Unrest in Brazil,* 176–80.

66. *Correio da Manha,* 14 and 15 Sept. 1962. Editorial, 20 Sept. 1962.

67. CIA Information Report, 14 Sept. 1962, NSF Co-K.

68. Dept. of State to AmEmbassy, Rio, 17 Sept. 1962, NSF Co-K.

69. Rusk to AmEmbassy, 21 Sept. 1962, NSF Co-K. Schlesinger complained that Draper was "incongruous. . . as a representative of the New Frontier" and "an appropriate appointment for the Eisenhower administration" (Schlesinger to Dungan, 15 Oct. 1962, Schlesinger Papers, Subject Files, JFKL).

70. For example, Paulo Ayres Filho, one of the founders of IPES, was a dinner guest of the mission during its São Paulo visit. See Braddock to DepState, Enclosure 4, Airgram A-109, 19 Oct. 1962, NSF Co-K; and Dreifuss, *1964,* n. 5, 398–99.

71. A "Preliminary Report," 24 Oct. 1962, and a final report entitled "Report of the Interdepartmental Survey Group," 5 Nov. 1962, are in NSF Co-K. All Draper quotations in preceding four paragraphs are from these two reports. See also the letter from Draper to the President, 11 Nov. 1963.

72. Draper to SecState, Airgram, Enclosure 7, 19 Oct. 1962, NSF Co-K. See also Gordon to President, 3 Mar. 1963, NSF Co-K.

73. Gordon to SecState, 2 Nov. 1962, NSF Co-K.

74. Vernon A. Walters, *Silent Missions* (New York, 1978), 364. Gordon, interview, 19 Oct. 1988.

75. Walters, *Silent Missions,* 374–75.

## Chapter 7

1. Richard J. Walton, *Cold War and Counterrevolution: The Foreign Policy of John F. Kennedy* (New York, 1972), 103–13; Henry Fairlie, *The Kennedy Promise: The Politics of Expectation* (Garden City, N.Y., 1973), 311–13; Geoffrey Perrett, *A Dream of Greatness: The American People, 1945–1963* (New York, 1979), 727. The chapter epigraph is taken from Gordon, Memorandum to the President, 7 Mar. 1963, NSF Co-K.

2. Gordon to SecState, 2 Nov. 1962, NSF Co-K.

3. Martin to Ambassador, 15 Nov. 1962, POF Box 112.

4. Martin to AmEmbassy, 29 Nov. 1962, NSF Co-K. See also Gordon to SecState, 28 Nov. 1962, NSF Co-K.

5. Keppel to DepState, Airgram 590, 23 Nov. 1962, NSF Co-K.

6. Gordon to SecState, 29 Nov. 1962, NSF Co-K; Hilsman to SecState, 5 Dec. 1962, NSF Co-K.

7. Keppel to DepState, Airgram, 23 Nov. 1962, NSF Co-K.

8. Bond to SecState, 3 Dec. 1962, NSF Co-K.

9. When Lincoln Gordon arrived in Brazil to take up his duties as ambassador, Heck arranged to meet him in order to inform him that Goulart was a Communist and would soon be overthrown by the "large" numbers of officers then preparing a "golpe" (Phyllis

R. Parker, *Brazil and the Quiet Intervention, 1964* [Austin, 1979], 10–11). At the time Gordon realized that the admiral was indulging in wishful thinking.

10. Compare the coverage in the *Estado de São Paulo* and the *Globo* with that of the *Correio da Manha* during November and December 1962. The anticommunist voice of Carlos Lacerda was not heard during this campaign. After the defeat of his candidates in the October election, he took off on a fifty-day vacation in Europe.

11. Joseph A. Page, *The Revolution That Never Was* (New York, 1972), 96–99. *Estado do São Paulo,* 6 Dec. 1962.

12. "Political Resolution of Communists, December 1962." Quoted in Edgard Carone, *O PCB (1943–1964)* (São Paulo, 1982), 2:253.

13. Mário Victor, *Cinco anos que abalaram o Brasil* (Rio de Janeiro, 1965), 446 N.

14. Preamble to the Charter of Punta del Este, Jerome Levinson and Juan de Onis, *The Alliance That Lost Its Way: A Critical Report on the Alliance for Progress* (Chicago, 1972), 352.

15. Joint Congressional Economic Committee, *Private Investment in Latin America, Hearings,* 88th Cong., 2d sess., 1964, (COMAP Report), 58.

16. Ibid., 101, (Memorandum by Three Members of COMAP).

17. Dungan to President, 11 Nov. 1962, POF Co.

18. Keppel to DepState, Airgram 590, 23 Nov. 1962, NSF Co-K.

19. The minutes of this NSC-Executive Committee meeting have not been declassified. Some idea of the proceedings can be reached by reading the State Department memorandums submitted to the Committee and by analyzing subsequent administration actions. See "Memorandum for the National Security Council Executive Committee Meeting of December 11," NSF Co-K.

20. Gordon to SecState, 14 Jan. 1963, NSF Co-K.

21. Lincoln Gordon, interview with author, Washington, D.C., 19 Oct. 1988. Even before December 1962 American efforts to conclude Alliance for Progress "impact" programs with the governors of Northeastern states had been opposed by representatives of the central government as "an attempt against the sovereignty of the nation." See Bond to SecState, Airgram A-590, 23 Nov. 1962, NSF Co-K.

22. Frank P. Sherwood, "A Report and Critique of USAID/Brazil Programs and Strategies in Urban Affairs," November 1966, USAID Reference Center.

23. *Public Papers of the Presidents of the United States: John F. Kennedy, 1962* (Washington, D.C. 1963), 871.

24. Ibid., 883, 887.

25. "Thus, Kennedy, without the slightest ceremony, aligned himself with the internal opposition to Goulart's government," concluded Luiz Alberto Moniz Bandeira in *O governo João Goulart* (Rio de Janeiro, 1977), 87. See also Luiz Alberto Moniz Bandeira, *Presença dos Estados Unidos no Brasil* (Rio de Janeiro, 1973), 432–33. Some Americans also were surprised. See Schlesinger to Bundy, memorandum, 13 Dec. 1962, NSF Co-K.

26. Gordon to SecState, 18 Dec. 1962; Airgram, 19 Dec. 1962, NSF Co-K.

27. E.g., *U.S. News & World Report,* "From Robert Kennedy: Tough Talk in Brazil," 31 Dec. 1962, 11.

28. CIA Information Report, 4 Mar. 1963, NSF Co-K.

29. Roberto de Oliveira Campos, interview with John E. Reilly, 29–30 May 1964, Rio de Janeiro, 44, Oral History Collection, JFKL. Campos was vilified by Brazilian nationalists as a pro-American *"entregista,"* but at this time he strongly supported Goulart.

30. See Bond to SecState, 3 Dec. 1962, NSF Co-K; and Memorandum for the National Security Council Executive Committee Meeting of December 11, 1962, NSF Co-K.

31. Gordon to SecState, 19 Dec. 1962, cables 1173 and 1174, NSF Co-K.

32. Martin to AmEmbassy, 29 Dec. 1962, NSF Co-K.

33. Gordon to SecState, 22 and 26 Jan. 1963; Martin to Amembassy, 23 Jan. 1963, and Rusk to AmEmbassy, 25 and 28 Jan. 1963, NSF Co-K.

34. Quadros had eliminated them once before, but subsidies in effect had been reintroduced by maintaining an artificial official exchange rate for the cruzeiros used to pay for these imports.

35. Cf. Peter Flynn, *Brazil: A Political Analysis* (London, 1978), 242.

36. *Globo,* 7 and 8 Jan. 1963; Gordon to SecState, 4 Jan. 1963, NSF Co-K.

37. Ambassador Gordon had to put in a vigorous argument in favor of the loan before it was granted. See Gordon to SecState, 2 Jan. 1963, and Rusk to AmEmbassy, 3 Jan. 1963, both NSF Co-K.

38. William H. Brubeck, Memorandum for Mr. McGeorge Bundy, 31 Jan. 1963, NSF Co-K. In its analysis of the new Goulart government, the embassy in Rio also expressed alarm. "The appointment of a number of highly suspect individuals to important posts in the new government on the subcabinet level, however, does not inspire confidence that Goulart has decided to free himself from influential pro-Communist or extreme nationalist advisors or to cease seeking support from Communist-dominated organizations" (Keppel to DepState, Airgram A-941, 18 Feb. 1963, NSF Co-K).

39. Thomas E. Skidmore, *Politics in Brazil, 1930–1964* (New York, 1967), 240.

40. See Roberto Campos, *Reflections on Latin American Development* (Austin, 1967), 91; and Schlesinger to Bundy, 13 Dec. 1962, NSF Co-K.

41. Campos, interview, 47.

42. *Wall Street Journal,* "ITT and Brazil Reach 'Interim Agreement' on Compensation for Firm Seized by State," 21 Jan. 1963, 7:2, and "ITT Said to Have Received $7.3 Million from Brazil for Expropriated Facilities," 1 Feb. 1963, 8:2; *Congressional Record,* vol. 109 (1963), 2140. Keppel to DepState, Airgram, 18 Feb. 1963, NSF Co-K. ITT eventually received $12.2 million. This sum included the Curitiba subsidiary. *Wall Street Journal,* "ITT Finishes Sale of Unit in Brazil for $12.2 Million," 20 June 1967.

43. Gordon to SecState, 17 Jan. 1963 and 6 Feb. 1963, NSF Co-K.

44. Carlos Castello Branco, *Introdução à revolução de 1964* (Rio de Janeiro, 1975), 1:132–33.

45. Memo, Background Information on Continental Congress for Solidarity with Cuba, undated, POF Co.

46. House Committee on Foreign Affairs, *Hearings on Castro-Communist Subversion in the Western Hemisphere,* 88th Cong., 1st sess., 1963, 247. Department of State, *Bulletin* 48 (1963): 434, 521.

47. See Mein to SecState, 20 and 22 Mar. 1963, NSF Co-K.

48. *Congressional Record,* vol. 109 (1963), 4428.

49. Memorandums of Conversations, 12, 13, and 25 March 1963, NSF Co-K. Cf. Gordon to SecState, 6 Feb. 1963, NSF Co-K.

50. Rusk (AID/W) to Embassy, 30 Mar. 1963, NSF Co-K. The entire agreement was published in the Department of State, *Bulletin* 48 (1963): 557–61.

51. Ball to AmEmbassy, 4 Apr. 1963, NSF Co-K.

52. Campos, interview, 48–49. Although it is not mentioned in the published U.S.-Brazil agreement, perhaps the AMFORP condition was not intended to be a secret. *Business*

*Week* states that AID administrator David E. Bell warned Dantas that aid would be suspended if the AMFORP purchase was not finalized. "Brazilian Brings Home the Bacon," 30 Mar. 1963, 82.

53. Bandeira, *Presença dos Estados Unidos,* 441, erroneously reports that the $30 million went to ITT and AMFORP. The amount and provenance of the $84 million are detailed in Rusk to AmEmbassy, 23 Mar. 1963, and in *Department of State Bulletin* 48 (1963): 561.

54. Gordon to SecState, 9 Apr. 1963, NSF Co-K.

55. Gordon to SecState, 25 Sept. 1964, Dec.DOS.Doc. *Revista Brasileira de Politica Internacional* 8 (Sept. 1965), 276. Skidmore (*Politics in Brazil,* 244–46), attributed the conclusion of the agreement to a whim of Dantas, while Jan Knippers Black (*United States Penetration of Brazil* [Philadelphia, 1977], 89), has Ambassador Campos signing the agreement "without his government's authorization." In fact, the refusal of the United States to release the promised funds forced Dantas's action, and Goulart had been advised and approved although he may not have actually read the document. See also Robert W. Dean to DepState, Airgram A-119, 23 Mar. 1964, NSF Co-K.

56. The annual report of Bond and Share, the parent company of AMFORP, revealed that an agreement had been reached. *Ultima Hora,* 15 May 1963.

57. For example, twenty-three UDN congressmen signed a "Bossa Nova" manifesto expressing support of the Three Year Plan. Maria Victoria de Mesquita Benevides, *A UDN e o udenismo* (Rio de Janeiro, 1981), 123.

58. Hélio Silva, *1964, golpe ou contragolpe* (Rio de Janeiro, 1975), 169–71.

59. Branco, *Introdução à revolução,* 1:126.

60. *Ultima Hora,* 9 Apr. 1963.

61. Branco, *Introdução à revolução* 1:124–25.

62. Even John Keppel, political analyst at the Rio embassy was impressed with the extent of Goulart's support. See Airgram A-941, 18 Feb. 1963 and Airgram A-1284, 9 May 1963, NSF Co-K. At the same time, however, White House analysts thought Goulart should be faulted for failing to publicly endorse the plan. Memorandum, Difficulties Confronting Brazil's Finance Minister San Tiago Dantas, 7 May 1963, POF 112.

63. Bandeira, *Governo João Goulart,* 99–103.

64. E.g., editorial, *Correio da Manha.* ("*Compra, nao*"), 7 June 1963.

65. See pt. 2 of "*A compra das concessionarias de energia electrica,*" *Revista Brasileira de Politica Internacional* 8 (Dec. 1965): 163–728.

66. Ball (Gordon and Martin) to President and Secretary, 29 June 1963. See also Mein to SecState, 2 and 10 June 1963, all in NSF Co-K.

# Chapter 8

1. Jean Jacques Faust, *A revolução devora seus presidentes* (Rio de Janeiro, 1965), 58. Another version of Goulart's remark has him saying "trying to find one's way through these things is like trying to find a black hat in a dark room." George W. Bemis, *From Crisis to Revolution: Monthly Case Studies* (Los Angeles, 1964), 15. Possibly he made this remark on a separate occasion.

2. Gordon to SecState, 23 Feb. 1963, NSF Co-K.

3. Hélio Silva, *1964, golpe ou contragolpe* (Rio de Janeiro, 1975), 268–73. Carlos Castello Branco, *Introdução à revolução de 1964* (Rio de Janeiro, 1975), 135–38, 153–55, 160, 173–75.

4. Silva, *1964,* 269.

5. John W. F. Dulles, *Unrest in Brazil: Political-Military Crises 1955–1964* (Austin, 1970), 246.

6. Goulart's opponents made much of the reported sale of two Czech machine guns by one Group of Eleven to incognito members of a right-wing anticommunist group. The purchase supposedly proved that Cuba (supplied by Czechoslovakia) was arming Brizola's terrorist forces. The machine guns were delivered to the U.S. embassy "because the North Americans had promised, in the event that Cuban intervention in favor of Brazilian communists was proved, the United States would give us official support in our struggle." José Stacchini, *Março 64: mobilização da audácia* (São Paulo, 1965), 87. Needless to say, this "proof" that the Groups of Eleven were heavily armed fighting groups seems a bit contrived.

7. *Correio da Manha,* 27 Dec. 1963.

8. João Candido Maia Neto, *La crises brasileña* (Buenos Aires, 1965), 128. See also Abelardo Jurema, *Sexta-Feira, 13: os ultimos dias do governo João Goulart,* 2d ed. (Rio de Janeiro, 1964), 82–83.

9. Abelardo Jurema, *Juscelino e Jango* (Rio de Janeiro, 1979), 109–10.

10. Ibid., 91.

11. The political analyst at the American Embassy was surprised by the cooperation. "As leader of the *grupo compacto,* he was very close to the Communists. Now, however, as Minister of Labor, he is apparently cooperating in the 'Dantas line' in trying to keep labor from raising excessive wage demands" (Keppel to DepState, Airgram 941, 18 Feb. 1963, NSF Co-K).

12. Kenneth P. Erickson, *The Brazilian Corporative State and Working-Class Politics* (Berkeley, 1977), 77–91.

13. Joseph A. Page, *The Revolution That Never Was* (New York, 1972), 170–76.

14. Paulo Cavalcanti, *O caso eu conto como o caso foi* (Recife, 1980), 1:324–30.

15. Luiz Alberto Moniz Bandeira, *O governo João Goulart* (Rio de Janeiro, 1977), 96. See also Keppel to DepState, Airgram 1284, 9 May 1963, NSF Co-K.

16. Keppel to DepState, Airgram 941, 18 Feb. 1963, NSF Co-K.

17. A number of political clichés were in use in the 1950s and 1960s to refer to possible Communists. Besides being "crypto" or "pro," one could be classified as "quasi-Communist," a "Commie-liner," a "Communist sympathizer" (or "Comsymp"), a "Communist dupe," or a "useful innocent." Even without earning any of the above labels, a person could be identified as "under Communist discipline." A new term for the Brazilian radical nationalists was coined in 1962: from this date on they were usually referred to as the "communo-nationalists." Third World political leaders were always advised to make a "clean break" with any of the above.

18. Mário Victor, *Cinco anos que abalaram o Brasil* (Rio de Janeiro, 1965), 436–37.

19. Maia Neto, *Crises brasileña,* 120.

20. Ronald H. Chilcote, *The Brazilian Communist Party: Conflict and Integration, 1922–1972* (New York, 1974), 153. Dulles, *Unrest in Brazil,* 165–66.

21. Erickson, *Brazilian Corporative State,* 113.

22. *O Globo,* 6 Feb. 1963.

23. Keppel to DepState, Airgram 941, 18 Feb. 1963, NSF Co-K.

24. *Ultima Hora* gave detailed coverage of the Lacerda-CGT quarrel from a pro-Goulart viewpoint, 27 Mar.–2 Apr. 1963. See also Gordon to SecState, 5 Apr. 1963, NSF Co-K.

25. Erickson, *Brazilian Corporative State,* 132–34. *Ultima Hora,* 4–9 Apr. 1963. See also Castello Branco, *Introdução à revolução,* 1:144–53.

26. Braddock to SecState, 10 May 1963, NSF Co-K.

27. Gordon to SecState, 17 July 1963, NSF Co-K.

28. Erickson, *Brazilian Corporative State,* 134–37. Dulles, *Unrest in Brazil,* 205–7.

29. Maia Neto, *Crises brasileña,* 127–28.

30. Ibid., 129.

31. Erickson, *Brazilian Corporative State,* 141–46.

32. Jurema, *Juscelino e Jango,* 131.

33. The figures are from Thomas E. Skidmore, *Politics in Brazil, 1930–1964* (New York, 1967), 257, 269.

34. CIA Information Report, 28 Aug. 1963, NSF Co-K.

35. Former AID official Philip Schwab, quoted by Peter D. Bell, "Brazilian-American Relations," in *Brazil in the Sixties,* ed. Riordan Roett (Nashville, 1972), 88.

36. *"As sombras do IRAD," Veja,* 16 Mar. 1977. See also Eloy Dutra, *IBAD, sigla da corrupção* (Rio de Janeiro, 1963).

37. See Rusk (AID/W) to Embassy, 30 Mar. 1963, NSF Co-K.

38. Mein to SecState, 10 June 1963, NSF Co-K.

39. Gordon to SecState, 3 July 1963, NSF Co-K. Castello Branco, *Introdução à revolução,* 194. Memorandum of Conversation, Robert Eakens and Jaime Rodrigues, Airgram 154, 22 July 1963, NSF Co-K. Gordon to SecState, 8 July 1963 and 7 Aug. 1963, NSF Co-K.

40. Ball (Martin and Gordon) to President and Secretary, 29 June 1963, NSF Co-K.

41. Kaysen to Klein, 30 June 1963, NSF Co-K.

42. Memorandum of Conversation, 3 July 1963, NSF Co-K. For subsequent Kennedy-Goulart correspondence on AMFORP see *Revista Brasileira de Política Internacional* 8 (Sept. 1965): 277–99; and Gordon to SecState, 3 and 18 July 1963, NSF Co-K. The Hickenlooper Amendment did not apply to the Brizola takeover in 1959 since the legislation's starting date was January 1962. The State Department felt the Pernambuco takeover was not covered since the question of compensation for possible residual rights was being determined in the courts. Mein to Rogers, 6 June 1963, NSF Co-K.

43. Martin to Gordon, 15 and 19 Aug. 1963, NSF Co-K.

44. Gordon to Martin, 21 Aug. 1963, NSF Co-K.

45. In December, Gordon referred to the fact that the embassy and the State Department were now in agreement. By this time Martin had been replaced as assistant secretary for Latin America by Thomas Mann. Mann was more concerned about protecting American investment and less interested in promoting development than Martin had been. Gordon to SecState, 20 Dec. 1963, NSF Co-J. See also Gordon, interview, 10 July 1969, 14, Oral History Collection, LBJL.

46. CIA Information Report, 14 Nov. 1963, NSF Co-K.

47. Gordon to SecState, 20 Nov. 1963, NSF Co-K. Goulart termed the American obsession with Communist strength in Brazil "another error."

48. Gordon, interview, 10 July 1969, 19.

49. The discussion was triggered by a consumer strike against the Espirito Santo subsidiary of the company and by threatened consumer action in Rio Grande do Norte. Gordon to SecState, 15, 24 and 27 Jan. 1964 and 4 and 5 Feb. 1964, Dec.DOS.doc.

Although the Brazilian officials thought the Memorandum of Understanding was no longer operative, Ambassador Gordon resurrected it as the basis for negotiation.

50. Gordon to SecState, 7 and 26 Mar. 1964; both Dec.DOS.doc.

51. Gordon to SecState, 26 Nov. 1963, NSF Co-J. "Memorandum of Conversation, Visit of John Buford," 31 Mar. 1964, Dec.DOS.doc.

52. Paulo Francis, "Tempos de Goulart," *Revista Civilização Brasileira* 1 (May 1966): 83, suggests that the only reason Goulart signed the legislation then was because aides to Finance Minister Carvalho Pinto had, without authorization, released the text to the press.

53. Bandeira, *Governo João Goulart,* 104-5.

54. Quoted in Frank Bonilla, "Rural Reform in Brazil," American University Field Staff Reports Service, *East Coast South America Series,* vol. 8, no. 4, 11.

55. This was essentially the position of the IPES study group on agrarian reform. It published the results of its research in a slick, hardcover book, *A reforma agraria,* in January 1964. IPES recommended the formation of rural cooperatives and reliance on private initiative to get greater mechanization and commercialization of agriculture. It thought the government might usefully do things such as carrying out pilot projects of colonization and providing additional credit for farmers.

56. Francisco Julião, *Que são as ligas camponesas?* (Rio de Janeiro, 1962), 84.

57. Maia Neto, *Crises brasileña,* 85.

58. Gordon to Martin, 21 Aug. 1963, NSF Co-K.

59. João Pinheiro Neto, interview with Aspasia Camargo, Helena Maria Bomeny, and Maria Luíza Heilborn, June 1977, 71, Oral History Collection, CPDOC.

60. The federal government could not use property taxes to force the sale of unutilized land, since the right to tax real estate lay with the state and local governments. In addition, although there were still vast areas of publicly owned land in Brazil on which landless peasants might be resettled, such land tended to be in remote areas, inaccessible, or otherwise unsuited for commercial agriculture.

61. Skidmore, *Politics in Brazil,* 260.

62. Under Lacerda's leadership, the majority faction of the UDN took a formal stand opposing any and all constitutional amendments. Lacerda argued that land redistribution was unnecessary and Goulart's championship of that cause was sheer demagoguery. See Maria Victoria de Mesquita Benevides, *A UDN e o udenismo* (São Paulo, 1981), 189-96.

63. Four existing agencies were combined to form the new one: the National Institute of Immigration & Colonization, the Rural Social Service, the Colonization Section of the Bank of Brazil, and the National Council on Agrarian Reform. Victor, *Cinco anos,* 468.

64. Dulles, *Unrest in Brazil,* 220-22.

65. Page, *Revolution That Never Was,* 166.

66. Peter Flynn, *Brazil: A Political Analysis* (London, 1978), 264-66.

67. Castello Branco, *Introdução à revolução,* 2:48-49.

68. Silva, *1964,* 179-80.

69. The decree is reprinted in Castello Branco, *Introdução à revolução,* 2:266-68.

70. The speeches were later published in book form. Bilac Pinto, *Guerra revolucionária* (Rio de Janeiro, 1964).

71. Marcio Moreira Alves, *A Grain of Mustard Seed,* Anchor Books ed. (New York, 1973), 29.

72. Gordon to SecState, 6 Dec. 1963, NSF Co-J. Paulo Francis, *"Tempos de Goulart,"* 75-76. Jurema, *Sexta-Feira,* 133.

## Chapter 9

1. The chapter epigraph is from *Eu, réu sem crime* (Rio de Janeiro, n.d.), 40. Castello is quoted in Vernon A. Walters, *Silent Missions* (New York, 1978), 383.

2. See Daniel Krieger, *Desde as missões: saudades, letras, esperanças,* 2d. ed. (Rio de Janeiro, 1977), 165.

3. John W. F. Dulles, *Unrest in Brazil: Political-Military Crises, 1955-1964* (Austin, 1970), 268. Alberto Dines et al., *Os idos de março e a queda em abril* (Rio de Janeiro, 1964), 199. The prayers of the São Paulo ladies were at first disturbed by loudspeakers broadcasting the proceedings at the rally until the head of the state police ordered the loudspeakers turned off. Carlos Castello Branco, *Introdução à revolução de 1964* (Rio de Janeiro, 1975), 2:260.

4. Dines, *Idos de março,* 309-10.

5. Hélio Silva, *1964, golpe ou contragolpe* (Rio de Janeiro, 1975), 323.

6. Dines, *Idos de março,* 310.

7. Ibid., 311. See also Dulles, *Unrest in Brazil,* 268, 270.

8. There are two easily accessible versions of Goulart's speech, one in Castello Branco, *Introdução à revolução,* 2:262-66; and the other in Silva, *1964,* 457-66. The two versions are quite close. The slightly longer one in Silva has the cadence of a spoken address and is probably the more accurate.

9. As soon as the rally was over, Goulart telephoned San Tiago Dantas to find out his reaction and to complain that Brizola's speech sounded the only discordant note at the rally. Renato Archer, interview with Lucia Hippolito and Helena Maria Bomeny, August 1978, 432, Oral History Collection, CPDOC, 432.

10. See, for example, Paulo Ayres Filho, "The Brazilian Revolution," in *Latin American Politics, Economics, and Hemispheric Security,* ed. Norman A. Bailey, (New York, 1965), 252.

11. Juracy Magalhães, *Minhas memórias provisórias* (Rio de Janeiro, 1982), 163.

12. Dines, *Idos de março,* 311-12.

13. Ibid., 36-37. See photographs of the rally in Dines and in Dulles, *Unrest in Brazil,* for samples of the placards.

14. *Estado do São Paulo,* 17 Mar. 1964; Silva, *1964,* 323-24. A spokesman for the Parliamentary Nationalist Front had earlier reported that the agents provocateurs who planned to attend the rally were linked to retired Admiral Heck and had been trained on plantations in Minas by foreign advisors. Castello Branco, *Introdução à revolução,* 2:191.

15. Abelardo Jurema, who, as minister of justice and domestic affairs, was in charge of the administration's domestic intelligence service, insisted that the "government was totally uninformed. There was no National Intelligence Service. There was no federal police agency. . . . Only the Information Section of the Army might know something from outside the country" (*Juscelino e Jango, PSD e PTB* [Rio de Janeiro, 1979], 250). However, Renato Archer asserted that Jango had a briefcase full of secret service reports on contacts by the Brazilian military officers with American agents. Archer believed Goulart was "well-informed" about this phase of the conspiracy. Archer, interview, 128-29. Luiz Alberto Moniz Bandeira, *O governo João Goulart* (Rio de Janeiro, 1977), 379-87, states that Goulart also knew all about CIA arms smuggling to right-wing vigilante groups.

16. Lacerda, for example, recalled running into Mourão in a São Paulo hotel corridor and being embarrassed by the general's loud and excited conversation about the need to overthrow Goulart (*Depoimento* [Rio de Janeiro, 1977], 277).

17. José Stacchini, *Março 64: mobilização da audácia* (São Paulo, 1965), 26–28.

18. Gordon to AID, 12 Oct. 1963, NSF Co-K.

19. *New York Times,* "Lacerda Scores Goulart Aides," 16 Oct. 1963, 15:1; *Correio da Manha,* 15 and 16 Oct. 1963; Dulles, *Unrest in Brazil,* 236–37.

20. Lacerda, *Depoimento,* 274.

21. Ibid., 278.

22. The Goulart administration believed that army attaché Vernon Walters, who worked for the Intelligence Section of the Defense Department, was in charge of the CIA and all covert operations in Brazil. At one point Goulart considered having him expelled. Walters, *Secret Missions,* 376. At this point in his career, Walters appears to have been working somewhat in competition with the CIA's Rio Station. It was considerably later, during the Nixon administration, that he became Deputy Director of the CIA.

23. Lacerda, *Depoimento,* 273. On the surface the option appeared reasonable, since until 1961 Guanabara had been the Federal District and all its public employees federal employees.

24. Ibid., 272.

25. See, for example, Castello Branco, *Introdução à revolução,* 1:157–58. When he visited the United States in November 1962, Adhemar assured President Kennedy that Goulart would be ousted within six months. Presumably he was in touch with conspirators at least that early. Memorandum of Conversation, 29 Nov. 1962, NSF Co-K.

26. Silva, *1964,* 265.

27. Castello Branco, *Introdução à revolução,* 1:181–82.

28. "If I could be certain that we could continue like this for another two years (until the elections of October 1965) and then begin following a genuine program, I would say: Let us continue. But the question isn't about continuing. I would prefer to see a new day dawning sooner rather than later. By that, I mean it could be within a few months. I don't believe things can go on like this until the end of the year." The entire Lacerda–*Los Angeles Times* interview is reprinted in Castello Branco, *Introdução à revolução,* 2:225–27.

29. Ibid., 82–88, 97. Luiz Alberto Moniz Bandeira, *Brizola e o trabalhismo* (Rio de Janeiro, 1979), 88–91. Dulles, *Unrest in Brazil,* 238–41. Thomas L. Hughes to Acting Secretary, Intelligence Note: Some Implications of Today's Moves by the Brazilian President, 4 Oct. 1963. CIA Information Reports, "Preliminary Evaluation...", 7 Oct. 1963, and "Developments in Brazilian Military...", 7 Oct. 1963, NSF Co-K.

30. CIA Information Report, "Developments in Brazilian Military," 7 Oct. 1963, NSF Co-K.

31. In fact Goulart's powers over appointments and promotions was a continual worry to American officials, who seemed to regard it as some sort of abuse of power. "Ultra-Nationalist officers who support President Goulart get promoted and get troop commands and desirable locations. Outspokenly prodemocracy pro-U.S. officers don't generally get promoted. They get passed over and retired" (Defense Information Report, 6 Aug. 1963, Schlesinger Papers, Classified Subject File). See also Gordon to SecState, 22 Feb. 1963, NSF Co-K.

32. Gordon to SecState, 14 Jan. 1963, NSF Co-K.

33. Cf. CIA Current Intelligence Memorandum, Plotting against Goulart, 8 Mar. 1963, POF Co; CIA Information Reports, 12 Apr. 1963, 30 Apr. 1963, 8 Aug. 1963, NSF Co-K; and Gordon to SecState, 22 and 23 May 1963, NSF Co-K. See also Walters, *Secret Missions,* 378.

34. Alfred Stepan, *The Military in Politics: Changing Patterns in Brazil* (Princeton, N.J., 1971), 174–83; Ronald M. Schneider, *The Political System of Brazil: Emergence of a "Modernizing" Authoritarian Regime, 1964–1970* (New York, 1971), 250–52. American influence in military education reached down into the lower ranks of the military hierarchy as well. For example, the Army Command and General Staff School (ECEME) was "modernized" in the postwar period by adopting American teaching methods and Cold War curriculum. Thus, Army Captain Hernani d'Aguiar, who taught military history there, reports that he and the other instructors staged a "virtual crusade against Communism and its rapid infiltration in Brazil." He credits the ECEME with molding the anti-Communist "ideological identity" that line officers shared at the time of the 1964 coup. As a conspirator, d'Aguiar belonged to the Costa e Silva "trooper" faction, not the Sorbonne group. Hernani d'Aguiar, *A revolução por dentro* (Rio de Janeiro, n.d.), 17. The U.S. training program for state police similarly devoted a substantial portion of instruction time to anticommunist indoctrination as part of counterinsurgency training. A. J. Langguth, *Hidden Terrors* (New York, 1978), 94–95.

35. René Armand Dreifuss, *1964: A conquista do estado. Ação política, poder e golpe de classe* (Petrópolis, 1981), 361–97. Stacchini, *Março 64,* 115–29.

36. Maxwell Taylor, Memorandum for Mr. Bundy: Counterinsurgency Doctrine. 13 Aug. 1962, NSF Meetings & Memorandums, Box 335A.

37. Work copy of Martin to Gordon, 15 Aug. 1963, NSF Co-K. This paragraph was "sanitized" out of the declassified final draft of the telegram.

38. Martin to Mann, 31 Dec. 1963, Schlesinger Papers, Box 2, JFKL.

39. Senate Foreign Relations Committee, *Hearings on Foreign Assistance Act of 1963,* 88th Cong., 1st sess., 1963, 256.

40. House Committee on Foreign Affairs, *Hearings, Winning the Cold War,* 88th Cong., 1st sess., 1963, pt. 2, 221–25. Senate Foreign Relations Committee, *Hearings, Training of Foreign Affairs Personnel,* 88th Cong., 1st sess., 1963.

41. E.g., Rusk testimony, Senate Foreign Relations Committee, *Hearings on Foreign Assistance Act of 1963,* 257; and Lincoln Gordon, "Castello perdeu a batalha," interview with Roberto Garcia, *Veja,* 9 Mar. 1977, 6.

42. Senate Foreign Relations Committee, *Hearings, Multinational Corporations and U.S. Foreign Policy,* 93d Cong., 1st sess., 1973, pt. 1, 97, 119.

43. House Committee on Foreign Affairs, *Winning the Cold War,* pt. 2, 140–45.

44. Senate Foreign Relations Committee, *Hearing, American Institute for Free Labor Development,* 91st Cong., 1st sess., 1969, 26.

45. Serafino Romualdi, *Presidents and Peons: Recollections of a Labor Ambassador in Latin America* (New York, 1967), 420.

46. Philip Agee, *Inside the Company: CIA Diary,* Bantam ed. (New York, 1976), 244–47, names both the first AIFLD director, Romualdi, and his successor, William Doherty, as CIA agents. In addition, he states that it was the CIA objective to have its salaried agents in control of all AIFLD field stations, the better to control and coordinate policies.

47. For a description of the program see Dreifuss, *1964,* 316–18; Romualdi, *Presidents and Peons,* 415–23; Eugene H. Methvin, "Labor's New Weapon for Democracy," *Readers Digest,* Oct. 1966, 21–28. See also Suzanne Bodenheimer, "U.S. Labor's Conservative Role in Latin America," *Progressive* 31 (1967): 26–30; Sidney Lens, "Labor and the CIA," *Progressive* 31 (1967): 23–28; and Ronald Radosh, *American Labor and United States Foreign Policy: The Cold War in the Unions from Gompers to Lovestone* (New York, 1970).

48. By 1969, AFL-CIO president George Meany was ready to play down the contribution of AIFLD to the coup. Cf. Senate Foreign Relations Committee, *Hearing, AIFLD,* 29.

49. Proposed Short Term Policy, 30 Sept. 1963, POF Co. The objective is reprinted verbatim in the AID Country Assistance Program. Brazil. FY 1965, AID Reference Center.

50. CIA Information Report, 26 May 1963, NSF Co-K.

51. E.g., *Ultima Hora,* 12 Mar. 1964.

52. Luiz Alberto Moniz Bandeira, *Presença dos Estados Unidos no Brasil* (Rio de Janeiro, 1973), 457–60. In *Governo João Goulart,* 135, he reports that an American submarine was sighted unloading weapons on a Pernambuco beach at midnight on July 16, 1963.

53. National Security Action Memorandum No. 57, Responsibility for Paramilitary Operations, 28 June 1961, NSF MM, Box 328.

54. Dulles, *Unrest in Brazil,* 257–63. Clarence W. Hall, "The Country That Saved Itself," *Readers Digest* (Nov. 1964), 145–46. There seem to have been surprisingly few attempts by the Left to retaliate by preventing Rightists from speaking. Aguiar cites one incident in which Lacerda was prevented from entering a college. He pounces on the incident as "proof" that a "revolutionary war" was in progress *(Revolução por dentro,* 88). In another incident, in Belo Horizonte on March 12, 1964, the left-wing Catholic Action prevented conservative Catholics from circulating a petition that expressed opposition to the liberal clergy and the Catholic Action activists. *Ultima Hora,* 13 Mar. 64; *Correio da Manha,* 13 Mar. 1964.

55. Bond to DepState, Airgram 282, 30 Apr. 1964, NSF Co-J.

56. Dulles, *Unrest in Brazil,* 230–33.

57. *Monthly Review,* April 1964, 671. The sergeants had a number of grievances besides their ineligibility to hold elective office: they were not covered by social security, they could be discharged at any time, there was no law governing promotions, and they were ineligible for admission to officers' schools.

58. Bilac Pinto, *Guerra revolucionário* (Rio de Janeiro, 1964), 4–6.

59. John W. F. Dulles, *Castello Branco: Making of a President* (College Station, Tex., 1978), 255–58. The sketch of Castello given here is drawn from this sympathetic biography. Castello Branco (White Castle) is one surname. Following current indexing practices, the name is indexed under "Branco," but the general was never called that. He was known as "Castello" instead of by his first name. To add to the confusion, the Castello Branco family retained the old spelling of "castle"—with the two "l's"—but many Brazilians (including his biographer) spelled the general's name with one "l."

60. Ibid., 324–25.

61. Beatrice Bishop Berle, *Navigating the Rapids, 1918–1971: From the Papers of Adolf A. Berle* (New York, 1973), 788.

62. The complete text of Castello's circular is printed in Dines, *Idos de março,* 392–93.

63. Cf. Juarez Tavora, *Uma vida e muitas lutas* (Rio de Janeiro, 1976), 3:176.

64. Silva, *1964,* 458.

65. Credit for the idea of the march has been generally given to a nun, Sister Ana de Lourdes. The women who headed the new conservative women's groups are credited with planning it and getting out the crowds. However, a number of men, especially Congressman Antonio Silvio da Cunha Bueno, a member of IPES, played a major role in planning and setting up the event. See Silva, *1964,* 335–40; Dines, *Idos de março,* 131–34; Sieckman, "When Executives Turn Revolutionaries," 214; and Dulles, *Unrest in Brazil,* 274–77.

66. Dines, *Idos de março,* 211, 319. American observers agreed that the march was primarily a middle-class performance "with limited lower-class participation." AmEmbassy São Paulo to SecState, 24 Mar. 1964, NSF Co-J.
67. *Ultima Hora,* 26 Mar. 1964.
68. Mein to SecState, 18 Mar. 1964, NSF Co-J.
69. Thomas E. Skidmore, *Politics in Brazil, 1930–1964* (New York, 1967), 289.

## Chapter 10

1. The chapter epigraphs: Gordon is quoted by Clarence Hall, "The Country That Saved Itself," *Readers Digest* (Nov. 1964), 137, and Gore's statement is from Senate Foreign Relations Committee, *Hearings, Foreign Assistance Act of 1964,* 88th Cong., 2d sess., 296. Darcy Ribeiro is cited in A. J. Langguth, *Hidden Terrors* (New York, 1978), 106.
2. Senate Foreign Relations Committee, *Hearing, Nomination of Lincoln Gordon,* 89th Cong., 2d sess., 1966, 36.
3. Mein to SecState, 18 Mar. 1964; Gordon to SecState, 25 Mar. 1964, NSF Co-J.
4. Mein to SecState, 18 Mar. 1964, NSF Co-J.
5. Lincoln Gordon, interview with Paige Mulhollan, 10 July 1969, Oral History Collection, LBJL, 21. Gordon was finally granted a semipersonal interview with the president on March 19. Johnson invited all of the ambassadors to Latin America in to see him, in groups of three or four at a time. Gordon Chase to Bundy, 19 Mar. 1964, NSF Co LA.
6. Johnson ordered a halt to all of the sabotage operations against Cuba that the Kennedy brothers had authorized. Even before Johnson explicitly disavowed such schemes, the CIA got the message and canceled plans to try to assassinate Castro. Thomas Powers, *The Man Who Kept the Secrets: Richard Helms and the CIA,* Washington Square Press ed. (New York, 1979), 181, 192, 198–99.
7. Philip Geyelin, *Lyndon B. Johnson and the World* (New York, 1966), 25–27, 69–70; Eric Goldman, *The Tragedy of Lyndon Johnson* (New York, 1969), 76, 381.
8. Thomas Mann, interview with Joe Frantz, 4 Nov. 1968, 12–13, Oral History Collection, LBJL. See also Geyelin, *Johnson and the World,* 79–80, 94–99.
9. Lincoln Gordon, interview, 10 July 1969, 14.
10. Bundy to President, 20 Sept. 1964, NSF Staff-J.
11. "Apparently somebody took notes and ran out and gave them to Tad Szulc," wrote Gordon Chase to Bundy, 19 Mar. 1964, NSF Co LA. See *New York Times,* "U.S. May Abandon Effort to Deter Latin Dictators," 19 Mar. 1964, 1:1.
12. E.g., Arthur M. Schlesinger, Jr., "The Alliance for Progress: A Retrospective," in *Latin America: The Search for a New International Role,* ed. Ronald G. Hellman and H. Jon Rosenbaum (New York, 1975), 78–80. See also Arthur M. Schlesinger, Jr., *Robert Kennedy and His Times* (Boston, 1978), 630–31.
13. The article was reprinted in Department of State, *Bulletin* 49 (1963): 698–700.
14. Apparently Castello Branco failed to establish contact with the most active group of conspirators in the navy because of status considerations: with four stars, General Castello Branco outranked three-star Vice Admiral Augusto Rademaker Grünewald, the leader of the navy conspirators. Castello therefore felt Grünewald should come to him, not vice versa. See John W. F. Dulles, *Castello Branco: The Making of a President* (College Station, Tex., 1978), 348.

15. Ibid., 354.

16. The Castello-Kruel rivalry dated back to their competition for power and honors as commanders of the Brazilian expeditionary force in Italy in World War II. In their youth, as classmates in military schools, they had been good friends.

17. Dulles, *Making of a President,* 337-40, 351-54.

18. Paulo Cavalcanti, *O caso eu conto como o caso foi* (Recife, 1980), 2:332-35; Thomas E. Skidmore, *The Politics of Military Rule in Brazil, 1964-1985* (New York, 1988), 121, 348N.

19. Abelardo Jurema, *Sexta-Feira 13: Os ultimos dias do governo João Goulart* (Rio de Janeiro, 1964), 151-61. See also John W. F. Dulles, *Unrest in Brazil: Political-Military Crises, 1955-1964* (Austin, 1970), 278-85.

20. Some blood was shed. Sentries at the Navy Ministry were ordered to fire on a group of 100 sailors who were trying to pass the building on their way to join the rebels in the union hall. Four sailors were wounded. Dulles, *Unrest in Brazil,* 283-84.

21. Abelardo Jurema, interview with Aspasia Camargo and Eduardo Raposo, July 1977, 316-17, Oral History Collection, CPDOC.

22. Dulles, *Unrest in Brazil,* 284-85.

23. "Entrevista do ministro da justiça, Abelardo Jurema, no dia 30 de março de 1964," in Alberto Dines et al., *Idos de março e a queda em abril* (Rio de Janeiro, 1964), 396. Cf. Jurema, *Sexta-Feira 13,* 161.

24. Mário Victor, *Cinco anos que abalaram o Brasil* (Rio de Janeiro, 1965), 500-501.

25. Denis de Moraes and Francisco Viana, *Prestes: lutas e autocríticas* (Petrópolis, 1982), 173.

26. Jurema, *Sexta-Feira 13,* 168-71. See also Dulles, *Unrest in Brazil,* 290-93.

27. Dines, *Idos de março,* 267.

28. E.g., Hernani d'Aguiar, *A revolução por dentro* (Rio de Janeiro, n.d.), 126; Araken Tavora, preface to *Brasil, 1e de abril* (Rio de Janeiro, 1964), n.p.

29. Dines, *Idos de março,* 338.

30. Ibid., 60.

31. The *Jornal do Brasil's* version of the speech is printed in the appendix of Dines, *Idos de março,* 396-400. Another version—in English—appears in *Political Power in Latin America: Seven Confrontations,* ed. Richard R. Fagen and Wayne A. Cornelius (Englewood Cliffs, N.J., 1970), 182-86.

32. Since this turned out to be Goulart's final nationally broadcast speech, it could be seen as his farewell message. Like Getúlio and Jânio before him, Jango was pinning the blame on corporate interests. In 1964 all evil was not yet attributed to the CIA.

33. Dines, *Idos de março,* 160.

34. José Stacchini, *Março 64: mobilização da audácia* (São Paulo, 1965), 7-8; Dulles, *Unrest in Brazil,* 313.

35. On his own initiative, Guedes had already begun the detention of suspected left-wing activists on the previous day. Dulles, *Unrest in Brazil,* 312.

36. The confusion and lack of coordination in the coup is apparent in the account presented by Dulles, *Making of a President,* 372-75. The rivalry among the military conspirators is discussed in René Armand Dreifuss, *1964: A conquista do estado* (Petrópolis, 1981), 390-97.

37. d'Aguiar, *Revolução por dentro,* 149.

38. d'Aguiar details the revolutionary activities of the officers in Rio on March 31 and April 1. Ibid., 131-69.

39. Carlos Lacerda, *Depoimento* (Rio de Janeiro, 1977), 286. For the story of Lacerda's activities during the revolution see Dines, *Idos de março,* 163–90.

40. Dulles, *Unrest in Brazil,* 328.

41. Dines, *Idos de março,* 183.

42. Jurema, *Sexta-Feira 13,* 205–6.

43. Ibid., 174.

44. Ibid., 188–89.

45. Fourth Army Commander Justino Alves Bastos also betrayed Goulart after assuring him of his loyalty early in the day on March 31. But the small Fourth Army in Recife did not play a critical role in the overthrow of the government. Unexplained is the behavior of Marine Commander Aragão, a Goulart loyalist, who directed his marines to seize radio and television stations and occupy newspaper offices but made no move to take the governor's palace or to try to arrest the leading conspirators.

46. Luiz Alberto Moniz Bandeira, *O governo João Goulart* (Rio de Janeiro, 1977), 177–85. The arrest of Castello would have involved the use of force. Castello's office was guarded by a large number of officers armed with pistols and eager for a fight. The most concise coverage of the military side of the 1964 coup can be found in Ronald M. Schneider, *The Political System of Brazil: Emergence of a "Modernizing" Authoritarian Regime, 1964–1970* (New York, 1971), 97–106.

47. Lacerda, *Depoimento,* 287.

48. Gordon mentioned discussing "various types" of contingency plans at the White House when in Washington in September 1963. Gordon to Martin, 16 Oct. 1963, NSF Co-K.

49. Gordon Chase to Bundy, 19 Mar. 1964, NSF Co LA.

50. JCS [Joint Chiefs of Staff] to CINCLANTFLT [Commander in Chief Atlantic Fleet] 31 Mar. 1964, and CINCLANTFLT to COMSECDFLT, 31 Mar. 1964, NSF Co-J. Phyllis R. Parker gives the most comprehensive account of the Brother Sam operation (*Brazil and the Quiet Intervention* [Austin, 1979], 73–87).

51. See JCS to CSAF, 31 Mar. 1964 and 1 Apr. 1964. JCS to USCINCSO [U.S. Commander in Chief Southern Forces] 1 Apr. 1964. NSF Co-J. Ambassador Gordon reached his conclusion that Goulart "is now definitely engaged on campaign to seize dictatorial power" even before Goulart had mishandled the sailor mutiny crisis. See Personal from Ambassador Gordon, 27 Mar. 1964, NSF Co-J.

52. Proposed Short-Term Policy—Brazil, 30 Sept. 1963, NSF Co-K.

53. Rusk to AmEmbassy, 1 Apr. 1964, NSF Co-J.

54. Andrade later insisted that he staged the impromptu ceremony installing Mazzilli as president in order to relieve the Third Army stationed in Rio Grande do Sul from the constitutional obligation of obeying Goulart. At the time he believed that Goulart was preparing to fight. Others applauded Andrade's move as a tactic to preserve civilian—not military—government, but Andrade was not concerned about possible military rule. He was so far out of the loop that he thought the coup was some sort of spontaneous eruption of the "people," untainted by military conspiracy. Auro Moura Andrade, *Um congresso contra o arbítrio* (Rio de Janeiro, 1985), 240–52, 267, 276, 357.

55. Department of State, *Bulletin* 50 (1964): 610. The statement had actually been drafted by the embassy in Rio. During a teleconference on April 2 the possible illegality of Mazzilli's succession was discussed. Telecon Rio-Washington, 2 Apr. 1964, Decl.Doc. #697–698, 1986.

56. Department of State, *Bulletin* 50 (1964): 610.

57. Gordon to SecState, 5 Apr. 1964, NSF Co-J.

58. See, for example. Mário Lago, *1 de abril, estórias para história* (Rio de Janeiro, 1964).

59. See Mann to AmEmbassy, 6 Apr. 1964, and Gordon to SecState, 6 Apr. 1964, both in NSF Co-J.

60. Marcio Moreira Alves, *Torturas e torturados* (Rio de Janeiro, 1966), 42. Presumably such heinous plans justified holding the trade officials incommunicado for weeks, denying even the Red Cross access to them. *Correio da Manha,* 21 Apr. 1964.

61. As quoted in Gordon to SecState, 4 Apr. 1964, NSF Co-J.

62. Gordon to SecState, 7 Apr. 1964, and 8 Apr. 1964, both in NSF Co-J.

63. Vernon A. Walters, *Silent Missions* (New York, 1978), 390.

64. Gordon to SecState, 7 Apr. 1964, NSF Co-J.

65. Gordon to SecState, 8 Apr. 1964, NSF Co-J.

66. See Cavalcanti, *O caso eu conto,* 1:374–83; Gregório Bezerra, *Memórias: Segunda parte, 1946–1969* (Rio de Janeiro, 1980), 193–203; José Coelho Pinto, *Um deputado no exilio* (Rio de Janeiro, 1965), 59–62; Alves, *Tortura e torturados.*

67. Quoted by José Murilo de Carvalho, "Organizational Roles, Belief Systems and Military Politics" in *Politics and Administration in Brazil,* ed. Jean-Claude Garcia-Zamor (Washington, D.C., 1978), 184.

68. Lacerda, *Depoimento,* 296. See also JANAF attachés to State, 4 Apr. 1964; CIA Intelligence Information Cable, 6 Apr. 1964; Gordon to SecState, 10 Apr. 1964; Olympio Mourão Filho, *Memórias: a verdade de um revolucionário* (Porto Alegre, 1978), 390–91, 405–9; Juracy Magalhães, *Minhas memórias provisórias* (Rio de Janeiro, 1982), 171–73.

69. Marcio Moreira Alves, "Urban Guerrillas and the Terrorist State" in *Contemporary Brazil: Issues in Economic and Political Development,* ed. H. Jon Rosenbaum and William Tyler (New York, 1972), 54. As has been the case in other witch-hunts in history, this one was also used to settle old personal quarrels that had nothing to do with political philosophy. See, for example, Mauro Borges, *O golpe em Goias; história de uma grande traição* (Rio de Janeiro, 1965), 161–62.

70. Solange de Deus Simões, *Deus, patria e familia: as mulheres no golpe de 1964* (Petrópolis, 1985), 121–22.

## Chapter 11

1. An earlier version of this chapter was published in *Prologue* (Summer 1981) 13:77–99. Dean Rusk's statement is from Department of State, *Bulletin* 50 (1964): 614. Alves's *Torturas e torturados* (Rio de Janeiro, 1966) is the source of the epigraph.

2. Gordon to SecState, 10 Apr. 1964, NSF Co-J.

3. Proposed Short-Term Policy—Brazil, 13 Aug. 1964, NSF Co-J.

4. Gordon to SecState, 10 Apr. 1964, NSF Co-J.

5. Gordon to SecState, 7 Apr. 1964, NSF Co-J.

6. Mann to AmEmbassy, 10 Apr. 1964, NSF Co-J.

7. House Committee on Foreign Affairs, *Hearings on Foreign Assistance Act of 1964,* 88th Cong., 2d sess., 1964, 307–8.

8. Senate Committee on Foreign Relations, *Nomination of Lincoln Gordon to be Assistant Secretary of State for Inter-American Affairs,* 89th Cong., 2d sess., 1966, 34–38.

9. Gordon to SecState, 7 Apr. 1964, NSF Co-J.

10. Gordon to SecState, 10 Apr. 1964, NSF Co-J. Gordon was so eager to get out the story on the the Red Menace that his superiors had to request that he allow all news about subversion to emanate from Brazilian sources. George Ball to AmEmbassy, 17 Apr. 1964, NSF Co-J. See Framework for AID Strategy, Country Assistance Program, Brazil, FY 1965–1966, 30 Nov. 1964, pp. 9–11 for embassy perceptions of the extent of subversive activity, AID Reference Center.

11. Clarence W. Hall, "The Country That Saved Itself," *Readers Digest* (Nov. 1964):133–59.

12. Chase to Bundy, 6 May 1964, Mann to Gordon, 9 June 1964, Mein to SecState, 11 June 1964, all in NSF Co-J.

13. Actually Juracy made the statement at the time he was named ambassador to the United States, before he became foreign minister. He subsequently spent a great deal of time explaining it away. See *Minhas memórias provisórias* (Rio de Janeiro, 1982), 176–77, 305–8.

14. Gordon to Dungan, 13 Apr. 1964, WHCF Co 37.

15. The failure of both U.S. and Latin American commentators to give him credit for his work on the Alliance for Progress irritated President Johnson. See Valenti to President, 15 Mar. 1966, Central Files, ExFO Co-37.

16. Gordon to Bell, Mann, Rogers, and Solomon, 8 June 1964, NSF Co-J.

17. Latin American Policy Committee, "Proposed Short Term Policy—Brazil," 13 Aug. 1964, NSF Co-J.

18. See the text of the Charter of Punta del Este, Appendix B in Jerome Levinson and Juan de Onis, *The Alliance That Lost Its Way: A Critical Report on the Alliance for Progress* (Chicago, 1972), 352–71.

19. John W. Tuthill, "Operation Topsy," *Foreign Policy* (Fall 1972): 66. American advisors were not always very discreet. See "Meddling in Brazil: The CIA Bungles On," *Commonweal* 87 (9 Feb. 1968): 553–54.

20. Lucia Maria Gaspar Gomes, *"Cronologia do governo Castelo Branco,"* *Dados* 1 (1967): 124.

21. CIA Intelligence Memorandum, 3 Apr. 1964, NSF Co-J.

22. Gordon to SecState, 22 Sept. 1965, NSF Co-J. See also Gordon to David E. Bell, 16 Sept. 1964, NSF Co-J.

23. See Wayne A. Selcher, "The National Security Doctrine and Policies of the Brazilian Government," *Parameters* 7 (Spring 1977): 10–24; Catherine Durandin, *"L'idéologie de la sécurité nationale au Brésil,"* *Notes et études documentaires* 44 (17 June 1977): 5–18; Roberto Calvo, "Church and National Security," *Journal of Interamerican Studies and World Affairs* 21 (Feb. 1972): 69–88; Alfred Stepan, "The New Professionalism of Internal Warfare and Military Role Expansion," in *Authoritarian Brazil,* ed. Alfred Stepan (New Haven, 1973), 47–65; Maria Helena Moreira Alves, *State and Opposition in Military Brazil* (Austin, 1985), 13–28.

24. See, for example, Hernani d'Aguiar, *A revolução por dentro* (Rio de Janeiro, n.d.), 292–301.

25. In his analysis of the National Security Doctrine, Comblin traced its "geopolitical" organic theme back to "all the devils" of nineteenth-century German idealism. He credits General Golbery do Couto e Silva with the major role in formulating the doctrine. José Comblin, *The Church and the National Security State* (Maryknoll, N.Y., 1979), 68.

26. *Revolução evolução. 6º aniversário da revolução.* Assessoria Especial de Relações Publicas da Presidência da Republica. (N.p., 1970), 37.

27. W. W. Rostow to Mann, Reflections and Recommendations on Brazil, 7 Sept. 1964, NSF Co-J; Chase to Bundy, 25 Aug. 1964, NSF LA; Valenti to President, 10 Aug. 1965, Confidential File, CO 37.

28. Luis Viana Filho, *O governo Castelo Branco* (Rio de Janeiro, 1975), 79–80. Gordon to SecState, 20 Apr. 1964 and 10 June 1964, NSF Co-J.

29. "He is hampered by a personal stiffness in manner and style, and this assumes proportions of a major defect through reluctance to embark on public relations projects aimed at building mass political support for his government," observed Gordon in Framework for AID Strategy, 30 Nov. 1964, p. 13, AID Reference Center. This was the most severe criticism Gordon ever made of the general.

30. See Mauro Borges, *O golpe em Goias: história de uma grande traição* (Rio de Janeiro, 1965); Dean to SecState, 16 Nov. 1964, NSF Co-J.

31. Covey T. Oliver, interview with Paige Mulhollan, 12 Dec. 1968, 19, Oral History Collection, LBJL.

32. This view was not limited to the Latin American experts of the executive branch. On August 7, 1965, Senator William J. Fulbright (soon to become a critic of Johnson's foreign policy) met with the Brazilian foreign minister and "expressed his view econ [*sic*] and social development must precede democracy, that some form authoritarianism almost necessary in early stages and in fact is one form of collective discipline, permitting country focus on its real problems" (Gordon to SecState, 7 Aug. 1965, NSF Co-J, [Box 9, Codel Fulbright]).

33. William D. Rogers to AmEmbassy, 19 June 1964; Bell and Mann to Gordon, 7 Aug. 1964, NSF Co-J. See also Gordon to SecState, 21, 23, and 25 Aug. 1964, Dec.DOS.doc.

34. Gordon to SecState, 15 and 21 May 1964, 9 June 1964, Dec.DOS.doc. See also Gordon to DepState, Airgram 1060, 5 Mar. 1964, Dec.DOS.doc.

35. Burton to AmEmbassy, 15 June 1964; Gordon to SecState, 16 and 22 June 1964; all are Dec.DOS.doc.

36. Gordon to SecState, 17 Aug. 1964, Dec.DOS.doc.

37. Gordon to SecState, 20 Apr. 1964, NSF Co-J.

38. Gordon to SecState, 20 and 29 July 1964, Dec.DOS.doc.

39. So bitter was the opposition in Brazil that Gordon discussed the possibility of completing the deal without submitting it to the Brazilian Congress. In the end, however, it was concluded that Brazilian funds to pay AMFORP would not be guaranteed without congressional approval. See Gordon to SecState, 29 and 31 July 1964, 19 and 20 Aug. 1964; Ralph Burton to AmEmbassy, 9 July 1964; Rusk to AmEmbassy, 5 Aug. 1964; all are Dec.DOS.doc.

40. See, for example, Robert Sayre to Bundy, 9 July 1964, NSF LA.

41. When Ambassador Gordon accompanied lawyer John J. McCloy, representing Hanna, to see Castello Branco, the opposition learned of it and raised a hue and cry. The incident was cited as proof that the ambassador was the tool of the American monopolies and that the monopolies were dictating policy to Castello Branco. Actually the hour-long visit was not decisive; Hanna did not definitely win the right to mine iron ore on its Brazilian properties until July 1968. See Gordon to DepState, Airgram A-444, 10 Nov. 1964, and Tuthill to DepState, Airgram 917, 23 July 1968; both Dec.DOS.doc.

42. *Public Papers of the Presidents of the United States: Lyndon B. Johnson, 1966* (Washington, D.C., 1967), 122.

43. See Hugh Sidey, *A Very Personal Presidency* (New York, 1968), 89–96 on LBJ's relationship with business.

44. John T. Connor to President, 4 Feb. 1964, WHCF-J, FO 3-2-1. Connor later became secretary of commerce. See also David Rockefeller to President, 29 Nov. 1963, and LBJ to David Rockefeller, 11 Dec. 1963; also WHCF-J, FO, 3-2-1.

45. David Rockefeller, in particular, became a White House confidant. See Name File, LBJL.

46. W. E. Knox to President, 24 Mar. 1965, WHCF-J, ExCo 1-8.

47. Compare, for example, David Rockefeller to President, 10 Sept. 1965, WHCF-J, FO 3-2-1, with Rockefeller's statement about the COMAP Report in 1962, reprinted in Joint Economic Committee, *Hearings, Private Investment in Latin America,* 88th Cong., 2d sess., 1964, 100–103.

48. Rostow to Mann, Reflections and Recommendations on Brazil, 7 Sept. 1964, NSF LA.

49. See Rubem Medina, *Desnacionalização, crime contra o Brasil?* (Rio de Janeiro, 1970), especially Tables 1:1–5, 46–50. However, the multinationals did reinvest a considerable share of profits earned in Brazil in the country—a factor not completely taken into account by Medina.

50. *Public Papers, Johnson, 1963-1964,* 1048–49. See also President's Staff File, DPT, Head of State Correspondence File, Brazil, LBJL.

51. Visit of President-elect Costa e Silva of Brazil, Background Paper, Brazil and Vietnam, 23 Jan. 1967, NSF Co-J; Viana Filho, *Governo Castelo Branco,* 441–43.

52. Carlos Castello Branco, *Os militares no poder* (Rio de Janeiro, 1976), 1:237–42.

53. William G. Bowdler to Bundy, 27 Oct. 1965, NSF Co-J.

54. Gordon to Rusk and Jack H. Vaughn, 29 Oct. 1965, NSF Co-J.

55. Vaughn to Gordon, 30 Oct. 1965, NSF Co-J.

56. AmEmbassy to SecState, 23 Nov. 1965, NSF Co-J.

57. Bundy to President, 27 Oct. 1965, NSF Co-J.

58. Gordon to Rusk, 14 Nov. 1965, NSF Co-J.

59. CIA memorandum, Political Situation in Brazil, 29 Nov. 1965, NSF Co-J.

60. Gordon to Bundy, AID Presentation on Brazil, 4 Nov. 1965, 24–27, NSF Co-J.

61. William S. Gaud, interview with Paige Mulhollan, 26 Nov. 1968, 5–6, Oral History Collection, LBJL.

62. Bundy to President, 7 Dec. 1965, and Mann to President, 8 Dec. 1965, both NSF Co-J. Project loans of $75–100 million and food funds of $35 million were not at issue in this dispute.

63. Bowdler to Bundy, 13 Dec. 1965, NSF Co-J.

64. Rostow to President, 30 Nov. 1965, WHCF-J, ExFO.

65. Juracy Magalhães to Mann, 30 Nov. 1965, NSF Co-J.

66. Castello Branco, *Os militares no poder,* 1:481.

67. Ibid., 584–86.

68. E.g., Thomas E. Skidmore, *The Politics of Military Rule in Brazil, 1964-1985* (New York, 1988), 18–65.

69. Rusk to President, Memorandum on Costa e Silva Visit, 23 Jan. 1967; Philip Raine to Rusk, Situation and Contingency Evaluation, 24 Jan. 1967; Gaud to President, Nov. 1966, p. 6; all in NSF Co-J. Senate Foreign Relations Committee, *Nomination of Lincoln Gordon,* 8.

70. See Bowdler to Rostow, 18 Nov. 1966, and Nicholas Katzenbach to Tuthill and D. K. Palmer, 8 Dec. 1966, both in NSF Co-J.

71. Carlos Lacerda, *Depoimento* (Rio de Janeiro, 1977), 382–89.

72. President Johnson was an exception to the rule. He was favorably impressed during Costa e Silva's preinauguration visit to the United States and later, at the 1967 OAS summit, Johnson singled out the general as the best president in Latin America. See Lincoln Gordon, interview with Paige Mulhollan, 10 July 1969, p. 111, LBJL. Reports by other officials of their encounters with Costa e Silva have a polite but strongly patronizing air. See, for example, Tuthill, Memorandum of Conversation, 23 Sept. 1966, and Rostow to President, 25 Jan. and 14 June 1967, NSF Co-J.

73. Anti-American sentiment was noted by State Department analysts before Costa e Silva took office. See Raine to SecState, Situation and Contingency Evaluation, 24 Jan. 1967, NSF Co-J.

74. Tuthill gives the full story in "Operation Topsy," *Foreign Policy* (Fall 1972): 62–85. There are some undated memorandums on the operation in NSF Co-J.

75. Tuthill, "Operation Topsy," 69–70, 72–74; Jan K. Black, *United States Penetration of Brazil* (Philadelphia, 1977), 221–24.

76. See Bowdler to Rostow, 19 Mar. 1968, NSF Co-J.

77. Philip Raine, *Brazil, Awakening Giant* (Washington, D.C., 1974), 207–8. See also A. J. Langguth, *Hidden Terrors* (New York, 1978).

78. Bowdler to Rostow, 19 June 1968, NSF Co-J. See also CIA Information Cable, 23 May 1967, NSF Co-J. Nevertheless the education reform that Costa e Silva had the Congress enact in September 1968 did include a number of the recommendations initially made by the USAID mission. Skidmore, *Politics of Military Rule,* 75–76.

79. E.g., *Ultima Hora,* 6 Feb. 1964. Cf. Barry Ames, *Rhetoric and Reality in a Militarized Regime: Brazil since 1964* (Beverly Hills, 1973), 16–26; and Janice E. Perlman, *The Myth of Marginality* (Berkeley, 1976), 195–241.

80. American Technical Assistance Corporation, Evaluation Report on AID Supported Programs to Improve Primary Education in Northeast Brazil, (1970), 14–17, AID Reference Center.

81. AID Program Memorandum, FY 1969, 29 Aug. 1967, AID Reference Center. See also Alliance for Progress Activities in Brazil, July 1968, AID Reference Center.

82. AID Spring Review, Country Paper. Land Reform in Brazil, Northeast, June 1970, AID Reference Center.

83. W. Alan Laflin, End of Tour Report, 30 July 1965, Northeast Regional Development, AID Reference Center.

84. Sidney Rocker, End of Tour Report, 13 Nov. 1964, Public Safety Program, AID Reference Center.

85. Roland Kelley, End of Tour Report, 9 Dec. 1965, Public Safety Program, AID Reference Center.

86. Robert J. Clark, End of Tour Report, 2 Apr. 1963, Public Safety Program, AID Reference Center.

87. Carl Gerbracht, End of Tour Report, 14 Feb. 1966, Vocational Education, AID Reference Center.

88. J. Russell Prior, End of Tour Report, 31 Oct. 1966, Public Safety Program, AID Reference Center.

89. Jack K. Ellis, End of Tour Report, 4 Feb. 1963, Public Safety Program, AID Reference Center.

90. House Committee on Government Operations, *Hearings, US AID Operations in Latin America under the Alliance for Progress,* 90th Cong., 2d sess., 1969, 450, 459.

91. C. R. Smith to Jim Jones, July 1968, WHCF-J, ExCo 37.

92. See Briefing Book, Costa e Silva Visit, Special Problems, 18 Jan. 1967, NSF Co-J; Costa e Silva to President, 10 Nov. 1967, and Rostow to President, 21 Nov. 1967, both in President's Staff File, Head of State Correspondence, LBJL.

93. Thomas C. Bruneau traces the growing opposition of the Church to the regime in *The Political Transformation of the Brazilian Catholic Church* (New York, 1974). See 177–209 for the 1964–1969 period.

94. Cf. CIA Information Cable, 30 Mar. 1968, NSF Co-J; *Time,* "Surpassing All Limits of Unpopularity," 5 July 1968, 34. See also Skidmore, *Politics of Military Rule,* 73–79.

95. See CIA intelligence memorandum, Brazil: The Road to Dictatorship, 23 Dec. 1968, NSF Co-J. The regime's systematic use of torture is discussed in Skidmore, *Politics of Military Rule,* 88–89, 119–22, 125–34, 185–86.

96. Sam Lewis to Rostow, 31 Dec. 1968, NSF Co-J.

97. Maxwell D. Taylor, Memo for Bundy, 13 Aug. 1962, NSAM 182, Box 335A–338, NSF MM.

98. John Tuthill, "Economic and Political Aspects of Development in Brazil and U.S. Aid," *Journal of Inter-American Studies* 11 (Apr. 1969): 201.

# Chapter 12

1. See Johnson's handwritten comments on the letter by Carlos Sanz de Santa Maria, 7 June 1965, WHCF-J, FO 3-2-1. The epigraph is from Bradlee's *Conversations with Kennedy* (New York, 1976), p. 122.

2. Bilac Pinto, *Guerra revolucionária* (Rio de Janeiro, 1964), 161–66; Antonio Carlos da Silva Muricy, *"Os motivos da revolução democratica brasileira,"* in *Palavras de um soldado* (Rio de Janeiro, 1971), 83.

3. Paulo Ayres Filho, "The Brazilian Revolution," in *Latin America, Politics, Economics and Hemispheric Security,* ed. Norman A. Bailey (New York, 1965), 254–56.

4. Sayre to Bundy, 15 June 1964, NSF Co-J.

5. José Stacchini, *Março 64: mobilização da audácia* (São Paulo, 1965), x.

6. In 1969 a guerrilla group looking for funds to finance their operations staged the robbery of a safe belonging to Adhemar. In it they found $2.5 million in U.S. currency. Thomas E. Skidmore, *The Politics of Military Rule in Brazil* (New York, 1988), 88.

7. Cf. Ronald M. Schneider, *The Political System of Brazil: Emergence of a "Modernizing" Authoritarian Regime, 1964–1970* (New York, 1971), 23–36; Riordan Roett, "A Praetorian Army in Politics: The Brazilian Military, 1946 to the Present," in *Politics and Administration in Brazil,* ed. Jean-Claude Garcia-Zamor (Washington, D.C., 1978), 265–301. Wanderley Guilherme dos Santos restates and attempts to systematize this "classic" explanation in *Sessenta e quatro: anatomia do crise* (São Paulo, 1986).

8. This argument has been best developed by Fernando Henrique Cardoso. A succinct statement of his theory can be found in *Authoritarian Brazil,* ed. Alfred Stepan (New Haven, 1973), 142–63. See also Peter Evans, *Dependent Development: The Alliance of Multinational, State, and Local Capital in Brazil* (Princeton, 1979).

9. See, for example, Robinson Rojas, *Estados Unidos en Brasil* (Santiago, Chile, 1965), 21–40, 46–51; Edmar Morel, *O golpe começou em Washington* (Rio de Janeiro, 1965); and Andrei Gromyko, *Through Russian Eyes: President Kennedy's 1036 Days* (Washington, D.C., 1973), 70–84, 93, 115.

10. Ralph Dungan, interview with Paige Mulhollan, 6 Apr. 1972, 28, Oral History Collection, LBJL.

11. Roger Blough, interview with Joe Frantz, 29 July 1971, 33, Oral History Collection, LBJL.

12. As quoted by Alan Wolfe and Jerry Sanders, "Resurgent Cold War Ideology," in *Capitalism and State in Latin America,* ed. Richard R. Fagen (Stanford, Cal., 1979), 49–50.

13. Michael Parenti, *The Anti-Communist Impulse* (New York, 1969) provides a discussion of anticommunism from the perspective of the Vietnam War years.

14. House Committee on Government Operations, *Hearings, US AID Operations in Latin America under the Alliance for Progress,* 90th Cong., 2d sess., 1969, 496.

15. Sylvia Ann Hewlitt, *The Cruel Dilemmas of Development: Twentieth-Century Brazil* (New York, 1980).

16. On the corruption issue, see Skidmore, *Politics of Military Rule,* 272, 398 nn. 53 and 54.

17. Carlos Lacerda, *Depoimento* (Rio de Janeiro, 1977), 289.

18. *Public Papers of the Presidents of the United States: John F. Kennedy, 1961* (Washington, D.C., 1962), 171.

19. The Death Squads of off-duty police and military, so useful for terrorizing civilians and executing alleged petty criminals, appeared first in Brazil. The disappearance of individuals arrested by the internal security agencies also happened first in Brazil, although not on the scale later practiced in Argentina or Chile or El Salvador. In analyzing the threat of the national security state to the Church, José Comblin credits Brazil with the dubious distinction of establishing this type of state as "a new government prototype" that military elites in other Latin countries copied (*The Church and the National Security State* [Maryknoll, 1979]), 104.

20. *Congressional Record,* 116 (10 Apr. 1970), 11212. See also the article on the use of torture in Brazil inserted in the record by Senator Harold E. Hughes, 11224–26.

21. *Congressional Record,* 117 (29 Oct. 1971), 38256.

22. E.g., Arthur M. Schlesinger, Jr., "The Lowering Hemisphere," *Atlantic* (January 1970): 81, and "The Alliance for Progress: A Retrospective," in *Latin America: The Search for a New International Role,* ed. Ronald G. Hellman and H. Jon Rosenbaum (New York, 1975), 78–80.

23. Bundy to President, Pierre Salinger and Brazil, 26 May 1964, NSF:NSC Staff.

24. *Congressional Record,* 117 (29 Oct. 1971), 38257.

25. *Public Papers: Harry S. Truman, 1949,* Inaugural Address, 115.

26. For a discussion of the continued power and prerogatives of the military in the New Republic, see Alfred Stepan, *Rethinking Military Politics: Brazil and the Southern Cone* (Princeton, 1988), 103–14, 121–28.

27. *Public Papers: John F. Kennedy, 1961,* Inaugural Address, 1.

# References

## Archives

AID Reference Center. Washington, D.C.

Centro de Pesquisa e Documentação de História Contemporâneo do Brasil, Instituto de Direito Público e Ciência Política, Fundação Getúlio Vargas. Rio de Janeiro.

Declassified documents. Many recently declassified documents are listed in Research Publications, Inc., *Declassified Documents Quarterly Catalog* and reproduced on microfiche. Available in research libraries.

Dwight D. Eisenhower Library. Abilene, Kansas. Presidential Papers (Ann Whitman File), International Series, Brazil.

John F. Kennedy Library. Boston, Mass.
   *National Security Files: Country: Brazil*
   *National Security Files: Meetings & Memos*
   *National Security Files: Trips & Conferences*
   *President's Office Files: Country: Brazil*
   *President's Office Files: Departments & Agencies*
   *President's Office Files: Staff*
   *Schlesinger Papers: Subject File: Brazil*
   *White House Central Files*

Lyndon B. Johnson Library. Austin, Texas.
   *National Security Files: Country: Brazil*
   *National Security Files: Country: Latin America*
   *National Security Files: National Security Council Staff File*
   *President's Staff File: Head of State Correspondence*

References

*White House Central Files*
*White House Central Files: Confidential CO 37*
*White House Central Files: Name Files*

## Published Documents

*Congressional Record.* 1961–71. Washington, D.C.
*Public Papers of the Presidents of the United States: Dwight D. Eisenhower, 1953–61.* 8 vols. Washington, D.C.: GPO, 1960–61.
*Public Papers of the Presidents of the United States: Lyndon B. Johnson, 1963–69.* 10 vols. Washington, D.C.: GPO, 1965–70.
*Public Papers of the Presidents of the United States: John F. Kennedy, 1961–63.* 3 vols. Washington, D.C.: GPO, 1962–64.
*Public Papers of the Presidents of the United States: Harry S. Truman, 1945–53.* 8 vols. Washington, D.C.: GPO, 1964.
U.S. Congress, House. Committee on Foreign Affairs. *Hearings, Castro-Communist Subversion in the Western Hemisphere.* 88th Cong., 1st sess., 1963.
———. *Hearings, Foreign Assistance Act of 1962.* 87th Cong., 2d sess., 1962.
———. *Hearings, Foreign Assistance Act of 1964.* 88th Cong., 2d sess., 1964.
———. *Hearing, Torture and Oppression in Brazil.* 93rd Cong., 2d sess., 1975.
———. *Hearings, Winning the Cold War: the U.S. Ideological Offensive.* 88th Cong., 1st sess., 1963.
U.S. Congress, House. Committee on Government Operations. *Hearings, U.S. AID Operations in Latin America Under the Alliance for Progress.* 90th Cong., 2d sess., 1969.
U.S. Congress, Joint Economic Committee. Subcommittee on Inter-American Relationships. *Private Investment in Latin America, Hearings.* 88th Cong., 2d sess., 1964.
U.S. Congress, Senate. Appropriations Committee. *Hearings on Foreign Assistance and Related Agencies Appropriations for 1964.* 88th Cong., 1st sess., 1963.
U.S. Congress, Senate. Armed Services Committee. *Inquiry into Strategic and Critical Material Stockpiles of U.S., Hearings, Hanna Nickel Contracts,* Part 6. 87th Cong., 2d sess., 1962.
U.S. Congress, Senate. Foreign Relations Committee. *Hearing, American Institute for Free Labor Development.* 91st Cong., 1st sess., 1969.
———. *Hearings, Foreign Assistance Act of 1962.* 87th Cong., 2d sess., 1962.
———. *Hearings, Foreign Assistance Act of 1963.* 88th Cong., 1st sess., 1963.
———. *Hearings, Foreign Assistance Act of 1964.* 88th Cong., 2d sess., 1964.
———. *Hearings, Multinational Corporations and U.S. Foreign Policy.* 93rd Cong., 1st sess., 1973.
———. *Hearing, Nomination of Lincoln Gordon to be Assistant Secretary of State for Inter-American Affairs.* 89th Cong., 2d sess., 1966.

# References

————. *Hearings, United States Policies and Programs in Brazil.* 92nd Cong., 1st sess., 1971.

U.S. Department of State. *Bulletin. The Official Weekly Record of United States Foreign Policy.* Vols. 44–59, (1961–68).

## Books and Journals

Agee, Philip. *Inside the Company: CIA Diary.* New York: Bantam, 1976.

Aguiar, Hernani d'. *A revolução por dentro.* Rio de Janeiro: Artenova, n.d.

Aguilar, Luis. *Marxism in Latin America.* New York: Knopf, 1968.

Alves, Marcio Moreira. *A Grain of Mustard Seed.* New York: Doubleday-Anchor, 1973.

————. *Torturas e torturados.* Rio de Janeiro: n.p., 1966.

————. "Urban Guerrillas and the Terrorist State." In *Contemporary Brazil: Issues in Economic and Political Development.* Edited by H. Jon Rosenbaum and William Tyler, 51–67. New York: Praeger, 1972.

Alves, Maria Helena Moreira. *State and Opposition in Military Brazil.* Austin: University of Texas Press, 1985.

Ames, Barry. *Rhetoric and Reality in a Militarized Regime: Brazil since 1964.* Beverly Hills: Sage, 1973.

Andrade, Auro Moura. *Um congresso contra o arbítrio.* Rio de Janeiro: Nova Fronteira, 1985.

Arriaga, Pablo H. "Brazil: Requiem for an Illusion." *Monthly Review* 16, no. 2 (June 1964): 84–89.

Ayres Filho, Paulo. "The Brazilian Revolution." In *Latin American Politics, Economics, and Hemispheric Security.* Edited by Norman A. Bailey, 239–60. New York: Praeger, 1965.

Balgooyen, H.W. "Problems of U.S. Investments in Latin America." In *Foreign Investment in Latin America.* Edited by Marvin Bernstein, 212–28. New York: Knopf, 1966.

Bandeira, Luis Alberto Moniz. *Brizola e o trabalhismo.* Rio de Janeiro: Civilização Brasileira, 1979.

————. *O governo João Goulart.* Rio de Janeiro: Civilização Brasileira, 1977.

————. *Presença dos Estados Unidos no Brasil.* Rio de Janeiro: Civilização Brasileira, 1973.

Barnet, Richard J. *Intervention and Revolution: The United States in the Third World.* New York: World, 1968.

Basbaum, Leôncio. *Historia sincera da republica.* Vol. 4, *De Jânio Quadros à Costa e Silva.* São Paulo: Fulgor, 1968.

Beaulac, Willard L. *A Diplomat Looks at Aid to Latin America.* Carbondale: So. Illinois University Press, 1970.

Bell, Peter D. "Brazilian-American Relations." In *Brazil in the Sixties.* Edited by Riordan Roett, 77–102. Nashville: Vanderbilt University Press, 1972.

301

Bemis, George W. *From Crisis to Revolution: Monthly Case Studies.* Los Angeles: University of Southern California Press, 1964.

Benevides, Maria Victoria de Mesquita. *A UDN e o udenismo.* Rio de Janeiro: Paz e Terra, 1981.

Berle, Adolf A. "As the Dust Settles in Brazil." *Reporter,* 23 April 1964.

————. *The Cold War in Latin America.* Storrs, Conn.: 1961.

Berle, Beatrice, and Travis Jacobs, eds. *Navigating the Rapids, 1918-1971: From the Papers of Adolf A. Berle.* New York: Harcourt Brace Jovanovich, 1973.

Bezerra, Gregório. *Memórias, segunda parte.* 2d ed. Rio de Janeiro: Civilização Brasileira, 1980.

Black, Jan Knippers. *United States Penetration of Brazil.* Philadelphia: University of Pennsylvania Press, 1977.

Blair, Joan, and Clay Blair, Jr. *The Search for JFK.* New York: Putnam's, 1976.

Blume, Norman. "Pressure Groups and Decision Making in Brazil." In *Studies in Comparative International Development.* St. Louis: Washington University Press, 1968. Vol. 3, no. 11, 205-23.

Bodenheimer, Suzanne. "U.S. Labor's Conservative Role in Latin America." *Progressive* 31 (1967): 26-30.

Bonilla, Frank. *"Jânio Vem Aí:* Brazil Elects a President." American Universities Field Staff Reports Service, East Coast South America Series, vol. 7, no. 2 (Oct. 1960).

————. "Rural Reform in Brazil." American University Field Staff Reports Service, East Coast South America Series, vol. 8, no. 4 (Oct. 1961).

Borges, Mauro. *O golpe em Goias: História de uma grande traição.* Rio de Janeiro: Civilização Brasileira, 1965.

Bradlee, Benjamin C. *Conversations with Kennedy.* New York: Pocketbooks, 1976.

Branco, Carlos Castello. *Introdução à Revolução de 1964.* 2 vols. Rio de Janeiro: Artenova, 1975.

————. *Os militares no poder.* 2 vols. Rio de Janeiro: Nova Fronteira, 1976.

Brazil. Assessoria Especial de Relações Publicas da Presidência da Republica. *Revolução evolução. 6⁰ aniversário da Revolução.* N.p., 1970.

Bronheim, David. "U.S. Military Policies and Programs in Latin America." In *Contemporary Inter-American Relations.* Edited by Yale H. Ferguson, 337-47. Englewood Cliffs, N.J.: Prentice Hall, 1972.

Bruneau, Thomas C. *The Political Transformation of the Brazilian Catholic Church.* New York: Cambridge University Press, 1974.

Burns, E. Bradford. *Nationalism in Brazil: A Historical Survey.* New York: Praeger, 1968.

Cabral, Carlos Castilho. *Tempos de Jânio e outros tempos.* Rio de Janeiro: Civilização Brasileira, 1962.

Calvo, Roberto. "Church and National Security." *Journal of Interamerican Studies and World Affairs* 21 (Feb. 1972): 69-88.

# References

Campos, Roberto. *Reflections on Latin American Development*. Austin: University of Texas Press, 1967.

Cardoso, Fernando Henrique. "Associated-Dependent Development: Theoretical and Practical Implications." In *Authoritarian Brazil*. Edited by Alfred Stepan, 142-76. New Haven: Yale University Press, 1973.

Carone, Edgard. *O PCB (1943-1964)*. São Paulo: Difel, 1982.

Carvalho, José Murilo de. "Organizational Roles, Belief Systems and Military Politics." In *Politics and Administration in Brazil*. Edited by Jean-Claude Garcia-Zamor, 173-206. Washington, D.C.: University Press of America, 1978.

Cavalcanti, Paulo. *O caso eu conto como o caso foi*. 2 vols. Recife: Guararapes, 1980.

Chilcote, Ronald A. *The Brazilian Communist Party: Conflict and Integration, 1922-1972*. New York: Oxford University Press, 1974.

Comblin, José. *The Church and the National Security State*. Maryknoll, N.Y.: Orbis, 1979.

"*A compra das concessionárias de energia elétrica*," *Revista Brasileira de Política Internacional* 8 (Sept. 1965): 163-728.

Dines, Alberto, Antonio Callado, Araújo Netto, Carlos Castello Branco, Cláudio Mello e Souza, Eurilo Duarte, Pedro Gomes, and Wilson Figueiredo. *Os idos de março e a queda em abril*. Rio de Janeiro: Alvaro, 1964.

Doria, João de Seixas. *Eu, réu sem crime*. Rio de Janeiro: Equador, n.d.

Dreifuss, René Armand. *1964: A conquista do estado. Ação política, poder e golpe de classe*. 3d ed. Petrópolis: Vozes, 1981.

Dulles, John W. F. "Communism under the Military: Efforts at Recovery, 1964-1969." In *Politics and Administration in Brazil*. Edited by Jean-Claude Garcia-Zamor, 207-64. Washington, D.C.: University Press of America, 1978.

———. *Castello Branco: Making of a President*. College Station: Texas A & M University Press, 1978.

———. *President Castello Branco: Brazilian Reformer*. College Station: Texas A & M University Press, 1978.

———. *Unrest in Brazil: Political-Military Crises, 1955-1964*. Austin: University of Texas Press, 1970.

Durandin, Catherine. "*L'idéologie de la sécurité nationale au Brésil.*" Notes et études documentaires. *Problème d'Amérique Latine* 44 (17 June 1977): 5-18.

Dutra, Eloi. *IBAD, sigla da corrupção*. Rio de Janeiro: Civilização Brasileira, 1963.

Eisenhower, Dwight D. *Waging Peace, 1956-1961*. Garden City, N.Y.: Doubleday, 1965.

Eisenhower, Milton S. *The Wine Is Bitter*. Garden City, N.Y.: Doubleday, 1963.

Erickson, Kenneth P. *The Brazilian Corporative State and Working-Class Politics*. Berkeley: University of California Press, 1977.

Evans, Peter. *Dependent Development: The Alliance of Multinational, State, and Local Capital in Brazil*. Princeton: Princeton University Press, 1979.

303

# References

Fairlee, Henry. *The Kennedy Promise: The Politics of Expectation*. Garden City, N.Y.: Doubleday, 1973.

Faust, Jean-Jacques. *A revolução devora seus presidentes*. Rio de Janeiro: Saga, 1965.

Figueiredo, Mário Poppe de. *A revolução de 1964: Um depoimento para a história patria*. Rio de Janeiro: APEC, 1970.

Flynn, Peter. *Brazil: A Political Analysis*. London: Ernest Benn, 1978.

Fonseca, Gondin da. *A miséria é nossa*. São Paulo: Fulgor, 1961.

———. *Os gorilas, o povo, e a reforma agrária*. São Paulo: Fulgor, 1963.

Francis, Paulo. *"Tempos de Goulart." Revista Civilização Brasileira* 1 (May 1966): 75–91.

Franco, Afonso Arinos de Melo. *Planalto: Memórias*. Rio de Janeiro: Olympio, 1968.

Galbraith, John K. *Ambassador's Journal*. New York: Signet, 1970.

Geyelin, Philip. *Lyndon B. Johnson and the World*. New York: Praeger, 1966.

Goldman, Eric. *The Tragedy of Lyndon Johnson*. New York: Knopf, 1969.

Gomes, Lucia Maria Gaspar. "Cronologia do governo Castelo Branco," *Dados* 1 (1967).

Gordon, Lincoln. *A New Deal for Latin America: The Alliance for Progress*. Cambridge: Harvard University Press, 1963.

Gromyko, Andrei. *Through Russian Eyes: President Kennedy's 1036 Days*. Washington, D.C.: International Library, 1973.

Gudin, Eugenio. *Analise de problemas brasileiros*. Rio de Janeiro: Agir, 1965.

Hall, Clarence W. "The Country That Saved Itself." *Readers Digest,* Nov. 1964, 133–59.

Hanson, Simon G. *Dollar Diplomacy, Modern Style: Chapters in the Failure of the Alliance for Progress*. Washington: Inter-American Affairs Press, 1970.

Hewlitt, Sylvia Ann. *The Cruel Dilemmas of Development: Twentieth-Century Brazil*. New York: Basic Books, 1980.

Horowitz, Irving. *Revolution in Brazil*. New York: Dutton, 1964.

Ianni, Octavio. *O colapso do populismo no Brasil*. Rio de Janeiro: Civilização Brasileira, 1968.

Ianni, Octavio, et al. *Politica e revolução social no Brasil*. Rio de Janeiro: Civilização Brasileira, 1965.

Instituto de Pesquisas e Estudos Sociais. *A reforma agrária, problemas, bases, solução*. N.p., 1964.

Julião, Francisco. *Que são as ligas camponesas?* Rio de Janeiro: Civilização Brasileira, 1962.

Jurema, Abelardo. *Juscelino e Jango. PSD e PTB*. Rio de Janeiro: Artenova, 1979.

———. *Sexta-Feira 13: Os ultimos dias do governo João Goulart*. Rio de Janeiro: Edições O Cruzeiro, 1964.

Kennedy, John F. *The Strategy of Peace*. New York: Harper & Row, 1960.

Khrushchev, Nikita S. "For New Victories of the World Communist Movement: Results of the Meeting of Representatives of the Communist and Workers' Parties." 2 vols. *Communism—Peace and Happiness for the Peoples*. Moscow: Moscow Foreign Languages Publishing House, 1963. 1:12–75.

Krieger, Daniel. *Desde as missões: Saudades, letras, esperanças*. 2d ed. Rio de Janeiro: Olympio, 1977.

Lacerda, Carlos. *Depoimento*. Rio de Janeiro: Nova Fronteira, 1977.

————. *O poder das idéias*. 4th ed. Rio de Janeiro: Record, 1964.

Lago, Mário. *1 de abril, estórias para história*. Rio de Janeiro: Civilização Brasileira, 1964.

Langguth, A. J. *Hidden Terrors*. New York: Pantheon, 1978.

Lens, Sidney. "Labor and the CIA." *Progressive* 31 (1967): 23–28.

Levinson, Jerome, and Juan de Onis. *The Alliance That Lost Its Way*. Chicago: Quadrangle, 1972.

Magalhães, Juracy. *Minhas memórias provisórias*. Rio de Janeiro: Civilização Brasileira, 1982.

Maia Neto, João Candido. *La crises brasileña*. Buenos Aires: Alvarez, 1965.

Martins, Wilson. "Brazilian Politics: Dialectic of a Revolution." *Luso-Brazilian Review* 3 (May 1966): 3–18.

Medina, Rubem. *Desnacionalização, crime contra o Brasil?* Rio de Janeiro: Saga, 1970.

Methvin, Eugene H. "Labor's New Weapon for Democracy." *Readers Digest*, October 1966, 21–28.

Mikesell, Raymond F. *Foreign Investment in the Petroleum and Mineral Industries*. Baltimore: Johns Hopkins University Press, 1971.

Millikan, Max F., and Walt W. Rostow. *A Proposal: Key to An Effective Foreign Policy*. New York: Harper, 1957.

Miroff, Bruce. *Pragmatic Illusions: The Presidential Politics of John F. Kennedy*. New York: David McKay, 1976.

Moraes, Denis de, and Francisco Viana. *Prestes: lutas e autocríticas*. 2d ed. Petrópolis: Vozes, 1982.

Morel, Edmar. *O golpe começou em Washington*. Rio de Janeiro: Civilização Brasileira, 1965.

Morrison, DeLesseps S. *Latin American Mission*. New York: Simon and Schuster, 1965.

Mourão Filho, Olympio. *Memórias: a verdade de um revolucionário*. Porto Alegre: L & PM, 1978.

Muricy, Antonio Carlos. "*Os motivos de revolução democratica brasileira: Palestras pronunciadas na TV Canal 2 em 19 e 25 de maio de 1964.*" In his *Palavras de Um Soldado*. Rio de Janeiro: Imprensa do exército, 1971. 77–139.

Nixon, Richard M. *Six Crises*. Garden City, N.Y.: Doubleday, 1962.

Oliveira, Franklin de. *Revolução e contrarevolução no Brasil*. 2d ed. Rio de Janeiro: Civilização Brasileira, 1962.

Operations and Policy Research, Institute for the Comparative Study of Political Systems. *Brazil 1962, Parties, Issues, and Political Personalities*. Washington, D.C.: n.d.

Page, Joseph A. *The Revolution That Never Was*. New York: Grossman, 1972.

Paper, Lewis J. *The Promise and the Performance: The Leadership of John F. Kennedy*. New York: Crown, 1975.

Parenti, Michael. *The Anti-Communist Impulse*. New York: Random House, 1969.

Parker, Phyllis R. *Brazil and the Quiet Intervention, 1964*. Austin: University of Texas Press, 1979.

Perlman, Janice E. *The Myth of Marginality*. Berkeley: University of California Press, 1976.

Perrett, Geoffrey. *A Dream of Greatness: The American People, 1945-1963*. New York: Coward McCann Geoghegan, 1979.

Pinto, Bilac. *Guerra revolucionária*. Rio de Janeiro: Forense, 1964.

Pinto, José Coelho. *Um deputado no exilio*. Rio de Janeiro: Leitura, 1965.

Poerner, Artur José. *O poder jovem: História do participação política dos estudantes brasileiros*. Rio de Janeiro: Civilização Brasileira, 1968.

*Political Power in Latin America: Seven Confrontations*. "Case 4. The Brazilian Coup of 1964," edited by Richard R. Fagen and Wayne A. Cornelius, 155-230. Englewood Cliffs, N.J.: Prentice Hall, 1970.

Powers, Thomas. *The Man Who Kept The Secrets: Richard Helms and the CIA*. New York: Washington Square Press, 1979.

Quadros, Jânio. "Brazil's New Foreign Policy." *Foreign Affairs* 40, no. 1 (Oct. 1961): 19-27.

Radosh, Ronald. *American Labor and United States Foreign Policy: The Cold War in the Unions from Gompers to Lovestone*. New York: Random, 1970.

Raine, Philip. *Brazil: Awakening Giant*. Washington, D.C.: Public Affairs Press, 1974.

Ray, Philip A. *South Wind Red*. Chicago: Regnery, 1962.

Reisky de Dubnic, Vladimir. *Political Trends in Brazil*. Washington, D.C.: Public Affairs Press, 1968.

Rico-Galan, Victor. "The Brazilian Crisis." *Monthly Review* 15, no. 12 (April 1964): 657-75.

Roett, Riordan. *The Politics of Foreign Aid in the Brazilian Northeast*. Nashville: Vanderbilt University Press, 1972.

———. "A Praetorian Army in Politics: The Brazilian Military, 1946 to the Present." In *Politics and Administration in Brazil*. Edited by Jean-Claude Garcia-Zamor, 265-301. Washington, D.C.: University Press of America, 1978.

———, ed. *Brazil in the Sixties*. Nashville: Vanderbilt University Press, 1972.

Rojas, Robinson. *Estados Unidos en Brasil*. Santiago, Chile: Latinoamericana, 1965.

Romualdi, Serafino. *Presidents and Peons: Recollections of a Labor Ambassador in Latin America*. New York: Funk & Wagnalls, 1967.

Rostow, Walt W. *The Diffusion of Power, 1957-1972*. New York: Macmillan, 1972.

———. *The Stages of Economic Growth: A Non-Communist Manifesto*. New York: Cambridge University Press, 1960.

———. *The United States in the World Arena*. New York: Harper & Row, 1960.

Rowen, Hobart. *The Free Enterprisers: Kennedy, Johnson and the Business Establishment*. New York: Putnam's, 1964.

Sampson, Anthony. *The Sovereign State of ITT*. New York: Stein & Day, 1973.

Santos, Wanderley Guilherme dos. *Sessenta e quatro: Anatomia da crise*. São Paulo: Vertice, 1986.

Schlesinger, Arthur M., Jr. "The Alliance for Progress: A Retrospective." In *Latin America: The Search for a New International Role*. Edited by Ronald G. Hellman and H. Jon Rosenbaum, 57-92. New York: Wiley, 1975.

———. "The Lowering Hemisphere." *Atlantic* 225 (January 1970): 79-88.

———. *Robert Kennedy and His Times*. Boston: Houghton Mifflin, 1978.

———. *A Thousand Days: John F. Kennedy in the White House*. Boston: Houghton Mifflin, 1965.

Schmitter, Philippe C. *Interest Conflict and Political Change in Brazil*. Stanford: Stanford University Press, 1971.

Schneider, Ronald M. *The Political System of Brazil: Emergence of a "Modernizing" Authoritarian Regime, 1964-1970*. New York: Columbia University Press, 1971.

Selcher, Wayne A. "The National Security Doctrine and Policies of the Brazilian Government." *Parameters* 7 (Spring 1977): 10-24.

Sidey, Hugh. *A Very Personal Presidency*. New York: Atheneum, 1968.

Sieckman, Philip. "When Executives Turn Revolutionaries." *Fortune* 70 (Sept. 1964): 147-49, 210-21.

Silva, Hélio. *1964, golpe ou contragolpe*. Rio de Janeiro: Civilização Brasileira, 1975.

Silveira, Jocl. *Meninos, eu vi*. Rio de Janeiro: Tribuna da Imprensa, 1967.

Simoes, Solange de Deus. *Deus, patria, e familia: as mulheres no golpe de 1964*. Petrópolis: Vozes, 1985.

Skidmore, Thomas E. *Politics in Brazil, 1930-1964*. New York: Oxford University Press, 1967.

———. *The Politics of Military Rule in Brazil, 1964-1985*. New York: Oxford University Press, 1988.

———. "United States Policy Toward Brazil: Assumptions and Options." In *Latin America: The Search for a New International Role*. Edited by Ronald G. Hellman and H. Jon Rosenbaum, 191-213. New York: Wiley, 1975.

*"Sombras do IBAD." Veja*, 16 March 1977, 3-6.

Sorenson, Theodore C. *Kennedy*. New York: Harper & Row, 1965.

Stacchini, José. *Março 64: mobilização da audácia*. São Paulo: Companhia Editora Nacional, 1965.

Stepan, Alfred. *The Military in Politics: Changing Patterns in Brazil.* Princeton: Princeton University Press, 1971.

———. "The New Professionalism of Internal Warfare and Military Role Expansion." In *Authoritarian Brazil.* Edited by Alfred Stepan, 47–65. New Haven: Yale University Press, 1973.

———. *Rethinking Military Politics: Brazil and the Southern Cone.* Princeton: Princeton University Press, 1988.

Tavora, Araken. *Brasil, 1º de abril.* 2d ed. Rio de Janeiro: Buccini, 1964.

Tavora, Juarez. *Uma vida e muitas lutas.* Vol. 3. Rio de Janeiro: Olympio, 1965.

Tejo, Aurelio de Limeira. *Jango: Debate sobre a crise dos nossos tempos.* Rio de Janeiro: Andes, 1957.

Tendler, Judith. *Electric Power in Brazil.* Cambridge: Harvard University Press, 1968.

Tulchin, Joseph L. "The United States and Latin America in the 1960s." *Journal of Interamerican Studies and World Affairs* 30, no. 1 (Spring 1988): 1–36.

Tuthill, John W. "Economic and Political Aspects of Development in Brazil and U.S. Aid." *Journal of Inter-American Studies* 11 (Apr. 1969): 186–208.

———. "Operation Topsy." *Foreign Policy,* no. 8 (Fall 1972): 62–85.

Viana Filho, Luis. *O governo Castelo Branco.* Rio de Janeiro: Olympio, 1975.

Victor, Mário. *Cinco anos que abalaram o Brasil.* Rio de Janeiro: Civilização Brasileira, 1965.

Wallerstein, Michael. "The Collapse of Democracy in Brazil: Its Economic Determinants." *Latin American Research Review* 15, no. 3 (1980): 3–40.

Wallis, Victor. "Brazil's Experiment with an Independent Foreign Policy." In *Contemporary Inter-American Relations.* Edited by Yale H. Ferguson, 35–50. Englewood Cliffs, N.J.: Prentice Hall, 1972.

Walters, Vernon A. *Silent Missions.* New York: Doubleday, 1978.

Walton, Richard J. *Cold War and Counterrevolution: The Foreign Policy of John F. Kennedy.* New York: Viking, 1972.

Welch, Robert H. *The Politician.* Belmont, Mass.: Privately printed, 1963.

Wolfe, Alan, and Jerry Sanders. "Resurgent Cold War Ideology." In *Capitalism and State in Latin America.* Edited by Richard R. Fagen, 41–75. Stanford: Stanford University Press, 1979.

## Interviews

Archer, Renato. Interview with Lucia Hippolito and Helena Maria Bomeny, Aug. 1978, Oral History Collection, CPDOC.

Blough, Roger M. Interview with Joe Frantz, 29 July 1971, New York, Oral History Collection, LBJL.

Cabot, John Moors. Interview with William W. Moss, 27 Jan. 1971, Oral History Collection, JFKL.

# References

Campos, Roberto de Oliveira. Interview with John E. Reilly, 29–30 May 1964, Rio de Janeiro, Oral History Collection, JFKL.

Dungan, Ralph. Interview with Paige Mulhollan, 6 Apr. 1972, Oral History Collection, LBJL.

Gaud, William S. Interview with Paige Mulhollan, 26 Nov. 1968, Oral History Collection, LBJL.

Gordon, Lincoln. Interview with John E. Reilly, 30 May 1964, Rio de Janeiro, Oral History Collection, JFKL.

———. Interview with Paige Mulhollan, 10 July 1969, Baltimore, Oral History Collection, LBJL.

———. Interview with Roberto Garcia, "Castello perdeu a batalha," *Veja,* 9 Mar. 1977, 3–8.

———. Interview with author, 19 Oct. 1988, Washington, D.C.

Jurema, Abelardo. Interview with Aspasia Camargo and Eduardo Raposo, April–July 1977, Oral History Collection, CPDOC.

Mann, Thomas. Interview with Joe Frantz, 4 Nov. 1968, Oral History Collection, LBJL.

Oliver, Covey T. Interview with Paige Mulhollan, 12 Dec. 1968, Oral History Collection, LBJL.

Pinheiro Neto, João. Interview with Aspasia Camargo, Helena Maria Bomeny, and Maria Luíza Heilborn, June 1977, Oral History Collection, CPDOC.

Smith, Bromley. Interview, 29 July 1969, Oral History Collection, LBJL.

## Newspapers

*Correio da Manha* (Rio de Janeiro), 1960–65.
*Estado do São Paulo* (São Paulo), 1960–68.
*O Globo* (Rio de Janeiro), 1962–65.
*Jornal do Brasil* (Rio de Janeiro), 1960–68.
*New York Times,* 1953–69.
*Ultima Hora* (Rio de Janeiro), 1962–64.
*Wall Street Journal,* 1961–69.
*Washington Post,* 1961–69.

# Index

# Index

314

316